Reluctant European

Reluctant European

Britain and the European Union from 1945 to Brexit

STEPHEN WALL

OXFORD
UNIVERSITY PRESS

OXFORD

UNIVERSITY PRESS

Great Clarendon Street, Oxford, OX2 6DP,
United Kingdom

Oxford University Press is a department of the University of Oxford.
It furthers the University's objective of excellence in research, scholarship,
and education by publishing worldwide. Oxford is a registered trade mark of
Oxford University Press in the UK and in certain other countries

First Edition published in 2020

Impression: 1

Published in the United States of America by Oxford University Press
198 Madison Avenue, New York, NY 10016, United States of America

British Library Cataloguing in Publication Data
Data available

Library of Congress Control Number: 2020933022

ISBN 978-0-19-884067-1

Printed and bound in Great Britain by
Clays Ltd, Elcograf S.p.A.

For my grandsons, Alex and Theo

Acknowledgements

The sources for this book have been many: my own memories of people and events; the views and recollection of those with, or for whom, I worked and, especially, the government documents of the day, now housed in The National Archives. I hope the book does justice to the politicians and officials who strove to advance the national interest and to make a success of Britain's membership of the European Community/Union, and of the EEC/EU as a whole.

I owe special thanks to Gill Bennett, formerly the Chief Historian at the Foreign and Commonwealth Office and herself an accomplished published historian. I drew on her work but, above all, on her kindness, generosity, and expertise. She read, commented on, and copy-edited the book, and her support and advice were invaluable.

I had strong backing for this book project from Dominic Byatt, Commissioning Editor for Politics and International Relations at Oxford University Press, and support from him and his colleagues throughout.

My husband, Ted (Dr Edward Sumner), read and commented on the book. He drew on his extensive experience as a journal editor to make suggestions and corrections. He gave me morale-boosting support and encouragement, with characteristic love and generosity.

Contents

List of Principal People

Acheson, Dean (1893–1971) US politician. Assistant Secretary of State for Congressional Relations and International Conferences, 1944–45; US Under Secretary of State, 1945–47; US Secretary of State, 1949–53

Allan, Sir Alex (1951–) British Civil Servant. Various appointments in HM Treasury and Customs &Excise, 1973–92; Principal Private Secretary to the Prime Minister (John Major), 1992–97; British High Commissioner to Australia, 1997–99; Chair of the Joint Intelligence Committee, 2007–11

Andreotti, Giulio (1919–2013) Italian Christian Democrat politician. Secretary of the Council of Ministers, 1947–54; Minister of Finance, 1955–58; Minister of the Treasury, 1958–59; Minister of Industry, Commerce and Craftsmanship, 1964–68; Minister of Defence, 1959–66 and 1974; Minister of Planning and the Budget, 1974–76; Minister of the Interior, 1954 and 1978; Minister of Foreign Affairs, 1983–89; Minister of State Participation, 1990–92; Minister of Culture and the Environment, 1991–92; Prime Minister, 1972–73; 1976–79; 1989–92

Armstrong, Robert (later Lord Armstrong of Ilminster) (1927–2020) Principal Private Secretary to the Prime Minister, 1970–75; Permanent Secretary, Home Office, 1977–79; Cabinet Secretary, 1979–87

Attali, Jacques (1943–) Special Adviser to President Mitterrand, 1981–91

Attlee, Clement (later, 1st Earl Attlee) (1883–1967) British politician. Labour MP for Limehouse, 1922–50 and Walthamstow West, 1950-55; Under-Secretary of State for War, 1924; Chancellor of the Duchy of Lancaster, 1930–31; Postmaster General, 1931; Lord Privy Seal, 1940–42; Secretary of State for Dominion Affairs, 1942–43; Lord President of the Council, 1943–45; Deputy Prime Minister, 1942–45; Prime Minister, 1945–51

Aznar, José Maria (1953–) Spanish politician. People's Party member of the Congress of Deputies, 1989–2004; Leader of the Opposition, 1989–96; Prime Minister, 1996–2004

Ball, George (1909–94) American diplomat. Under Secretary of State for Economic Growth, Energy and the Environment, 1961; US Under Secretary of State, 1961–66; US Ambassador to the UN, 1968

Balladur, Edouard (1929–) French politician. Secretary-General of the French Presidency, 1973–74; Minister of Finance, 1986–88; Prime Minister of France, 1993–95

Balls, Ed (1967–) British politician. Labour MP for Morley and Outwood Normanton, 2005–10; Economic Secretary to the Treasury, 2006–7; Secretary of State for Children, Schools and Families, 2007–10

Barber, Anthony (1920–2005) British politician. Conservative MP for Doncaster, 1951–64, and Altrincham and Sale, 1965–74; Parliamentary Secretary to the PM, 1957–59; Economic Secretary to the Treasury, 1959–62; Financial Secretary to the Treasury, 1962–63; Minister of Health, 1963–64; Chairman of the Conservative Party, 1967–70; Chancellor of the Duchy of Lancaster, 1970; Chancellor of the Exchequer, 1970–74

Barnier, Michel (1951–) French politician. Member of the National Assembly for Savoie, 1978–93; Minister of the Environment, 1993–95; Minister for European Affairs, 1995–97; European Commissioner for Regional Policy, 1999–2004; Minister of Foreign Affairs, 2004–5; Minister of Agriculture and Fisheries, 2007–9; European Commissioner for Internal Market and Services, 2010–14; European Commission Chief Negotiator for Brexit from 2016

Barre, Raymond (1924–2007) French politician. Minister of Economy and Finance, 1976–78; Prime Minister, 1976–81

Barroso, José Manuel Durão (1956–) Portuguese Social Democratic politician. Member of the Portuguese Assembly, 1985–2004; Minister of Foreign Affairs, 1992–95; Leader of the Opposition, 1999–2002; Prime Minister of Portugal, 2002–4; President of the European Commission, 2004–14

Benn, Tony (Anthony Wedgwood Benn) (1925–2014) British politician Labour MP for Bristol South East, 1950-60 and 1963-83, and Chesterfield, 1984-2001. Secretary of State for Industry, 1975–75; Secretary of State for Energy, 1975–79

Berlusconi, Silvio (1936–) Italian media tycoon and Forza Italia politician. Member of the Italian Chamber of Deputies, 1994–2013; Senator, 2013; Prime Minister of Italy, 1994–95; 2001–6; 2008–11; Member of the European Parliament, 2019

Bevin, Ernest (1881–1951) British Trade Union leader and politician. General Secretary of the Transport and General Workers Union, 1922–45; Labour MP, for Wandsworth Central, 1940–50 and Woolwich East, 1950-51; Minister of Labour and National Service, 1940–45; Secretary of State for Foreign Affairs, 1945–51; Lord Privy Seal, 1951

Blair, Tony (1953–) British politician. Labour MP for Sedgefield, 1983–2007; Leader of the Opposition, 1994–97; Prime Minister, 1997–2007

Brandt, Willy (1913–92) German politician. President of the Berlin House of Representatives, 1955–57; President of the Bundesrat, 1957–58; Governing Mayor of West Berlin, 1957–66; Federal Minister for Foreign Affairs, 1966–69; Vice Chancellor of West Germany, 1966–69; Chancellor of West Germany, 1969–74; Leader of the Social Democratic Party, 1964–87

Bridges, Sir Tom (later, 2nd Baron Bridges) (1927–2017)HM Diplomatic Service, 1951-87; Private Secretary to Prime Minister Harold Wilson, 1972–74; Ambassador to Italy, 1983–87

Brown, George (later, Lord George-Brown of Jevington) (1914–85) British politician. Labour MP for Belper, 1945–70; Minister of Works, 1951; Secretary of State for Economic Affairs, 1964–66; First Secretary of State, 1964–66; Secretary of State for Foreign Affairs, 1966–68

Brown, Gordon (1951–) British politician. Labour MP for Dunfermline East, 1983-2005, and Kirkcaldy and Cowdenbeath, 2005-2015; Chancellor of the Exchequer, 1997–2007; Prime Minister, 2007–10

Bullard, Sir Julian (1928–2006) HM Diplomatic Service, 1953–88; Minister, British Embassy, Bonn, 1975–79; DUSS, FCO, 1979–84; Deputy PUS and Political Director, FCO, 1982–84; Ambassador to the FRG,1984–88

Butler, Sir Michael (1927–2013) HM Diplomatic Service, 1950–85; Assistant (later Deputy) Under-Secretary for European Community questions, FCO, 1974–79; Permanent Representative to the European Community, 1979–85

Butler, Rab (later, Lord Butler of Saffron Walden) (1902–82) British politician. Conservative MP for Saffron Walden, 1929–65; Minister of Education, 1941–45; Minister of Labour and National Service, 1945; Chancellor of the Exchequer, 1951–55; Lord Privy Seal, 1955–59; Leader of the House of Commons, 1955–61; Home Secretary, 1957–62; First Secretary of State, 1962–63; Deputy Prime Minister, 1962–63; Secretary of State for Foreign Affairs, 1963–64; Father of the House of Commons, 1964–65

Butler, Robin (later, Lord Butler of Brockwell) (1938–) British Civil Servant. Official in HM Treasury. Private Secretary to Prime Ministers Heath and Wilson, 1972–75; Principal Private Secretary to Prime Minister Thatcher, 1982–85; Second Permanent Secretary, Treasury, 1985–87; Secretary of the Cabinet and Head of the Home Civil Service, 1988–98

Callaghan, James (later Lord Callaghan of Cardiff) (1912–2005) British politician. Labour MP for Cardiff South, 1945-50 and Cardiff South East, 1950-83; Chancellor of the Exchequer, 1964–67; Home Secretary, 1967–70; Foreign and Commonwealth Secretary, 1974–76; Prime Minister, 1976–79

Cameron, David (1966–) British politician. Conservative MP for Witney, 2001–16; Prime Minister, 2010–16

Carrington, Peter (Lord Carrington) (1919–2018) British politician. Defence Secretary, 1970–74; Foreign & Commonwealth Secretary, 1979–82

Carter, James Earl ('Jimmy') (1924–) US Democrat politician. Member of the Georgia State Senate, 1963–67; Governor of Georgia, 1971–75; President of the United States, 1977–81

Cartledge, Sir Bryan (1927–) HM Diplomatic Service, 1966-88; Head of East European and Soviet Department, FCO, 1975–77; Foreign Office Private Secretary to the Prime Minister, 1977–79; Ambassador to Hungary, 1980–83; Assistant Under-Secretary, FCO, 1983–84; Deputy Secretary of the Cabinet, 1984–85; Ambassador to the Soviet Union, 1985–88

Castle, Barbara (later, Baroness Castle of Blackburn) (1910–2002) British politician. Labour MP for Blackburn, 1945–79; MEP for Greater Manchester, 1979–89; Minister for Overseas Development, 1964–65; Minister for Transport, 1965–68; Secretary of State for Employment and Productivity, 1968–70; Secretary of State for Health and Social Services, 1974–76

Chamberlain, Neville (1869–1940) British politician. Conservative MP for Birmingham Ladywood, 1918–29 and Birmingham Edgbaston, 1939-40; Minister of Health, 1931; Chancellor of the Exchequer, 1931–37; Prime Minister, 1937–40; Lord President of the Council, 1940

Cheysson, Claude (1920–2012) French politician. Minister of Foreign Affairs, 1981–84; Member of the European Commission responsible for Mediterranean Policy and North/South relations, 1985–89

Chirac Jacques (1932–2019) French politician. Minister of Agriculture, 1972–76; Prime Minister, 1974–76 and 1986–88; President of the Republic, 1995–2007

Churchill, Sir Winston (1874–1965) British politician. Conservative MP, 1900–22 and 1924–64; President of the Board of Trade, 1908–10; Home Secretary, 1910–11; First Lord of the Admiralty, 1911–15; Chancellor of the Duchy of Lancaster, 1915; Minister of Munitions, 1927–19; Secretary of State for War, 1919–21; Secretary of State for Air, 1919–21; Secretary of State for the Colonies, 1921–22; Chancellor of the Exchequer, 1924–29; First Lord of the Admiralty, 1939–40; Prime Minister, 1940–45 and 1951–55

Clarke, Kenneth (1940–) British politician. Conservative MP for Rushcliffe, 1970–2019; Lord Commissioner of the Treasury, 1974; Parliamentary Under-Secretary for Transport, 1979–82; Minister of State for Health, 1982–85; Minister of State for Employment, 1985–87; Paymaster General, 1985–87; Minister of State for Trade and Industry, 1987–88; Chancellor of the Duchy of Lancaster, 1987–88; Secretary of State for Health, 1988–90; Secretary of State for Education and Science, 1990–92; Home Secretary, 1992–93; Chancellor of the Exchequer, 1993–97; Secretary of State for Justice and Lord High Chancellor of Great Britain, 2010–12; Minister without portfolio, 2012–14; Father of the House of Commons, 2017–19

Clegg, Nick (1967–) British politician. Member of the European Parliament for East Midlands, 1999–2004; Liberal Democrat MP for Sheffield Hallam, 2005–17; Leader of the Liberal Democrat Party, 2007–15; Deputy Prime Minister, 2010–15

Cook, Robin (1946–2005) British politician. Labour MP for Edinburgh Central, 1974-1983 and Livingston, 1983-2005; Foreign and Commonwealth Secretary, 1997–2001;

Leader of the House of Commons and Lord President of the Council, 2001–3; Resigned from the government over Iraq, 2001; President of the Party of European Socialists, 2001–4

Couve de Murville, Maurice (1907–99) French politician. Foreign Minister, 1958–68; Prime Minister, 1968–69

Couzens, Ken (1925–2004) Deputy Secretary, HM Treasury, 1977–83; Permanent Secretary, Department of Energy, 1983–85

Craxi, Bettino (1934–2000) Italian politician. Secretary of the Italian Socialist Party and Member of the Italian Chamber of Deputies, 1976–83; Prime Minister, 1983–87

Cresson, Edith (1934–) French Socialist politician. Minister of Agriculture, 1981–83; Minister of Foreign Trade and Tourism, 1983–84; Minister of Industrial Redeployment and Foreign Trade, 1984–86; Minister of European Affairs, 1988–90; Prime Minister, 1991–92; European Commissioner for Research, Innovation and Science, 1995–99

Cromer, George Rowland ('Rowley'), 3rd Earl of Cromer (1918–91) British banker and diplomat. Governor of the Bank of England, 1961–66; British Ambassador to the United States, 1971–74

Crosland, Anthony (1918–77) British Politician. Labour MP for South Gloucestershire, 1950-55 and Great Grimsby, 1959-77; Secretary of State for the Environment, 1974–76; Secretary of State for Foreign and Commonwealth Affairs, 1976–77

Cunliffe, Sir Jon (1953–) British Civil Servant. Official of HM Treasury. Managing Director (later, Second Permanent Secretary) of Macroeconomic Policy and International Finance; Head of the European and Global Issues Secretariat, Cabinet Office and Adviser to the PM on International Economic Affairs and the EU, 2007–11; UK Permanent Representative to the EU, 2012–13; Deputy Governor of the Bank of England from 2013

Darling, Alistair (later, Lord Darling of Roulanish) (1953–) British politician. Labour MP for Edinburgh Central, 1987–2005 and Edinburgh South West, (2005-15; Chief Secretary to the Treasury, 1997–8; Secretary of State for Work and Pensions, 1998–2002; Secretary of State for Transport, 2002–6; Secretary of State for Scotland, 2003–6; Secretary of State for Trade and Industry and President of the Board of Trade, 2006–7; Chancellor of the Exchequer, 2007–10

Davies, John (1916–79) British business leader and politician. Conservative MP for Knutsford, 1970–78; Director of the CBI, 1965–69; Minister of Technology, 1970; Secretary of State for Trade and Industry, 1970–72; Chancellor of the Duchy of Lancaster, 1972–74

Davignon, Etienne (1932–) Belgian official and politician. Foreign Ministry official, 1959–65; Head of International Energy Agency, 1974–77; European Commissioner for

Internal Market, Customs Union and Industrial Affairs, 1977–81; European Commissioner for Industry and Energy, 1981–85

Davis, David (1948–) British politician. Conservative MP for Boothferry,1987-1997 and Haltemprice and Howden since 1997; Minister of State for Europe, 1994–97; Chair of the House of Commons Public Accounts Committee, 1997–2001; Chair of the Conservative Party, 2001–2; Shadow Home Secretary, 2003–8; Secretary of State for Exiting the European Union, 2016–18

Debré, Michel (1912–96) French Gaullist politician. Prime Minister, 1959–62; Minister of Economy and Finance, 1966–68; Minister of Foreign Affairs, 1968–69; Minister of Defence, 1969–73

De Gaulle, Charles (1890–1970) French General and politician. Leader of the Free French, 1940–44; President of the Provisional French Government, 1944–46; Prime Minister of France, 1958–59; President of the Republic, 1959–69

Dehaene, Jean-Luc (1940–2014) Belgian politician. Minister of Social Affairs and Institutional Reform, 1981–88; Deputy Prime Minister, 1988–92; Prime Minister of Belgium, 1992–99

Delors, Jacques (1925–) French politician. Member of the European Parliament, 1979–81; Minister of Finance, 1981–84; President of the European Commission, 1985–95

Denman, Sir Roy (1924–2006) Head of the European Secretariat, Cabinet Office, 1975–77; Director-General for External Affairs, European Commission, 1977–82; European Commission Representative in Washington, 1982–89

Dixon, Sir Pierson ('Bob') (1904–65). HM Diplomatic Service. British Ambassador to Czechoslovakia, 1948–50; UK Permanent Representative to the UN, 1954–60; British Ambassador to France and concurrently Head of the Official Delegation to the EEC, Brussels, 1960–64

Dooge, James (1922–2010) Irish politician. Minister of Foreign Affairs, 1981–82; Leader of Fine Gael in the Irish Senate, 1982–87; Chair of the European Community Committee on the Single European Act, 1985

Douglas-Home, Alec (Earl of Home, 1951–63; Sir Alec Douglas-Home, 1963–64; Lord Home of the Hirsel, 1974–95) (1903–95) British politician. Conservative MP for Lanark,1950-51 and Kinross and West Perthshire, 1963–74; Secretary of State for Commonwealth Relations, 1955–60; Foreign Secretary, 1960–63; Prime Minister, 1963–64; Foreign & Commonwealth Secretary, 1970–74

Dumas, Roland (1922–) French politician. Minister of European Affairs, 1984; Minister of Foreign Affairs, 1984–86 and 1988–93

Eden, Anthony (later 1st Earl of Avon) (1897–1977) British politician. Conservative MP for Warwick and Leamington, 1923–57; Lord Privy Seal, 1933–35; Secretary of State for Dominion Affairs, 1939–40; Secretary of State for War, 1940; Leader of the

House of Commons, 1943–45; Secretary of State for Foreign Affairs and Deputy Prime Minister, 1951–55; Prime Minister, 1955–57

Eisenhower, Dwight D. (1890–1969) US General and politician. Supreme Allied Commander, Europe, 1943–45; 1st Supreme Allied Commander NATO, 1951–52; President of the United States, 1953–61

Erhard, Ludwig (1897–1977) German CDU politician. Vice-Chancellor of the Federal Republic of Germany, 1957–63; Federal Chancellor, 1963–66

Ewart-Biggs, Christopher (1921–76) HM Diplomatic Service, 1949-76; Minister, British Embassy, Paris, 1971–76; British Ambassador in Dublin, 1976. Assassinated by the Provisional IRA.

Fitzgerald, Garrett (1926–2011) Irish politician. Fine Gael MP for Dublin SE, 1969–92; Minister of Foreign Affairs, 1973–77; Taoiseach, 1981–82 and 1982–87

Foot, Michael (1913–2010) British politician. Labour MP for Devonport (1945–55), Ebbw Vale (1960–83) and Blaenau Gwent (1983–92). Secretary of State for Employment, 1974–76; Leader of the House of Commons, 1976–79; Leader of the Labour Party, 1980–83

Franklin, Sir Michael (1927–2019) Bitish Civil Servant. Deputy Director-General for Agriculture, European Commission, 1973–77; Deputy Secretary and Head of the European secretariat, Cabinet Office, 1977–81; Permanent Secretary, Department of Trade, 1982–83; Permanent Secretary, MAFF, 1983–87

Fretwell, Sir John (1930–2017) HM Diplomatic Service, 1953-90; Head of European Integration Department, FCO, 1973–76; AUSS for European Affairs, FCO, 1976–79; Minister, British Embassy Washington, 1980–81; British Ambassador to France, 1982–87; Political Director and Deputy to the PUS, FCO, 1987–90

Gaitskell, Hugh (1906–63) British politician. Labour MP for Leeds South, 1945–63; Minister of Fuel and Power, 1947–50; Chancellor of the Exchequer, 1950–51; Leader of the Opposition, 1955–63

Garel-Jones, Tristan (later, Lord Garel-Jones) (1941– 2020) British politician. Conservative MP for Watford, 1979–97; Minister for Europe in the FCO, 1990–93

Genscher, Hans-Dietrich (1927–2016) German FDP politician. Minister of Interior, 1969–74; Foreign Minister and Vice-Chancellor, 1974–82 and 1982–92

Gilmour, Ian (later, Lord Gilmour of Craigmillar) (1926–2007) British politician. Conservative MP for Central Norfolk, 1962-74 and Chesham and Amersham, 1974–92; Minister for Defence Procurement, 1971–74; Secretary of State for Defence, 1974; Lord Privy Seal, 1979–81

Giscard d'Estaing, Valéry (1926–) French politician. Minister of Finance and Economic Affairs, 1962–66 and of Economics and Finance, 1969–74; President of the Republic, 1974–81

Goldsmith, Peter (later, Lord Goldsmith of Allerton) (1950–) British lawyer and politician. Attorney General for England, Wales and Northern Ireland, 2001–7

Gonzalez, Felipe (1942–) Spanish Socialist politician. Secretary-General of the Spanish Socialist Workers Party, 1979–97; Prime Minister, 1982–96

Hague, William (later, Lord Hague of Richmond) (1961–) British politician. Conservative MP for Richmond (Yorkshire), 1989–2015; Parliamentary Private Secretary to the Chancellor of the Exchequer, 1990–93; Parliamentary Under-Secretary for Social Security, 1993–94; Minister of State for Social Security, 1994–95; Secretary of State for Wales, 1995–97; Leader of the Conservative Party, 1997–2001; Secretary of State for Foreign and Commonwealth Affairs, 2010–14; Leader of the House of Commons, 2014–15; First Secretary of State, 2010–15

Hallstein, Walter (1901–82) German academic and politician. Member of the Bundestag, 1969–72; State Secretary, Federal German Foreign Ministry, 1951–58; 1st President of the European Commission, 1958–67

Hannay, David (later, Lord Hannay of Chiswick) (1935–) HM Diplomatic Service, 1959-95; Chef de Cabinet to Sir Christopher Soames, European Commission, Brussels, 1973–75; Assistant Under-Secretary of State for EEC issues, FCO, 1979–84; Minister, British Embassy Washington, 1974–75; UK Permanent Representative to the European Community, 1985–90; UK Permanent Representative to the UN, 1990- 95

Hattersley, Roy (later, Lord Hattersley of Sparkbrook) (1932–) British politician. Labour MP for Birmingham Sparkbrook, 1964-97; Minister of State, FCO, 1974–75; Secretary of State for Prices and Consumer Affairs, 1976–79; Secretary of State for the Environment, 1979–80; Shadow Chancellor of the Exchequer, 1983–87; Deputy Leader of the Labour Party, 1983–92

Hayward, Ron (1917–96) British Labour Party official. Labour Party Organizer for the Southern region, 1959–69; General Secretary of the Labour Party, 1972–82

Healey, Denis (later, Lord Healey of Riddlesden) (1917–2015) British politician. Labour MP for Leeds South East, 1952-55 and Leeds East, 1955-92; Secretary of State for Defence, 1964–70; Chancellor of the Exchequer, 1974–79; Deputy Leader of the Labour Party, 1980–83

Heath, Sir Edward (1916–2005) British politician. Conservative MP for Old Bexley and Sidcup, 1950-83; Chief Whip, 1955–59; Minister of Labour, 1969–60; Lord Privy Seal, 1960–63; President of the Board of Trade, 1963–64; Leader of the Opposition, 1965–70 and 1974–75; Prime Minister 1970–74

Henderson, Sir Nicholas (Nicko) (1919–2009) HM Diplomatic Service, 1944-82; Private Secretary to Foreign Secretary, 1963–65; Ambassador to Poland, 1969–72; to Federal Republic of Germany, 1972–75; to France, 1975–79; and to the United States, 1979–82

Heseltine, Michael (later, Lord Heseltine of Thenford) (1933–) British politician. Conservative MP for Tavistock, 1966-74 and Henley, 1974-2001;1966-2001; Parliamentary Secretary to the Ministry of Transport, 1970; Parliamentary Under-Secretary for Environment, 1970–72; Minister of State for Aerospace and Shipping, 1972–74; Secretary of State for Defence, 1983–86; Secretary of State for the Environment, 1990–92; Secretary of State for Trade and Industry and President of the Board of Trade, 1992–95; Deputy Prime Minister and First Secretary of State, 1995–97

Heywood, Jeremy (later, Lord Heywood of Whitehall) (1961–2018) British Civil Servant. HM Treasury official; Principal Private Secretary to chancellors Lamont, Clarke, and Brown; Economic and Domestic Policy Secretary to Prime Minister Blair, 1997–98; Principal Private Secretary to the Prime Minister, 2009–10; Chief of Staff, Downing Street, 2008–10; Permanent Secretary, 2010–12; Cabinet Secretary, 2012–18

Hibbert, Sir Reginald (1922–2002) HM Diplomatic Service, 1946-82; British Ambassador to France, 1979–82

Hill, Jonathan (later, Lord Hill of Oareford) (1960–) Politician. Number 10 Policy Unit, 1991–92; Political Secretary to the Prime Minister and Head of the PM's Political Office, 1992–94; Parliamentary Under-Secretary for Schools, 2010–13; Leader of the House of Lords and Chancellor of the Duchy of Lancaster, 2013–14; European Commissioner for Financial Stability, Financial Services and Capital Markets Union, 2014–16.

Hogg, Sarah (later, Baroness Hogg of Kettlethorpe) (1946–) Journalist and business leader. Head of the Prime Minister's Policy Unit, 1990–95

Howard, Michael (later, Lord Howard of Lympne) (1941–) British politician. Conservative MP for Folkestone and Hythe, 1983–2010; Minister of State for Local Government, 1987–88; Minister of State for the Environment, 1988–89; Minister of State for Housing, 1989–90; Secretary of State for Employment, 1990–92; Secretary of State for the Environment, 1992–93; Home Secretary, 1993–97; Leader of the Opposition, 2003–5

Howe, Sir Geoffrey (later, Lord Howe of Aberavon) (1926–2015) British politician. Conservative MP for Bebington, 1964-66; Reigate, 1970–74 and East Surrey, 1974-92; Solicitor General for England and Wales, 1970–72; Minister of State for Trade and Consumer Affairs, 1972–74; Chancellor of the Exchequer, 1979–83; Secretary of State for Foreign and Commonwealth Affairs, 1983–89; Deputy Prime Minister, Leader of the House of Commons, and Lord President of the Council, 1989–90

Hunt, Sir John (later Lord Hunt of Tanworth) (1919–2008) Second Permanent Secretary, Cabinet Office, 1972–73; Cabinet Secretary, 1973–79

Hurd, Douglas (later Lord Hurd of Westwell) (1930–) British politician. HM Diplomatic Service, 1952–66; Private Secretary to the Leader of the Opposition

(Edward Heath), 1968–70; Political Secretary to the Prime Minister, 1970–74; Conservative MP for Mid Oxforshire, 1974–83 and Witney, 1983–97; Opposition spokesman on European Affairs, 1976–79; Minister of State FCO, 1979–83; Minister of State, Home Office, 1983–84; Secretary of State for Northern Ireland, 1984–85; Home Secretary, 1985–89; Secretary of State for Foreign and Commonwealth Affairs, 1989–85

Ingham, Sir Bernard (1932–) Journalist and Government Press Officer. Government Press and Public Relations Officer, 1967–79; Chief Press Secretary to the Prime Minister, 1979–90

Jackling, Sir Roger (1913–86) HM Diplomatic Service, 1939-76. Economic Minister, British Embassy, Bonn, 1953–57; Deputy Permanent Representative to the UN, 1963–67; Deputy Under-Secretary, FCO, 1967–68; Ambassador to the Federal Republic of Germany, 1968–72; Leader of the UK Delegation to the UN Conference on the Law of the Sea, 1973–76

Jenkins, Roy (later Lord Jenkins of Hillhead) (1920–2003) British politician. Labour MP for Southwark Central, 1948-50 and Birmingham Stretchford,1950-77; SDP MP for Glasgow Hillhead, 1982–87; Minister of Aviation, 1964–65; Home Secretary, 1965–67 and 1974–76; Chancellor of the Exchequer, 1967–70; Deputy Leader of the Labour Party, 1970–72; President of the European Commission, 1977–81

Jobert, Michel (1921–2002) French official and politician. Directeur de Cabinet of the French Prime Minister, 1966–69; Secretary-General of the Elysée, 1969–73; Minister of Foreign Affairs, 1973–74; Minister of External Commerce, 1981–83

Johnson, Lyndon B. (1908–73) US politician. Democratic Congressman for Texas, 1937–49; Senator for Texas, 1949–61; Senate Majority Leader, 1955–61; Vice-President of the United States, 1961–63; President of the United States, 1963–69

Jospin, Lionel (1937–) French Socialist politician. Minister of Sport, 1988–91; Minister of National Education, 1988–92; First Secretary of the Socialist Party, 1995–97; Prime Minister, 1997–2002

Juncker, Jean-Claude (1954–) Luxembourg politician. Christian Social People's Party Member of the Luxembourg Chamber of Deputies, 1984–2013; Minister for Work and Employment, 1984–99; Minister of Finance, 1989–2009; Minister for the Treasury, 2009–13; Prime Minister, 1995–2013; President of the European Commission, 2014–19

Karamanlis, Constantine (1907–98) Greek politician. Prime Minister, 1961–63, 1974–80, 1980–85; President of Greece, 1990–95

Kennedy, John F. (1917–63) US politician. Democratic Congressman for Massachusetts, 1947–53; Senator for Massachusetts, 1953–60; President of the United States, 1961–63

Kerr, John (later Lord Kerr of Kinlochard) (1942–)HM Diplomatic Service, 1966–2002; Assistant Under-Secretary, FCO, responsible for EEC policy, 1987–90; UK Permanent Representative to the EEC/EU, 1990–95; Ambassador to the USA, 1995–97; Permanent Under Secretary, FCO, 1997–2002

Kiesinger, Kurt Georg (1904–88) German CDU politician. Minister–President of Baden–Württemberg, 1955–66; Chancellor of the Federal Republic of Germany, 1966–69

Kinnock, Neil (later, Lord Kinnock of Bedwellty) (1941–)British politician. Labour MP for Bedwellty, 1970-83 and Islwyn, 1983-95; Shadow Secretary of State for Education and Science, 1979–83; Leader of the Opposition, 1983–92; European Commissioner for Transport, 1995–99; Vice-President of the European Commission and Commissioner for Administrative Reform, 1999–2004

Kissinger, Henry (1923–) US National Security Adviser, 1969–75: US Secretary of State, 1973–77

Kohl, Helmut (1930–2017) German Christian Democrat politician. Minister President of Rhineland–Palatinate, 1969–76; Leader of the Christian Democratic Union (CDU) Party, 1973–98; Chancellor of the Federal Republic of Germany, 1982–98

Lamont, Norman (later, Lord Lamont or Lerwick) (1942–) British politician. Conservative MP for Kingston-upon-Thames, 1972–97; Minister of State for Trade and Industry, 1983–85; Minister for Defence Procurement, 1985–86; Financial Secretary to the Treasury, 1986–89; Chief Secretary to the Treasury, 1989–90; Chancellor of the Exchequer, 1990–93

Lawson, Nigel (later, Lord Lawson of Blaby) (1932–) British journalist and politician. Conservative MP for Blaby, 1974–92; Financial Secretary to the Treasury, 1979–81; Secretary of State for Energy, 1981–83; Chancellor of the Exchequer, 1983–89

Lee, Sir Frank (1903–71) British Civil Servant. Colonial Office, 1926–40; HM Treasury, then Permanent Secretary, Ministry of Food, 1940–51; Permanent Secretary Board of Trade and later Joint Permanent Secretary, HM Treasury, 1951–62

Legras, Guy (1938–) French Civil Servant. Head of European Community Affairs, French Ministry of Foreign Affairs, 1982–85; Director-General for Agriculture, European Commission, 1985–89

Leigh-Pemberton, Robin (later, Lord Kingsdown) (1927–2013) British banker. Governor of the Bank of England, 1983–93

Letwin, Oliver (1956–) British politician. Conservative MP for West Dorset, 1997–2019; Minister of State for Government Policy, 2010–15; Chancellor of the Duchy of Lancaster, 2014–16

Lubbers, Ruud (1939–2018) Dutch politician. Minister of Economic Affairs, 1973–77; Prime Minister of the Netherlands, 1982–94; UN High Commissioner for Refugees, 2001–5

Macmillan, Harold (later the Earl of Stockton) (1894–1986) British politician. Conservative MP for Stockton on Tees, 1924–29 and 1931–45, and for Bromley, 1945–64; Minister Resident in the Mediterranean, 1943–45; Secretary of State for Air, 1945; Minister of Housing, 1951–54; Minister of Defence, 1954–55; Foreign Secretary, 1955; Chancellor of the Exchequer, 1955–57; Prime Minister, 1957–63

Major, Sir John (1943–) British politician. Conservative MP for Huntingdon, 1979–2001; Minister of State for Social Security, 1986–87; Chief Secretary to the Treasury, 1987–89; Foreign and Commonwealth Secretary, 1989; Chancellor of the Exchequer, 1989–90; Prime Minister, 1990–97

Makins, Sir Roger (later 1st Baron Sherfield) (1904–96) HM Diplomatic Service,1928–56. Minister, British Embassy Washington, 1945–47; Assistant Under-Secretary of State, FO, 1947–48; Deputy Under-Secretary of State, FCO, 1948–52; British Ambassador to the United States, 1953–56; Joint Permanent Secretary to the Treasury, 1956–60; Chairman of the UK Atomic Energy Authority, 1960–64

Mandelson, Peter (later, Lord Mandelson of Foy) (1953–) British politician. Labour MP for Hartlepool, 1992–2004; Minister without Portfolio, 1997–98; Secretary of State for Trade and Industry and President of the Board of Trade, 1998; Secretary of State for Northern Ireland, 1999–2001; European Commissioner for Trade, 2004–8; Secretary of State for Business, Innovation and Skills, 2008–10; Lord President of the Council and First Secretary of State, 2009–10

Marsh, Richard (later Lord March of Mannington) (1928–2011) British politician. Labour MP for Greenwich, 1959–71; Parliamentary Private Secretary, Ministry of Labour, 1964–65 and Ministry of Technology, 1965–66; Minister of Power, 1966–68; Minister of Transport, 1968–69; Chairman of British Railways Board, 1971–76

Marshall, George (1880–1949) US soldier and statesman. Chief of Staff of the US Army, 1939–45; US Secretary of State, 1947–49; President of the American Red Cross, 1949–50; Secretary of Defence, 1950–51

Maudling, Reginald (1917–79) British politician. Conservative MP for Barnet, 1950–74; Paymaster General,1957–59; President of the Board of Trade, 1959–61; Secretary of State for the Colonies, 1961–62; Chancellor of the Exchequer, 1962–64; Home Secretary, 1970–72

Merkel, Angela (1954–) German CDU politician. Member of the Bundestag since 1991; Minister for Women and Youth, 1991–94; Minister for the Environment, Nature Conservation and Nuclear Safety, 1994–8; Leader of the CDU, 2000–18; Chancellor of Germany since 2005

Miliband, Ed (1969) British politician. Labour MP for Doncaster North, 2005–19; Minister for the Third Sector, 2006–7; Minister for the Cabinet Office and Chancellor of the Duchy of Lancaster, 2007–8; Secretary of State for Energy and Climate Change, 2008–10; Leader of the Labour Party and Leader of the Opposition 2010–15; Shadow Secretary of State for Business, Enrgy and Industrial Strategy from 2020

Mitterrand, François (1916–96) French politician. Minister of 'Overseas' France, 1950–51; Minister of Interior, 1954–55; Minister of Justice, 1956–57; Leader of the French Socialist Party, 1971–81; President of the Republic, 1981–95

Monnet, Jean (1888–1979) French political economist. French Planning Commissioner, 1945–52; President of the High Authority of the ECSC, 1952–55; Creator of the Action Committee for a United States of Europe, 1955

Nairne, Sir Patrick (1931–2013) British Civil Servant. Second Permanent Secretary, Cabinet Office, 1973–75; Permanent Secretary, Department of Health and Social Security, 1975–81; Master, St Catherine's College, Oxford, 1981–88

Nield, Sir William (1913–94) British Civil Servant. Under-Secretary, MAFF, 1959–64; Deputy Under-Secretary, Department of Economic Affairs (DEA), 1964–66; Deputy Under-Secretary, Cabinet Office,1966–68; Permanent Secretary (DEA) 1968–69; Second Permanent Secretary, Cabinet Office coordinating British policy towards the EEC, 1969–72; Permanent Secretary, Northern Ireland Office, 1972–73

Nixon, Richard M. (1913–94) US politician. Republican Congressman for California, 1947–50; Senator for California, 1950–53; US Vice-President, 1953–61; President of the United States, 1969–74

O'Neill, Sir Con (1912–88) British Civil Servant and Member of HM Diplomatic Service; Ambassador to the EEC, Brussels, 1963–65; Deputy Under-Secretary, FO, 1965–68; and FCO, 1969–72, as Official Leader of the UK Delegation negotiating UK accession to the EEC.

Ortoli, François-Xavier (1925–2007) French politician. *Directeur de Cabinet* for President Pompidou, 1962–66; Minister of Housing and Supply, 1967–68; Minister of Economy and Finance, 1968–69; Minister of Scientific and Industrial Development, 1969–72; President of the European Commission, 1973–77; Vice-President of the European Commission for Economic and Financial Affairs, 1977–84

Osborne, George (1971–) British politician. Conservative MP for Tatton, 2001–17; Chancellor of the Exchequer, 2010–16; Editor of the London *Evening Standard* since 2017

Owen, David (later, Lord Owen of the City of Plymouth) (1938–) British politician. Co-founder, and later leader, of the Social Democratic Party (SDP); MP for Plymouth Sutton (Labour, 1966–81; SDP, 1981–92); Under-Secretary for Defence, 1968–70; Minister of State at the DHSS, 1974–76; Minister of State at the FCO, 1976–77; Secretary of State for Foreign and Commonwealth Affairs, 1977–79

Palliser, Sir Michael (1922–2012) HM Diplomatic Service, 1947-1982; UK Permanent Representative to the European Community, 1973–75; Permanent Under-Secretary, FCO and Head of HM Diplomatic Service, 1975–82

Papandreou, Andreas (1919–96) Greek economist and politician. Member of the Hellenic Parliament, 1974–96; Prime Minister of Greece, 1981–89 and 1993–96

Peart, Fred (later, Lord Peart of Workington) (1914–88) British politician. Labour MP for Workington, 1945–76; Minister of Agriculture, Fisheries and Food, 1964–68 and 1974–76; Leader of the House of Lords, 1976–79

Peyrefitte, Alain (1925–99) French scholar and politician. French Minister of Information, 1962; Minister of Information, 1962–66; Minister for Scientific Research, 1966–67; Minister of Education, 1967–68; Minister for Administrative Reform, 1973–74; Minister for Culture and the Environment, 1974; Garde des Sceaux, Ministry of Justice, 1977–81

Peyrefitte, Roger (1907–2000) French diplomat, novelist and campaigner for homosexual rights. Best known for his novel *Les Amitiés Particulières*

Pleven, René (1901–93) French politician. Member of De Gaulle's Free French Forces, 1940–44; Minister of the Economy and Finance, 1944–46; President of the Democratic and Socialist Union of the Resistance (USDR), 1946–53; Minister of Defence, 1949–50; Prime Minister, 1950–51 and 1951–52; Defence Minister, 1952–54; Foreign Minister, 1857–58; Minister of Justice, 1969–73

Pöhl, Karl Otto (1929–2014) German economist. President of the Deutsche Bundesbank, 1980–91

Pompidou, Georges (1911–74) French Gaullist politician. Trained and taught as a teacher; banker, 1953–62; Prime Minister, 1962–68; President of the Republic, 1969–74

Powell, Charles (later, Lord Powell of Bayswater) (1941–) British diplomat and businessman. Member of HM Diplomatic service, 1963–91; Private Secretary for Foreign Affairs to the Prime Minister, 1983–91

Powell, Enoch (1912–98) British politician. Conservative MP for Wolverhampton, 1950–74; Ulster Unionist MP,1974–77; Minister of Health, 1960–61

Pym, Francis (later, Lord Pym of Sandy) (1922–2008) British politician. Conservative MP for Cambridgeshire, 1961–87; Government Chief Whip, 1970–73; Secretary of State for Northern Ireland, 1973–74; Secretary of State for Defence, 1979–81; Postmaster General and Chancellor of the Duchy of Lancaster, 1981–82; Secretary of State for Foreign and Commonwealth Affairs, 1982–83

Reagan, Ronald (1911–2004) US politician. Governor of California, 1967–75; President of the United States, 1981–89

Rees-Mogg, William (later, Lord Rees-Mogg) (1928–2012) British journalist. Editor of *The Times*, 1967–81; Chairman of the Arts Council of Great Britain, 1982–89

Reilly, Sir Patrick (1909–99)HM Diplomatic Service, 1933–68; British Ambassador to the Soviet Union, 1957–60; Deputy Under-Secretary, Foreign Office, 1960–65; British Ambassador to France, 1965–68

Renwick, Robin (later, Lord Renwick of Clifton) (1937-) HM Diplomatic Service, 1963-95; Assistant Under-Secretary, FCO, 1984-87; British Ambassador to South Africa, 1987-91; British Ambassador to the United States, 1991-95

Rifkind, Sir Malcolm (1946-) British politician. Conservative MP for Edinburgh, 1974-97; Parliamentary Under-Secretary, FCO, 1982-83; Minister of State for Europe, FCO, 1983-86; Secretary of State for Scotland, 1986-90; Secretary of State for Transport, 1990-92; Defence Secretary, 1992-95; Foreign and Commonwealth Secretary, 1995-97

Rippon, Geoffrey (later, Lord Rippon of Hexham) (1924-97) British politician. Conservative MP for Norwich South, 1955-64, and for Hexham, 1966-87; Minister of Technology, 1970; Chancellor of the Duchy of Lancaster, 1970-72; Secretary of State for the Environment, 1972-74; Shadow Foreign Secretary, 1974-75

Rocard, Michel (1930-2016) French Socialist politician. Mayor of Conflans-Sainte-Honorine, 1977-94; Minister of Territorial Development, 1981-83; Minister of Agriculture, 1983-85; Prime Minister, 1988-91; Member of the European Parliament, 1994-2009

Rostow, Walt Whitman (1916-2003) US economist and academic. Deputy National Security Adviser to the President of the United States, 1961; Director of Policy Planning, 1961-66; National Security Adviser, 1966-69

Santer, Jacques (1947-) Luxembourg politician. Member of the Chamber of Deputies, 1974-95; Prime Minister of Luxembourg, 1984-95; President of the European Commission, 1995-99

Schmidt, Helmut (1918-2015) German politician. Minister of Defence, 1969-72; Finance Minister, 1972-74; Chancellor of the Federal Republic of Germany, 1974-82

Schröder, Gerhard (1910-89) German CDU politician. Member of the Bundestag, 1949-80; Federal Minister of the Interior, 1953-61; Federal Minister of Foreign Affairs, 1961-66; Federal Minister of Defence, 1966-69

Schröder, Gerhard (1944-) German SPD politician. Member of the Bundestag, 1980-86 and 1998-2005; Minister President of Lower Saxony, 1990-98; President of the Bundesrat, 1997-98; Leader of the SDP, 1999-2004; Chancellor of the Federal Republic of Germany, 1998-2005

Schulz, Martin (1955-) German Socialist politician. MEP, 1994-2017; Member of the Bundestag for North Rhine-Westphalia since 2017; President of the European Parliament, 2012-17; Leader of the Social Democratic Party, 2017-18

Schuman, Robert (1886-1963) French politician. Prime Minister, 1947-48; Foreign Minister, 1948-53; President of the European Parliament, 1958-60

Shore, Peter (later, Lord Shore of Stepney) (1924-2001) British politician. Labour MP for Stepney, 1964-74, Stepney and Poplar, 1974-83 and Bethnal Green and Stepney,

1983-97; 1964-87; Parliamentary Private Secretary to Harold Wilson, 1964-67; Secretary of State for Economic Affairs, 1967-69; Minister without Portfolio, 1969-70; Secretary of State for Trade, 1974-76; Secretary of State for the Environment, 1976-79

Silkin, John (1923-87) British politician. Labour MP for Deptford, 1963-74 and Lewisham Deptford, 1974-87; Minister of Public Building and Works, 1969-70; Minister of Local Government and Planning, 1974-76; Minister of Agriculture, Fisheries and Food, 1976-79

Smith, John (1938-94) British politician. Labour MP for Monklands East, 1970-94; Minister of State for Energy, 1975-76; Minister of State for the Privy Council Office, 1976-78; Secretary of State for Trade and President of the Board of Trade, 1978-79; Leader of the Opposition, 1992-94

Soames, Sir Christopher (later, Lord Soames of Fletching) (1920-87) British politician. Conservative MP for Bedford, 1950-66; Secretary of State for War, 1958-60; Minister of Agriculture, Fisheries and Food, 1960-64; British Ambassador to France, 1968-72; Vice-President of the European Commission, responsible for External Relations and Trade, 1973-77: Lord President of the Council and Leader of the House of Lords, 1979-81; Governor of Rhodesia, 1979-80. Married to Mary Soames, youngest daughter of Winston Churchill

Soares, Mario (1924-2017) Portuguese politician. Secretary-General of the Portuguese Socialist Party, 1973-86; Minister without Portfolio, March–August, 1975; Minister of Foreign Affairs, 1974-75 and 1977-78; Prime Minister, 1976-78 and 1983-85; President of Portugal, 1986-96; Member of the European Parliament, 1999-2004

Spaak, Paul-Henri (1899-1972) Belgian politician. Foreign Minister of Belgium, 1936-38; 1939-49; 1954-58; 1961-66; Prime Minister, 1938-39; 1946; 1947-49

Spreckley, Sir Nicholas (1934-94) HM Diplomatic Service; Head of European Communities Department, FCO, 1979-83; Ambassador to the Republic of Korea, 1983-86; High Commissioner to Malaysia, 1986-91

Stalin, Joseph (1878-1953) Russian revolutionary and politician. General Secretary of the Communist Party of the Soviet Union, 1922-52; Chairman of the Council of Ministers of the Soviet Union, 1941-53

Stewart, Michael (later, Baron Stewart of Fulham) (1906-90) British politician. Labour MP for Fulham, 1945-59; Foreign Secretary, 1965-66 and 1968-70; Secretary of State for Economic Affairs, 1966-67; First Secretary of State, 1966-68

Straw, Jack (1946-) British politician. Labour MP for Blackburn, 1979-2015; Home Secretary, 1997-2001; Foreign and Commonwealth Secretary, 2001-6; Leader of the House of Commons, 2006-7; Secretary of State for Justice and Lord Chancellor, 2007-10

Thatcher, Margaret (later Baroness Thatcher of Kesteven) (1925–2013) British politician. Conservative MP for Finchley, 1959–92; Secretary of State for Education, 1970–74; Leader of the Opposition, 1975–79; Prime Minister, 1979–90

Thomson, George (later Lord Thomson of Monifieth) (1921–2008) British politician. Labour MP for Dundee East, 1952–72; Minister of State, Foreign Office, 1964–66; Chancellor of the Duchy of Lancaster, 1966–67 and 1969–70; Secretary of State for Commonwealth Affairs, 1967–68; Member of the European Commission, 1973–77

Thorn, Gaston (1928–2007) Luxembourg politician. Foreign Minister and Foreign Trade Minister, 1969–80; Prime Minister, 1974–79; President of the European Commission, 1981–85

Thorpe, Jeremy (1929–2014) British politician. Liberal MP for Devon North, 1959–79; Leader of the Liberal Party, 1967–76

Tindemans, Leo (1922–2014) Belgian Christian Democrat politician. President of the European People's Party, 1976–85; Prime Minister, 1974–78; Foreign Minister, 1981–89

Tomkins, Sir Edward (1915–2007) HM Diplomatic Service, 1939-75. Ambassador to The Netherlands, 1970–72; Ambassador to France, 1972–75

Truman, Harry S. (1884–1972) US politician. Presiding Judge of Jackson County, Missouri, 1927–35; US Senator for Missouri, 1935–45; Vice-President of the United States, 1945; President of the United States, 1945–53

Tugendhat, Christopher (later, Lord Tugendhat of Widdington) (1937–) British politician. Conservative MP for the Cities of London and Westminster, 1970–77; Member (latterly Vice-President) of the European Commission for Budgetary Issues, 1977–85

Turnbull, Andrew (later, Lord Turnbull of Enfield) (1945–) British Civil Servant. Official of HM Treasury; Principal Private Secretary to the Prime Minister, 1988–92; Permanent Secretary to Department of Environment (DEFRA) 1992–98; Permanent Secretary to the Treasury, 1998–2002; Cabinet Secretary and Head of the Home Civil Service, 2002–5

Verhofstadt, Guy (1953–) Belgian Liberal politician. Member of the Belgian Chamber of Representatives, 1985–2009; Minister of Budget, 1985–92; Deputy Prime Minister, 1985–92; Prime Minister of Belgium 1999–2008; Member of the European Parliament since 2009; Leader of the Alliance of Liberals and Democrats for Europe Group in the European Parliament, 2009–19

Walker, Peter (later, Baron Walker of Worcester) (1932–2010) British politician. Conservative MP for Worcester, 1961–92; Minister of State for Housing and Local Government, 1970; Secretary of State for the Environment, 1970–72; Secretary of State for Trade and Industry, 1972–74; Minister of Agriculture, Fisheries and Food, 1979–83; Secretary of State for Energy, 1983–87; Secretary of State for Wales, 1987–90

Walters, Sir Alan (1926–2009) British economist. Chief Economic Adviser to Prime Minister Margaret Thatcher, 1981–83 and 1989

Werner, Pierre (1923–2002) Luxembourg politician. Prime Minister of Luxembourg, 1959–74 and 1979–84

Wicks, Sir Nigel (1940–) British Civil Servant. Joined HM Treasury, 1968; Private Secretary to Prime Ministers Wilson and Callaghan, 1975–78; Economic Minister, British Embassy Washington and UK Executive Director of the IMF and IBRD, 1983–85; Principal Private Secretary to the Prime Minister (Margaret Thatcher), 1983–85; Second Permanent Secretary at HM Treasury, 1985–2000

Williams, Shirley (later, Baroness Williams of Crosby) (1930–) British politician. Labour MP for Hitchin, 1964-74 and Hertford and Stevenage, 1974-79; SDP MP for Crosby, 1981–83; Secretary of State for Prices and Consumer Protection, 1974–76; Secretary of State for Education and Science, 1976–79

Williamson, David (later, Lord Williamson of Horton) (1934–2015) British Civil Servant. Joined the Ministry of Agriculture, Fisheries and Food, 1958; Deputy Director-General for Agriculture in the European Commission, 1977–83; Deputy Secretary and Head of the European Secretariat, Cabinet Office, 1983–87; Secretary-General of the European Commission, 1987–97; Convenor of the Crossbench Peers, House of Lords, 2004-7

Wilson, Harold (later, Lord Wilson of Rievaulx) (1916–95) British politician. Labour MP for Ormskirk, 1945-50 and Huyton, 1950 –83; Parliamentary Secretary to the Ministry of Works, 1945–47; Secretary for Overseas Trade, 1947; President of the Board of Trade, 1947–51; Prime Minister, 1964–70 and 1970–74

Wood, Stewart (later, Lord Wood of Anfield) (1968–) British academic and political adviser. Member of the Chancellor of the Exchequer's Council of Economic Advisers, specializing in education policy, local government, and EU policy; Adviser to the Prime Minister on foreign policy, Northern Ireland, culture, media and sport, 2007–10; Adviser to Ed Miliband (Leader of the Opposition) 2010–15

Wright, Sir Oliver (1922–2009) HM Diplomatic Service, 1946-86;. Assistant Private Secretary, and then Private Secretary, to the Foreign Secretary, 1960–63; Private Secretary to the Prime Minister (Douglas-Home and Wilson), 1964–66; Ambassador to Denmark, 1966–69; to the Federal Republic of Germany, 1975–81; and to the United States, 1982–86

List of Abbreviations

ACP	African, Caribbean and Pacific Group of States
AfD	Alternative für Deutschland
AUSS	Assistant Under-Secretary of State
BBC	British Broadcasting Corporation
BOAC	British Overseas Airways Corporation
BSE	Bovine Spongiform Encephalopathy
CAB (and CC)	Minutes of Cabinet meetings
CAP	Common Agricultural Policy
CBI	Confederation of British Industry
CDU	Christian Democratic Union (Germany)
CFP	Common Fisheries Policy
CJD	Creutzfeldt-Jakob Disease
CO	Cabinet Office
COREPER	Committee of Permanent Representatives of the European Community/European Union
CSU	Christian Social Union of Bavaria
DTI	Department of Trade and Industry
ECJ	European Court of Justice
ECOFIN	Economic and Financial Affairs Council of the EEC/EU
ECR	European Conservatives and Reformists Group (European Parliament)
ECSC	European Coal and Steel Community
EEC	European Economic Community
EFTA	European Free Trade Association
EMS	European Monetary System
EMU	Economic and Monetary Union
EP	European Parliament
EPP	European People's Party
ERDF	European Regional Development Fund
ERM	European Exchange Rate Mechanism
ESF	European Social Fund
EU	European Union
FAC	Foreign Affairs Council of the EEC
FCO	Foreign and Commonwealth Office
FPD	Free Democratic Party (Germany)
FRG	Federal Republic of Germany

GAC	General Affairs Council (Foreign Ministers, of the EEC/EU)
GATT	General Agreement on Tariffs and Trade
GDP	Gross Domestic Product
GDR	German Democratic Republic (East Germany)
GNP	Gross National Product
HMG	Her/His Majesty's Government
HMT	Her Majesty's Treasury
IBRD	International Bank for Reconstruction and Development (the World Bank)
IGC	Intergovernmental Conference
IMF	International Monetary Fund
MAFF	Ministry of Agriculture, Fisheries and Food
MCA	Monetary Compensatory Amount
MEP	Member of the European Parliament
MP	Member of Parliament
MUA	Monetary Unit of Account
(N)AFTA	North Atlantic Free Trade Area
NATO	North Atlantic Treaty Organization
NEC	National Executive Committee of the Labour Party
NFU	National Farmers' Union
OECD	Organisation for Economic Co-operation and Development
OEEC	Organisation for European Economic Co-operation
OR	Own Resources (the financing mechanism of the EEC/EU)
PLP	Parliamentary Labour Party
PPS	Parliamentary Private Secretary *or* Principal Private Secretary
PREM	Prime Ministerial (Number 10 Downing Street) papers held at The National Archives
PUS	Permanent Under-Secretary of State
PUSS	Parliamentary Under-Secretary of State
QMV	Qualified Majority Voting
RAF	Royal Air Force
SACEUR	Supreme Allied Commander Europe
SDP	Social Democratic Party
SEA	Single European Act
SPD	Social Democratic Party (Germany)
TNA	The National Archives
TUC	Trades Union Congress
UKIP	UK Independence Party
USSR	Union of Soviet Socialist Republics
VAT	Value Added Tax
WEU	Western European Union
WTO	World Trade Organization

Introduction

I stand in the Frick gallery in New York, staring at the two sixteenth-century Holbein portraits on the wall in front of me. On the left is Thomas More, on the right, Thomas Cromwell. They look as they must have been. Both lost their heads to the tyrant Henry VIII, whom they both served. But their portraits are timeless, modern in their precision, acute in their revelation of character. No way can the piggy-eyed, clever thug that Holbein saw in Cromwell be reconciled with the sympathetic version created by Hilary Mantel in *Wolf Hall*. By the same token, it is hard to reconcile the statesmanlike More with the man whose scatalogically virulent attacks on Martin Luther went far beyond the bounds of anything we would today consider normal or acceptable.

In a way, the two men represent the two sides of the schism that was the Reformation: a schism that went beyond religious difference and encapsulated two different views of the world. More was a Renaissance scholar, fluent in the Latin and Greek in which he educated his daughter, Meg, at a time when his own wife, more usually for the time, was illiterate. He was the friend of the Dutch philosopher and scholar Erasmus. They both saw themselves as part of an international, and especially European, cultural and spiritual order: that of Christendom. For More, the son of a lawyer, and himself the most senior guardian and dispenser of the law in the England of his day, the Church and State were umbilically linked and the laws of God and the laws of Man had to be in harmony. When Henry VIII sundered that harmony by declaring himself Head of the Church and breaking from the authority of Rome he was not, in More's eyes, simply rebelling from a pontiff who was more of a temporal ruler than a spiritual one. Henry's action was, as More saw it, an assault on the very foundations on which the English state was built.

Cromwell, by contrast, was the supremely transactional politician. What the king wanted, the king would get, be it the cruel and wanton dissolution of the monasteries and the seizure of their wealth, or a divorce from one wife and marriage to another. Or, when it came to it, the execution of the new wife, Anne Boleyn, on trumped up charges. Cromwell asserted the new Englishness without a moment of hesitation, remorse, or nostalgia for the old order. In many ways, he was more ruthless than his master who clung to the old forms of Catholic Christianity even while rejecting its right to dictate to him how he conducted the business of his life and of his kingdom.

More, the 'Remainer'; Cromwell, the 'Brexiteer', I think to myself as I stand there. I am woken from my reverie by two people standing behind me. They too are looking at the portraits. 'No', opines one of them 'I like 'em fuzzy'. Maybe my thinking is a bit fuzzy, or certainly wishful. But I do believe that you cannot explain Brexit without tracing a path which extends back at least as far as the Reformation in our island story, and probably further: the thousand years of history of Hugh Gaitskell's description.

If this suggests a kind of ordained inevitability to Brexit, it is not meant to do so. The 2016 referendum result was close enough that it could easily have tilted the other way. It is no surprise that the 'For Want of a Nail' proverb has many versions across many countries and centuries. Because we are mortal, cannot see the future and are perilously insecure, we seek patterns of inevitability in our interpretation of the past. Thus, the Second World War 'inevitably' followed the First because of the humiliations inflicted on Germany by the Treaty of Versailles. The roots of new conflict are certainly there at Versailles but, without the economic crash of the late 1920s, or the ferocious genius of a second-rate artist and would-be architect, would the Second World War have happened?

The speculation is pointless, but retracing the course of events is instructive. In the case of Britain and continental Europe, there is a consistent pattern of centuries-long British (or at least English) engagement with the continent in order to resist conquest or domination by any one foreign power or group of powers. As an island nation we found in the sea both our peril and our security. You have only to look at the attempts of Napoleon or Hitler to cut off our sea routes so as to starve us out, to appreciate the peril. And you have only to see the difficulties for Hitler of mounting an invasion once the Battle of Britain had been won by young allied heroes, and the *Blitzkrieg* had failed, to appreciate the part that the sea, and naval superiority, paid in our security, but also in our prosperity as a nation dependent on international trade. So, even if you do not accept a thousand years of conflicted history as a paradigm for our more modern behaviour, it is hard to argue that the Brexit vote was a total aberration compared with the rest of our European history, since 1945 at least. Winston Churchill, who summoned up the new world of post-war continental integration to redress the balance of the old world of conflict, nonetheless wanted Britain to be 'with' Europe, not 'of' it.

The conventional wisdom of those senior civil servants for whom I worked in the 1970s and 1980s was that the generation above them, of both politicians

and officials, had made a signal error of judgement in not seeing the significance of the European Community at its foundation. We had missed the
European train in the 1950s and had ultimately had to scramble aboard.
I believe they were right that a mistake had been made. But the post-war
attitudes I describe in early chapters of this book were not just the product of
misplaced vanity, though there was some of that. They were, much more, the
product of a world where the UK was still an imperial power, where Germany
was still perceived as a potential threat, and where hard experience had bred
faith in the robustness of British political institutions and lack of faith in those
on the European continent. The successive post-war Labour and Conservative
governments had very different prescriptions for domestic policy. But their
world view was very similar: it was about defence rooted in the American
protective shield, NATO, and resistance to Soviet aggression. Churchill clung
to dreams of empire, but it was his successor but one, the Conservative, Harold
Macmillan, who most presciently described the winds of change blowing
through what, at the time, was still colonial Africa. Both political parties,
therefore, faced up to the end of empire. But both clung for too long to a
belief in the economic, and therefore political, importance that the independent nations of the Commonwealth would represent for British interests.

It was Macmillan, too, who saw, sooner than his colleagues, that Britain
could not defeat the fledgling EEC through the rival EFTA. But Macmillan did
misread de Gaulle, just as he mishandled Adenauer, the German Chancellor.

In 1958, when de Gaulle returned to power, he did so as a sceptic about the
supranational Treaty of Rome to which France had signed up a year earlier. It
was Adenauer, sitting with de Gaulle as they looked out over the woods and
fields at Colombey-les-deux-Églises, who persuaded the French President that
EFTA was a blind alley and that the future lay with the EEC. And when, in the
same year, Soviet Russia tried to starve West Berlin out of existence, it was de
Gaulle who championed the German cause while Macmillan, preoccupied by
his desire to get alongside Moscow, hung back. The British were still trying to
play the great game, to the neglect of their own neighbourhood.

For the British, joining the European Community was always a distress
purchase: the reluctant outcome of the failure of other post-war strategies. For
the original Six, there had been more positive motivations in terms of politics,
economics, and security. The rules of the EEC that the UK joined in 1973 had
been made in Brussels, Paris, and Bonn. Such accommodations as were made
to the UK were, at British request, concentrated on the interests of the
Commonwealth: New Zealand butter trumped the escalator of budget costs
to the British Exchequer. But it was the latter that would prompt, in Margaret

Thatcher's five-year battle for 'my money back', the biggest row between the UK and her partners and the one that would etch into British DNA the notion that EEC membership was a battle: us versus them; win or lose.

In the meantime, the Labour Party had opposed membership in 1961–3, supported it between 1966 and 1970, opposed it again between 1970 and 1974 and had then papered over the cracks through a largely optical renegotiation and a referendum. That 1975 referendum appeared to be decisive in public terms. But it did little to heal the divisions in the Labour Party which, after its defeat by Thatcher in 1979, once again, and for several years, became a party which opposed continued British membership of the Community.

Throughout most of the years from 1961, the Conservative Party considered itself 'the Party of Europe' (as did the Liberals, who had only small representation in Parliament). But Prime Minister Edward Heath faced significant opposition from within his own ranks in taking Britain into the EEC and Thatcher turned negotiation into warfare. And neither main party came to terms with the EEC as it was, or as the rest of the membership wanted it to be.

'Ever closer union among the peoples of Europe' is a primary objective of the EEC/EU as set out in its founding treaty, the Treaty of Rome. It is a goal that came to be interpreted in the UK as synonymous with a European super state; or as ever greater centralization led by a power hungry European Commission. Few attempts were ever made by British politicians to explain that ever closer union was built into the DNA of the EEC.

The European treaties gave to the EEC's institutions only those powers which the Member Governments chose to grant. But the accretion of power to the institutions was an inevitable consequence of each decision by the membership to take on more cooperation through the EEC mechanisms, rather than through intergovernmental treaties agreed under separate international law. The logic was impeccable. In order to avoid the dominance of the smaller states by the larger, decisions as to what areas of cooperation should be proposed for common action had to lie with an independent body. The composition of that body, the European Commission, did not disregard the relative size of the different Member States, but was devised in such a way that proposals by the Commission could not be dictated by the more powerful members.

The proposals the Commission put forward for action required the agreement of the Member States (through the Council of Ministers, representing national Member Governments) and, in later years that of the European Parliament. The Commission had, in the early days, to seek the unanimous agreement of the member governments. Gradually, for reasons of efficiency and progress, more majority voting was introduced. And once a Commission proposal had been adopted by the Council, i.e. by the membership as a whole, it could not be gainsaid by any one government or national parliament. A 'competence', be it over environment, trade, agriculture, social protections, or energy policy, became a competence of the EEC and no longer of each government. The sovereignty of national parliaments was therefore retained in a global sense: any parliament could decide to leave the club. But, while remaining in the club, governments and parliaments had to accept that their power of individual decision and action was curtailed. There was, in the legal sense, a continuous loss of sovereignty.

In this respect the EEC/EU Treaties were, and are, unlike any other international treaty the UK has entered into. The North Atlantic Treaty, for example, has been amended over time, by unanimous agreement, to take in new members. But its binding terms and commitments have remained unchanged since the 1950s. By contrast, the binding terms and commitments inherent in the EEC Treaties have been in constant evolution. And where the competences granted by those Treaties have no longer been thought adequate, the Member States have got together to increase them: notably through the Maastricht, Amsterdam, Nice, and Lisbon Treaties. Each time, more power has gone from the member nations to the institutions of the EEC.

Each of those treaties has required the unanimous consent of the Member Governments and the approval of their national Parliament. That has been an essential safeguard. The individual measures subsequently adopted have had to be within the legal scope of the Treaties and have required the negotiated assent of the Member Governments (increasingly by majority vote) and the approval of the European Parliament, whose members are directly elected by European citizens.

For most Member States, for most of the first half century of the EEC's existence, the system was, not just acceptable, but well regarded and even popular. The gain outweighed any pain. Germany achieved post-war respectability and a market for her industry. Through the EEC's mutual obligations, France gained a degree of control over a Germany the French still feared. And the French ensured that the main EEC policy of the early years was an agricultural support policy (the CAP) that favoured an economy dominated by farming. The smaller Member States felt protected by the EEC structures from dominance by the large. The poorer Member States, such as Ireland, Greece, Portugal, and Spain benefited from large financial subsidies to bring them out of poverty. In the early years, only the Germans paid more of their national wealth over to the Community than they got back. Everyone else got back more than they had put in. Loss of national sovereignty was more than acceptable when set against the gain in prosperity, overall influence, and weight in the world.

Britain joined late, and paid a price, both political and economic. The price of membership that it had to accept to join an already existing and flourishing club was steep financially. It was uncomfortable, too, in that the policies of the club were better suited to agricultural, and protectionist, economies than to a country that depended on open trade with the world and had been obliged to negotiate, not just in its own interests, but in those of its Commonwealth partners as well. And, more than in any other Member State, Britain's sense of national identity was centred on the sovereignty of Parliament.

This book is the story of why Britain did not foresee that the efforts of post-war continental Europe to come together would succeed, why it then hesitated to join, why it joined on bad terms, and why, and how, it wrestled with the conditions and contradictions of membership almost without ever feeling at ease with the decision it had taken. This is the story of the long and troubled road to June 2016 and the vote to leave the European Union.

1

A Thousand Years of History

The air in the room was heady with excitement and anticipation, the mood buoyant. Students, wearing medieval costumes of scarlet, purple, yellow, and green, waved brilliant banners. Surprisingly perhaps, they were waiting, not for a newly elected young Lochinvar of a leader but, instead, for an elderly man who was no longer even in office. But to them he was a hero and, being a man who loved to think about the future, he had quite deliberately chosen to speak to a young audience because, as he was to tell them, on them would 'devolve the great task of rebuilding a world devastated by war and sundered by hatreds'.

On that warm autumn day in September 1946, Mr Churchill's progress towards the great Zurich hall was slow as crowds showered upon his car huge bunches and sprays of flowers. When he did arrive and rose to speak, those who heard him were not disappointed. Perhaps because he was making the speech in Switzerland, neutral during the world war which had ended barely a year earlier, Churchill started by conjuring up the dark European landscape which lay beyond the Swiss border, a world of 'a vast grieving mass of tormented, hungry, careworn and bewildered human beings who wait in the ruins of their cities and their homes and scan the dark horizons'.

As ever with Churchill, the 'sovereign remedy' which he proposed was bold. 'We must', he proclaimed, 'build a kind of United States of Europe'. Why should there not be, he asked, a European grouping which would give a sense of enlarged patriotism and common citizenship to the 'distracted peoples of this mighty continent'? For Churchill, such a new venture was to be rooted in the ideas put forward in the pre-war years by the French patriot and statesman Aristide Briand, who had advocated a pan-European union. It would not, said Churchill, in any way conflict with the new world organization of the United Nations. The new European grouping, like the British Commonwealth of nations, would support, not undermine, the global peace structure which the wartime allies had set in place.

For Churchill, the two world wars of the twentieth century had arisen because of the vain passion of the newly united Germany to play a dominating part in the world. The guilty must be punished but then there must be an end to retribution. There must be instead an act of faith in the European family.

'I am now going to say something which will astonish you', Churchill continued. 'The first step in the recreation of the European family must be a partnership between France and Germany. In this way only, can France recover the moral and cultural leadership of Europe. There can be no revival of Europe without a spiritually great France and a spiritually great Germany. The structure of the United States of Europe will be such as to make the material strength of a single state less important. Small nation states will count as much as large ones ... If at first all the states of Europe are not willing or able to join a union, we must nevertheless proceed to assemble and combine those who will and those who can.'

For Churchill, 'in all this urgent work, France and Germany must take the lead together ... Therefore, I say to you "Let Europe arise"'.[1]

This, and other post-war speeches of Churchill's, have fuelled a debate in Britain as to whether the great man would have favoured Britain first joining, and then remaining in, the European Community which, a decade after the Zurich speech, was to become the realization of his early rallying call. But, in the conclusion of his speech, Churchill foreshadowed what was to be the consistent position of post-war British governments until the beginning of the 1960s: 'Great Britain, the British Commonwealth of nations, mighty America and, I trust, Soviet Russia must be the friends and sponsors of the new Europe and must sponsor and champion its right to live'. In other words, Britain would imagine, encourage and support, but not take part in, a project which was to be led by, and comprise, the countries of continental Europe.

Behind Churchill's view of Britain's place in the world lay, not just his experiences in a long lifetime, or even a sense of the empire which he had served as a young subaltern in imperial India, but an idea of Britain—or at least of England—much older than that. 'Je me suis toujours fait une certaine idée de la France' was the first line of General de Gaulle's memoirs. For de Gaulle, France as an entity could always somehow transcend the failings and foibles of its people. That notion may seem fanciful but, if de Gaulle created his own myth of French nationhood, he was hardly unique in doing so. No nation is without myths, and the myth may be essential to creating and sustaining a sense of national—or at least tribal—unity. The British myth, or at any rate the story we tell ourselves, is a mixture of geographical and historical fact, a product of language, of selective memory, of the sense of ourselves we get

---

[1] *The Times*, 20 September 1946.

from our families. Like Churchill himself—as much an American as a Briton by ancestry—it is full of paradoxes.

In Britain's case, the impact of geography is self-evident. To an extent, we still define ourselves as Shakespeare's 'precious stone set in the silver sea' despite the grey coldness of our maritime environment and the urban sprawl that has overtaken much of our landscape. But, of course, in John of Gaunt's famous speech in *Richard II*, the stone and the silver sea are far more political metaphors than they are geographical descriptions. What John of Gaunt is conjuring up is a world of order and stability threatened by the 'rash fierce blaze of riot' of the young king, Richard. So too, Hugh Gaitskell, the leader of the Labour Party in 1962, when Conservative Prime Minister, Harold Macmillan, was embarked on a negotiation to take Britain into the European Economic Community (EEC). At the Labour Party conference in Brighton in October of that year, Gaitskell told his audience: 'Now we must be clear': 'it does mean, *if* this is the idea, the end of Britain as an independent nation state, the end of a thousand years of history'.

The phrase 'the end of a thousand years of history' has echoed down the years, but the nuance Gaitskell added has not: 'You may say, All right! Let it end! But, my goodness, it's a decision that needs a little care and thought.'[2]

Gaitskell, dead only a few months later, was wildly cheered by Conference delegates albeit, as his wife Dora tartly remarked, by 'the wrong people'. Right or wrong, Gaitskell had no need to explain what he meant by 'a thousand years of history'. He would have conjured in the minds of his audience a picture of a nation of ancient Britons cut down by Roman swords; of the heroic and tragic uprising of Boudicca (though to Gaitskell's audience she would have been 'Boadicea'); of dark ages following the fall of Rome; of the Norman conquest of 1066; of the gradual absorption of the Normans and their foreign language into the landscape and language of England; of a country never since then successfully invaded from continental Europe; of wars against continental encroachment; of Magna Carta; of a Reformation which severed England from the corruption and overweening power of popery; of empire and of two twentieth-century wars, in the most recent of which Britain had stood alone against the forces of tyranny.

The point about those images and historical memories is not that they lack truth but that they airbrush out inconvenient facts or simply ignore certain realities which might otherwise inform Britain's view of itself. For different parts of the United Kingdom the images will be different, but still rooted in

---

[2] Michael Charlton, *The Price of Victory* (London: British Broadcasting Corporation, 1983), p. 274.

'our island story'. Self-image and self-awareness, let alone self-interest, do not always coincide. What patriotic Scot would not rather picture Rob Roy pitting his heroism against the cruel cunning of the English, than contemplate the more prosaic modern fact of a succession of Scots who have dominated British national life, including three Prime Ministers in the space of two decades?

In other words, the 'thousand years of history' conjured by Gaitskell was based on a view of Britain's place in the world which, by giving a simplistic picture of a glorious past, was equally deceptive in its assessment of Britain's place in the post-war world. 'The end of a thousand years of history' implies that the end of past successes will inevitably mean the end of future ones as well. And the 'little care and thought' Gaitskell would probably have given to the subject had he lived was lost in the applause of an enthusiastic political audience.

Geography is inescapable and does ineluctably define much of the separateness of Britain from the rest of Europe. The sea has been Britain's safeguard. Julius Caesar only achieved a secure foothold at the second attempt. William the Conqueror had to await a storm-free tide. The Spanish Armada of 1588 was dashed to pieces on the Irish and Scottish rocks. And the sea defeated two further Spanish attempts, in 1596 and 1597. Once Hitler had lost the battle of the air in the Second World War, he would have had to invade by sea. 'We are', Churchill told the people of France in a broadcast in October 1940, 'waiting for the promised invasion. So are the fishes.'

Command of the seas helped save England from Napoleon and became the safeguard of Britain's imperial trading ascendancy. Political neglect of naval defence lost the Falkland Islands in 1982. The political significance of the fishing industry far exceeds its statistical economic significance. You are much more likely to think of Europe as being elsewhere if you cannot simply walk across the same piece of land to get there. Psychologically, too, the horizons of an island maritime nation are different. You may set sail and make a day's trip to Calais; or a year-long voyage to China.

In reality, there have been almost as many invasions of Britain by native claimants to the throne as by foreign conquerors, though often the native pretenders were supported by continental backers. Lambert Simnel and Perkin Warbeck were impostors. But Edward IV achieved his final victory over Henry VI when he invaded from exile in the Low Countries, and Henry Tudor landed on a beach in Wales before, at Bosworth Field, he consigned Richard III to a battlefield death and subsequent burial beneath a future Leicester car park. Apart from the role of France in supporting Scottish rebellion against England, French forces made attacks and landings over the centuries, notably Kent

(1295), Southampton (1338), Winchelsea (1360), the Isle of Wight (1545), and Teignmouth (1690).

This intertwining of the British Isles and the continent was continuous and intense. The life of Roman Britain, at least for the settler, was sophisticated. The communications found preserved at Vindolanda on Hadrian's Wall bear witness to the familiar normality of social life: a plea to the quartermaster for more beer for the troops, an invitation to an afternoon party, a contemptuous reference to the local British natives as 'Britunculi' ('wretched little Brits'). The invasions of the Saxons and the Vikings were brutal, but the period coincided with the spread of Christianity as a unifying cultural and belief system across much of Europe, including Britain. The central and western European empire of Charlemagne did not include the British Isles, so a defining event in the history of continental Europe, and a marker of subsequent continental history, made no direct impact on our shores, save in the form of a trading arrangement and a common currency which both led to diplomatic dispute. Nevertheless, by the year 1000 England was a relatively advanced society with 'a universal land tax, an efficient bureaucracy, a single recognised coinage, and a single system of justice and administration'.[3]

It was not therefore a country lacking identity and structure that the Normans invaded in 1066, and it would be wrong to light upon Hastings as the place which defined our future as an island race. But that one act of conquest and its aftermath have provided the framework of political alliances, rivalries, and conflicts which has shaped our history and sense of identity to this day.

Before 1066, there were no recognizable national quarrels between France and England. Such relations as there were between England and the continent were primarily between England and Normandy. The *English* king, Edward the Confessor, was the son of a Norman mother. From the great Norman abbey at Jumièges came one of the early Archbishops of Canterbury. So the Normans had a foothold of benign occupation well before the conquest.

The language of the Normans, despite their Viking origins, was French. French was to remain the language of the aristocracy in England for several centuries after the conquest, and to weave into the fabric of English life vocabulary and place names which resonate to this day. But the Normans defined their interests as being in opposition to the power of the *French* kings. So, from the outset, as Norman power and settlement spread across the land, the nature of that occupation and subjugation was not one of France

---

[3] Ibid.

conquering England but, rather, of the French-speaking Normans establishing a power base from which they could pursue their quest for superiority in continental France.

The ebb and flow of battle, conquest, occupation, and resistance gave the ruling house of England, the Plantagenets, control of half of France. But most of that empire was lost to the French king by that most un-English of English hero-kings, Richard the Lion Heart, who spoke not a word of English, barely set foot on English soil and, save in modern cinema, never had any detectable dealings with that other English hero of the period, Robin Hood.

Thanks to Shakespeare and, nearer to our own times, Laurence Olivier, the cry of 'God for England, Harry and St George' echoes vibrantly down the centuries from the Battle of Agincourt in 1415. The present Duke of Sussex cultivates that 'little touch of Harry' to good effect. The fact that France and England both draw powerful support for our respective national myths from the Hundred Years War is a reflection of its endurance as a conflict and of the changing fortunes on the battlefield. Crécy and Agincourt stiffen British sinews and summon up our blood, just as Bertrand du Guesclin and Joan of Arc do for the French. The extent of England's defeat was perhaps disguised by the changing fortunes of war, but England was ultimately forced out of all of France except Calais, to which it clung until 1588. With a quaint and slightly ridiculous sense of fantasy, English monarchs continued to call themselves Kings of France until the beginning of the nineteenth century. (Perhaps it was a similar touch of Osymandian hubris that later led Queen Victoria to accept the advice of her favourite Prime Minister, Disraeli, and to style herself Empress of India.) The other reason, perhaps, for the Hundred Years War to be so embedded in our respective national cultures is that out of it emerged, more clearly than ever before, a sense in both countries of national identity: a politically united France and an England whose kings (whatever they might pretend) were now, not Normans using England to fight their dynastic battles, but Englishmen fighting for England.

My father's family arrived in England as Norman foot soldiers and settled in Derbyshire. Their name gradually morphed from Du Val to Wall and they became what a book on the old families of Derbyshire called 'knights of the field': yeoman farmers who reared livestock on land of which they were the owners. My great-grandfather sold his produce at his butcher's shop in Buxton. Along with everyone else in Britain, they were Christians and, until the mid-sixteenth century, being Christian meant owing allegiance to Rome. The most famous conflict between Church and State is personified in the quarrel between Henry II and Thomas à Becket, ending in that Archbishop of

Canterbury's murder on the altar steps of his own cathedral in 1170. The Pope in Rome exercised both temporal and spiritual sway. The Church was wealthy, owned land, and was a main source of employment and education. The Pope could summon to arms successive waves of crusaders to defend the frontiers of Christendom from the infidel Ottomans and Moors. Modern central European attitudes to migration reverberate to an echo from the past when Don John of Austria (with a precocious young Spaniard called Miguel de Cervantes in his retinue) faced down the invaders at the Battle of Lepanto in 1571.

So the Reformation that swept through sixteenth-century Europe was a revolution both of religious and political thought. The very act of translating the Bible into the vernacular (English) was seen by traditionalists as an act of theological heresy and intellectual, and therefore political, rebellion. The fact that the Reformation in England took a unique form was undoubtedly because of a rather typical English mixture of accident and opportunism. The accidents were that King Henry VIII's Spanish wife, Catherine of Aragon, was unable to bear a male child; and the king's probably genuine conviction that he had committed a mortal sin by marrying her (his brother's widow) in the first place. Henry VIII was not the first, let alone the last, statesman to be led by lust. But a combination of his genuine scruples about his marriage, and his insatiable yearning for Anne Boleyn, triggered an opportunistic chain reaction which set the English crown at loggerheads with Rome and led to deep cultural and political fissures between England and France and Spain, in particular.

One of Henry's most loyal courtiers, the Lord Chancellor, Sir Thomas More, ultimately laid down his life, not because he opposed the king's divorce from Catherine and subsequent marriage to Anne, but because the Act of Supremacy, by which Henry made himself head of the Church in England, was for him a civilizational cataclysm. For More, stern, incorruptible, ardent burner of heretics, superlative lawyer to his fingertips, the stability of society depended on the symbiotic partnership of Church and State. For the king to challenge the authority of the Church was to set himself against the centuries-long authority vested in St Peter and his successors by Christ himself. 'Thou art Peter (the rock) and upon this rock I will build my Church' meant to More, and others who gave up their lives at Tower Hill and Tyburn, something literal, tangible, and eternal. If the temporal power pitted itself against that divine order, then all order in society was in peril.

More's view of the world was shared by a greater proportion of his fellow countrymen than is now recalled. Although primarily a phenomenon of northern England, an estimated 40,000 people took part in the so-called

Pilgrimage of Grace to protest against Henry's actions. But most of the establishment of the day went with Henry. He exercised power with a toxic blend of ruthless cruelty and magnetic charisma. He never saw himself as a Protestant in the theological sense, and made no substantive changes to the Mass (other than to remove references to loyalty to the Pope). The dissolution and desecration of the monasteries was in part an attack on power, but more relevantly a quick and ruthless way of accruing wealth to his fast-emptying coffers. Thomas Cromwell, More's successor as Lord Chancellor and the instrument of the king's wrath, had more mixed motives. Cromwell was a convinced religious reformer and also, unlike More, readily tempted by personal enrichment and aggrandizement. To study the Holbein portraits of the two men as they regard each other across the centuries on the same wall of the Frick collection in New York, is to look from the ending of one world, that of the European renaissance, of which More was a leading scholar, to the beginning of a new, much more Anglo-centric one. Protestantism in England came to symbolize English island virtues standing up to the encroachment of a corrupt continental and alien popery.

That it so came about is scarcely surprising. Religious division fuelled political rivalry. England's defiance of papal authority, combined with the insult and humiliation inflicted on Catherine of Aragon, were reason enough for the Spanish king to want revenge. Philip II's dynastic marriage with Henry VIII's heir, Mary Tudor, was accompanied by her reign of terror against the new religion and the serial martyrdom of men who came to symbolize, not just their religious values, but the whole notion of defending freedom against tyranny. It was also Mary's misfortune to preside over the loss of Calais. That humiliation first established, as the historian Brendan Simms puts it, 'the fatal link in the minds of many Englishmen between popery and strategic incompetence'.[4]

In France, the king persecuted the Protestant Huguenots, many of whom sought refuge in England. The Huguenot community, which established itself in Spitalfields, and what is modern-day Wandsworth, continued to deploy their silk weaving skills to make hats for cardinals. The French embraced and supported Mary Queen of Scots (born of a French mother who became regent in Scotland). But their embrace proved to be a suffocating one. Catholic France came to be seen in Scotland as more of a threat than did England and, under Elizabeth I, Mary Tudor's Protestant successor, the French were evicted.

---

[4] Brendan Simms, *Britain's Europe: A Thousand Years of Conflict and Cooperation* (London: Allen Lane, 2016), p. 28.

Elizabeth pursued a treatment of Catholics which, though hardly benign, was characteristically pragmatic. She would not, she said, 'open a window into men's souls' and her policy was one of calculated penalization rather than terrorizing persecution. Even before the stormy sea put paid to the Spanish Armada, English Catholics were more disposed to see Spain as a threat than an opportunity. They were Englishmen first. Protestant England was bound to feel threatened by the power of Catholic Spain, not least because Philip II's ambitions to create a Catholic empire in continental Europe and beyond, took his conquests to the Low Countries and he made no secret of his aim to be 'lord of everything in east and west'.[5]

There began a pattern of English engagement with the continental powers which, through shifting alliances and in different theatres of war, was designed to prevent the establishment of a universal (Catholic) monarchy in which England would become a vassal state. As the power of Spain declined and that of France grew, English attention came to be focused on France and the territorial ambitions of Louis XIV. The Glorious Revolution of 1688 (a kind of invasion by invitation by William of Orange) was conceived by William as necessary to ensure that Protestant England took part in resisting the encroachment of Catholic France. Before that, there had been a degree of ambivalence in English attitudes. Charles I lost his head over the issue of who (King or Parliament) had the right to control taxation, but dissent over his leadership had begun with his perceived weakness in support of the Protestant cause in Germany. During the period of the Commonwealth, following the execution of Charles I in 1649, Cromwell pursued a vigorous policy of foreign military engagement in which the Protestant and the national interest were usually, though not invariably, synonymous. Yet, on the restoration, Charles II was ready to ally himself with Louis XIV in the interest of shoring up his own position and James II, openly Catholic, was determined to restore the Catholic faith in England. As Duke of York, James had warned his brother, Charles II, of a plot to overthrow him. 'Jamie, Jamie', the king is said to have replied, 'who is going to kill me to make *you* king?' After his brother's death James destroyed his reign by his own actions in a bare three years. As he escaped by boat, he dropped the Great Seal of the Realm into the Thames, believing that tradition and formality would trump the self-interest of his opponents. But national self-interest was with England's political and religious leaders and a foreign Protestant was preferable to a native Catholic. Thus, just over a decade after

---

[5] Geoffrey Parker, *The Grand Strategy of Philip II* (New Haven and London: Yale University Press, 1998), p. 4.

their successful assault on the English fleet, the Dutch were back when the leaders of the Glorious Revolution invited James's daughter, Mary, and her Dutch husband, William, to assume the English throne.

England's continental wars were at this time less wars of conquest than wars based on the principle that the best defence lay in attack. Trade rivalries also loomed large. The Plague of 1665 and the Great Fire of London of 1666 are known to every student of English history. We give less attention to the ease with which, in 1667, in an Anglo-Dutch war over dominance of the seas, the Dutch successfully sailed up the Thames into the heart of the Royal Navy fleet, captured thirteen ships and towed away the English flagship, *HMS Royal Charles*. Samuel Pepys, as a senior Admiralty clerk, was a key witness to the humiliation. In his diary of 29 July he noted that 'thus in all this, in wisdom, courage, force, knowledge of our streams, and success, the Dutch have the best of us, and end the war with victory on their side'.

The Anglo-Dutch war of the seventeenth century was essentially about predominance in trade via dominance of the sea routes. Britain's prosperity from the wool trade, from medieval times, depended on exports. It was easier and faster to sail to the near continent than to travel on horse or foot to the remoter parts of England.[6] Go today to a small town such as Topsham in Devon, which flourished from the wool trade until the mid-nineteenth century, and you see houses built of Dutch brick, brought back as ballast on ships plying the wool trade. Not for nothing did the Lord Chancellor sit in the House of Lords on a sack of wool.

The Nine Years War of the late seventeenth century was fought by England and her continental allies to curb the expansion of Louis XIV's territorial conquests in mainland Europe. The peace of 1697 with which it culminated, was short-lived and within four years England, as part of a Grand Alliance, was engaged in what was to be a ten-year conflict. '*Français, c'est moi, Churchill qui vous parle*', said the great man in one of his wartime broadcasts (the same one in which the 'fishes' were summoned to a prospective feeding frenzy on the threatened Nazi invader). But the first Churchill to come to French attention, the future Duke of Marlborough, summoned up quite different feelings in French hearths and homes as French mothers allegedly enjoined their fractious children to sleep lest Malbrouck should come and get them. Blenheim Palace is so much part of our rural and historical landscape that we tend to forget that Blenheim is a small town in Bavaria. Marlborough, so the victory column at Blenheim Palace tells the world, 'asserted and confirmed the

---

[6] Simms, *Britain's Europe*.

liberties of Europe' by his military successes.[7] Safety and prosperity at home were secured by continental wars, and a national sense of England as the home of liberty was enshrined in the national psyche, despite the signal lack of what we would recognize as popular representation.

Marlborough's victories led to the Treaty of Utrecht in 1713 and to a relatively peaceful quarter century in which Britain established maritime, commercial, and financial pre-eminence. But the second half of the century saw the old rivalry between France and Britain played out in wars of mixed fortunes: wars which included the establishment of British rule in India and Canada but a naval defeat at the hands of the French at Yorktown in 1781: the culminating battle in the American War of Independence. The cost of that victory to the French, in terms of debt, was to be a factor in establishing the conditions which precipitated the French Revolution of 1789.

From 1714, this increasingly predominant Britain was ruled by a succession of Hanoverian monarchs, the first of whom, George I, was a rather distant cousin of his predecessor, Queen Anne. There were many closer claimants to the throne but the Catholic Stuarts were debarred by the Act of Succession of 1701 which ruled out any idea of a Catholic monarchy. It is one of the many curiosities of Britain's chequered European history that Protestantism should so definitively have trumped Catholicism that a German-speaking prince, with no knowledge of Britain or of the English language, was able to displace those who had a better claim to the throne by birth. But, by then, Catholic France was firmly established in the minds of Protestant England as England's natural enemy. French support for the Stuart cause only served to reinforce the prejudice. When, in 1931, my Protestant father became engaged to my Roman Catholic mother, his aunt in Derbyshire wrote to him in stern terms. He must not betray his heritage (centuries of Protestant family members, 'yeomen stock, the breath and backbone of England') by consenting to the requirement of the Catholic Church that any children of the marriage should be baptized and brought up as Catholics. In our post-Christian society, those sentiments scarcely survive. But they were still evident as late as the 1950s. In Surrey, where I grew up, it was believed by the French nuns in the Catholic convent school I attended in Epsom, that the County Council had a policy of discriminating against Catholics in the award of Grammar School scholarships.

The attitude many in the West had to the Arab Spring in our own times was mirrored in English attitudes to what was happening in France at the outbreak

---

[7] Ibid., p. 45.

of the revolution of 1789. Apart from satisfaction at the discomfiture of the French state, there was an initial upsurge of enthusiasm for the apparent espousal of liberal values: 'bliss was it in that dawn to be alive', as Wordsworth had it. The carnage which ensued, as the revolution ate its children in the reign of terror, killed off those hopes. But Britain was not among the countries who combined to try to restore the French monarchy after the luckless, bewildered Louis XVI was led to the guillotine and the watching crowds jostled for who would be first to dip their handkerchiefs in his spurting blood. It was revolutionary France that declared war on Britain.

If French mothers had warned their recalcitrant children to obey or face a malevolent Marlborough, so English children in the early years a century later, were warned that 'Boney' would get them. Bonaparte's conquest and occupation of much of continental Europe, the defeat of his fleets at the Battles of the Nile and Trafalgar, and his ultimate downfall at the hands of English and Prussian troops in 1815, confirmed in English politics, policy, and psychology the sense of existential danger posed by continental dominance and of Britain's unique role in resisting it.

Napoleon is one of those rare tyrants whose genius left an enduring legacy and whose excesses, and not just in French eyes, were outstripped by his achievements. Napoleon effected a revolution in the organization of French society which shapes French life to this day. It could only have been done in the aftermath of a revolution in which Frenchmen had taken the lives of some 40,000 of their fellow citizens.[8] Napoleon recognized the craving for order and stability and set in place 'a centralised despotism which brought better justice and greater security to [France's] subjects than had been known before'.[9] Our conception of peace and orderliness in the lives of citizens derives from the rule of Napoleon. At the price of individual liberty, he established stability and security in national life. Old inequalities and injustices were swept away. He created an efficient police force operating under a new, clear and equitable system of law. It was no longer necessary for people to own and carry a weapon; they could live and work in peace. The *Code Napoléon* became one of France's most successful exports. Under it, a new law which required property to be divided among a man's heirs on his death, led to the spread of small holdings of land in France. There grew up a new class of peasant proprietors. Not only did they stand by Napoleon, even to his final 100 days

---

[8] An estimated 25,000 to 30,000 'collaborators' were killed in the immediate aftermath of the liberation of France in 1944.

[9] Oliver J. G Welch, C. J. P. Hughes, H. E. Howard, and P. C. G. Walker, *A Modern History of Europe 1046–1918* (London: Victor Gollancz, 1935).

after his escape from Elba in 1815, they defined much of the economy and politics of nineteenth-century France and, a hundred and fifty years later, shaped the founding policies of the European Community.

As with the Roman Empire, the price of prosperity and stability was the denial of personal freedom. Bonaparte allowed no dissent. He created a state education system which, more ordered than any other in Europe at the time, indoctrinated its pupils in the benefits of Napoleonic rule. Freedom of the Press was denied. An exception, based on rivalry rather than respect, was the introduction of religious tolerance, not just in France but in all the countries that Napoleon conquered.

Along with societal reform, Napoleon also brought modern communication—public works, roads, canals: innovations for which the state had not, since Roman times, assumed responsibility. These radical improvements in the conditions of life were not confined to France. Wherever his armies conquered, Napoleon swept away the fabric of medieval life. At the height of his power, around 1810, he controlled, either directly or through subject states, great swathes of continental Europe: Italy, Switzerland, a large area of what is now Germany, part of modern-day Poland, and Spain. The paradoxical consequence of Napoleon's system of government, for example bringing most of Germany under one authority, was to foster the very sense of nationhood which he sought to destroy. In the end, the resentments fostered by his revolution would contribute to his downfall.

At this period, England far outstripped the rest of the world in terms of industrial revolution. Napoleon too had a vision of an industrialized France and, to achieve it, he devised a Continental System designed to exclude English goods from all of the European continent which he controlled. Russia joined the Continental System in 1807. Sweden too was compelled to comply. When Napoleon's ambitions turned to the Iberian Peninsula, he threatened England with having no continental access for her goods or for imports except through Turkey. To the Battle of Vimiero, in Portugal, in which the future Duke of Wellington defeated the French General Junot, was soon added Spanish resistance to Napoleonic domination. Ultimate defeat in Spain, and the failure of his Russian campaign, led to Napoleon's defeat, abdication, and exile to the island of Elba. Characteristically, Napoleon, in his brief period of exile, completely revolutionized Elba's governance. But it was too small to contain his genius and his ambition. In the spring of 1815, he escaped from Elba. With the restored Bourbon monarchy fleeing before him, his old soldiers rallying to the flag and the peasant landowners he had fostered egging him on, he reached Paris without a single shot being fired. But there was now a coalition of

English, Dutch, Belgian, and German forces to confront him. And at Quatre Bras, on 15 June 1815, thanks to the thin red line of the English red-coat square formations, and the timely arrival of Blücher and his Prussian troops, Napoleon met his final defeat.

As we shall see, the history of Britain's troubled relationship with the European Community/Union in our own time is dominated by continuous, intense, and, above all, instinctive mistrust of the French by the English and of the English by the French. That mistrust had long-established roots. When, in 1963, France's President de Gaulle first vetoed Britain's application to join the European Community, his rationale was rooted in his desire for French dominance in Europe and by deep-seated resentments. These were not just about his perceived mistreatment by his Anglo-Saxon allies in the Second World War but harked all the way back to Fashoda. The Fashoda Incident was by then long forgotten in Britain. But it was embedded in the mind of de Gaulle. In 1898, French troops laid claim to an area of Southern Sudan and were forced by a British force under General Kitchener to withdraw and cede control to Britain. British insistence on the immediate and unconditional French withdrawal from Fashoda was perceived as a national humiliation. Nothing, de Gaulle wrote, in the very first page of his memoirs, excited him more as a child than the reminders all around him of France's glorious history: dusk over the cathedral of Notre Dame, the majesty of the evening sky at Versailles, the Arc de Triomphe bathed in sunlight, the flags of the conquered stirring in the crypt of the Invalides. And nothing saddened him more deeply than France's weaknesses and errors which he heard about, and read in people's faces, in his youth. And first among those was the retreat from Fashoda.[10]

This Anglo-French rivalry was one of the aspects of a potent nationalism in both countries. Yet the period from 1815 and the Congress of Vienna up to the year of revolutions (1848) was one in which the statesmen of Europe tried hard to stuff the genie of national self-expression back into the bottle of monarchical servitude. The central preoccupation at the Congress of Vienna was the so-called Balance of Power. This was partly about dividing up the spoils of victory, in which dogfighting England was happy to keep her mastery of the seas, with the bonus of a few extra colonies. It was also about insuring against renewed French aggression by a form of encirclement. Belgium was joined to Holland; Prussia was given German lands in northern Saxony and on the west bank of the Rhine, together with the two million new citizens who went with

---

[10] Charles de Gaulle, *Mémoires de Guerre et Mémoires d'Espoir* (Paris: Librairie Plon, 1954), p. 1.

the territory; Swiss independence was guaranteed; Savoy was given to Piedmont; Russia kept most of Poland and Finland; Norway was added to Sweden. Scant, if any, regard was paid to what the inhabitants of these countries and regions wanted. The following half century was turbulent enough as Belgium sought (and achieved) independence from Holland, Norway secured liberation from Sweden, and powerful movements for national unity arose in both Italy and Germany.

In the immediate aftermath of the ending of Napoleonic rule, out of the Congress of Vienna arose the Quadruple Alliance between Great Britain, Russia, Austria, and Prussia which pledged the four powers to support any one of them that might be attacked by France. The respective governments committed themselves to regular meetings. Curiously, by 1818, the Quadruple Alliance had become a five-power one with France allowed back in as a Great Power, though the original four powers maintained their mutual guarantee, just in case. One idea of the time was that the army of 150,000 which had been settled in France under Wellington should be redeployed as an international police force, with its headquarters in Brussels. But, weary of war, British public opinion was by now resolutely pacifist and the British government under Castlereagh realized that neither Parliament nor People would stomach it.

The first outbreaks of popular revolt against the restoration of the old order across continental Europe were not long in coming, as the desire for freedom was met by a countervailing illiberal repression. Even supposedly liberal England imposed, in 1819, laws which placed a punitive impost on all news-papers so as to discourage freedom of expression, and outlawed all public meetings. It is no accident that 1819 was the year of the Peterloo Massacre. Repression was the order of the day in Spain and Naples (both under Bourbon rule), Russia (despite the formerly liberal instincts of the tsar, Alexander), Prussia and the Austrian Empire. But when revolt erupted in Spain, Portugal, and Naples and the Austrian statesman Metternich called the Great Power Alliance to a meeting in the autumn of 1820, the British (perhaps prefiguring their reaction to the Messina conference of 1955) declined to send any representative of note. The meeting drew up a Protocol which engaged the members of the Great Alliance to bring back into line any country in the European concert of nations which changed its constitution as a result of internal revolt, 'if need be by arms'. But the government in London (perhaps conscious that, twice in the seventeenth century, England's own constitution had been changed by internal revolt) adamantly refused to sign up—rejecting strenuously the whole idea of outside interference in the internal affairs of other countries.

As usual in the messy world of real life, consistency did not always rule the day. When the French occupied Spain by force in 1823, the English Foreign Secretary, Canning, protested but took no further action. A full-fledged war with France was unthinkable. But when the French sought to interfere in the Spanish colonies of Latin America, Canning persuaded the US President, Monroe, to warn European powers not to meddle in the affairs of the American continent. Canning was not slow to claim credit for what became known as the Monroe Doctrine. He had, he said, 'called a new world into existence to redress the balance of the old'. By his action, and his support for liberalism in Portugal, Canning also effected the *de facto* end of the Concert of Europe. While Metternich, pulling the levers of power at the heart of the Austrian Empire, strove to fulfil his dictum: 'Govern and change nothing', and to give his life to, as he put it 'propping up a mouldering edifice', various attempts were being made to hasten that edifice's collapse.

The great Ottoman Empire which, in the mid-sixteenth century, ruled over some fifty million people (compared with a population in the British Isles of some four million), had, over the ensuing two centuries, been in decline. But it still ruled over the Balkans, including Greece and, in particular, controlled Constantinople. For England, this presented a problem. For Russia had had her eye on Constantinople since the time of Peter the Great. If Russia could control the straits joining the Black Sea and the Mediterranean, she was assured of her status as a great European power. But Russian control of Constantinople would also encourage the revolt of the Baltic States against Austria. England (and increasingly her public) was apprehensive that Russian control of the Dardanelles would potentially threaten British access to India whose neighbourhood with Russia was a further source of nervous rivalry. So British policy towards Turkey was one of ambivalent tolerance. But when the Greeks rebelled against their Turkish oppressors in 1821, and the Turks retaliated with the mass slaughter of Christians and the execution of the Patriarch of Constantinople and three archbishops, opinion in England was outraged. It found in Lord Byron its most romantic and charismatic champion in verse, in his presence among the rebels and in his death at Missolonghi which raised him to the pantheon of Greek national heroes. When the Turks, in 1824, called to their aid their Egyptian vassal, Mehmet Ali, who occupied Crete and devastated the mainland, France and Britain felt obliged to intervene.

Each year to this day, in Navarino in the Peloponnese, the Greeks celebrate the anniversary of the naval battle which took place there in 1827. Combined French and English fleets, under Admiral Sir Edward Codrington, sailed into

Turkish waters with instructions to enforce mediation but avoid enemy action. In Navarino Bay, the Turks fired on one of Codrington's ships, *HMS Dartmouth*. The French flagship responded with fire and, in the ensuing battle, the Turkish fleet was destroyed.

This was not what the government in London wanted. Wellington, now Prime Minister, apologized to the Turks for what he called in the House of Commons 'an untoward event', a phrase which was both pusillanimous in itself and only encouraged the Turks to continue in their unequal struggle with the Russians which ended in 1829 with a treaty which effectively confirmed Greek independence and advanced Russian power.

The Battle of Navarino is largely lost to English history, but it provides a memorable example of the triumph of a determined person, with right on their side. Admiral Codrington's victory was deemed by the government at Westminster to be politically inconvenient and a disreputable campaign was mounted to discredit him. Moreover, so complete had been the destruction of the Turkish fleet that there were no prizes taken and the government, despite the loss of English life in the battle, refused to grant any prize money.

Codrington stood for Parliament, with the sole aim of achieving redress. He won the support of the House of Commons against the government and secured the sum of £60,000 for his men. His reputation was enhanced and his career resumed. On his death, he was acclaimed in the Greek Chamber of Deputies as an 'illustrious philhellene'. One of Codrington's sons, a young midshipman, was wounded in the battle. Years later, when he was himself a senior naval officer, he met Tahir Pasha, who had been one of the Turkish admirals at the battle: '*Figlio di Codrington, figlio mio*', said the old man as he warmly welcomed the son of his old adversary.[11]

British and French fear of Russian dismemberment of Turkey was a main cause of the one significant European war which Britain fought in Europe between 1815 and 1914: the Crimean War of 1854. On the British side, it started as a very amateur enterprise, led by inadequate commanders. It was also the first war to be exposed to Press scrutiny (with no censorship on the British part) and to the powerful witness of photography. Public shock at the evidence from the front brought Palmerston back into power by popular demand and he professionalized the management of the campaign as far as he could. The outcome was not in the end strategically decisive. But it was a campaign which took the lives of three quarters of a million combatants, half a million of them Russians. It was significant for being a war which, unlike those

[11] C. M. Woodhouse, *The Battle of Navarino* (London: Hodder & Stoughton, 1965).

that succeeded it, had no economic motivation. It did, for twenty years, to some extent constrain Russian influence in the Balkans. And it confirmed the French ruler, Napoleon III as the 'Emperor of Europe', and as the man who had avenged his uncle's retreat from Russia in 1812 and dented the notion of Russian potency. Napoleon was to play a confused, sometimes disreputable but nonetheless determinant role in the lengthy struggle for the unification of Italy and its freedom from Austrian rule. France's armed presence on Italian soil was only to end when French troops were obliged to leave to face the Prussian attack on France of 1870 that brought this second Napoleon's reign to an end.

Louis Napoleon, born in 1808, spent his childhood with his mother, living variously in Italy, Switzerland, and Bavaria. He spoke French with a German accent, and German with a Swiss one. He was an ardent admirer of his uncle Bonaparte. In 1830, he took part in the liberal uprisings in Italy but he saw his destiny as being to rule France. He made two attempts at a military putsch, in 1836 and 1840. Both failed. The monarchy of Louis-Philippe, 'the bourgeois king', did not take him seriously enough to imprison him but he took the wise precaution of fleeing to America, whence he returned to Europe, settling in England. When his uncle's remains were brought back from St Helena for burial in France, with a few intrepid followers he mounted an attempted coup, landing at Boulogne where he was promptly captured and sentenced to life imprisonment. In prison, he set about writing vaguely socialist pamphlets which had a wide circulation and an increasingly popular following. In 1846, Louis Napoleon escaped from prison dressed as a workman. Once again, he set himself up in England where he cut quite a figure in society, having made the decision, flattering to his slightly bemused hosts, to take an English mistress. Such was his engagement in English life that when, in 1848, the Chartists marched on London, Napoleon enrolled as a special constable and patrolled in Park Lane.

The year 1848 was one of revolutions across Europe as populations, often welded together by political boundaries which bore little relationship to historical or ethnic and tribal identity, rebelled: in France, Prussia, Hungary, Austria, and Italy. It was in the aftermath of the revolution in France, which overthrew the rule of Louis-Philippe, that Louis Napoleon came to power. He became, for nearly two decades, a dominant figure in European politics, intervening in Italy, where he annexed Savoy and Nice, and defeated the Austrians at Solferino, and in Mexico where he tried and failed to gain a foothold in Central America.

By 1870, his early liberalism had turned somewhat arbitrary and, while he was a considerable social reformer, his half-baked political reforms only served to encourage bolder democratic opposition. The views of Karl Marx were being heard in Paris and the voice of Victor Hugo's outrage thundered in Paris all the way from his exile in the Channel Islands.

The cause of Napoleon's downfall was not, however, internal strife but external defeat. Prussia under Count Otto von Bismarck was expansionist. Bismarck set about, and succeeded, in extending the Prussian monarchy so as to rule a united Germany. The expansion of Prussia required the defeat of Austria. For Prussia to gain the whole of southern Germany, France would have to be defeated as well. For thirty years, the Prussian military genius, von Moltke, plotted the defeat of France. When it came, in 1870, Louis Napoleon, despite personal courage in defiance of ill health, was defeated at Sedan. He was to spend his last years, as he had spent several of his early ones, as an exile in England. He had a considerable popular following. My paternal grandfather changed his first name by deed poll from Lewis to Louis out of admiration. Since my grandfather died before my birth, I never got to ask him what particular Napoleonic virtue it was that so caught the imagination of a middle-class Derbyshire bank manager.

To the victors the spoils. In the so-called Peace of Frankfort, Germany annexed Alsace and eastern Lorraine. Metz and Strasbourg also went to Germany. In the Hall of Mirrors at Versailles, King William of Prussia was proclaimed the first Emperor of Germany. This was a lesson in national humiliation which Hitler was to draw on in a different setting some seventy years later. The arrogant humiliation of France of course bred its counterpart in an ardent desire for revenge.

German strength could not yet compete on an equal footing with British imperial power. Britain had a huge empire and controlled the world's shipping. But German industrial expansion in the last two decades of the nineteenth century posed a serious competitive threat to manufacturing, shipbuilding, and banking in Britain. A German policy, later copied by Japan and later still China, of producing cheap commodities enabled them to beat all tariffs.

In Britain, there were conflicting attitudes to the rise of Germany. France was England's traditional enemy and the removal of the maritime threat from Britain's nearest coastal neighbour was greeted with relief. But, as France grew closer to Russia in the late 1880s, unease increased. In 1889, the Royal Navy proclaimed the two-power standard: Britain should ensure its naval security by shipbuilding 'to a standard strength equivalent to that of the combined forces of the next two biggest navies in the world'.[12]

British fears were seemingly justified by the global imperial ambitions articulated by Queen Victoria's grandson, Kaiser Wilhelm II. The growth of modern communications (the railway, later followed by the aeroplane) called into question the adequacy of naval power alone, rather as, in our own time, cyber and chemical warfare have undermined our own confidence in the adequacy of conventional and nuclear defence.

When, in 1899, the South African Boers rebelled against British rule, Britain was perceived as the global bully-boy. Britain's sense of military and moral superiority was severely damaged by the Boers' near success, on the one hand, and Britain's scandalous invention of the concentration camp, on the other. There followed a crisis of national confidence: an outpouring of Edwardian-era books and dramas all seeking to explain and correct the loss of national moral fibre. Baden Powell's Boy Scout movement was one answer to the perceived crisis. Another, fuelled by German aggressiveness towards France in Morocco, was a rapprochement between Britain and France which led to the *entente cordiale* of 1904.

It is yet another historical curiosity that the English author of rapprochement with France and hostility to the appeasement of Germany was a British diplomat who was born in Leipzig and educated in Düsseldorf, Berlin, and France. Eyre Crowe had not even visited England until he was seventeen, and traces of a German accent were detected in his spoken English even late in his life. On 1 January 1907, Crowe submitted to his Foreign Office superiors a *Memorandum on the Present State of British Relations with France and Germany*. He had, I imagine, penned it during the Christmas break.

Central to Crowe's argument was the position of Britain as a maritime power. Sea power, Crowe argued, was more potent than land power 'because it is as pervading as the element in which it moves ... A maritime State is, in the literal sense of the word, the neighbour of every country accessible by sea.' For Crowe, this maritime superiority made the state that enjoyed it the object of universal jealousy and fear and, accordingly, exposed that state constantly 'to the danger of being overthrown by a general combination of the world'. It followed that 'England, more than any other, non-insular, power, has a direct and positive interest in the maintenance of the independence of nations.'

The greatest threat, as Crowe saw it, came from the insatiable quest for power of Germany, 'the foremost power on the European continent'. German

---

[12] Simms, *Britain's Europe*, p. 134.

ambitions were to Crowe, writing in 1907, as much a threat to the balance of power in Europe as had been Spain and France in centuries past.

So, in 1914, when the Austrian Archduke Ferdinand was assassinated in Sarajevo, a chain of events was triggered which posed for Britain the existential threat of which Crowe had warned. France backed Russia against Austria and Germany backed Austria. The prospect of a French defeat at the hands of Germany aroused Britain's deepest fears. Britain's formal commitment to the integrity of Belgium was the trigger for Britain's engagement, but the underlying rationale for Britain's declaration of war lay centuries-deep.

It is now part of historical received wisdom that the Treaty of Versailles of 1919 so humiliated Germany after the First World War that it sowed the seeds of Hitler's rise to power and of the next war with Germany barely twenty years later. Under the treaty, Germany lost land, colonies, and her navy. British troops formed part of an allied army of occupation of the Rhineland. The treaty adopted a punitive approach demanded by the French; 1870 still rankled. Britain favoured, but did not insist on, a more conciliatory approach. A liberal, prosperous Germany would be less susceptible to the blandishments of Bolshevism. Economic recovery in Europe, so the economist Maynard Keynes argued, depended on industrial recovery in Germany.

When, in 1923, France occupied the Ruhr because Germany had failed to make reparation payments, British atavistic fears were aroused. To the British, France's action looked like a return to the days of French territorial aggrandizement in Europe and was condemned accordingly. In France, Britain's failure to support France is seen to this day as a factor in Hitler's calculations that he could defy international opinion with impunity.

The British government was not inactive. In 1925, in the magnificent surroundings of what is today known as the Locarno Suite in the Foreign Office, a treaty of non-aggression was hammered out between France, Germany, and Belgium. It was guaranteed by Britain and Italy. But those guarantees did not extend to the east and Germany made no commitment in respect of her borders with Poland and Czechoslovakia. Germany was admitted to membership of the League of Nations and, for Stresemann, the German Foreign Minister, the treaty represented a return to respectability and status, backed up by industrial strength. In 1984, German Chancellor, Helmut Kohl, made a speech in Oxford in which he cited Stresemann as he set out German ambitions for a united Europe. For Kohl, the goal of European union was, first and foremost, the means by which German reunification could be achieved with the acceptance and blessing of the rest of the European continent. One prominent British journalist was moved to comment that once again, albeit benignly, a prominent German leader was questioning the status quo in Europe.[13]

The Locarno Treaty was a characteristically thorough, practical, and professionally competent approach to the problems posed by the aftermath of Versailles. Far less to British liking (because of its implications for national sovereignty) was a proposal in 1930 by the French statesman Aristide Briand for a European Federal Europe involving economic and military cooperation coordinated by an executive. The British Chancellor of the Exchequer had set out an imaginative, but more constrained, approach five years earlier. He wanted to see Germany and France so united economically, socially, and morally that mutual interdependence would prevent rivalry and conflict. 'Europe could rise again' said the Chancellor. But, by 1930, that same politician, Winston Churchill, was of the view that 'We are with Europe, but not in it...linked but not compromised...interested and associated but not absorbed'. There must, Churchill argued, be a 'kind of United States of Europe' but with Britain and the British Commonwealth of Nations, and the United States in the role of friends and sponsors of the new Europe.

That vision of Europe was to be dramatically expounded once again. But by the time Churchill stood in the great hall in Zurich in 1946, to be rapturously received by his audience, sixteen years had passed and seventy million lives had been lost.

---

[13] Stephen Wall, *The Official History of Britain and the European Community, Volume III* (London: Routledge, 2019), p. 278.

2

The Price of Victory

The Rocky Road to Europe, 1945–1961

All history is written with the benefit of hindsight and, in writing it, part of the task is to try to assess what might have been known, but wasn't, at the time (the 'knowable unknown' as US Defence Secretary, Donald Rumsfeld, later called it).

Neville Chamberlain, on his deathbed in 1940, told his sister that he thought it would take a hundred years before the Munich agreement was seen in true perspective. Yet in 1938, the agreement (now seen as a betrayal of Czechoslovakia) was hugely popular in the United Kingdom, which had been through a devastating war only twenty years earlier. That was the prevailing view. But it was not the *only* view. There were prescient voices (Churchill and Eden prominent among them) who correctly assessed that Hitler would not treat the Munich agreement between himself and the French and British Prime Ministers as more than a scrap of paper and that his appetite would be fed, not assuaged, by conceding his spurious claim to authority over the Sudeten Germans of Czechoslovakia.

In the case of Britain's approach to her global and European interests after the Second World War, there were almost *no* voices, in either of the main political parties, calling for a different approach to the one taken; no significant statesman challenging the orthodoxy; no Press or public pressure for Britain to take a different course. Only when the measurable evidence changed, did British attitudes change.

Thus, most of the officials and politicians who had a leading role in the formation of Britain's European policy in the 1950s did later come to believe that they had got it wrong. They acknowledged that they had failed to predict the extent of the change in Britain's status and economic interests and had not imagined that the countries of continental Europe could successfully combine in an organization that would survive, prosper, and outstrip Britain economically.

That this was so did not result from post-war hubris. Britain was too impoverished by the war for that. If there was a divide in Britain, it was domestic. Returning service personnel had contributed to turfing Churchill out of office in the General Election of July 1945 in favour of the economic and social reforms promised by the Labour Party. On foreign policy, there was only one significant foreign policy disagreement between Labour and Conservative: over early independence for India though, even there, a different Tory leader than Churchill would have been less vocal in the defence of empire.

The lack of disagreement on foreign policy was not surprising since Clement Attlee, the new Prime Minister, and Foreign Secretary Ernest Bevin, had served in the wartime coalition under Churchill. Attlee, as Deputy and, after the 1945 election, as Prime Minister, had attended the Potsdam Conference that determined the shape of post-war Europe. The struggles which rapidly developed between the Soviet Union and her wartime allies, and the Soviet suppression or annexation of much of democratic east and central Europe, were to be the major defining events of the 1950s, raising an existential threat to global peace. The threat of nuclear war between the democratic countries of the West and the communist Soviet Union and its conscripted allies loomed large in the lives of all of us, at least until the resolution of the Cuban missile crisis in 1962. When, at my school, we debated 'This house believes that nuclear war is inevitable', it was not an exercise in political theory; we were teenagers anxiously asking ourselves whether we would live to adulthood.

Post-war Britain was a country struggling for economic recovery. The Labour government had a radical programme of nationalization: the railways, steel, and coal; and of tax redistribution. Building on plans laid by the wartime coalition, it revolutionized health care through the creation of the National Health Service and embarked on a programme of public housing unprecedented in British politics.

Impoverished though the country was (retaining food rationing after the countries of continental Europe had abandoned it) the United Kingdom was nonetheless a global power. The empire still existed and its system of trade (imperial preference) gave Britain privileged access to the markets of its member countries, and vice versa. In 1951, the USA and the six countries of what was to become the EEC, took the same proportion of UK trade by value: 10 per cent. The Commonwealth countries and the colonies took 55 per cent. This huge imbalance in Britain's trade was a relatively recent phenomenon, fuelled by European and US protectionism in the 1930s. The trend was exacerbated by the UK's post-war import quotas, designed to protect the UK balance of payments and mostly directed against goods from the rest of Europe and the USA.[1]

Post-war Britain was caught between its dependence on Commonwealth trade, on the one hand, and its wartime commitment to the United States to reduce or remove those same Commonwealth preferences (in exchange for US aid on which no interest would be paid for the duration of the war) on the other. For the Attlee government, therefore, economic recovery was seen in global terms. Britain had been one of the creators of a post-war economic infrastructure, whose architecture was designed at the Bretton Woods hotel in the New Hampshire hills in 1944. The International Monetary Fund and the World Bank were conceived as instruments of global economic management and support in a world which would move towards liberalized trade. The rules of that trade would be set by another post-war creation, the General Agreement on Tariffs and Trade (GATT), which would outlaw new tariffs between its members, save in the case of customs unions which lowered previous tariffs.

The UK's approach to international order in the immediate aftermath of the war was that of a country, virtually unique in Europe, whose national democratic institutions had survived the onslaught of a monstrous tyranny and had emerged unbowed. By contrast, much of the rest of Europe had been laid waste, its democratic structures vandalized by Nazi Germany or, in the case of Germany and its ally, Italy, defeated and disgraced. The UK saw itself as a global power, still seeking cooperative leadership with its wartime allies. As Churchill's Zurich speech in 1946 had shown, a year after the war, it was still just possible to envisage the Soviet Union as an ally in peaceful global management. But only just. A few months earlier, in Memphis, Churchill had delivered his Iron Curtain speech, vividly describing how all the great capitals of eastern and central Europe (Berlin, Vienna, Bucharest, Sofia, Budapest, Prague and Warsaw) had fallen under Soviet enforced control. Churchill gave his warning about these events in order, as he put it, to 'safeguard the future' against the threat of a new world war.

The British Labour Foreign Secretary, Ernest Bevin, seems to have found Churchill's interventions irritating. Bevin had his own vanity, and being upstaged by Churchill evidently offended him. But Bevin, like Churchill, instinctively saw Anglo-US collaboration and partnership as natural and obvious. What other European country could provide the necessary stability,

---

[1] Alan S. Milward, *The Rise and Fall of a National Strategy 1945–1963* (London: Whitehall History Publishing, 2002), p. 4.

experience, and capability to support the United States? France under the Fourth Republic seemed unstable. Both there and in Italy, the largest parties in parliament were Communist parties. Germany, under four-power control, was still the conquered enemy and one of the fears that Churchill evoked in his Iron Curtain speech was that Soviet malign meddling in Berlin might empower a future resurgent Germany to play off East versus West.

The picture of Europe in 1947 was one of complexity, danger, and uncertainty. Germany was perceived as a potential threat. In January, Britain and France signed the Treaty of Dunkirk, committing both countries to mutual defence from German attack. At the same time, in Washington thoughts were turning to the idea of some kind of European customs union. It would make West Germany a partner, not a potential adversary, and that would require a shift in French thinking, not least on the question of control of German coal and steel production in the Ruhr. Binding France in was also an important objective given the perceived threat to French democracy from the power of the Stalinist Communist Party there.

The main immediate driver of such closer European cooperation was the new situation created by the division of Europe between East and West as a result of Soviet aggressive annexation. In the spring of 1947, the three western wartime allied Foreign Ministers (France, Britain, and USA) and the Foreign Minister of the Soviet Union came to a point of terminal disagreement over the future of Germany and later that year their meetings (the one surviving instrument of four-power collaboration) came to an end. In 1948, the Russians attempted to choke off the lifeblood of West Berlin (controlled by the USA, France, and the UK) and they soon established in their zone of control in East Germany a separate communist state. In the aftermath, US Secretary of State, George Marshall, came to see peace in Western Europe as dependent on economic recovery and collaboration *in* Europe by the countries *of* Europe as a critical ingredient.

It was here that British ambivalence first became manifest. The economies of Europe were in dire straits. In mid-1947 the US government took the bold decision, under President Truman and Secretary of State George Marshall, to give aid on a massive scale ($12 billion) to Europe under the Economic Recovery Programme, the so-called Marshall Plan. Britain was one of the beneficiaries and its Foreign Secretary, Ernest Bevin, played a significant role in establishing the Committee (later the Organisation) for Economic Co-operation and Development (OEEC) through which Marshall Aid was administered. At the same time, Bevin resented Britain, America's wartime comrade in arms, being treated as 'just another European country'.[2] As American minds turned towards a customs union in Europe, so it became harder for the British to reconcile such a union with their perception of their national interests.

The idea of a customs union was not new. A union, amounting to political union, had been proposed by Churchill to the French government in 1940. The initiative had come from the Frenchman Jean Monnet, who had used his friendship with Chamberlain to sell the idea to Churchill. It was a last-ditch attempt to save France from collapse in the face of German aggression and, as such, fell to earth as France fell to the Nazis. There had been some further discussion of a customs union in Europe during the war and in 1942, the three Benelux governments in exile (Belgium, Luxembourg, and Netherlands) began work on what was to become such a union between the three countries when the war ended.

At various points in the late 1940s, work was done in Whitehall on what a customs union might look like. At no point does it seem to have been conceived in the form in which we know it today in the European Union. Certainly, there was nothing of supranationality, i.e. independent institutional structures, anywhere in British thinking, although the US government tried to make it a condition of Marshall Aid at one point. When such an idea was raised in the context of the OEEC, Britain stamped on it firmly. In British thinking, a customs union was as much a political as an economic construct in that it had to address the reconstruction of a Europe by now divided by the actions of the Soviet Union, but at a time when the full extent of Soviet imperial control of eastern and central Europe was not yet clear. It had to be compatible with Britain's Commonwealth responsibilities and economic interests. It had to ensure that Britain and other European countries were not vassals of the United States, while furthering good relations and remaining compatible with the shared British and US wish for global trade liberalization.

At two points, there was a failure of British perception. The British were slow to realize the extent to which the United States was prepared to subordinate her wider economic agenda to the shorter-term requirement of European economic reconstruction and, even more importantly, political stability. The genius of Jean Monnet, who had lived and worked in Washington in the war, was to understand the American mind and to use this understanding, in what became the European Coal and Steel Community, to invent something which satisfied the United States, resolved Franco-German

---

[2] Ibid., p. 13.

tensions, and had the potential to hand to France the political leadership of Europe.

The second British failure was a lack of comprehension of the power of the federal idea in much of the rest of Europe. Perhaps because Churchill was there, and made a great European speech, Bevin paid scant attention to the Congress of Europe at The Hague in May 1948. Yet it brought together most of the prominent politicians of Western Europe, launched the European Movement to work for European unity, demanded the establishment of a Council of Europe, and called for the establishment of a European Assembly.[3] Like the OEEC, the Council of Europe was to be intergovernmental but its terms of reference were drawn more widely: it was to be a framework for consultation and cooperation between the governments of Europe.[4]

Churchill's speech at the Congress went a good deal further than he had done in Zurich: 'Mutual aid in the economic field and joint military defence', Churchill said, 'must inevitably be accompanied step by step with a parallel policy of closer political unity. It is said with truth that this involves some sacrifice or merger of national sovereignty. But it is also possible, and no less agreeable, to regard it as the gradual assumption by all the nations concerned of that larger sovereignty which can alone protect their diverse and distinct customs and characteristics.'

Did Churchill regard Britain as being encompassed in his advocacy of a federal Europe? His later record in government was to be very different. But at the time he readily assented to the unanimous adoption the next day of a political resolution in which the Congress recognized 'that it is the urgent duty of the nations of Europe to create an economic and political union in order to assure security and social progress'. Among Churchill's enthusiastic hearers was a prominent Conservative politician named Harold Macmillan.[5]

The Council of Europe was quickly established. It was to provide for international consultation between governments in a Committee of Ministers and between members of national parliaments in a Consultative Assembly. But, over the six months in which the shape of these institutions was hammered out, there arose a disagreement—a foretaste of things to come—between the French and Belgian governments on one side and the British and Scandinavian governments on the other. The French and Belgians

---

[3] Miriam Camps, *Britain and the European Community 1955–1963* (Princeton: Princeton University Press, 1964), p. 6.

[4] Roger Morgan, *West European Politics since 1945: The Shaping of the European Community* (London: Batsford, 1972), p. 84.

[5] Charles Williams, *Harold Macmillan* (London: Weidenfeld & Nicolson, 2009), p. 194.

wanted an autonomous Assembly with the authority to give direction to the work of the Committee of Ministers. The British insisted that the Assembly should be strictly consultative, and similarly succeeded in restricting the Committee of Ministers to the voluntary coordination of the policies of national governments. The British would not accept that Ministers should be bound to execute majority decisions.[6]

Macmillan, who, in Opposition, played a prominent role in the Assembly, later noted the conflict between the 'functional' views of people such as himself and the 'federal' views of some of the continental delegates.[7] At the very least, these stark differences clearly signalled to the French and other continental governments the limitations of Britain's ambition. 'When you open that Pandora's box', Bevin is said to have remarked of the Council of Europe, 'you'll find it's full of Trojan horses'. Nor was British reluctance lost on the US government. At a meeting in the US State Department in September 1949, senior US official George Kennan summarized the American view: 'The UK', Kennan told the meeting, 'tended to exert a retarding influence on Western European plans for closer political and economic integration. The UK was most wary of entering into any arrangements which might tend to derogate from her sovereignty and she was continuously preoccupied with her Empire commitments. The net result was that UK participation tended to place a ceiling on Western European attainments towards unification.'[8]

Bevin had a concept—Western Union—which he first explained to the House of Commons in January 1948.[9] The time for the consolidation of Western Europe was ripe, he said. Britain was to take a lead in bringing the countries of Western Europe together. But what did it mean? From the interviews which the journalist Michael Charlton conducted years later with Bevin's contemporaries in Westminster and Whitehall, it seems that the speech had no very coherent European political philosophy behind it. Paul-Henri Spaak, the Belgian Foreign Minister who did more than any other single European leader to bring the European Community into fruition, recounted in his memoirs his incomprehension at the failure of Bevin to put flesh on the bones of his basic idea. Spaak saw the ideas he himself later championed as springing from Bevin's initiative and could not understand why Bevin was

---

[6] Morgan, *West European Politics*, p. 85.

[7] Stephen Wall, *A Stranger in Europe: Britain and the EU from Thatcher to Blair* (Oxford: Oxford University Press, 2008), p. 1.

[8] *Foreign Relations of the United States (FRUS)*, 1949 (I), p. 521. Quoted in Alan Bullock, *Ernest Bevin Foreign Secretary 1945–1951* (London: William Heinemann, 1983), p. 703.

[9] See *Documents on British Policy Overseas (DBPO)*, Series I, Vol. X, No. 42.

dismayed when continental politicians started, as they saw it, to put his ideas into practice.

In truth, Bevin's ideas seem to have contained a large degree of wishful thinking. 'Provided', he wrote in a Cabinet paper in January 1948, 'we can organise a Western European system such as I have outlined... backed by the power and resources of the Commonwealth and of the Americas, it should be possible to develop our own power and influence to equal that of the United States of America and the USSR... By giving a spiritual lead now, we should be able to carry out our task in a way which will show clearly that we are not subservient to the United States of America or to the Soviet Union.'[10]

Economic reconstruction was part of Bevin's thinking, but the hard core was military security. If there was one pressing post-war reality it was the increasing threat from the Soviet Union. Bevin and his contemporaries were confronted with a post-war Europe which, in the two years after one world war, became the likely theatre of the next one. The Communist seizure of power in Czechoslovakia in 1948 convinced France to join Britain and the Benelux in the Brussels Treaty. The Treaty was a defensive mutual assistance pact of which Bevin was a leading architect. It was conceived in large part as a defensive measure against the risk of German military resurgence. But, under Bevin's leadership, it led to an approach by the signatory countries to the United States and to the signature of the North Atlantic Treaty in the following year. It would take another year for what became the now-familiar military structure of NATO to be established. And by then, not only was the Supreme Allied Commander in Europe (SACEUR) an American, so too was the battle plan. And the battle plan by then was not a battle plan for combating German aggression but the much more real threat of attack by the Soviet Union. The American presumption was that US bases in Europe could withstand a Soviet attack for up to six weeks. Thereafter, Europe could only be rescued by re-conquest.[11]

Through his involvement in the establishment of OEEC to administer Marshall Aid and of NATO, Bevin thus played a decisive role in the creation of the pillars of post-war western stability. His ideas on European union did include a degree of harmonization of industrial and social systems. 'Diplomats in London asked me', Bevin once said, 'what the aim of my foreign policy really was. And I said, to go down to Victoria Station, get a railway ticket and

---

[10] 'The First Aim of British Foreign Policy', 4 January 1948, CP (48)6, printed ibid., No. 7. See also Michael Charlton, *The Price of Victory* (London: BBC, 1983), p. 54.
[11] Milward, *Rise and Fall*, p. 34.

go where the hell I liked, without a passport or anything else.'[12] But his world view was influenced by Britain's global role and her uniquely close relationship with the United States. America's treatment of Britain as just another European country for the purposes of Marshall Aid, and other instances of US hard-headedness, did not undermine British confidence in trying to persuade successive US governments of Britain's fundamentally intergovernmental view of how European political development should be steered. This approach was to persist even as Britain's approach to Europe diverged from that of her continental neighbours and as the approach of those same continental neighbours was increasingly espoused by the United States.

British reluctance, after the Congress of The Hague, to cooperate in the kind of European institutional structures which Churchill's speeches and Bevin's 'Western Union' had seemed to promise, was already causing friction with the UK's European neighbours when, in 1950, the most radical of post-war ideas was proposed: a European Coal and Steel Community (ECSC).

Some historians and commentators have seen Britain's unwillingness to participate in the ECSC as the decisive moment at which Britain irrevocably failed to shape the politics and economics of post-war Europe. Of itself, the British government's decision to take no part in the ECSC did not preclude it, had it so wished, from becoming a founder member of the European Community in 1956. It would have been possible for Britain to associate itself fully with the European Community project despite having had no part in the ECSC. But, there was, for Britain, in both 1950 and 1956, a Rubicon which no politician could contemplate crossing, and that river carried the strong current of 'federalism' to which no British government then, or since, would commit itself. And 'federalism' was at the heart of the ECSC. As with the later, bigger European project, the ECSC was a mixture of the lofty and visionary and of hard-headed self-interest and shared interest on the part of its participants.

Disagreements between France and Germany over the Ruhr and the Saar had bedevilled the 1920s and 1930s: they were among the seeds of the Second World War. In the post-war world of the late 1940s, France was confronted with conflicting interests. Helped by Marshall Aid, West German industrial production was allowed by the victorious allies to rise after 1948. For France, that economic recovery aroused fears. France had secured formal control of the Saarland in 1947. In 1949, German and American pressure persuaded France to relinquish political control of the Saarland. Formal French cession of political control was not matched by the reality: the economic union of the

---

[12] Charlton, *The Price of Victory*, p. 43.

territory with France continued. The coal and steel production of both the Ruhr and the Saarland were of critical importance to France. As seen from France, German industrial revival potentially presaged the revival of a dangerous militarism. At the same time, West Germany was claiming her place as a western democracy. The Federal Republic was an essential bulwark against Soviet aggression. Jean Monnet, author of the 1940 plan for Anglo-French union and, in 1949, Head of the 'Plan' in France, was the genius behind the notion that, if control of coal and steel represented the principal threat to peace between France and Germany, then the radical but conceptually simple solution was to place both under a separate European authority.

Monnet's idea captured the imaginations of leaders in both countries. But it was to London that Monnet first brought his thinking. It was at that stage more of a concept than a plan. One of those who took part in the discussions with Monnet, Robert Hall (Director of the Economic Section of the Cabinet Office), told Michael Charlton that the British side had expected Monnet to propose detailed talks on what the new authority would be. But, instead, 'his idea was that we should, as it were, marry first. Then, with that commitment, we'd be under pressure to make it work.' But that was not something the British could accept, and Monnet soon received, with some shock, the response that the British government were not interested in collaborating.[13]

Edwin Plowden (later Lord Plowden) who was the British government's Chief Planning Officer at the time, recalled that Ministers and officials did not appreciate just how far, politically, Monnet wished to go. Had they done so, he believed, the plan would have frightened them even more. As it was, Bevin felt that the plan would go too far in surrendering sovereignty. 'I don't think', Plowden told Charlton 'that we really believed in the vision [Monnet] had of forming a nucleus around which a new Europe could be built. After all, for I don't know how many hundreds of years, Britain had kept out of Europe. And suddenly to ask it to give up its external, its worldwide, role in order to join with a Europe which was down and out at the time, required a vision which I'm quite sure I hadn't got and I doubt whether very many people in the United Kingdom had. Some may now think they had, but I don't think they did.'[14]

It is perhaps characteristic of a British political inability to comprehend the politics of non-English speaking countries, or accurately to assess and accept their attitudes to the UK, that Bevin's reaction to the Monnet plan, when it was made public, on 9 May 1950 was one of anger and resentment that he had not

---

[13] Ibid., p. 85.   [14] Ibid., p. 87.

been forewarned, particularly since it emerged that the US Secretary of State, Dean Acheson, had been shown the proposals two days earlier. The French Foreign Minister who launched the plan which bore his name was Robert Schuman. He and Bevin had disagreed before, over the nature of parliamentary representation for the Council of Europe. The two men were as different as two French and British politicians could possibly be. Acheson described them in his memoirs. Schuman was slender, stooped, with a long nose and shy, surprised eyes and smile. He looked as if he could have been a painter, musician, or scholar rather than, as he was, a former President of France. Bevin, as Acheson saw him, was 'short and stout, with broad nose and thick lips'. Where Schuman's humour was 'quiet, gentle and ironic, Bevin's was broad and hearty'.[15]

However humorous Bevin may have been, the Foreign Secretary, only just out of hospital for treatment for the cancer that would kill him, had furious rows with both Schuman and Acheson when the three leaders met in London on 11 May. In announcing his plan on 9 May, Schuman had said: 'The pooling of coal and steel production will immediately provide for the establishment of common bases for economic development as a first step *in the federation of Europe*, and will change the destinies of those regions which have long been devoted to the manufacture of munitions of war, of which they have been the most constant victims.'[16]

What irked Bevin was the fact that the French had not shared the announcement with the British government in advance, whereas they had done so with the Americans; the fact that the Americans supported the plan and the fact that it undermined the collaboration of the three allied powers in their dealings with Germany. To an extent not foreseen in Britain at the time, a new Franco-German European dynamic was being born. The French stuck to their guns. According to Foreign Office official Sir Roger Makins (later Lord Sherfield), when he and others called on Monnet at the Hyde Park Hotel on the morning of the three-power talks, Monnet was clear that a condition precedent for participating in the project was that the UK would accept the principle of a federal Europe. The officials said to Monnet 'Now, look, does this mean that if we are not prepared to accept the principle of a Federal Europe, that we're not in, we're not wanted?' 'Yes', Monnet replied, 'that is the position.'[17]

---

[15] Dean Acheson, *Present at the Creation* (New York: W. W. Norton, 1987), pp. 270–1.
[16] The text of Schuman's communiqué, together with the record of subsequent discussions, is printed in *DBPO*, Series II, Vol. I.
[17] Charlton, *The Price of Victory*, p. 99.

All governments, however high minded, act out of national—and narrower political—interest. For West Germany, the ECSC was a route back into the Western European family, the removal of a humiliation and an assurance of stable control of the principal elements of a German industrial regeneration which was quickly to make the country the wealthiest in Europe. For France too, it provided economic stability. It enabled France to clasp Germany tightly to her bosom, less out of affection than for reassurance as the United States, faced with a Soviet threat, sought to accelerate Germany's rehabilitation.

For Britain, on the other hand, the idea of a supranational authority—beyond the control of national parliaments—was, and remained, conceptually alien and politically nigh on impossible to contemplate. We live with that political reality to this day. In addition, the Labour government had just implemented one of the manifesto pledges on which it had been elected: nationalization of the coal mines. At the time, British coal production outstripped that of the rest of all of Western Europe combined. The idea that the defeated Germany would grow as fast as it did had no more taken hold of British minds than had the duration and extent of what was to become Britain's own economic decline. France under the Fourth Republic was unstable: governments rose and fell in a multi-party system where the Communist Party was a potent force. Britain's two-party system (with the Liberals a very minor player at the time), rooted in the sovereignty of Parliament, seemed by contrast a model of stability. The testimony of Ministers and officials from the period suggests that, at most, the British establishment considered the Schuman initiative somewhat offensive. It was not considered significant. According to a future Prime Minister, Harold Wilson, the idea was not taken very seriously at all by either Attlee or Bevin. The man who was to launch Britain's bid for EEC membership just over a decade later, Harold Macmillan, told the House of Commons that he was not having anyone in Europe telling him which pits to close down.

Churchill did, at the time, urge the government to discuss the Plan and then decide whether to take part in it. But on his return to power in 1951, in a memorandum to Cabinet, Churchill wrote: 'Our attitude towards further economic developments on the Schuman lines resembles that which we adopt about the European Army. We help, we dedicate, we play a part, but we are not merged and do not forfeit our insular or Commonwealth-wide character...I am not opposed to a European Federation...provided that this comes about naturally and gradually. But I never thought that Britain or the British Commonwealth should either individually or collectively become an integral part of a European federation and have never given the slightest support to the idea...'[18]

The fact that Churchill assumed that any British participation in a federation might encompass the Commonwealth is evidence of how much the UK's approach was rooted in instinct rather than analysis.

Revealingly, in the same memorandum, Churchill showed awareness that the UK's policies were diverging from those of the United States. 'I should', he wrote, 'resist any American pressure to treat Britain as on the same footing as the European states, none of whom has the advantages of the Channel and who were consequently conquered.'

The Channel was a psychological as well as a geographical frontier. When I was working on the second volume of the *Official History of Britain and the European Community*, covering the years 1963-75, Sir Michael Palliser generously read and commented on my draft. Palliser was a former Permanent Under-Secretary at the Foreign Office. He had been a Guards officer in the war, was married to the daughter of Belgian Foreign Minister Spaak, served in the British Embassy in Paris, and became Britain's first Permanent Representative (Ambassador) to the European Community in 1973.

We were talking one day about Giscard d'Estaing, whose attitudes to Britain when he was President of France (from 1974-81), loomed large in my draft. My book recorded the views of Sir Nicholas (Nicko) Henderson, who had been Britain's Ambassador in Paris at the time. Henderson considered Giscard to be profoundly unsympathetic to Britain. For Palliser, this was no surprise. Giscard was, he said, from Alsace. He was one of a significant number of French people who, for reasons of intertwined history and geography, were culturally and instinctively more at home in Germany and in German than they were in England or English.

Something similar was true of Schuman (President and then Foreign Minister of France) and German Chancellor Adenauer. Adenauer was from the Rhineland, where parts of the region had been under French government for decades. Adenauer, and others like him, felt naturally close to France and the French people. For his part, the Frenchman, Schuman, had actually fought on the German side in the First World War. He had studied in Bonn and spoke German like a native. These were therefore facts and factors which no Briton could share and which very few either knew or could understand.

'When all is said and done', according to an article in *The Economist* in June 1950, 'the fact remains that at the bar of world opinion, the Schuman proposal

---

[18] C (51) 32, CAB 129/48, 19 November 1951: see *DBPO* Second Series, Vol. I, No. 406.

has become a test. And the British Government have failed it.'[19] In turning down the opportunity first to design, and then to participate in, the European Coal and Steel Community, Britain did not inevitably and for all time, miss the 'European train'. But, on both sides of the Channel, a fundamental difference of approach was confirmed and entrenched: for Britain the intergovernmental; for Europe, the federal. For Britain, the Atlantic and Commonwealth rather than Europe; for continental Europe: Europe with Britain if possible, but without Britain if necessary. For Britain, the relationship with the United States remained predominant. For the United States, the relationship with Britain remained of great importance, but the United States would pursue its national interests in Europe with or without British consent. Over time, it would become clear that, for the United States, British acquiescence in US policies towards Europe was a necessary part of the close bilateral relationship.

A Conservative government, led by Churchill and with Eden as Foreign Secretary, was returned to power in the General Election of October 1951. The Britain now under Churchill's Prime Ministership had made a significant contribution, through its espousal of the Marshall Plan and through the creation of NATO, to fostering peace and stability in Europe. The new government, even more than its Labour predecessor, would have to wrestle with the twilight of empire and the development of determined liberation movements in its colonies. The significance of sterling as a global currency would contribute to Britain's economic sluggishness compared with accelerating growth in continental Europe. The Conservatives in power would be led by three successive Prime Ministers (Churchill, Eden, and Macmillan) who believed in Britain's global role and who saw themselves as potential brokers of détente between East and West. For all of them, their lifetime experiences, including as soldiers in one world war and prominent politicians in the second, governed their view of the world. Churchill had rallied the fallen people of Europe to the flag of a visionary regeneration, but one of which Britain was to be an observer. By 1951 he was, as his old comrade General, now President, Eisenhower, confided to his diary, not able 'to think in terms of today...He no longer absorbs new ideas'. Eden, unlike Churchill and Macmillan, had played no part in the stirring congresses that had given rise to the Council of Europe. He too, supreme tactician more than strategist, saw international politics in global terms.

The new government, as Churchill's memorandum shows, shared the view of its predecessor on the European Coal and Steel Community. The ECSC was,

---

[19] *The Economist*, 10 June 1950.

however, an accomplished fact and, for that reason, had to be accommodated within Britain's foreign policy, albeit at a low level of interest. So, when Britain and the ECSC entered into an Association Agreement, the British sent, as their first head of Britain's permanent commission to the ECSC High Authority in Luxembourg, an able economist named Sir Cecil Weir who had served as Economic Adviser to the British Control Commission in post-war Germany. Weir quickly became an enthusiast for the ECSC, 'always dashing back... rushing around the corridors of the Foreign Office, the Treasury and the Board of Treasury... singing the praises of an organisation which they all regarded as totally insignificant'.[20]

This slightly uneasy accommodation with the first European supranational institution was set a further challenge by the other major attempt at a post-war supranational structure: the European Defence Community. The war in Korea which broke out in 1950 saw British troops as part of a UN force defending south Korea from an invasion by forces backed by Russia and China. The possibility of nuclear war loomed. The threat from the Soviet Union required, in US eyes, the remilitarization of Western Europe, in which West Germany (as the country most immediately vulnerable to Russian attack) would have to play a prominent part. For any French government of a country which had been brutally attacked by Germany three times in some eighty years, the idea that there could once again be a German army, a German War Ministry, and a German General Staff was unacceptable. Might the answer lie, thought Monnet and others, in extending to the field of defence the underlying principles of the ECSC? In October 1950, the French Minister of Defence, René Pleven, put forward what was basically Monnet's plan. At its heart was the notion that West German soldiers should be, not German soldiers under German command, but European soldiers, in European uniform, under European command. Pleven hoped to attract British support by drawing inspiration from the proposal for a common European army which had been adopted in Strasbourg that same year on a motion put forward by Winston Churchill.

The Attlee government had declined to participate, Bevin observing that the French plan looked 'like a mere shop-window force'.[21] So, European hopes ran high when, in October 1951, the very man who could claim co-authorship with Monnet of the idea, Churchill, once again became Prime Minister. The

[20] Sir Con O' Neill, quoted in Charlton, *The Price of Victory*, p. 138.
[21] Milward, *Rise and Fall*, p. 84. The West German initial reaction was that the Pleven Plan was 'a deliberate insult to the German nation and was wholly unacceptable': *DBPO* Second Series, Vol. II, No. 81.

new Cabinet worked on, and agreed, a statement of policy to be delivered by the new Home Secretary, David Maxwell Fyfe, at a meeting of the Consultative Assembly of the Council of Europe in Strasbourg. The key passage of Maxwell Fyfe's carefully honed text stated: 'I cannot promise our full and unconditional participation but I can assure you of our determination that no genuine method shall fail through lack of thorough examination...There is no refusal on the part of Britain.' Just a few hours later, at a Press conference in Rome where he was attending a NATO meeting, Eden made clear that Britain would *not* participate in a European army.[22]

Anyone familiar with the nuances of carefully crafted government prose can see that Eden's statement was not a complete contradiction of Maxwell-Fyfe's. But whereas Maxwell-Fyfe's rather ambiguous statement had kept alive the expectations and hopes of continental Europeans that a Churchill government would herald a new era of cooperation, Eden's comment dashed those hopes. Spaak resigned as the President of the Council of Europe in protest. In reality, British policy had shifted to the extent that Churchill's government—and Eden personally—wanted the European Defence Community (EDC) to work, but not with British participation in a European army. Lord Sherfield recalled a meeting in the British Embassy in Paris early in 1952. Churchill was preparing a speech: 'Writing Sir Winston Churchill's speeches was quite an undertaking and it was a collective operation! It took a long time...and he would talk a lot about it. I can remember him saying, "European Army, European Army: it won't be an army, it'll be a sludgy amalgam! What soldiers want to sing is their own marching songs!" And then he burst into song...'[23]

Both Churchill and Eden saw more clearly than many in France that, if the EDC did not come into being, German rearmament would still have to be accepted in another form. They were prepared to go as far as agreeing a Treaty of Association with the EDC which presaged the inclusion of a British army division in an EDC corps. This was a considerable concession. But France's five EDC partners were determined to retain the supranational institutional structures of the EDC intact and Britain's partial engagement was not enough to persuade them to accede to France's demand that the supranational elements should be weakened.

The EDC eventually foundered, after three years of debate in France, on the refusal of the French Parliament to approve its own government's proposal. In the aftermath of the war, the allies had resolved to abolish German militarism for ever. The French army was being asked to merge its independent existence

---

[22] Charlton, *The Price of Victory*, p. 146.   [23] Ibid., p. 151.

into co-existence with Germany. With much of the French army locked in a war in Indochina, the European army would be dominated by Germany. This proved too much to swallow.[24] Sir Con O'Neill, who later led Britain's team of officials in the negotiations for entry to the EEC, looked back on the EDC as a mistaken concept, no more than a device to reconcile the French to the rearmament of the Germans 'by putting German rearmament in a framework where it would have been meaningless and useless'.[25]

If Britain's refusal to be a member of the EDC had played a part in its failure, Eden subsequently played a leading and crucial role in creating European defence structures of a much more substantial and enduring kind. Into a critical situation in 1954, including American uncertainty about what to do after the failure of the EDC, Eden stepped forward with a plan which was to bring Italy and West Germany into the Brussels Pact, already composed of Britain, France, and the Benelux—and thence into NATO. The expanded Brussels Pact became the Western European Union, with a defence commitment (Article V) which went beyond that of NATO in scope, requiring its signatories, in the event of any one of them coming under attack, to render 'all the military aid and other assistance in their power'. Spaak considered that Eden had saved the Western alliance. In doing so, Eden had also sought to demonstrate the potential for effective action at intergovernmental, rather than supranational, level.

Britain's success in taking the initiative to save Western defence through intergovernmental means, following the collapse of the supranational EDC, reinforced the UK's belief in the validity of its approach and made the government complacent about the prospect of further supranational initiatives. At the same time, and paradoxically, Britain had helped create the secure conditions in which such imaginative thinking could thrive and had, by bringing West Germany into the core of western defence, given France an added motive for binding Germany into a political structure which would limit the risk of an uncontained German resurgence.

It was not solely for those reasons that the British paid scant attention to a discussion among the six members of the ECSC in Messina in June 1955. The discussion followed a series of initiatives. The Six were edging towards extending the ECSC model to other sectors such as nuclear energy and transport. Led by the Dutch Foreign Minister, the Benelux countries put forward proposals for 'a new stage in European integration'. Since evolution to a full customs union would be the logical outcome of the ECSC's existing sectoral approach,

---

[24] Morgan, *West European Politics*, p. 138.   [25] Charlton, *The Price of Victory*, p. 163.

why not go the whole way in one go? Monnet was about to step down as President of the ECSC's High Authority and was already mulling what soon became his Action Committee for the United States of Europe. There was almost a competition of ideas, with the Italian government calling for greater cooperation in economic and social development and the Germans proposing a European University. In June, Spaak was invited by his colleagues to chair a committee to examine these ideas. It met in Brussels between July 1955 and March 1956. The British government was invited, without prior conditions on the part of the Six, to participate.

In May 1955, Eden, who had succeeded Churchill as Prime Minister, comfortably won the British General Election. Although it was in that same year that Germany recaptured and surpassed its pre-war share of European markets, no alarm bells were ringing in London. The Spaak committee was not dismissed as of no importance. Macmillan, now Foreign Secretary, was more open-minded than most in the Cabinet, instructing his officials that 'if we were to exert proper influence on the latest efforts to "re-launch Europe" we should not appear stuffy but should go in at the beginning and try to keep as many initiatives as possible in a form in which we could join'.[26]

British expectations of the Spaak committee were, however, not notably coherent. It was not obvious to the British at the outset that the outcome would be a proposal for a customs union, though such an outcome was considered in Whitehall and the view reached that it would present difficulties given the predominance of Britain's Commonwealth trade and the unaccept-ability of French requirements for the acceptance of her agricultural exports. Rab Butler, Chancellor of the Exchequer, was bored and hostile. Thorneycroft, at Trade, still favoured a one-world strategy as opposed to a regional approach. Macmillan was ambivalent. Eden was not opposed to the idea: but it was for others, not for Britain. The government took solace in the belief that the French, given their protectionist tendencies, would not accept a Common Market. If necessary, some kind of accommodation with the work of the OEEC might, however, be possible.

Gerald Bretherton, the senior Board of Trade official sent as Britain's representative on the Spaak committee, has been maligned in popular history as indifferent, or even contemptuous, of the proceedings. In reality, Bretherton was sent with no very clear instructions, and certainly no detectable negotiat-ing mandate. He realized sooner than most in London that Spaak was bringing his committee's work to a recommendation in favour of a common market

---

[26] FO 371/116042, quoted in Milward, *Rise and Fall*, p. 198.

and a customs union. By the late summer of 1955 Bretherton was advising London that the evolution of the Spaak committee was much more serious than had initially been thought. His advice was not ignored but it appears to have been weighed against a background in which officials, perhaps reflecting ministerial reservations and lack of interest, looked for reasons why Britain should not take part in a Common Market project.

The Mutual Aid Committee (MAC) in which these matters were considered collectively by officials, concluded in October 1955 that 'on the whole the establishment of a European Common Market would be bad for Britain and if possible should be frustrated. But if it came into being with us outside it we should pay an increasing price commercially. But even this would not necessarily outweigh the political objections to joining.'[27]

A month earlier, Macmillan, preoccupied by problems in the British colony of Cyprus, had declined an invitation to attend a meeting of Foreign Ministers to review the progress of the Spaak committee. According to Bretherton's own later account 'there was no Press interest at all. Public opinion was not interested. Most Ministers were not interested. Macmillan...took no active part in this. The Foreign Office line on it was that nothing would happen...'[28]

Britain's participation in the Messina conference terminated in November. Bretherton was sent to the meeting of the Spaak committee with rigid instructions, at the instigation of the Foreign Office, for him to say, quite formally, that while the United Kingdom was interested in the work of the committee, it could not take part in the design of a Common Market and that as many as possible of the issues should be referred back to the OEEC.

Spaak, in his memoirs, implies that the British simply withdrew of their own accord. Bretherton's recollection was different. Spaak had, Bretherton told Michael Charlton, reacted strongly to his statement: 'I am astonished and very hurt at this. You are just sticking to your guns. England has not moved at all, and I am not going to move either...Well, clearly you can't take part in the completion of a Final Report...You must not attend any more...[The] final report must be completed by people who are committed to recommendations.'[29]

Rab Butler, who held all the great offices of state save that of Prime Minister, was Chairman of the OEEC at the time, a job he held for four years. He spoke French and German. 'At that time', Butler told Charlton, 'Britain was regarded as the normal chairman of Europe...I remember giving almost my final

---

[27] CAB 134/1026, (MAC (55) 45th Meeting), 27 October 1955.
[28] Charlton, *The Price of Victory*, p. 185.   [29] Ibid., pp. 188–9.

dinner in Paris to the OEEC...and making a remark saying that excavations were proceeding at Messina at which we were not taking part...I always remember that because it was, in my view, a definite lack of foresight on the part of myself, and a much bigger lack of foresight on the part of the Treasury, and a very big lack of foresight on the part of the Foreign Office...That is where we started to go wrong in regard to the EEC of today.'[30]

The Treaty of Rome, the founding treaty of the European Economic Community, was signed in Rome on 25 March 1957. For an organization largely conceived by Catholic Christian Democrats, the choice of the Feast of the Annunciation was an appropriate one. By now, Macmillan had succeeded Eden as Prime Minister. 'What I chiefly fear', Macmillan wrote to a friend in April, 'and what me must at all costs avoid, is the Common Market coming into being and the Free Trade Area never following...However, I will do my best.'[31] History belongs to the victors, and President de Gaulle's claim, when in 1963 he vetoed Britain's application to join the EEC, that Britain had tried to promote a European free trade area in order to destroy the fledgling Common Market, has carried more credence than is merited by the facts.

In the EEC, Britain faced an accomplished fact. At the heart of the project lay a customs union which was, of its very nature, protectionist. If goods were to be freely traded without tariff barriers within the customs union, then there had to be an external tariff wall to make the project economically viable for its members. The danger this posed to Britain, whose trade with its European neighbours was increasing, even as its share of world markets was declining, was obvious. At the same time, the Commonwealth still accounted for 43 per cent of the UK's trade, and cheap food imports from the Commonwealth were an economic imperative both for Britain, as its domestic economy stuttered, and for the exporting countries of the Commonwealth.

In the British government's perception of political priorities, the Commonwealth loomed large. The political resonance, of the old Commonwealth especially, was great: these were the countries where many Britons had close relatives. They had fought alongside Britain in the war and had helped sustain her food supplies in the stark times after the war had ended. So, for any British government, managing the Commonwealth trading relationship was an essential ingredient of any arrangement with the EEC. From the British perspective, the answer lay in a free trade area bringing together the customs union of the EEC and the non-EEC countries such as Britain, Sweden,

---

[30] Ibid., p. 195.
[31] Harold Macmillan, *Riding the Storm 1956–1959* (London: Macmillan, 1971), p. 435.

and Denmark. The idea also fitted with Britain's traditional intragovernmental, as opposed to supranational, view of the global order.

From a continental perspective, things looked different. EEC members such as Netherlands and West Germany were sympathetic to a free trade agreement: they too wanted to develop the fledgling GATT as an instrument of liberalized global trade. France was less sympathetic. What was to become the Common Agricultural Policy of the EEC (occupying 90 per cent of the Community budget) had yet to be developed but France's agricultural economy was bound to be undermined if a Free Trade Area (FTA) with Britain included (as, for the British it must) privileged access to European markets for cheap Commonwealth agricultural exports.

Reconciling two very different systems was hugely fraught technically, and even more so politically. The Six prioritized their hard-won unity above doing a deal with Britain and her friends. But that unity was itself still fragile, as historian Miriam Camps explained in her forensic analysis: 'With considerable reason, the "Europeans" feared that if the free trade area offered comparable commercial advantages with fewer obligations, those who supported the Common Market principally to gain the benefits of a larger market (and there were many, particularly in Germany, who did so) would lose interest in giving content to those provisions of the treaty [of Rome] which were designed, not simply to bring about a customs union, but to go further and to open the way to a far-reaching economic union.'[32]

In May 1957, Macmillan appointed Reginald Maudling, the young Paymaster General, to lead Britain in negotiations in the OEEC on how a free trade area with the EEC might be constructed. Maudling was later to become Chancellor of the Exchequer and an (unsuccessful) candidate for the leadership of the Conservative Party. Talks got underway in October 1957 and soon hit an issue which, in navigating today's post-Brexit European landscape, looks disturbingly familiar: trade deflection. The EEC was a customs union with a common external tariff on imports from outside the union. Members of an FTA, by contrast, were free to negotiate their own tariff regimes with individual countries. 'It meant', as John W. Young, describes it, 'that imports from countries outside the FTA might be able to enter a member state with low external tariffs, but could then be traded freely within the FTA. For high-tariff states such as France and Italy, this was unacceptable.'[33]

[32] Camps, *Britain and the European Community*, p. 167.
[33] John W. Young, *Britain and European Unity 1945–1999* (London: Macmillan, 1999), p. 57.

The British government, for its part, sent conflicting signals. In speeches given within weeks of each other in 1957, Sir David Eccles, the President of the Board of Trade, described the new European Community to a French audience as 'one of the masterpieces of history' and, to a Commonwealth audience, as 'a treaty to do exactly what, for hundreds of years, we have always said we could not see done with safety to our own country'. Even in 1957 what was said in one place was widely reported in others. Three years later Macmillan, on a visit to Washington, was still muttering darkly to his hosts that if the split between the EEC and Britain and the other free-traders continued, Britain would have no alternative but to lead another peripheral coalition, much as it had done in the days of Napoleon. He even seems to have threatened to reduce British troop numbers in Europe.[34]

Suspicion of British motives was therefore prevalent on the continent. So much so that when, in 1960, the British government was gradually coming to terms with the idea of applying for EEC membership, Foreign Secretary Selwyn Lloyd felt it necessary to address the question head on in a speech to the Consultative Assembly of the Council of Europe. 'We regard ourselves as part of Europe', he told his audience, 'for reasons of sentiment, history and geography . . . I shall be told: "It is all very well for you to say that you are part of Europe, but you have done nothing to promote European unity since the war. You did not come into the European Coal and Steel Community. You did not come into the European Defence Community. You are opposed to the Six. You prefer a Europe which is divided and in which you play one group off against another. What is more, when you are being your nicest you are most to be suspected".'[35]

The difficulty of reconciling two very different economic and political approaches was to assume even larger proportions when the Fourth Republic in France collapsed in May 1958, and General de Gaulle returned to power as Prime Minister. Within months, the French people had approved a new constitution by 79 per cent of the votes cast in a referendum; had given de Gaulle and his allies an overwhelming majority of 331 out of the 465 members of the National Assembly; and had (albeit by a system of indirect representation) chosen de Gaulle as their new President with 77.5 per cent of the votes, compared with 13.6 per cent for his nearest rival.[36]

De Gaulle disliked the supranational elements of the Treaty of Rome over which, in self-imposed exile in Colombey-les-deux Églises, he had had no say.

[34] Camps, *Britain and the European Community*, pp. 124 and 284.   [35] Ibid., p. 278.
[36] Morgan, *West European Politics*, p. 150.

During his ten years in office as President, de Gaulle, in Roger Morgan's persuasive analysis, was to try three classic variants of French policy towards West Germany: alignment with the maritime powers, the US and the UK, to exercise joint control over Germany; close agreement with Germany to keep any dangerous tendencies under control, and even to use Germany against the Anglo-Saxons; and looking beyond Germany to eastern Europe to control her through understandings with the Soviet Union and the smaller Slavonic states.[37]

De Gaulle's grand design eventually succumbed to the brutal reality of the Soviet invasion of Czechoslovakia in 1968. In the intervening period, a combination of his love-hate relationship with the British, his single-minded pursuit of French national interests, and the other factors which Morgan identifies were important elements in Britain being at the margins of the great post-war European project and in the establishment of a Franco-German duopoly into which successive British governments failed to insert themselves.

Even before de Gaulle's return to power, French opposition to the FTA was evident, as were signs of German support for France. But de Gaulle quickly proved to be an especially formidable obstacle. Macmillan's memoirs convey a picture of two leaders talking past each other. For Macmillan, two distinct economic organizations at loggerheads within Europe would be a recipe for conflict. De Gaulle, writing to Macmillan on 30 June 1958, claimed that 'France is not at all unfavourable, quite the contrary, to an enlargement of economic cooperation in Europe, in which Great Britain is naturally included...But we must find means of arriving there without destroying the equilibrium of France's economy and finances...and without basically putting at issue the agreements existing between the six member countries of the European Common Market.'[38]

On 14 November 1958, the French delivered the *coup de grâce*. 'It is not possible', the French government said in a formal statement, 'to create a Free Trade Area as wished by the British—that is, with free trade between the Common Market and the rest of the OEEC, but without a single external tariff barrier round the seventeen countries, and without harmonisation in the economic and social spheres.'[39] It is hard to find fault with the logic of the French position.

In the aftermath, Macmillan continued 'to brood over this uncertain and potentially dangerous disarray into which Europe seemed to have drifted...

---

[37] Ibid., p. 157.   [38] Macmillan, *Riding the Storm*, p. 450.   [39] Ibid., p. 457.

Can we organise another European Free Trade Area out of the European countries *not* in the Rome community?'[40] The Swedish government were of similar mind and, in the nearly twelve months between the November breakdown and Macmillan's decisive victory in the 1959 General Election, negotiations took place on what became the European Free Trade Association (EFTA) of Britain, Sweden, Norway, Denmark, Austria, Switzerland, and Portugal.

In its own terms, EFTA worked well enough. I personally have fond memories of it. On holiday, aged 16, in Norway with my parents in 1963, I received a telegram containing my A-level results. On the strength of them, my father bought me the Omega watch after which I hankered: under EFTA arrangements, it was importable into Britain with very low customs duty. Fifty-seven years later, the watch's Swiss craftsmanship has proved more enduring than the Association of which the Swiss were members.

Macmillan saw the Seven as 'a first line of defence in the economic field', but also as 'a rather tender plant'.[41] It was very soon clear that the value of the British market to the other EFTA members was greater than the value of their market to Britain. In 1961, UK exports to the rest of EFTA represented 10.5 per cent of the country's export total. The comparable figure for UK exports to the EEC was 15.4 per cent.[42] The existence of EFTA did nothing to prompt merger between the EEC and EFTA: rather the reverse. Across the Atlantic, the US government were prepared to accept the trade rivalry of the EEC in the interests of European political unity and stability. They saw EFTA by contrast as, if anything, an obstacle to their goal of global trade liberalization through GATT and were, for similar reasons, even less sympathetic to the idea of a merger between EFTA and the EEC.

Macmillan's evolving reflections led, in April 1960, to the establishment of an interdepartmental examination of Britain's European policy, led by Sir Frank Lee, who had moved from the Board of Trade to become Permanent Secretary at the Treasury. At the same time, Macmillan appointed Rab Butler (now Home Secretary) to chair the relevant Cabinet subcommittee. Butler was very candid in his interviews with Michael Charlton. Butler had been partly educated in, and had lived, in France. He was no little Englander. But he had made a shrewd appraisal of de Gaulle, foreseeing that he 'was going to be a great nuisance – because I met de Gaulle when he first came over, with Winston, and you know how rude he was to him. De Gaulle, of course, had

[40] Harold Macmillan, *Pointing the Way 1959–1961* (London: Macmillan, 1972), p. 50.
[41] Ibid., p. 55.   [42] UN Statistical papers quoted in Milward, *Rise and Fall*, p. 313.

a most wonderful patriotic record for his own country, but he didn't want us ... he thought we might take the lead from him.'

Butler, as an MP from a farming constituency knew that, as a later Conservative Minister, Sir Geoffrey Howe put it, 'if the Church of England was the Conservative Party at prayer then the Conservative Party was the National Farmers' Union (NFU) at prayer'. He knew of the enormous power of the farming lobby in France and of the NFU's reluctance to give up the British system of support payments. But Butler, travelling round the country at Macmillan's behest, began to detect a change of mood towards the EEC among the farming community, not least because the British agricultural support system was becoming unaffordable.[43]

Meanwhile, Sir Frank Lee's committee had been asked by Macmillan to look at a range of options, including membership of the EEC, albeit with special provisions for the Commonwealth. Lee's conclusion was that Britain faced two realistic choices. One was to join the EEC but there were serious political obstacles, including the impact on the Commonwealth, domestic opinion, the possible opposition of the Six, and the risk of destroying EFTA. These obstacles, the Committee concluded, might be 'perhaps decisive against any immediate decision to make joining our objective'. The second option was that of near-identification with the EEC, i.e. acceptance of most of the EEC's policies without formal membership. Of this approach Lee wrote: 'If we cannot join the Common Market it is, in my view, the objective which seems at once the most practicable, the least harmful to our basic political interests, and the most likely to secure for the UK the great benefits of a single European market.'[44]

The striking thing about Lee's paper is its acknowledgement that, in any decision, politics might trump economics. The issue of British membership of the EEC had by this time become an issue in the Press and Macmillan scheduled a discussion in Cabinet in July 1960. Cabinet that July took no decisions, but it was clear from the discussion that, if membership was to be contemplated, it could only be on special terms to safeguard the interests of the Commonwealth. Britain could not accept EEC membership on the basis of the terms laid down in the Treaty of Rome.[45]

It is not surprising then that Macmillan, when he reshuffled his Cabinet later in the month, put the pro-Europeans Heath, Soames, and Sandys into

---

[43] Charlton, *The Price of Victory*, p. 245.   [44] Milward, *Rise and Fall*, pp. 326–7.
[45] Gill Bennett, *Six Moments of Crisis: Inside British Foreign Policy* (Oxford: Oxford University Press, 2013), p. 71.

prominent positions in the Foreign Office, the Ministry of Agriculture, and the Commonwealth Office. Heath's boss at the Foreign Office was Lord Home, newly promoted from Commonwealth Secretary. Home was all too conscious of Commonwealth reservations over possible EEC membership, but he was a loyal colleague. Heath had overall responsibility for the development of the government's European policy and, because he was in the House of Commons, while the Foreign Secretary sat in the Lords, was in a new role of considerable prominence.

The British Press interpreted these changes as a clear signal that the government were moving towards an application for membership. But the relevant Cabinet committee held no meetings between October 1960 and March 1961. Moreover, as Milward points out, there were a set of contradictions at the heart of the British dilemma. First of all, de Gaulle had given the British no reason to think that he was willing to admit the UK to EEC membership. When the new British Ambassador to France, Sir Pierson ('Bob') Dixon, presented his credentials to the French President in October, de Gaulle told him that Britain had her Commonwealth and France had her Community, which had a certain usefulness, principally from the point of view of Franco-German relations. It was obvious to de Gaulle that Britain, an island with connections throughout the world via the Commonwealth, could not come into Europe.[46] At the same time, since the federal objectives of the EEC were not palatable to the British government, it was part of Macmillan's calculation that Britain would need to join, if she did, while de Gaulle was around to help dilute the supranational nature of the Community.

At the turn of the year 1960/61, Macmillan penned what he somewhat wryly called his 'Grand Design'. Britain, Macmillan wrote, was '...harassed with countless problems: the narrow knife-edge on which our economy is balanced; the difficult task of changing an Empire into a Commonwealth...the uncertainty about our relations [with] the new economic, and perhaps political, state which is being created by the Six countries of continental Western Europe; and the uncertainty of American policies towards us...'[47]

The new US President, John F. Kennedy, was seen by Macmillan as a potential source of influence on de Gaulle, and Macmillan had in his mind the possibility of a sweetener, in the form of some kind of collaboration between the UK, USA, and France in a nuclear strike force. Macmillan, when he met de Gaulle at Rambouillet in January 1961, made rather Delphic

[46] PREM 11/3131, quoted in Milward, *Rise and Fall*, p. 335.
[47] Macmillan, *Pointing the Way*, p. 324.

allusion to his nuclear ideas but got very little response. On the key issue of British membership of the EEC, de Gaulle was friendly in tone but unaccommodating on substance.

Macmillan flew to Washington in April for the beginning of what was to prove a close and affectionate relationship with the President. Kennedy had no particular prior convictions on the question of EEC membership. But his advisers, George Ball most prominently among them, were clear in their advice to him. For them, France was an ally of uncertain reliability and it was in American interests to see Britain as a full EEC member.

Macmillan's attempt to interest Kennedy in some arrangement which would give France a privileged position in NATO was received politely by the President, but without evident enthusiasm. Macmillan followed up the meeting with a letter setting out his ideas. He also neatly encapsulated the British government's view: 'We cannot sign the Treaty of Rome as it is ... To do so would mean abandoning the Commonwealth and going back on our pledges to EFTA, to say nothing of our difficulties with agriculture at home.'[48]

When Cabinet met on 20 April, on Macmillan's return from Washington, the Prime Minister played the American card of influence to good effect. For the first time, Cabinet addressed the constitutional implications of potential accession, on the basis of advice from the Lord Chancellor, Lord Kilmuir. As historian Gill Bennett explains, and contrary to a modern belief that the issues were either unseen or neglected at the time, Kilmuir was clear and precise. At Heath's request, he had given his legal advice some weeks earlier. This was: that Parliament would have to surrender some of its functions to the European Community; the crown would have to transfer part of its treaty-making powers; and the British courts would become subordinate in some respects to the European Court of Justice. Kilmuir thought these facts needed to be made public, though they were not in his view decisive. Nonetheless, it would not be easy to persuade Parliament or the public to accept them.[49] At the Cabinet meeting itself, Kilmuir, after explaining his advice, nonetheless pronounced himself in favour of membership.

When the Cabinet discussion resumed on 26 April, Rab Butler picked up the legal argument, saying that he stood by the decision taken by Cabinet nine months earlier when it had rejected full acceptance of the Treaty of Rome. Heath sought to refute Butler's contention, using arguments which were self-deludingly employed down the years by successive generations of politicians

---

[48] PREM 11/3311 quoted in Milward, *Rise and Fall*, p. 343.
[49] Bennett, *Six Moments of Crisis*, pp. 88–9.

and officials. The loss of sovereignty, Heath claimed, would be confined to specific commercial policies. Federalism was not in the Treaty of Rome. Not all Member States wanted it anyway. If Britain and others joined, the idea of a federal Europe would recede.

Cabinet was inching towards a decision to apply. There had already been extensive consultation of the Commonwealth, and a special Commonwealth Heads of Government meeting had been held. Now, Cabinet decided to send out one more mission to the Commonwealth. Despite continuing reservations, notably on the part of Maudling, consensus was building around the belief that only by lodging an application could the government ascertain whether membership would be attainable on terms which offered suitable arrangements for the Commonwealth. This position was one of the minuted outcomes of an ad hoc meeting of senior Ministers at Chequers on 18 June: 'Discussion showed general agreement that provisions which safeguarded Commonwealth interests during the transition period only, would not be acceptable to Commonwealth countries or to public opinion in the UK. It would be necessary to secure permanent provision for at least some Commonwealth imports into the UK at broadly the present level of trade.'[50]

On 21 June, Cabinet took the decision which is encapsulated in what Rab Butler said at the meeting: his political inclinations were strongly against going into Europe but he favoured an announcement that the government would apply to join the EEC in order to 'find out what terms we can get'.[51]

This ambivalence was reflected in the difference between the terms of the announcement which Macmillan made to Parliament on 31 July and the terms of the government motion tabled two days later on 2 August. In his statement, Macmillan announced 'a formal application under Article 237 of the Treaty [of Rome] for negotiations with a view to joining the Community if satisfactory arrangements can be made to meet the special needs of the United Kingdom, of the Commonwealth and of the European Free Trade Area'. Two days later, the government motion which Macmillan commended to the House of Commons sought support for 'the decision of HMG to make formal application under Article 237 of the Treaty or Rome in order to initiate negotiations *to see if satisfactory arrangements can be made* to meet the special interests of the UK, of the Commonwealth and of EFTA'. No agreement affecting those interests, or involving British sovereignty, would be taken,

---

[50]   CAB 128/135, quoted in Milward, *Rise and Fall*, p. 350.
[51]   Bennett, *Six Moments of Crisis*, p. 86.

the Government promised, without a decision by the House of Commons after full consultation with other Commonwealth countries.[52]

Thus Britain's bid for accession to the EEC was exploratory rather than full-hearted. Macmillan's responses to the questions of MPs reflected the ambiguity. He assured one Member that 'of course, we are far more committed by our present commitments in NATO and WEU than we are under this, which is a purely economic and trading negotiation and not a political and foreign policy negotiation'. But a minute later, he was more revelatory of his own assessment, warning that, if the negotiations failed 'we ought to be quite clear ourselves, and perhaps the countries with which we are to negotiate ought to be quite clear, that quite a lot of things will happen and quite major changes may have to be made in the foreign policy and the commitments of Great Britain ... We have to recognise what will be the state of the world if this agreement cannot be made.'

The government's chosen course was approved by the House of Commons with only five dissenting votes. Neither Press nor public paid much attention. Insofar as the government saw the journey on which they had embarked as in any way perilous, the peril lay in the implications for Britain's relations with the Commonwealth and her overall place in the world. Few would have predicted the next decade of European rejection that Britain was to experience.

[52] *Hansard* of 31 July and 2 August 1961. Author italics.

3

Second Thoughts, 1961–1969

If Anthony Eden's reputation rested on his pre-eminence and achievements as Foreign Secretary, and not on the debacle of Suez, he would be remembered with an honour and respect that are largely denied him. Something similar could be said of Edward Heath. He is remembered now for the three-day week, for losing a General Election which he called to determine 'who governs Britain' and for his defeat as Tory Leader at the hands of Margaret Thatcher. But, just as Eden became Prime Minister because of his success as Foreign Secretary, so Heath climbed to the top very largely for his performance in the first negotiation for British entry into the EEC. The esteem in which he was held is the more remarkable for the fact that the negotiation which he led on behalf of the government of Harold Macmillan ultimately failed. But Heath's conduct of the negotiation was respected in Britain, even by his political opponents, while in continental Europe the perception of him as a convinced European laid the groundwork for his eventual success as Prime Minister in securing French agreement to British accession.

Heath was helped by his own European convictions, born of wartime army experience on the battlefield. But the task which faced him in the autumn of 1961 was a huge one. Public opinion in Britain was at best lukewarm on the subject of British membership of the EEC. In Parliament, the Tory benches were not united in support of the government's policy. Bipartisanship across the House of Commons soon turned into Labour Party hostility. The Heads of Government in the rest of the Commonwealth had reluctantly acquiesced in Britain's bid, on the basis of assurances that EEC membership would not weaken, and might even strengthen, their economic ties with the UK. On the continent, the six EEC Member Governments had a long experience of Britain's indifference, ambivalence, and even hostility to their great project. Britain's other European partners, in EFTA, now feared that Britain would desert them.

Heath's first task at the first session of the accession negotiations in October 1961 was to convince the Six that Britain's application was not born of narrow opportunism but was a decision rooted in the realization that, as Heath put it, 'our destiny is intimately linked with yours'. It was a decision, Heath continued, 'arrived at, not on any narrow or short term grounds, but as a result of a thorough assessment over a considerable period of the needs of our own country, of Europe and of the Free World as a whole. We recognise that it is a great decision, a turning point in our history, and we take it in all seriousness. In saying that we wish to join the EEC, we mean that we desire to become full, wholehearted and active members of the European Community in its widest sense and to go forward with you in the building of a new Europe.'[1]

The British government embarked on the negotiations hoping that they would be allowed to work with the Six in the formulation of policies that were still in embryo, notably what became the Common Agricultural Policy (CAP). This was not to be. The French government of President de Gaulle had already perceived that the EEC's embryonic agricultural policy could be shaped to suit French national farming interests and that British interests would run contrary to their own. The British system of farm support through deficiency payments was very different from the emerging EEC system of subsidies to encourage production and to promote exports. The EEC system was based on so-called Community preference, i.e. on a degree of self-sufficiency which implied that a newly joining country such as Britain would have to replace food imports from outside the EEC with imports from within it. The fact that those imports from outside were mostly from Commonwealth countries, which would face tariff and other barriers on British accession, posed a threefold problem for the British government. They would have to confront Commonwealth governments with unpalatable truths that had lain partly concealed. They would have to accept that the levies they collected on food imports from outside the EEC were to be regarded as EEC revenue, and they would have to come to terms with the fact that their own domestic agriculture was too small to be a major generator of subsidy revenue to compensate.

On all these points, British hopes and aspirations were to be disappointed. They were denied by the Six any say in the formulation of the CAP; their request for lengthy transition periods to ensure gradual adaptation was denied. Negotiations on the terms of access for Commonwealth agricultural exports were both technically complex and politically fraught. A special Commonwealth summit in London in 1962 revealed the extent of unhappiness among the leaders, especially those from the old Commonwealth.

That some of these issues (notably in respect of New Zealand) were still unresolved by the late autumn of 1962 gave some credence to the subsequent

---

[1] *The United Kingdom and the European Economic Community* (Cmnd. 1556, HMSO, November 1961).

French claim that the negotiations as a whole were clearly doomed to failure. Indeed, the breakdown of the negotiations in January 1963 was not unrelated to the issue of agriculture. But that was not in the narrow sense of an argument about tariffs or import conditions, for the British had made, and were prepared to make, concessions. It lay, rather, in the mind, prejudices, ambitions, convictions, and policies of one man: President Charles de Gaulle.

'Now that we are in secret session', Churchill told one such meeting of the House of Commons in December 1942, 'the House must not be led to believe that General de Gaulle is an unfaltering friend of Britain. On the contrary, I think he is one of those good Frenchmen who have a traditional antagonism, ingrained in French hearts by centuries of war against the English.'[2]

Macmillan and de Gaulle shared a long history, going back to Algeria in the Second World War. Macmillan was used to what Jean Monnet had then described to him as de Gaulle's capacity to 'vary from comparative calm to extreme excitability' which had led Monnet to find it 'difficult to make up his mind whether the General is a dangerous demagogue or mad, or both'.[3]

Macmillan and his ministerial colleagues had known from the start that de Gaulle would be difficult. 'I knew', Macmillan confided to his diary, 'from my many intimate talks with de Gaulle during the war how obsessed he was by his almost insane hatred for Roosevelt and even for Churchill; by his jealousy of Britain, and by his mixture of pride in France's splendid history and humiliation by her ignoble fall in 1940'. It would be difficult, Macmillan reflected on de Gaulle's return to power in May 1958, 'to lead him away from the nostalgic concepts of France's position in Europe towards the new picture of what a United Europe might mean in a changed and changing world'.[4] But the government could not be certain of de Gaulle's attitude. In particular, de Gaulle's unconcealed dislike of the supranational institutions of the EEC gave some room for hope that he might value Britain's similar perception. But de Gaulle's policies were soon rooted in Franco-German reconciliation and in a bilateral partnership in which France would grant Germany respectability in exchange for a French leadership which exceeded her real economic weight.

Unlike Macmillan, de Gaulle did not see a western interest that would bring Europe and the United States together in a common cause. He suspected US motives in NATO as being designed to make Europe subordinate. He thought

[2] Stephen Wall, *The Official History of Britain and the European Community Volume II 1963–1975* (London: Routledge, 2013), p. 9.
[3] Harold Macmillan, *War Diaries: The Mediterranean 1943–1945* (London: Macmillan, 1984), p. 97.
[4] Harold Macmillan, *Riding the Storm 1956–1959* (London: Macmillan, 1971), p. 444.

Europe, under French leadership, could stand between the United States and Russia. Britain's close relationship with the United States, including her dependence on the USA for nuclear defence collaboration, allowed de Gaulle, however disingenuously, to portray Britain as a Trojan Horse for America. And de Gaulle was not wrong in fearing that Britain's global Commonwealth interests implied a world of free trade which would challenge the EEC's protectionist customs union (with French agricultural interests at its heart), as well as presaging further enlargement to other European countries whose policies would correspond more closely to British interests than to French.

Prior to a meeting with de Gaulle at the Château de Champs in June 1962, Macmillan had a long talk with Heath. Macmillan noted that Pierson Dixon, the British Ambassador in Paris, believed that de Gaulle had already decided to exclude Britain from the EEC. Macmillan himself was not convinced de Gaulle had made up his mind. He saw him as torn between emotion and reason.

When the two men met, de Gaulle proved to be a charming host and seemed to be struck by how far Macmillan was prepared to give priority to Britain's European role, and to adjust her relations with the United States and the Commonwealth accordingly. The change of mood was picked up in the French and British Press.[5] That the change was either illusory or transitory was shown sharply when the two men next met in the cold fog of a December day at Rambouillet. In what today seems a deeply eccentric prelude to a serious discussion, Macmillan and others of the party (though not de Gaulle himself) spent the first morning at Rambouillet shooting. They killed a total of 385 pheasants, of which Macmillan bagged 77.

On the Saturday afternoon, and again on Sunday morning, the two leaders met alone with a note-taker on each side. The talks were conducted in French, mostly without interpretation, though an interpreter was on hand. Macmillan took the opportunity to inform de Gaulle that, in his forthcoming talks with President Kennedy, he would be asking the President to give the UK access to the Polaris intercontinental nuclear missile which was likely to replace the Skybolt missile, whose development programme was to be cancelled. Neither then, nor in a somewhat later discussion with Dixon, did de Gaulle suggest that he saw this as surprising or as a sign of the UK's inability to commit to Europe as opposed to the United States. Nevertheless, both meetings between de Gaulle and Macmillan went badly. De Gaulle based his opposition to British

---

[5] Miriam Camps, *Britain and the European Community 1955–1963* (Princeton: Princeton University Press, 1964), p. 428.

accession on the difficulties in the negotiations themselves, especially over agriculture, but even more on his pessimism about the scope for building any true kind of European organization. He cited the failure of the Fouchet plan (a plan for a European intergovernmental foreign and defence policy proposed by de Gaulle in 1961) as proof of the lack of will among other European countries.

When other Ministers joined the leaders, Macmillan reproached de Gaulle for his pessimism. The whole future of Europe was at stake. Europe had destroyed itself twice already in the twentieth century. The Second World War resulted from the failures of the western allies following the peace of 1919. Now, if the moment to build a strong Europe in alliance with the United States was lost, it would be a tragic failure.

De Gaulle admitted to being impressed by Macmillan's vision. But the fact was that, in the Six, France had some weight. She could say 'no' to policies with which she disagreed. She could say 'no' to the Germans. With Britain in, and others following, and the rest of the world demanding special trading arrangements, the result would be a sort of world free trade area. That might be desirable in itself. But it would not be European. Macmillan, after a pause, described de Gaulle's statement as most serious. It was in fact, he said, a fundamental objection to the whole idea of Britain's entry into the Common Market.

There the meeting between the two leaders ended. In a subsequent private discussion, the French Foreign Minister, Couve de Murville, tried to suggest that Macmillan had misunderstood what de Gaulle had said, but he admitted that he himself was not quite sure what the General *had* meant. The French Prime Minister, Georges Pompidou, was more informative: the whole point was that France did not want to have to renegotiate the Community's agricultural policy all over again in eight years' time.

The French Minister of Information at the time was Alain Peyrefitte. The Peyrefitte name remains known thanks to the lasting reputation of his cousin, Roger, whose novels of gay life were considered scandalous at the time. The 'respectable' member of the family, Alain, known to the British Embassy as 'a particularly malicious man', briefed the French Press after the Rambouillet meeting. President de Gaulle, he told them, had given the Council of Ministers (the French equivalent of the Cabinet) an account of his discussion with Macmillan. He had told them that he had known Macmillan for twenty years and had great personal esteem for him. It was with regret that he had had to refuse Macmillan, who was in difficulties. However, major French interests were at stake and he could not do other than refuse. When

Macmillan had left he had felt sorry for him. Indeed, so upset had Macmillan been, that the President had felt like consoling him with the words of Edith Piaf's song: 'Ne Pleurez Pas Milord'.[6]

Within days of the Rambouillet meeting, Macmillan was in Nassau for a meeting with President Kennedy at which he secured the promise of Polaris to replace the scrapped Skybolt missile programme. For Macmillan, a lot was at stake: not just the potential end of Britain's nuclear capability, but the perception and reality of the country's place in the world. The meeting was a political and personal success, cementing what Kennedy called 'the intimate family atmosphere with the flavour of a close family gathering'.

Macmillan flew home for Christmas and, on Boxing Day, wrote a letter to Heath reflecting on the Rambouillet meeting. His assessment was that de Gaulle was personally friendly and wanted good relations with Britain but did 'not want us now in the Community because he is in a mood of sulks about the future of Europe politically and would prefer to stay where he is, with France dominating the Five'.[7]

It was not clear at the start of the year (1963) that de Gaulle's hostility would bring Britain's bid for EEC membership to a halt. Serious negotiating issues, mostly relating to agriculture, remained unresolved. But Heath told Cabinet on 10 January that, with the exception of the French, the EEC members were earnestly seeking to reach a settlement. On the following day, in Paris, Heath asked Couve de Murville whether the French would oppose British entry even if the outstanding economic issues were resolved. Couve de Murville replied that, if the economic problems could be solved, nothing could prevent Britain from acceding. Couve also said that he did not expect de Gaulle to say anything at his scheduled Press conference on 14 January that would bring the Brussels negotiations to a halt. British expectations, therefore, were that the French tactic would be to drag out the negotiations and make difficulties in the hope that the British would eventually conclude for themselves that the price of entry was too high.

De Gaulle's Press conferences were set-piece, stage-managed affairs, often with questions planted among collaborating journalists. On 14 January, when de Gaulle was asked about 'the political evolution of Europe', he was ready with his answer. He gave a lengthy disquisition on the Treaty of Rome, the shared interests of the EEC members in industry, agriculture, and foreign trade. He highlighted the fact that what the member countries produced,

---

[6] D. R. Thorpe, *Supermac: The Life of Harold Macmillan* (London: Chatto & Windus, 2010), p. 534.
[7] PREM 11/4412, TNA.

bought, sold, and consumed was intended to be bought, sold, and consumed within their own group. They were bound in solidarity.

France, de Gaulle continued, had insisted on agricultural arrangements satisfactory to her interests as an absolute condition of the Common Market and its further evolution. How could Britain's agricultural trade and practices be anything other than incompatible with the system established by the Six? If Britain joined, her entry would completely change everything that the Six had established and would bring in its wake the accession of others. 'Then', de Gaulle added, with considerable foresight, 'it will be another Common Market whose construction ought to be envisaged, but one which would be taken to eleven and then thirteen and perhaps eighteen and would no longer resemble, without any doubt, the one the Six built'. Under those circumstances, de Gaulle concluded, with rather less sharp vision, the cohesion of the Six would not long endure and 'ultimately it would appear as a colossal Atlantic community under American dependence and direction'. With huge condescension, de Gaulle then expressed his unchanging respect for Britain ('this great state, this great people') and offered Britain an association agreement 'if the Brussels negotiations were shortly not to succeed'.

'I think this man has gone crazy–absolutely crazy', Macmillan told Kennedy over the transatlantic telephone a few days later. 'He is', Macmillan continued, 'inventing any means whatever to knock us out and the simple thing is he wants to be the cock on a small dunghill instead of having two cocks on a larger one'.[8]

In Cabinet, three days after de Gaulle's Press conference, some hope was expressed that Chancellor Adenauer of West Germany might bring pressure to bear on de Gaulle. But Adenauer was about to go to Paris to sign a Franco-German treaty which would set the seal on the post-war reconciliation between the two countries. Both Walter Hallstein, the President of the European Commission, and Jean Monnet, did call on Adenauer at the Bristol Hotel shortly after his arrival in Paris and sought to persuade him to ask de Gaulle to back down. Adenauer, for his part, did raise the issue, albeit rather tentatively, with de Gaulle, but he appears to have been readily persuaded by de Gaulle's contention that Britain was not suitable as a European partner. The Franco-German Treaty represented for Adenauer the culmination of all his post-war aims. He had little love for the British.

Such residual hopes as there were on the British side rested with the clear hostility of the Five to France's stand. There was even a mood among the

[8] Wall, *Official History*, p. 7.

delegations of the Five to consider an empty chair policy in which they, without France, would continue to negotiate with the British. But the Germans and Italians were reluctant. So too were the British. They did not want to be seen to be trying to break up the Six, and they feared that any concessions they made to secure agreement with the Five would then be trumped by French demands for yet more. At the end of the day, Britain could not join without the agreement of France.[9]

There were other reasons for British reluctance to go ahead with the Five alone. Heath, sitting in Brussels, was sent clear instructions in a telegram from Macmillan and Lord Home. 'As regards defence', it said, 'we do not want to do anything which would detract from NATO. Discussion in a smaller European group would almost certainly mean pressure on us for increased commitments to the defence of Europe and...we might soon expect pressing German demands. It would also, as you suggest, be a mistake to make any move in this direction without prior American agreement...Thirdly, as regards the political future of Europe, we must bear in mind that the Five are all in varying degrees in favour of Federalism...We have concluded that it would not at this stage be advantageous to commit ourselves to a further early meeting with the Five.'[10]

The axe fell on 29 January 1963, when Heath was asked to join a meeting of the Six. Over the preceding two days, attempts had been made by the Five to keep British hopes alive, in the form of a report to be made by the European Commission on the outstanding points in the negotiation. But the French would not accept that such a report should include suggestions as to how the remaining issues might be resolved.

In Heath's presence, Spaak, the Belgian Foreign Minister, spoke first. He had good claim to be one of the principal founders of the Community, and was one of those whose pro-British sentiments and hopes had been disappointed by the British. Now, he described France's action as a spectacular reversal of previous French policy. 'As soon as one member of a Community', Spaak said, 'wishes to compel the others to take decisions which are of capital importance, the Community spirit ceases to exist'. Others spoke with similar regret, though Herr Schröder, the German Foreign Minister, did not indulge in criticism of the French. For the time being, he could not see what was to be done but he promised that the German government would not give up the idea of British entry.[11]

[9] Camps, *Britain and the European Community*, p. 485.   [10] Wall, *Official History*, p. 35.
[11] Camps, *Britain and the European Community*, p. 490.

In a moving response, which contributed to the respect, and even affection, in which he was held by his continental colleagues, Heath was clear where the blame lay. 'The plain fact is', he said, 'that the time had come when the negotiations were, for some, too near to success...They have been halted, not for any technical or economic reasons, but on purely political grounds and on the insistence of a single government.' He concluded with a pledge: 'And so I would say to my colleagues: they should have no fear. We in Britain are not going to turn our backs on the mainland of Europe or on the countries of the Community. We are a part of Europe: by geography, tradition, history, culture and civilisation. We shall continue to work with all our friends in Europe for the true unity and strength of this continent.'[12]

'All our policies at home and abroad are in ruins', Macmillan confided to his diary on 28 January.[13] In public, he put a brave face on what was clearly a debacle. In Parliament, he asserted the importance of good Anglo-German and good Anglo-French relations, though the government did cancel a visit to Paris by HRH Princess Margaret on the grounds that de Gaulle was going to turn it into a great jamboree—a decision which was much criticized in Britain at the time and which Macmillan later regretted. As for the future, Macmillan made no secret of the fact that negotiations would not be reopened quickly. Britain's external plan of action would be based on close cooperation with the Commonwealth, the USA, EFTA, and, he hoped, the Six.

On the other side of the Chamber sat the new Leader of the Opposition, Harold Wilson. The two men knew each other, since Wilson had been appointed Shadow Chancellor when Macmillan was still Chancellor of the Exchequer. Wilson had succeeded Gaitskell as Leader of the Labour Party on Gaitskell's sudden death in mid-January. As Shadow Chancellor, Wilson had opened the second day of the debate in August 1961 on the government's decision to open negotiations and had won Macmillan's admiration for 'the most brilliant speech of the debate'. The two men were to combine public sparring with privately good fellow feeling, in what Wilson called 'a happy and stimulating relationship'.[14]

Wilson has gone down in contemporary history as the 'artful dodger': the first 'modern' political leader with a command of television, a supreme manipulator; a man who had few convictions, the supreme opportunist on matters European. There is much truth in the characterization. Wilson was a

---

[12] Ibid., p. 492.

[13] Harold Macmillan, *At the End of the Day 1961–1963* (London: Macmillan, 1973), p. 367.

[14] Thorpe, *Supermac*, p. 323.

superb tactician and Heath, who defeated him at the polls once and who was beaten by Wilson three times, regarded him as totally untrustworthy. At home, Wilson's second term from 1966 ended in defeat and his final term, and that of his successor, Jim Callaghan, were marked by record levels of inflation and industrial strife. On Europe, Wilson's record is that of a man who was not by nature an internationalist and whose heart lay primarily with the Commonwealth, especially with New Zealand, where he had 'kith and kin', a phrase with both family and racial connotations, much used at the time. But Wilson's European record, against a background of ever-growing hostility towards the EEC within the Labour movement, tells a more principled and strategic story than he is usually given credit for.

As Shadow Chancellor, Wilson had spoken, in the speech much admired by Macmillan, of the debt of gratitude owed by Britain to New Zealand. 'We cannot, consistently with the honour of this country, take any action now that would betray friends such as those. All this and Europe too – if you can get it... But if there has to be a choice, we are not entitled to sell our friends and kinsmen down the river for a problematic and marginal advantage in selling washing machines in Düsseldorf.'

That was vintage Wilson: concealing the fair wind he was giving to the negotiations with an emotive appeal to sentiment and an entertaining disparagement of what was at stake in Europe. More surprising perhaps was what he had to say about sovereignty:

'The whole history of political progress is a history of gradual abandonment of sovereignty... We abrogated it – some would say that we did not abrogate it enough – when we joined the United Nations. One cannot talk about world government in one breath and then start drooling about the need to preserve national sovereignty in the next... The question is not whether sovereignty remains absolute or not, but in what way one is prepared to sacrifice sovereignty, to whom and for what purpose... The vital question in the political sense is whether to join the Common Market explicitly or implicitly means a move towards a federal Europe. There is nothing in the Treaty of Rome enjoining federalism, although there is a great deal of supranationalism... It is a little myopic of the Prime Minister [Macmillan] to refer to it as a 'purely economic negotiation and not a political and foreign policy negotiation'. But, all the same, we warmly welcome his statement of yesterday associating himself with President de Gaulle's approach... There should be no doubt on this federal issue. There should be no double talk with

Europe about it...I hope that we make it clear that we shall not go into a federal system.[15']

In the wake of de Gaulle's veto, Wilson offered the House an upbeat view of what Britain's approach should be. It should encompass a pragmatically positive approach to greater European unity, involving regular meetings of western European Heads of Government. But Wilson also made a rousing call for national endeavour: 'Our future lies now clearly in our own hands, on our sense of purpose, of dynamism, of self-discipline, of sacrifices, if sacrifices there must be, fairly shared. If this failure of the Brussels negotiations has brought this home to us as never before, I thank God for it, because this is the first condition for reasserting our national strength and our national independence...[Macmillan's] speech today was one of abdication on behalf of a whole government. The recovery of Britain's lost dynamic is a task that must and will now pass into other hands.'[16]

Later that month, Wilson made a Party Political broadcast that attracted the largest audience for any television programme until then. Sixty-four per cent of those polled by Gallup approved. By March, Labour's lead over the Conservatives stood at 17 per cent, and was to rise to 20 per cent by June. At the same time, Wilson's approval ratings showed a 19 per cent lead over Macmillan's.[17]

On 18 October 1963, Macmillan resigned on grounds of ill health. He was replaced by Lord Home (who then renounced his title and won a seat in the House of Commons as Sir Alec Douglas-Home). Barely a month later, it fell to Macmillan to speak from the back benches in tribute to President Kennedy, assassinated in Dallas on 22 November. Kennedy did not, Macmillan said, 'regard it as a statesman's duty to yield to public opinion, but to strive to lead it...He seemed sometimes to be almost a lonely figure, but always true to his own integrity and his own faith...When this terrible news came in on Friday everyone in this country – and, I think, in every country – felt stunned by the shock of what seemed to us – to each one of us – a personal bereavement, and to the whole of humanity, struggling in this world of darkness, the sudden and cruel extinction of a shining light. We mourn for him and for his bereaved family...and we mourn him – and this is perhaps the greatest tribute to Jack

[15] *Hansard*, 3 August 1961, cols. 1667–9.   [16] *Hansard*, 11 February 1963, col. 979.
[17] Ben Pimlott, *Harold Wilson* (London: HarperCollins, 1963), p. 266.

Kennedy's life and work – for ourselves, for what we and all the world have lost.'[18]

In the summer of 1964, with a General Election only weeks away, Sir Con O'Neill, head of the UK Delegation to the European Communities in Brussels, put pen to paper to address the European issues which the next British government would have to face. It was possible, O'Neill argued, to see the EEC as the most hopeful experiment in international relations embarked on in generations. At the other end of the spectrum, it could be seen as having succeeded, by stealth, in achieving what Napoleon and Hitler had failed to achieve by force: a Europe united, without Britain and, therefore, against her.

The tide of indignation at de Gaulle's veto had, O'Neill argued, ebbed fast and now the EEC members thought little about Britain's exclusion. The European Community looked as if it would endure and prosper over the next decade. On balance, Britain would probably gain economically from entry. But the key argument was political. For the rest of the century, there would be three great centres of effective power: the United States, the Soviet Union, and Western Europe. If Britain did not join the EEC 'our decline towards isolation and comparative insignificance, which it seems to me has already begun, is likely to continue, and cannot be arrested'.[19]

Whatever the prescience of O'Neill's views, they found little resonance in either the Conservative or Labour manifestos for the General Election in October 1964. 'Entry into the EEC is not open to us in existing circumstances and no question of fresh negotiations can arise at present', said the Conservatives. As for Labour, 'Though we shall seek to achieve closer links with our European neighbours, the Labour Party is convinced that the first responsibility of a British Government is still to the Commonwealth.' The Labour manifesto characterized the policy of the Conservative government as being one of readiness 'to accept terms of entry to the Common Market that would have excluded our Commonwealth partners, broken our special trade links with them, and forced us to treat them as third class nations'.

It is of course a trick of politics so to caricature your opponent's policies that your own appear starkly different even if, in reality, they are much the same. Given the state of opinion in the Labour Party and the country, the manifesto would have seemed hopelessly naïve had it espoused membership of the EEC at a time when de Gaulle was still firmly guarding the door. By the same token, across the Channel, it suited the French to cite Labour's approach as evidence of further British backsliding. Less than two weeks after Wilson's narrow

---

[18] *Hansard*, 25 November 1963, col. 42.   [19] PREM 11/1548, TNA.

election victory (Labour had an overall majority of four seats), the French Foreign Minister, Couve de Murville, told the National Assembly that the will of Great Britain 'truly to participate in European construction [had] evolved in a more and more pessimistic direction'.[20] That de Gaulle's high-handed humiliation of Britain might have contributed to this state of affairs was not of course alluded to.

It was partly in response to Couve's disobliging comments that Patrick Gordon-Walker, the new Foreign Secretary, recommended to Cabinet that the government's most effective counteraction would lie in strengthening EFTA, whose morale he described as being low. This was not altogether surprising, since one of the first acts of the new Labour government had been to impose a surcharge on imports which, in the case of EFTA, was against the rules of the club, and done with no prior consultation. The anger of the other EFTA members was soon to force the British to climb down.

Two months later, the death of Winston Churchill on 24 January 1965, brought de Gaulle to London and gave Wilson his first opportunity to meet and evaluate the French leader. De Gaulle began the conversation with a characteristically self-serving account of the failed negotiations. The British had said they wanted to join the EEC but it was evident that, for domestic and Commonwealth reasons, that was simply not possible. Yet Britain now bore a grudge against the French simply because the French had stated the obvious.

Wilson pandered to de Gaulle's prejudices. Labour, he said, had consistently pointed out the difficulty of reconciling Britain's links with the Commonwealth with the spirit of the Common Market. The Labour Party had strongly opposed the supranational element in the Treaty of Rome and was certainly not prepared to abandon to a supranational authority control over foreign policy and defence. He found the President's view entirely realistic.

What, beyond ingratiation, Wilson's policy amounted to at this early stage of his premiership, was perhaps best expressed in his meeting with West German Chancellor Erhard the next day. Membership of the EEC, Wilson said, was not in the realm of practical politics 'at present'. But the new government were not neutral on the issue. On the contrary, the Labour Party regarded the formation of the Common Market as a historic landmark and Franco-German reconciliation as a great step forward. On the political side, the British government wanted to be closely associated with any

---

[20] PREM 13/1042, TNA.

development for political union. On the economic side, they wanted to take 'all steps' to increase trade between Britain and the EEC.[21]

The first sign of different thinking came in a minute of January 1965 from Michael Stewart (who had replaced Gordon-Walker as Foreign Secretary). A range of factors, Stewart argued, were 'resulting in what may be described as a creeping isolation of Britain from Europe'. The EEC had passed the point of no return and was bound to become more dominant and assertive. The Six would have conversations about political union, including defence issues, from which Britain would be excluded. EFTA would be no more than an industrial free trade area. French obstruction in NATO and the WEU prevented Britain from using either organization for effective consultation or integration. A few days later, in the House of Commons, Wilson said that 'if a favourable opportunity were to arise for negotiating entry into the EEC, we would be prepared to negotiate if, and only if, the necessary conditions relating to essential and British and Commonwealth interests could be fulfilled'. Wilson added that the government would 'do anything in our power to avoid the further economic division of Europe and [would do] all we can to build a bridge between EFTA and the EEC'.[22]

That was Wilson's preferred approach: a rapprochement between the EEC and EFTA, leading to a nil-tariff trading relationship over a five-year period. So the Wilson plan was not very different in concept from the earlier failed Maudling plan, but the circumstances were even less propitious for its fulfilment: EFTA was muddling along; the EEC was motoring. The British government's decision that same year to move to the metric system was a symbolic shift towards Europe and away from the Commonwealth. Some of the signals emanating from the Elysée also appeared propitious. Alain Peyrefitte, both his master's voice and with no detectable liking for Britain, made a speech in July 1965 in which, he suggested, 'two great nations, France and Britain, are fated...together to build a future based on exchanges, cooperation and friendship'.[23] But the French had just flounced out of the EEC Council of Ministers in a row about further integration, and Peyrefitte's speech was probably intended to pour salt on the tails of France's integrationist-minded EEC partners rather than to sweet-talk the British. After six months of the empty chair, which brought EEC business to a halt, the French settled their dispute with their partners, at some cost to themselves.

While Wilson's mind was turning ever more towards the EEC, there was little substantive evidence that de Gaulle had changed his mind since the 1963

[21] PREM/306, TNA.   [22] *Hansard*, 16 February 1965, col. 1003.   [23] PREM 13/904, TNA.

veto. But Wilson wanted to give himself a margin of manoeuvre. In his day, Prime Ministers could seek a dissolution of Parliament and a General Election at a time of their own choosing. In March 1966, Wilson did just that, buoyed up by opinion polls which predicted the handsome victory he in fact secured in the General Election, transforming an overall majority of 4 into one of 96.

During the campaign, Wilson talked up the improvement in Anglo-French relations, in a less than honest attempt to disparage the Tory record compared with his own. 'We believe', Wilson went on, 'that given the right conditions, it would be possible to join the EEC as an economic Community... The Common Market is no cure-all for Britain's economic problems... Unless we modernise, streamline our industries, base our attitudes on a full day's work for a full day's pay... then the Common Market choice is simply a choice between being a backwater inside Europe and a backwater outside Europe. If the conditions are right, and we are able to enter the wider Community from a situation of industrial strength, we shall be facing a challenging adventure...'[24]

In the post-election Cabinet there were some, most notably Wilson's nominal deputy, George Brown, openly arguing for EEC membership. Wilson and much of the rest of the Cabinet were more cautious. Should they wait upon the demise of de Gaulle, or press forward in the hope that de Gaulle could be outflanked by the combined pressure of Britain and the Five? What state did the British economy need to be in before Britain joined, or applied to join? Were acceptable conditions of membership attainable? Wilson himself was reluctant 'to invite the political controversy which would undoubtedly be aroused if we gave any public indication that we were prepared formally to accept the Treaty [of Rome]'.[25] An official visit to London by French Prime Minister Georges Pompidou, and other Ministers in July provided no helpful clarification, and certainly no indication that, on substance, de Gaulle had changed his mind. But waiting for de Gaulle to die or retire could mean waiting a long time. In that time, yet further integration of the EEC members would take place. There were already embryonic indications of an emerging EEC foreign policy. A Europe dominated by France and Germany, with Germany being courted by the United States both to keep it onside and because of its economic strength, represented a threat to Britain's status as the USA's closest ally.

Indecision might have prevailed but for the domestic economic travails of the British economy in the summer of 1966. Europe offered a new horizon.

---

[24] PREM13/905, TNA.   [25] PREM 13/906, TNA.

At a special Cabinet on Europe, held at Chequers in October, Wilson proposed that he and George Brown (who had become Foreign Secretary in a job-swap with Michael Stewart) should make a joint tour of EEC capitals to explore the scope for a bid. There were differing views within Cabinet. Wilson emphasized the non-committal nature of the exploration and the fact that no decision on whether to join had yet been taken. That question would come back to Cabinet. But he did put some of his cards on the table at Cabinet a few weeks later, telling his colleagues that 'as regards the balance of advantage of membership of the Community, in his view the arguments based on the advantages of scale to be derived from membership of a much larger market were of greater weight than those related to the "cold douche" of competition to be expected in those circumstances'.[26] According to a Gallup poll two days later, the public had become decidedly more favourable to the idea. Sixty-eight per cent of those questioned were in favour of accession with barely any difference in enthusiasm detectable across the three main political parties.

In mid-January 1967, Wilson and Foreign Secretary George Brown set out on their fact-finding mission. They were politely received everywhere, though without notable enthusiasm. The German Chancellor, Kurt Kiesinger, was civil and supportive but gave no indication that the German government would bring pressure to bear on de Gaulle. The General, for his part, was friendly, warm in his appreciation of Britain but in no way encouraging. Wilson concluded that it was clear de Gaulle continued to want to keep Britain out. The question was whether he would again defy the Five in vetoing a British application. It was also recognized in London that any renewed accession negotiation would have to be short, confined to major issues only, preferably as pre-cooked as possible and, crucially, timed to coincide with a resurgence in Britain's economic fortunes.

Cabinet met over two days at the end of April to consider whether to go ahead. There were a number of doubters, and the political case for joining was more readily accepted than the economic one. Jim Callaghan, as Chancellor of the Exchequer, saw long-term advantages from accession through the impetus to industrial investment and economic growth. But the immediate impact on the balance of payments would, he advised, be 'disadvantageous and serious'. Richard Crossman (Lord President of the Council) raised the possibility of devaluing the pound but Wilson cautioned against any hint of it being discussed, even if it was an option. Callaghan said that so long as he was

---

[26] Wall, *Official History*, p. 147.

Chancellor, he would not devalue: he had given too many pledges to holders of sterling to make that credible.[27]

Wilson did not sum up the discussion, but all were clear where things were headed. On 1 May, the Foreign Office telegraphed to its overseas posts, warning them of an imminent announcement and Wilson sent a message to de Gaulle, asking him to consider a bid by Britain to join 'with the utmost care and in a spirit of friendship and goodwill'. 'Whatever may happen', de Gaulle replied, 'rest assured that, so far as France is concerned, she will act in the spirit of friendship which characterises the relationship between our two countries.'[28]

On 2 May, Wilson sought the approval of Cabinet for the announcement he was to make in the House, of the government's decision to apply for membership. Only two Cabinet Ministers, Richard Marsh (Minister of Power) and Barbara Castle (Minister of Transport) dissented. The decision was, Wilson told the House of Commons later in the day, 'a historic decision which could well determine the future of Britain, Europe, and indeed of the world, for decades to come'.[29]

On 10 May, the House of Commons voted by 487 votes to 26 in favour of the United Kingdom applying for EEC membership. It was the highest majority recorded in the House on any issue for a century. On the following day, the EEC Council of Ministers agreed to consider the application, though the French Foreign Minister's comments reportedly bordered on the sarcastic. Wilson and de Gaulle had met at the funeral of Chancellor Adenauer on 25 April. De Gaulle had promised Wilson that, at the Press conference he was due to hold on 16 May, he would say nothing that would cause offence. In the event, he repeated most of the arguments against British accession that he had made four years earlier. He was willing, he said, to offer Britain some sort of free trade area or Association Agreement with the EEC or, he added, why not wait 'until this great people, so magnificently endowed with capabilities and courage, should themselves have accomplished, first of all, and by themselves, the profound economic and political transformation which is required so that its union with the continental Six can be effected...If one day, this were to come about, with what joy would France greet this historic conversion.'[30]

The British Press were convinced de Gaulle had once again vetoed the British application. The British Ambassador in Paris, Patrick Reilly, thought the whole of what de Gaulle had said to be so negative as to be not so much a

[27] CC (67) 26th Conclusions, CAB 128/42, TNA.   [28] PREM 13/1481, TNA.
[29] *Hansard*, 2 May 1967, col. 314.   [30] Wall, *Official History*, p. 203.

veto as a block on negotiations even starting. Jean Monnet, on the other hand, took comfort from the fact that de Gaulle (of whom he was no great admirer) had not actually said 'no'. It was vital that the British did not treat what he had said as if it was a veto. More realistically, Hervé Alphand, the Secretary General at the French Foreign Ministry, told the US Ambassador in Paris that what his President had said was, quite categorically, a rejection of the British application.

Macmillan had taken de Gaulle's 1963 veto as terminal and his government had withdrawn Britain's membership application. Wilson determined on a formula, which he used in Parliament and the media from de Gaulle's Press conference onwards, which was to say that he would not take 'no' for an answer. On the one hand, in quite a clever way, the phrase took some of the sting out of de Gaulle's antagonism and implicitly reminded people that de Gaulle was ageing and would not be around forever. On the other hand, it also took the sting out of earlier British threats, which Wilson repeated when he met de Gaulle at the Grand Trianon palace on 19 June, that, if Britain were not able to enter the EEC she would pursue a quite un-European course—possibly seeking a free trade arrangement (NAFTA) with the United States.

If Britain was not taking 'no' for an answer, that implied that she would stick with her EEC-based strategy. But the very mention of a NAFTA of some sort gave de Gaulle the opening to argue that the United Kingdom was still closely tied to the United States and would always be pulled towards the United States. Would Britain bring to the European enterprise something that would really be European; or would her entry, on the contrary, simply lead to an Atlantic community or some loose free trade arrangement? One day, said de Gaulle, some such Atlantic concept might submerge the EEC. In that case, there would be no Europe—or at least no European Europe, and no specifically European character or personality. France, on the other hand, had made its choice. In both the Middle East and the Far East, de Gaulle argued, France had disengaged. US disputes were not France's disputes. France had done this, not from hostility, but from realism. The USA, as the greatest power in the world, would consider only themselves and their own interests.

De Gaulle's belief that Europe could only be built by a kind of exceptionalism vis-à-vis the United States was not shared by his EEC partners, least of all the West Germans who depended on US armed support for their survival in the face of a hostile Soviet Union. By contrast, de Gaulle's assessment that the UK would always look first and foremost to the United States was close to the mark at the time—and has remained so. Paradoxically, Wilson had been given a nod and a wink from President Johnson that the Americans would tolerate

Britain playing up to de Gaulle's prejudices. When Wilson and Johnson met on 2 June, Wilson explained to the President that he might need to make some tactical gestures towards de Gaulle 'that might seem a bit non-American, or even anti-American'. He (Wilson) might need 'a Nassau in reverse'. Johnson, supreme wheeler-dealer that he was, apparently 'took this well and grinned'. Insofar as Wilson played these cards (and he did paint a prospective picture of advanced industrial collaboration between Britain and France), de Gaulle was not convinced.[31]

Wilson himself, as he wrote in a personal letter to Foreign Secretary George Brown, came away from the Elysée with mixed feelings. 'The picture looks pretty sombre for our prospects', he wrote.

'But...I believe this to have been a useful visit...I think he [de Gaulle] was genuinely attracted at the possibility of Britain and France playing a more effective role together in world issues...while in the European context he showed unmistakable interest in what I told him about our willingness to cooperate (if we got in) in the advanced technologies and particularly the civil nuclear field...He accepted that in these major economic and industrial areas we are now becoming increasingly independent of the Americans. To sum up (and even if this sounds a shade far-fetched) I found myself watching this lonely old man play an almost regal 'mine host' at Trianon, slightly saddened by the obvious sense of failure and, to use his own word, impotence, that I believe he now feels. His concept of France's role as he described it is oddly reminiscent of the days of the Maginot line. There is nothing he can do but sit behind his *Force de Frappe* and watch the world move towards Armageddon...I feel paradoxically encouraged. He does not want us in and he will use all the delaying tactics he can...But if we keep firmly beating at the door and do not falter in our purpose or our resolve I am not sure that he any longer has the strength finally to keep us out – a dangerous prophecy, as prophecy always is with the General...'[32]

A few days later, Roy Jenkins, the British Home Secretary, held meetings in Paris with Valéry Giscard d'Estaing, former French Finance Minister, and with François Mitterrand, Leader of the French Socialist Party. Both men were destined to become President of France (though Giscard, who lost the Presidency to Mitterrand in 1984, in 1967 confidently predicted to Jenkins that Mitterrand, as a man of no principles, would never become President).

---

[31] PREM 13/1731 and 13/1906, TNA.   [32] PREM 13/1521, TNA.

Mitterrand told Jenkins that de Gaulle was unlikely to relax his opposition to British accession. But Gaullism would not survive de Gaulle. Giscard, so the British Embassy in Paris reported, was 'generally favourable' to Britain joining.[33]

From accounts of de Gaulle's conversations with other European leaders over the summer, there was plenty of evidence of the General's continuing opposition to Britain. But the British had lodged a formal application, and it fell to the European Commission to produce a formal Opinion for the EEC Council of Ministers. That Opinion, when it came at the end of September, was broadly favourable to the British cause. The Commission were clear in recommending that negotiations be opened. However, the passages in the Opinion on the state of the British economy, heavily influenced by one of the French members of the Commission, Raymond Barre, were very unfavourable. In the Commission's view, the British economy was in a better state than it had been in 1963/64. But the fundamentals had not changed. Industrial investment had stagnated. The marked improvement in the balance of payments situation achieved towards the end of 1966 had been reversed. Violent fluctuations in the sterling balances could not be excluded. Those could upset the UK economy and, if the UK were by then a member of the EEC, could upset the economies of the rest of the EEC as well.

De Gaulle wasted no time. On 5 October, he summoned the British Ambassador in Paris, Patrick Reilly. There was, de Gaulle told him, no objection of principle to British accession either from him personally or from France. On the contrary, when Britain was ready to come in, she would be welcome. But Britain was not ready and her accession would break up the Community. Britain would have to take political and economic decisions before she was ready to join. Her economic problems: the balance of payments, the stability of the pound, the international role of sterling all, he implied, amounted to an insurmountable obstacle.[34]

Uncertainty once again prevailed in London as to whether de Gaulle was strong enough to go as far as another veto. Various alternative, or even retaliatory, scenarios were considered and rejected. Then, on 18 November 1967, in the face of a severe run on the pound in international currency markets, the British government devalued the pound from a parity of $2.80 to $2.40. Wilson sent messages to each Head of Government of the Six asserting that 'the decision...does not affect our resolve to pursue our

---

[33] PREM 13/1653, TNA.   [34] PREM13/1485, TNA.

declared European policy and that it is our intention to prosecute an application to the Community with energy'.[35]

On 27 November, de Gaulle, in a tone which mixed heavy sarcasm with lofty condescension, dismissed Britain's application out of hand. In Reilly's account, the President had 'displayed the greatest contempt for normal standards of international behaviour'. His references to Britain had been 'tinged with hostility and malice'. He had suggested that the recent devaluation might explain the extraordinary haste with which Britain had been pressing to start negotiations. He as good as said that Britain was only now trying to join the Common Market because her earlier efforts to break it up or dominate it had failed, and because she was being left behind by the EEC while it was the Commonwealth that was breaking up. He gestured dismissively when he referred to Britain's industrial problems.[36]

The British responded by reiterating that they had made an application to join in formal and due form and that it was for the European Community as a whole to respond. When the Council of Ministers met, on 18 December, five Member States clearly wanted negotiations with the UK to open but, as the formal statement from the Council put it, one Member State had said that the process of recovery of the British economy must be brought to its conclusion before the British application could be recognized.

Once again, the Five were dismayed by de Gaulle's veto. But there was less anger than there had been in 1963, partly because the sands of time were running out for de Gaulle but also because the prospect of an economically weak UK joining the EEC, and perhaps needing some kind of bail-out, was not especially attractive.

De Gaulle had once again suggested some kind of association agreement between the EEC and Britain. Over the ensuing weeks, various ideas did the rounds as to how progress could be made, falling short of actual membership. The British were doubtful, wary of anything that would bind them to decisions taken by the EEC whilst having no role in taking those binding decisions in the first place.

Other events intervened. In May, 1968, student riots in Paris quickly spread to strikes by the French workforce. De Gaulle was on a state visit to Romania as the crisis worsened. On his return, on 24 May, he broadcast to the French nation, but his performance was lacklustre. Would de Gaulle be forced to resign? The French government seemed close to collapse when, on 29 May, de Gaulle failed to preside over the Council of Ministers. In fact, he had flown to

[35] PREM 13/1860, TNA.   [36] PREM 13/2646, TNA.

Baden Baden to secure an assurance that the army would remain loyal. On his return, de Gaulle found his form in a strong broadcast, defying the Communists and their allies, rousing his supporters, rallying the police and deploying troops and tanks around Paris. The rebellion subsided. The British government had throughout maintained a tactful silence.

Jean Monnet was one of those who had hoped that de Gaulle's opposition to the United Kingdom could be overcome. But, in July, he told Harold Wilson that he had reluctantly concluded that there was no hope of a change of heart. The Gaullists had been returned to power in the post-May election. This was not, according to Monnet, a positive vote for de Gaulle but a vote against either chaos or communism. De Gaulle's attitude would not change. The Germans would not break with the French for the sake of Britain. Indeed, the Germans themselves were suspicious of British intentions.

As most of Europe took to its August deckchairs, Soviet tanks rolled into Prague, crushing the Prague Spring of democracy. The invasion was a brutal demonstration of Soviet power. Wilson contemplated sending a message to the French President as a gesture of shared European outrage and in the hope that de Gaulle might be induced to second thoughts about his threatened withdrawal from the military structures of NATO. His Foreign Secretary, Michael Stewart advised against: 'at a time when General de Gaulle has clearly suffered the reversal of so many of his hopes, it might seem patronising for these to be rubbed into him so quickly', Stewart wrote. Wilson agreed. No message was sent.

In the wake of the Soviet invasion of Czechoslovakia, the Cabinet met in emergency session. Parliament was recalled. I joined the Foreign Office, at the age of 21, straight from university, that September. I was dispatched almost immediately to New York as a so-called Reporting Officer (a euphemism for general factotum) at the UK Mission to the United Nations. The extent of our sanction against the Soviets, as I recall, was to boycott all the social events organized by the Soviet mission to the UN and its satellite countries in what they chose to call their 'Commonwealth'. The tender shoots of democracy had been crushed. The West had little choice but to accept that the countries of eastern and central Europe would remain under a harsh tyranny.[37]

In the days before international telephoning, and long before the almost monthly meetings of EU leaders we know today, Ambassadors were a conduit of communication between Heads of Government. It is striking how often de

---

[37] See *Documents on British Policy Overseas*, Series III, Vol. I, pp. 66–75 for discussion of the crisis by British Ministers.

Gaulle talked to successive British Ambassadors in Paris on issues where he wanted his views recorded and reported. No modern Ambassador has such access and governments do not need their Ambassadors to have the conversations which now take place directly between leaders on the phone or face to face. Against that background, it is to the credit of the Wilson government that, at this vexed juncture in Anglo-French relations, they made an original but inspired decision in appointing as Britain's new Ambassador to Paris a former Cabinet Minister, Christopher Soames. Soames was a Conservative, so the move was controversial in Labour circles. But his credentials were exceptional: he had been Minister of Agriculture and understood the excruciating detail of the issues at the heart of the accession negotiation. He had served as a Defence Attaché in the Embassy in Paris and spoke fluent French. He was married to Winston Churchill's youngest daughter, Mary. He was a big man: imposing, wealthy, extrovert, and shrewd. As a politician, he would be guided by the instructions he received from the Foreign Office, but he would not necessarily follow them blindly. If this occasionally riled the Foreign Secretary, Michael Stewart, who was as quiet and self-effacing as Soames was boisterous, it did not dismay Wilson who wanted as his Ambassador a politician who would do a politician's job.

The issue which faced Soames as he arrived in the ornate Residence in the Faubourg St Honoré, the decorative candles lit in the windows as they always were to greet a new Ambassador, was how to reopen a fruitful dialogue with the French government and, more especially, with de Gaulle. Foreign Office policy, as Soames saw it, was to try to get round the French veto by isolating them. Soames correctly judged that the Germans would never cooperate in isolating the French.

A variety of initiatives was under consideration in London when, on 5 February 1969, Soames paid his first call on de Gaulle. De Gaulle treated Soames to his familiar views on Britain and the EEC. Soames replied that what de Gaulle had said took no account of Britain's efforts to participate in the creation of a European economic and political entity. De Gaulle said that the whole essence of a European entity must be its independence in world terms and he doubted if it was possible for Britain to accept that. In response to a question from Soames as to whether this meant, in de Gaulle's eyes, Britain leaving NATO, de Gaulle said that he was not looking for that but, in his view, once there was a truly independent Europe, there would be no need for NATO as such 'with its American dominance and command structure'.

De Gaulle then went on to say that he wanted to see the European Community changing into a looser form of a free trade area with suitable arrangements for agricultural trade. He would be quite prepared to discuss with Britain what should take the place of the Common Market as an enlarged European Economic Association, with a small inner council (a European Political Association) consisting of France, Britain, Germany, and Italy. There should be private talks between the British and French on economic, monetary, political, and defence matters to see whether the differences between the two countries could be resolved. His proposal should be secret until a decision to hold talks had been taken. If talks took place, then the fact that they were happening should be disclosed. He specifically asked for his proposal to be transmitted to the Prime Minister and Foreign Secretary.

Soames, despite his own fluent French, took the precaution of checking his report of the conversation with the Elysée staff, who confirmed its accuracy. He then proposed to London that he be authorized to probe matters further with the French Foreign Minister, Michel Debré, and others close to the President.

Wilson was of similar mind. But Stewart, the Foreign Secretary, egged on by senior official advice within the Foreign Office, was profoundly suspicious. He instructed Soames to take no action and sent a separate message to Wilson (to which Soames was not made privy) in which he misrepresented what de Gaulle had said, advised Wilson to inform the German Chancellor when he saw him the following week and to alert other European partners. Soames was already due to meet Debré, and Stewart instructed him to say nothing of substance on what de Gaulle had proposed. But Debré, for his part, had quite a lot to say and left Soames with the clear impression that he (Debré) had been working on the General for some time to bring him to the point where he was prepared to make the serious overture to the British which was what his proposal for talks amounted to.

Soames suggested that he travel to London to discuss de Gaulle's initiative with Wilson and Stewart, but Stewart refused. Instead, a senior Foreign Office official was sent to the Paris Embassy to tell Soames of the plan hatched in London to spill the beans about the conversation to the German and other European governments, as well as to the Americans. Soames remonstrated with London about what would, he said, 'amount to a betrayal of General de Gaulle's confidence…This is tantamount to rebuffing the French in a way which I fear could have adverse long term consequences.'

At a meeting in Number 10, the senior official from the Foreign Office who had been sent to Paris, told the meeting dismissively that Soames found it difficult to accept that he was 'now only an Ambassador', a comment that prompted Wilson's Foreign Office Private Secretary, Michael Palliser, to warn Wilson that the Foreign Office's treatment of Soames might provoke the latter's resignation.

Wilson was about to leave for Bonn and told Stewart that he would test the atmosphere with Chancellor Kiesinger before deciding how to proceed.

Stewart was not satisfied with this and sent Wilson a follow-up message urging him to tell Kiesinger 'the whole story'. As to any French accusation of a breach of confidence, it was the French who had breached confidences by proposing such secret bilateral talks on matters which vitally affected the interests and security of their partners and allies. The French anyway had more respect for those who looked after their own interests and spoke plainly.

Into this heady mix of Stewart's animus against Soames, political miscalculation, and sheer professional incompetence was injected the characteristic organizational efficiency of the Foreign Office. Instructions were sent to British Ambassadors in all EEC capitals putting them on notice of what they were to say to the governments in their host countries once they received a trigger telegram telling them to do so. Their message was to be that the British government rejected de Gaulle's views on NATO and maintained their position on entry to the EEC. At the same time, Soames was instructed to seek a meeting with Debré, accepting the idea of talks provided other partners were fully in the picture. In a personal message, Stewart told Soames that he did 'not believe that in the longer run the reply I am now asking you to return to Debré will damage either our policies or your position in France. On the contrary, I am convinced that both will benefit.'

Wilson, in Bonn, briefed Kiesinger, and then authorized the release of the instructions to Ambassadors. News of de Gaulle's initiative then began to spread and, in response, the Foreign Office took the unprecedented step of releasing to the Press a comprehensive account of de Gaulle's conversation with Soames. This provoked a furious backlash in Paris.

Soames, who was blameless in the affair, offered his resignation, which was refused. In a letter to Wilson he wrote: 'As I see it, the General handed me a cup which I handed on to Whitehall. It may have been full of peace or poison. This, only time and discussion would have told. I saw it as the beginning of what you wanted me to achieve when you sent me here. So of course I was dismayed when it was deliberately smashed to pieces.' Wilson, in his memoirs, judged the Foreign Office to have presented Britain 'as a rather priggish Little Lord Fauntleroy who had resisted the General's anti-EEC blandishments'.

Had de Gaulle remained in office, there is little doubt that the incompetent misjudgements made in London, and de Gaulle's anger and bitterness at their consequences, would have caused lasting and serious damage to Anglo-French relations. But, just a few weeks later, de Gaulle put to the French people a referendum on constitutional change. In the event of a 'no', he would, he said, resign. In consequence, on 28 April 1969, he did just that.[38]

---

[38] Account of the Soames Affair based on several sources cited in Wall, *Official History*, pp. 320–30.

4

Good Result or Bad Deal?

The Price of Entry, 1970–1973

In the spring of 1965, President de Gaulle toured the French provinces, attended by various of his Ministers. It did not escape the attention of the French Press that de Gaulle had shown an unprecedented mark of favour to his Prime Minister, Georges Pompidou, by allowing him to share the same platform. Pompidou, the French media suggested, was now the heir apparent, the Dauphin. On seeing a telegram from the British Embassy in Paris reporting this news, Harold Wilson, doubtless a student of Shakespeare's *Henry V*, wrote in the margin in his characteristic green ink: 'No objection to the dauphin. Send tennis balls?'[1]

Pompidou had, sometime before de Gaulle's departure, taken the deliberate step of standing down from government, not in hostility to his leader but as a way of putting some distance of time and perception between him and the dominant President. Now, following de Gaulle's resignation, Pompidou was the clear favourite to succeed, and duly won the second round of the Presidential election by a large margin. He and Wilson had met before, and Pompidou had not taken a liking to the British leader. While the new President's statements on UK accession to the EEC gave reason to believe that de Gaulle's absolute veto of principle would be withdrawn, they gave no guarantee that the door to the United Kingdom would be opened. Pompidou had cast doubt on Britain's European convictions and had not committed himself to the goal of full membership for the UK.

On the English side of the Channel, Wilson had an advantage denied to Macmillan: the Conservative Party in Opposition would support, not oppose, accession, though even within that Party there was some anti-European sentiment which coalesced round the charismatic and controversial politician Enoch Powell. Wilson's own assessment of the parliamentary situation was

---

[1] PREM 13/2653, TNA. In Shakespeare's *Henry V*, in a lull in the Hundred Years War, the French Dauphin sends the young English king a barrel of tennis balls, enjoining him mockingly to focus on games, not warfare.

that support for membership of the EEC had cooled, but not turned into significant hostility. Public opinion, meanwhile, was scarcely enthusiastic after two attempts to join that had ended in humiliating rejection. Inside the Cabinet, the determination to pursue negotiations for accession was not exactly wholehearted.

When Cabinet discussed the issue in July 1969, the Foreign Secretary drew comfort from the fact that an anti-EEC Early Day Motion in the House of Commons had drawn little support. But it was natural, he believed, for hostile sentiment to become more vocal as the prospect of membership became more attainable. It was the government's settled policy to seek membership and nothing should be said by Ministers to imply any loss of serious intent.

Michael Stewart's advice did not go wholly unchallenged. Both Peter Shore (Secretary of State for Economic Affairs) and Fred Peart (Lord President) argued that circumstances had changed since 1967 and that an up-to-date appraisal was needed before the government sought membership 'at any cost'. Denis Healey (Secretary of State for Defence), who had been an opponent of membership, argued that nothing need be decided in a hurry. Elections were imminent in West Germany. There would be an internal crisis in the EEC as its members argued over the future financing of the Common Agricultural Policy (CAP). A confrontation between Enoch Powell and Heath over Europe might split the Tory Party.

One of Wilson's great skills was in summing up a difficult discussion and, especially, in judging when to reach for an agreement and when to hold back. On this occasion, he held back. The government was indeed confronted, he said, with problems that were even more difficult than those it had faced in 1967, in particular the consequences of the devaluation of sterling and developments within the EEC, especially over the CAP. There was no need for a reappraisal of policy. The UK application remained on the table; the various problems on which decisions might later be needed were being studied. Decisions should in due course be taken collectively in Cabinet and not be pre-empted by individual pronouncements by Departmental Ministers.[2]

The particular issues requiring study were the implications for the UK of whatever policy on the CAP was adopted by the Six, and what the economic impact of membership might be. On the first, it was clear that the CAP offered, for the French, the principal practical advantage of being in the EEC in the first place. The CAP was at the time the only common policy of the European Community within the basic core framework of a customs union. The EEC

---

[2] CC (69) 35th Conclusions, CAB 128/44, TNA.

Member States were committed by the Treaty of Rome to the creation of a single market in goods, services, and capital, and tariffs between the members had already been abolished. But all the policies of today's European Union on issues such as energy, environment, social policy, harmonization of product standards, security and foreign policy, and even a common (let alone a single) currency were, in the late 1960s, only just being thought about. So the common budget of the EEC, when definitively agreed, would be spent almost entirely on agriculture, and who would pay, and how, and who would then benefit from the resulting expenditure, were existential questions. There was no way a French government was going to allow those matters to await the arrival of the British, who would want to go on importing agricultural produce on a large scale from the Commonwealth and were instinctively and practically averse to the notion of Community preference—i.e. buying from within the borders of the EEC and not from outside them.

Any British assessment of the economic costs of membership was, against this background, bound to focus sharply on the costs of the CAP. Modern economics has largely discarded the balance of payments as a key measure of prosperity. But, in 1969, it was *the* key monthly measure of the state of the economy, and successive British governments struggled, usually without success, to achieve and maintain a surplus, i.e. that the value of British exports exceeded the cost of imports. The main measure of the balance of payments did not include services (then a relatively small part of the UK economy). Looking at the EEC in 1969, economists calculated that the direct balance of payments cost to the UK arising from the devaluation of the pound and the cost of financing surplus EEC agricultural production would be of the order of £400 to £600 million. On top of that, the cost of the CAP would push up food prices, and industrial costs would rise as the workforce tried to compensate itself for the higher cost of living through higher earnings. So the total cost to the balance of payments from joining the EEC might be as high as £1,000 million. How, the economists asked, could the government achieve a balance of payments surplus under those conditions? And even if they could, would consumers accept that the economies of scale arising from membership were big, and tangible, enough to outweigh the increases in food prices that they would experience every time they went to the shops? Andrew Graham, an Oxford economist (later Master of Balliol College) who advised Wilson, concluded that 'accepting the CAP is exactly identical to giving aid—only it is to the French farmer rather to the underdeveloped world and it may be doubted whether [that] is the best use of our resources'.[3]

With this kind of advice in his mind, Wilson must have wondered why he, along with the other main Party leaders, had agreed to speak at a pro-European dinner at the Guildhall in July 1969. As it turned out, Heath seems to have had some of the same preoccupations because, uncharacteristically, he used some of his speech to express concern about the financial costs, and the weakening of Britain's national identity, that membership would entail. Wilson, for his part, focused on the political advantages of membership, while being careful to avoid any commitment to political union. It must be doubtful whether thoughts about the likely state of British debate on Europe half a century later were anywhere in his mind when he went on to say: 'The immediate task of this generation is to work, as we are pledged to work, for that degree of political unity which is within our immediate grasp. That is *our* task in the months and years that lie ahead of us. But we are not here to legislate for the views, still less prejudice the views, of those young people whose personal identification with the ideals and aspirations of a wider Europe is one of the hopes of all of us here tonight. They will choose their own course. They will fashion the institutions they think right for the Europe of which they will be part. Our duty is to create something on which they can build.'[4]

While Wilson continued to stress the political advantages of accession in public, behind the scenes the British government was seeking to persuade the EEC Member Governments of the need for flexibility in the decisions to be taken by the Six on agriculture. But those arguments rested on the British interest in preserving a flexibility which would give them some influence on the eventual shape and cost of the CAP. As such, they did not commend themselves to the French.

When the EEC Heads of Government met in The Hague at the beginning of December 1969, President Pompidou argued that what the Community had already achieved must be 'jealously preserved'. Completion (meaning on the funding arrangements for the Community) must take place according to the established timetable and Community action should be increased, especially in the field of economic and monetary cooperation. As regards enlargement of the EEC, 'the candidatures of Great Britain and the three other countries

[3] PREM 13/2629, TNA.

[4] Harold Wilson, *The Labour Government 1964–1970: A Personal Record* (London: Weidenfeld & Nicolson, 1971), pp. 687–8.

[Ireland, Denmark and Norway] must be approached in a positive spirit but without losing sight of the interests of the Community and its members'.

The German Chancellor, Willy Brandt, spoke next and was outspoken in his support of enlargement. Without Britain and the other candidate countries, Europe, he argued, could not become what it should and could be. The candidates should be told that the Six expected to be able to open negotiations in the spring of 1970.

That evening, the German delegation, in private, told the French of their disappointment at the lukewarm tone on enlargement adopted by Pompidou. Brandt, unlike his predecessor as Chancellor, Kiesinger, was taking a proactive hand in promoting the British case and the following day Pompidou spoke in more forthcoming terms about enlargement. The final communiqué was somewhat oblique but implied the opening of enlargement negotiations no later than the middle of 1970.

William Nield, the senior Cabinet Office official advising Wilson on EEC issues, described the outcome to the Prime Minister as 'the first small breach in the dyke of French obstruction'. But he warned Wilson that the stagnation of the Community and the obstruction of de Gaulle had left Britain with a ten-year syndrome of being 'unwanted' by a Community whose problems had been more in the public eye than its achievements. The image of a not very good club with a high subscription and expensive meals persisted. Even if the Community had been a public triumph, Britain's own problems in respect of membership would be great. The government, according to Nield, were, in effect, asking the public to look beyond the price of butter tomorrow to the position of Britain and Europe in the last three decades of a twentieth century dominated in all fields by America, Russia, and perhaps China.[5]

The high agricultural price Britain would have to pay for entry into the club was made all too clear when the French Finance Minister, Valéry Giscard d'Estaing, visited London in December. At the summit in The Hague, Pompidou had, Giscard told his British hosts, insisted on the urgency of reaching agreement among the current EEC members on agricultural policy and the agricultural financial regulations. The main source of funding, which the French supported, would come from all the agricultural levies and customs duties collected on imports from outside the EEC being paid into a common EEC agricultural fund. That would still leave a shortfall of around 30 per cent (somewhere between $600 and $750 million) of the necessary funding for

<hr>

[5] PREM 13/2631, TNA.

agriculture. That funding would have to come from other financing methods, for example a key related to national GNP.

Wilson made the obvious response, namely that the highest contributions under the proposed scheme would come from the countries, notably the UK, with the highest levels of imports. This argument made little impact on Giscard, a man described by the British Embassy in Paris as having 'lack of popular appeal due to his arrogance, coldness of manner and the silver spoon he allows too obviously to stick out of his mouth'. The kind of settlement he had outlined was, said Giscard, important for France, politically as well as financially. France had not got a good bargain industrially out of the EEC and needed agriculture to offset it.

Barely a week later, Nield was warning Wilson that the Six looked likely to adopt a definitive agricultural financing regulation 'which would make it impossible for us to join the Community unless it was very substantially modified'. By the same token, it would be very difficult to secure the modifications the UK would need. Only Britain and Germany, Wilson was warned separately, were likely to be substantial net contributors to the funding of the EEC.[6]

Prediction was borne out by reality. Just before Christmas, the Six agreed an arrangement much along the lines described by Giscard. It would put the British in a very disadvantageous negotiating position. De Gaulle had twice vetoed a British application, in large part to preserve the protectionist safeguards he wanted the Community to provide for French agriculture. Now, his successor was about to open the door to negotiations with the British, but only after ensuring that the core Community policy, and its financing, were moulded to French national interest and would be secure from British amendment.

Wilson's Christmas reading was the draft of a White Paper, promised by the government, containing an economic assessment of EEC membership. The draft did not make for comfortable reading. The realistic estimate of the cost of membership to the UK balance of payments was between £500 and £700 million a year. Wilson, however, did not take this too tragically, telling Cabinet in the New Year of 1970 that it would only take a very small increase in the growth of Britain's GDP to provide the additional resources needed to meet the cost of membership.

When the White Paper was published it gave rise to some sceptical continental Press speculation. Was Wilson cooling in his attitude to membership? Or

---

[6] Ibid.

was he trying to give himself a weapon to use in the negotiations? Both views were lent some credence by Wilson's decision not to write an introduction to the White Paper offering an assertion of the political advantages to offset the disadvantages of the economic costs. Wilson's counterargument to the case for giving the document a political spin was that it 'should be as factual as possible, not argumentative'.[7] What he clearly wanted was to avoid reopening the whole argument about membership within the Labour Party, or more broadly. He had good reason for caution. Even with low-key handling of the document in the House of Commons, an opinion poll at the time found 72 per cent of those asked, to be against Common Market membership. At the same time, 76 per cent thought that the UK would nonetheless join eventually.[8]

Britain's Ambassadors in the EEC countries were called to London in March 1970 to discuss the government's negotiating strategy. George Thomson, the Cabinet Minister in charge of the process, told the assembled envoys that the lesson from the recent White Paper was that the short-term economic disadvantages of membership were quantifiable, whereas the medium-term advantages were not. At the end of the day, the government would have to make a historic political judgement on whether the conse-quences of membership outweighed those of exclusion. These were not calcu-lations which could be made in a little black book. The government would negotiate toughly but in good faith.

The discussion among the Ambassadors was led by Christopher Soames. The French, he said, had got what they wanted in the Community. Now that they had secured their national interests, they were stressing their *commu-nautaire* approach to the forthcoming enlargement negotiations because in such an approach the French national, and wider Community, interests could be brought to coincide. Britain should negotiate in a similarly *communautaire* way. So, for example, instead of arguing in Brussels for a ceiling on the UK's budget contribution, it might be preferable to seek an assurance that the evolution of agricultural production and prices would be such that the British would not find themselves with an excessive burden at the end of what was hoped could be a long transitional period.

Soames's view was met with general assent: a *communautaire* approach was better than the UK asking for national derogations from Community policy, the so-called *acquis communautaire*. It took Sir Con O'Neill, who would be the senior Foreign Office official in the negotiations, to pour cold water on this emerging optimism. The governments of the Six might be 'attired in the white

[7] PREM 13/3198, TNA.   [8] PREM 13/3201, TNA.

sheets of Community purity'. But if the system the Six had agreed was applied to the UK without modification it could easily leave the United Kingdom with a share of the EEC's costs amounting to £670 million. Every other member of the Community would see their contributions fall as a result. Sir William Nield put the problem in even starker terms. A transfer of resources from the UK to the Community on the scale that seemed realistically likely would cut the growth the UK was hoping to secure from membership. If the effect was severe, then it would be wrong to join. So, whether or not Britain could afford to join the EEC would depend on whether the Community financing problem could be solved. No country in the world could afford a burden of the size that might fall on Britain.[9]

It is unlikely that the assembled Ambassadors appreciated the portentous nature of Nield's intervention. They were men who had waited for much of their careers to see the door opened to UK accession. Britain's Ambassador in Bonn, Sir Roger Jackling, for example, argued that it would be difficult to persuade the Germans of the British financial case and he backed what he called Soames's 'plea' for a *communautaire* approach. Jackling based his argument on the judgement that the Germans were becoming increasingly *communautaire* in their attitudes. But what did that mean? It sounded as if it meant that they were prepared to subordinate their national interest to the common Community good. And it is true that Germany became and remained the largest net contributor to the EEC budget. But for Germany, and the other founder members, the common good and national advantage would easily coincide, for the obvious reason that they would not have agreed and signed the Treaty of Rome in the first place had it not been so. Giscard d'Estaing had pointed to the industrial advantages that EEC membership had given to Germany, and he was following closely in the footsteps of de Gaulle in insisting that France must have a *quid pro quo* in terms of agricultural advantage. The other Member States would all be net beneficiaries from the budget mechanism they had just agreed. So each of the Six had tangible benefits from membership, readily sellable to their electorates.

Britain, by contrast, had no clear tangible benefit it could point to. To sell the project to the British people, the government had to rely on its expect-ations of benefits from a growing European market and on the fact that Britain would recoup some of its declining global political influence through mem-bership of a larger organization. But, at heart, the British people were being told that the previous post-war strategy of the Labour and Conservative

[9] Ibid.

governments had failed; that the Commonwealth was a wasting asset economically; that the United States attached more importance to a Britain that was
inside the EEC than outside; that Britain was not strong enough to go it alone,
and therefore that they had no choice but to attach themselves to the organization that had succeeded where the UK had failed—the EEC. The fact that de
Gaulle (the refugee who had been given succour in wartime London) had twice
humiliated Britain by keeping her out, that defeated Germany now outstripped Britain in prosperity, and that Britain would now have to accept
club rules written by countries to whom she felt morally superior were all hard
realities (or at least perceptions of reality) to come to terms with. It is not
surprising that a Europe-wide opinion survey, taken in March 1970, showed
only 19 per cent of Britons in favour of joining. Across the Six, by contrast,
support for British accession ran at an average of 64 per cent.[10]

It is clear from the archives of the time, and from what was said by the
Wilson government in public, that the principal anxiety about accession arose
from the likely financial burdens. The political aspects of membership were
less of an issue. When, in February 1970, the Chancellor of the Exchequer, Roy
Jenkins, visited Paris he told Giscard d'Estaing that some people had suggested
that the UK might find it difficult to move towards the EEC goal of monetary
union because that might disturb relations with the United States. In no sense
was that true, said Jenkins. The United Kingdom would not find it difficult to
move as far and as fast as any member of the Six. When Giscard observed that,
in due time, there might be just two currencies of any importance–a European
currency and the US dollar, Jenkins did not disagree, asserting that the British
government were 'prepared to move far in this field'. When Wilson read an
account of the meeting he minuted: 'Interesting. Chancellor seems to me to
have given all the right answers.'[11] A few months later, when Wilson met the
Luxembourg Foreign Minister, Gaston Thorn, in London, Thorn referred to
the work being done on the practicalities of economic and monetary union on
behalf of the EEC by his Prime Minister, Pierre Werner. Wilson commented
that he thought a supranational political federation was still a long way off but
that the British government were prepared to go as far and as fast as the Six
would wish to. The very next day, Wilson told the Economic Committee of the
TUC that the government's decision on entry into the Common Market would
ultimately depend on the terms that could be obtained. It was true that, if the
terms were crippling, then that would nullify the dynamic advantages of

---

[10] Ibid.   [11] Ibid.

accession but, on better terms of entry, there could be important dynamic advantages.

The Prime Minister went on to spell out some of the obligations of membership. Britain would have to accept the constitution of the EEC. This did not, however, entail a total loss of sovereignty and absorption into a single unit. A federal Europe might come in time. But that was not what was involved in acceding to the Treaty of Rome. Nor was it a present reality.[12]

These pieces of evidence are significant in two respects. They show positive attitudes to the European Community which were a far cry from those which the Labour Party would soon adopt in Opposition. And they are evidence of a government more open than any subsequent British government to the concept of a federal Europe and the possibility of economic and monetary union.

In British politics, before the adoption of the Fixed Term Parliament Act in 2011, it was rare for a Parliament to run its full five-year course. There was a general expectation that no government with a working majority (and the Wilson government had a comfortable majority) would 'go to the country' in its first three years. But it was generally expected that, at some time in the fourth year, a government which was well ahead in the opinion polls would capitalize on its advantage by asking the Queen for Parliament to be dissolved and a General Election held. On Sunday, 17 May 1970 Wilson told the assembled Cabinet that he was going to do just that. Parliament would be dissolved and a General Election would be held on 18 June.

The last recorded account of the Labour government's approach to the EEC is the record of the first meeting of the Ministerial Cabinet subcommittee on the EEC negotiations which met under George Thomson's chairmanship on 11 May. The meeting was tasked with examining three options for tackling the huge balance of payments problem that the UK was expected to face on accession. The options were: (i) to insist on a reshaping of the EEC's arrangements; (ii) to seek a special favourable arrangement for the UK; and (iii) to accept the EEC's arrangements but to adopt some of the Community's 'own devices' to find a tolerable solution. The committee decided not to determine a precise course until the problem had been examined by the Six but they accepted that neither of the first two options would be negotiable.[13]

Thus the policy of the Labour government, on the eve of an election that, with strongly favourable opinion polls, it was confident of winning, was one of positive engagement on the most difficult issue of the prospective EEC

---

[12] Ibid.   [13] CAB 134/2596, TNA.

negotiation. Its declared ambition for the economic and political evolution of the Community was on a par with that of the existing Six.

It cannot be said that the election manifestos of either of the two main political parties dealt at great length with Europe, or showed conspicuous enthusiasm. If anything, the Conservative manifesto was the more guarded, noting that there was 'obviously ... a price we would not be prepared to pay ... Our sole commitment is to negotiate; no more, no less.' Labour were somewhat more upbeat, promising that the negotiations would 'be pressed with determination with the purpose of joining an enlarged Community provided that British and essential Commonwealth interests can be safeguarded'. Sharp-eyed Commonwealth leaders might have noticed that, while, by implication, *all* British interests were to be protected, only those Commonwealth interests judged to be *essential* were to receive similar safeguards.

The Labour manifesto was that of a Party in government and expecting to remain so; the Conservative manifesto that of a Party with ground to make up and with one of its most prominent members, Enoch Powell, openly and articulately opposed to EEC membership. Powell had been sacked from the Conservative front bench team by Heath after making a speech in 1968 in which he predicted interracial strife in Britain if immigration from Britain's former colonies continued at its actual and expected rate. Powell's constituency was in the west Midlands, an area of large-scale immigration. In his speech, he predicted that 'the black man will have the whip hand over the white' and that, filled with foreboding, he, like the Roman of old (Powell was a classical scholar) seemed 'to see the River Tiber foaming with much blood'.

Following his dismissal from the front bench, Powell never again held government office. But his inflammatory speech found a ready echo among white working-class voters, so that when, in 1969, Powell came out publicly against EEC membership his anti-European views found a similarly receptive audience.

Throughout the General Election campaign of June 1970, the opinion polls put Labour well ahead of the Tories. Then, one poll on the eve of the vote showed Heath winning—which he did with an overall majority of thirty-one seats. It has been suggested that Powell's anti-Europeanism helped swing the vote in favour of the Conservatives, a claim that has never been substantiated persuasively. A bad set of trade figures late in the campaign, showing a deterioration in Britain's balance of payments, undoubtedly did play a part. So too may have complacency in the Labour camp. When I joined the Number 10 Press Office in 1976, to work for Prime Minister James Callaghan, those long-serving members of the small Press team who had worked for Wilson cited one particular set of Press photos of Wilson eating strawberries and cream at a village fête in the middle of the campaign as the fateful moment when the tide turned.

The first brief by officials on the forthcoming EEC negotiations for the new Conservative government set out in detail the potential budget costs of membership to the UK, warning that Britain risked being faced with a burden that would be 'both intolerable and inequitable, as compared with other members'. But, the paper argued, securing changes in the budgetary arrangements recently agreed by the Six during the course of the accession negotiations would not be achievable. The way through lay, not in challenging the rules, but in seeking some alleviation in the way they were applied.[14]

The new Conservative Foreign Secretary, Alec Douglas-Home, followed this line in his opening statement to the Six in Luxembourg on 30 June 1970.[15] But the Foreign Secretary balanced his warning of a potential burden which risked becoming intolerable and would make it impossible for any British government to join, with a commitment to share the determination of the Six to work together in economic and monetary matters, foreign policy and defence.[16]

The man chosen by Edward Heath to do the job of chief negotiator that he himself had done under Macmillan was Anthony Barber. But Barber's tenure was short. In October, the Chancellor of the Exchequer, Iain Macleod, died suddenly of a heart attack and Barber was promoted to replace him, a move wickedly described by Wilson as 'the only thing Mr Heath has ever done to suggest that he has a sense of humour'.[17] Barber was replaced as negotiator by Geoffrey Rippon, MP for Hexham in Northumberland, and an experienced lawyer.

Rippon's list of difficult issues, so he told the French Foreign Minister, Maurice Schumann, at their first meeting was confined to four: access for New Zealand dairy products, access for Commonwealth sugar, transitional arrangements, and Community finance. No mention was made of fish, but the 'fishes' who, in Churchill's wartime broadcast, had been complacently awaiting the long-threatened Nazi invasion, were soon to swim into prominence. The Six, in an act of pre-emptive and ruthless self-interest, had decided to equip themselves with a Common Fisheries Policy (CFP) before the British, Danes, Norwegians, and Irish (all significant fishing nations) were allowed to join.

---

[14] Ibid.
[15] Under one of the compromises reached within the Six at the founding of the EEC, all meetings of the Council of Ministers took place in Brussels, except in April, June, and October, when they were (and are) held in Luxembourg.
[16] PREM 15/062, TNA.   [17] Speech at the Labour Party Conference on 29 September 1970.

From their perspective, it made perfect sense. Total fish production in a Community of ten would be four times that of the Six. British landings of fish for human consumption were of the order of 900,000 tonnes in 1969, i.e. greater than the landings of any other applicant country or of any existing Member State. Forty per cent of those British landings were caught by the British inshore fleet. The British sought discussions on how the proposed new Common Fisheries Policy would work. But Rippon found to his dismay that the Community's procedures were even more wooden than they had been in 1962. In meetings between the British delegation and the Six, Rippon complained to Heath, 'only the Chairman is allowed to speak while we are present, and he can neither agree to, nor comment on, anything we say, however trivial, without prior agreement within the Community or an adjournment. This in turn means that the Community tends to progress – or regress – on the basis of elaborately worked out texts.'[18]

The death of General de Gaulle gave Heath his first opportunity as Prime Minister to meet Pompidou. In retirement, de Gaulle had sat at his desk in his country house (La Boisserie) in the village of Colombey-les-deux Églises in the Haute-Marne, writing his magnificent *Memoirs*. The house is charming and tranquil. From his desk, de Gaulle could look out over the woodland and valleys of a timeless French countryside. Sitting there in the dark of an autumn evening in November 1970, he suffered an aneurism that killed him instantly. As he had ordained, de Gaulle was buried privately at Colombey. Heath, together with Eden, Macmillan, and Wilson, all attended the formal Requiem Mass at Notre Dame Cathedral in Paris, three days later. For all that de Gaulle had been a thorn in the side of Prime Ministers from Churchill onwards he was, in Macmillan's succinct verdict 'a great man who saved France'.

Pompidou and Heath exchanged *politesses* at their brief meeting after the funeral. Then, so Heath recorded in a note of the discussion, Pompidou produced from a tray on his desk a copy of that day's *Le Monde* newspaper, opened at a page containing an advertisement placed there by BOAC, the forerunner of today's British Airways. The advertisement, headlined '*L'Amérique commence à Londres en VC10 BOAC*', vaunted London and the airline as the fastest, most luxurious way of getting to the United States. Neither Pompidou nor Heath commented on the advertisement. Was Pompidou suggesting that, as de Gaulle had always feared, Britain in Europe would be a Trojan Horse for the Americans; or that British entry would

---

[18] PREM 15/062, TNA.

threaten France commercially? The page from the newspaper remains, tantalizingly, in the Number 10 archive. Heath, for his part, noted Pompidou's acknowledgement during the conversation of the European orientation of the new British government's policies, and Heath detected 'none of the scepticism I had noticed when we last met in the spring'.[19]

The year 1971 would be the crucial one for the United Kingdom in the accession negotiations. A conversation between Soames and Pompidou in late November 1970 confirmed the view Heath had formed. Pompidou told Soames explicitly that he wanted the negotiations with Britain to succeed. He was, however, concerned at the role of sterling, not because, as some had suggested, the reserve role of sterling gave Britain an unfair advantage but, rather, because he saw the role as a disadvantage. As Pompidou's advisers in the Elysée explained subsequently, for Pompidou, the key issue was how to avoid the entry of sterling into the EEC leading *ipso facto* to the establishment of a new European reserve currency aligned against the dollar. Nor did the French want to see a requirement on the EEC to have to support what was now a solely British obligation of economic management because of events, say, in Hong Kong.

In December, Cabinet held its first detailed examination of the likely financial implications of membership. The European Commission had proposed that, at the end of a five-year period, the British share of EEC financing should be either 22.5 per cent or 25 per cent. Rippon suggested to Cabinet that he might be able to get this figure down to 17 per cent. That would represent a balance of payments cost to the UK of £460 million in the sixth year of membership. Even if the economic advantages of membership turned out to be only half as good as the Labour government had suggested in their own economic assessment, they would still be sufficient to cover the costs of membership. And Rippon's estimate of the likely costs also suggested that they would be substantially less than those given in the Labour government's White Paper. A pro-European Conservative government could hardly, Rippon implied, jib at terms which were likely to be better than those considered acceptable to a supposedly less pro-European Labour administration. At the end of the Cabinet discussion Heath concluded that 'it was not...suggested that the burden would so clearly be intolerable that no useful purpose would be served by continuing the negotiations'.[20]

British public opinion at the end of 1970 remained lukewarm, with one opinion poll showing 61 percent of the electorate opposed to membership and

[19] Ibid.   [20] CM (70) 45th Conclusions, CAB 128/47, TNA.

only 24 per cent in favour. Even within the Conservative ranks in the House of Commons, one authoritative estimate suggested that not more than two thirds of Tory MPs would go into the 'Aye' lobby in a vote on accession. Sir Tufton Beamish, Chairman of the Conservative Group for Europe, warned, in what Heath described as 'a very good paper', that, even if the government obtained favourable entry terms, public and parliamentary opposition might be so well organized as to expose the government to the risk of defeat. According to Beamish, this was exactly what Enoch Powell was waiting for and explained his recent tactics. In the June General Election, Beamish continued, in constituencies where the Tory candidates held strong anti-EEC views, they had not hesitated to make that their platform even though it conflicted with official Party policy. The left wing of the Labour Party, including all the crypto-Communists, was in an unholy alliance with the Tory anti-Marketeers, most of whom were on the right wing of the Party. The impression had gained ground, both in the country and in Parliament, that there was no clear official policy and that it was perfectly acceptable for a Tory MP to defy the government pleading, of course, 'conscience'. Many Conservative MPs who had been enthusiastic for entry were now uncommitted, either because they were not sure the terms would be good enough or because they dared not risk losing favour with their constituents. Some had promised to demand a referendum before a decision on entry was taken. The Labour Party, according to Beamish, was even more divided.[21]

Little progress was made in the accession negotiations in the early months of 1971. In Brussels the French played hardball and it began to look as if relying exclusively on the routine Brussels process would not break the logjam. Accordingly, Heath sought the advice of Christopher Soames on other options, in particular the idea of a summit of the Ten (the Six and the four applicants: Denmark, Ireland, Norway, and the UK) under Pompidou's chairmanship (since the French held the six-monthly rotating chairmanship of the Community) or a talk between Prime Minister and President to unblock the logjam, with the negotiations being concluded at ministerial level in Brussels thereafter. Soames had established a good relationship with Michel Jobert, the Secretary-General at the Elysée, and on the basis of talking to him Soames was clear in his advice to Heath. A summit of the Ten risked being unproductive. Soames was sure Pompidou would want to settle the main outstanding issues in a bilateral meeting with Heath, though the initiative for such a meeting would have to come from the British side. Heath agreed and, while conflicting

<hr>

[21] PREM 15/030, TNA.

views on the advisability of a bilateral summit still circulated in Whitehall, Soames lost no time in getting back to Jobert. The two men agreed on the key issue: a meeting should take place. As to tactics, Jobert posed the question as to how much of a crisis atmosphere would be desirable to enable the meeting to take place successfully. He then answered the question himself: 'the best situation would be one that was short of a crisis', but with sufficient of an impasse to make the need for the meeting obvious to people in both countries. The meeting should be well prepared in advance, but the French Foreign Ministry should not be informed or involved since they would create 'many difficulties'.[22]

Despite these favourable auguries, the two sides danced round each other for several weeks before the scene could be set. How much progress should be made in Brussels before the summit of the two leaders; what should be reserved for them to discuss? Jobert insisted that sugar should be one of the issues in order, so Soames speculated, to allow Pompidou to make a concession on sugar at the meeting while hanging tough on access for New Zealand dairy produce. At the end of April, Pompidou himself, in a lunch with political journalists, one of whom gave his notes of the meeting to Michael Palliser (Soames's deputy), pronounced himself less optimistic than he had been a few months previously. The English had, he said, not progressed an inch but were, on the contrary, bringing forward new issues every week for which they sought a special regime: first it was butter, then sugar and now pears. In the meantime, the essential point was being forgotten: was England now ready to play the European game? Had she renounced the idea of entering in order to upset everything? Was she prepared to be a loyal partner? Pompidou then half floated the idea of a summit with Heath. If the two men met, the Brussels dialogue of the deaf could not continue. The two men could not for much longer continue to avoid each other; but nothing had been fixed as regards a meeting.[23]

The meeting that eventually took place between the two leaders on 20 and 21 May 1971 was a heady mixture of theatre and substance. Over the two days, the two men held four meetings entirely on their own, apart from the presence of interpreters. Even Palliser, who was Heath's interpreter, had to be guarded in what he reported to those such as Soames, and Douglas Hurd, then one of Heath's advisers, who were anxiously awaiting news.

At a formal dinner at the Elysée at the end of the first day, the exchange of toasts and speeches suggested that things were going well. On the second day,

[22] PREM 15/368, TNA.   [23] PREM 15/371, TNA.

Pompidou came to lunch at the British Embassy. This was a rare event which, as Soames later recorded, was 'quickly noted by the Press of a country which, despite its claims of civil egalitarianism, in fact observes the nuances of protocol and social relations with an attention which recalls Byzantium'.[24]

As to the talks themselves, the records (produced, on the British side, by Palliser who combined the roles of note-taker and interpreter with rare talent) were very tightly held within both administrations. The British records show a subtle performance on Heath's part. He had prepared meticulously so that, on the detail, he had a greater mastery than Pompidou. But he had also heeded Soames's advice to start with the big picture. He did so in terms which Macmillan might have used—indeed had used—with de Gaulle, addressing himself in particular to French fears of Britain as a country magnetically pulled towards the United States. For Heath, there could be no real partnership between two powers one of which was barely a quarter the size of the other. European countries could not hope to exercise influence unless they were united, with an economic base comparable in size to that of the United States or the Soviet Union. For his part, Heath continued, he wanted to see a strong Europe speaking with one voice. World affairs should not be left to be settled between the two superpowers. All this was exactly what Pompidou wanted to hear and, unlike de Gaulle, who had heard it all before and discounted it, Pompidou was receptive.

For his part, the French President wanted assurances from Heath on the matter of the institutions of the European Community. He referred to the crisis of the mid-1960s when France had left her chair at the Council chamber empty for six months. For France, it was critical that, if vital national interests were at stake, whatever the theoretical arrangements (i.e. the provision for majority voting) there must be unanimous agreement before a decision could be reached. The statement reached in Luxembourg at the end of the six-month dispute, the so-called Luxembourg Compromise, was not, Pompidou said, a matter of legal interpretation. The idea that, where a Member State's very important national interests were at stake, discussion should continue until agreement was reached was a matter of political fact. If some unacceptable decision affecting vital French interests were taken by majority vote, France would not allow it to be imposed on her.

The key thing was that everyone in the Community should know that if vital interests concerning Britain, Germany, or Italy (just as much as France) were at stake, then any decision in the matter must be unanimous. Some Member

---

[24] PREM 15/372, TNA.

States, notably the smaller ones, were constantly trying to undermine the French interpretation of the Luxembourg Compromise. France was resolutely determined to stick to her interpretation and hoped that Britain would be ready to behave likewise. Heath agreed enthusiastically, going so far as to say that the Luxembourg Compromise was a significant element in the willingness of the British government to accept the Treaty of Rome, its regulations, its institutions, and its voting arrangements.

This part of the discussion between Heath and Pompidou was one of the most significant of the accession negotiations. At the time, it was also the view of the German Chancellor that, in practice, the essential interests of any of the large Member States could not be overridden by a vote. But neither the German nor the Italian government had accepted the French interpretation of the Luxembourg Compromise. British Ministers (admittedly in the previous government to Heath's) had been advised by officials at the time that the Luxembourg Compromise was a political statement, not a legal text. Now, however, Pompidou gave it huge weight and, in so doing, led the Heath government, and the later Wilson government of 1974, to interpret the Luxembourg Compromise as if it really was a veto and to sell it to the British people as such. This fortress construction was later to be shown to be built on shifting sand.

On the substance of the Brussels negotiations, Heath and Pompidou reached an understanding which appeared to offer a way forward. On New Zealand dairy exports. Pompidou, good Auvergnat that he was, and no doubt mindful of his home province's native blue cheese, was much more worried about New Zealand cheese exports than about butter. He was prepared to contemplate a five-year transition period in which guaranteed access for New Zealand cheese degressed to a very low figure, while New Zealand butter exports declined by only a small amount.

On EEC finance, the two men agreed that the European Commission's most recent proposal provided an acceptable framework. A notional British contribution to the EEC budget would be calculated for each of the years of the transition. However, in order to determine the actual amount payable each year, the notional contribution would be reduced by a proportion which became progressively smaller as the transition period progressed. Rippon had told Cabinet on 18 May that, provided the sums corresponding to these proportions were themselves reasonable, this approach could provide a satisfactory solution. Heath, as recorded in the formal Conclusions of the talks, told

Pompidou that this 'problem was simply one of transition'.[25] In this he was to be proved seriously mistaken.

After so many years of Britain's knocking at the door only to have it slammed in her face by de Gaulle, it was a powerful and moving moment when Heath and Pompidou, in the very room from which de Gaulle had pronounced his first veto, proclaimed that agreement had been reached. Heath himself, in his memoirs, described the moment as 'wildly exciting'. He spoke in similarly elegiac terms when he reported to the House of Commons on 24 May 1971, claiming that the divisions and suspicions of the past had now been removed and that Britain could approach the final phase of the negotiations, and the development of Europe thereafter, with the prospect of 'a degree of unity, and thus peace and prosperity, in Western Europe which our continent has never seen before, and which would be of profound significance for Britain, for Europe and for the whole world'.[26]

Harold Wilson, who, a year earlier could have assumed that it would fall to him as Prime Minister to strike the deal, offered no congratulations but confined himself to asking pertinent questions of detail. In the intervening year, the European mood of the Labour Party had soured. Defeat at the General Election had come as a shock; Wilson's own standing as leader had taken a battering and he faced criticism for devoting more time to writing his lucrative memoirs than to the business of Opposition; the Party was determined to find any lever with which they might prise Heath and the Conservatives from office. One day after Heath's statement to the House of Commons on the Paris talks, Jim Callaghan, who had been a supporter of the 1967 application for EEC membership, made a speech which positioned him both as an anti-Marketeer and as a potential rival to Wilson for the leadership of the Labour Party.

I worked in the Foreign Office when Callaghan was, in the 1970s, Foreign Secretary and, when he became Prime Minister in 1976, I went to Number 10 as one of his Press officers. He was a fundamentally decent man and grew in stature as Prime Minister, but his self-proclaimed image as 'sunny Jim' was belied by the fact that he could be a bully, and he was, until he climbed to the top of the greasy pole, opportunistically ambitious. In the 1966 Labour government, he had sided with the trade unions to defeat the attempt of Wilson and Barbara Castle to reform trade union law. Now, in 1971 he used

---

[25] Ibid.
[26] Edward Heath, *The Course of My Life* (London: Hodder & Stoughton, 1998), and *Hansard*, 24 May 1971, col. 35.

Europe to advance his standing in the Labour Party. On 25 May, Callaghan gave a much-trailed speech in Southampton. Days earlier, Pompidou had given an interview to the BBC's flagship news programme, *Panorama*. During the interview, Pompidou had referred to French as the language of Europe. It was at the time the principal language used in documents and was the *lingua franca* of EEC negotiations in Brussels. The French were worried that English might usurp their position and Heath had made an appropriately reassuring response at the Paris summit. Now, said Callaghan in his speech, the British people must expect that the language of Chaucer, Shakespeare, and Milton was to be regarded as an undesirable import. 'If', he continued, 'we have to prove our Europeanism by accepting that French is the dominant language in the Community, then my answer is quite clear, and I will say it in French in order to prevent any misunderstanding: *Non, merci beaucoup*'.

Callaghan had reportedly told at least one journalist that the speech would be that of the next leader of the Labour Party. If true, then Callaghan was right—but it would take him five years to get there. The speech was correctly, and universally, interpreted as Callaghan saying 'no' to the EEC. It faced Wilson with a loss of support for the EEC project by three of his most senior colleagues, all of them ambitious for his job: Healey, Crosland, and now Callaghan. It is true that Wilson had received assurances from Roy Jenkins, then the biggest of the big beasts in the Party, that the Labour pro-Europeans would not side with Callaghan or anyone else against him if he stayed true to the European policies the Party had pursued in government. But Jenkins too was a rival for Wilson's job and his assurances can have given Wilson no comfort.[27]

Callaghan's speech added to pressure on Wilson to call a special Labour Party Conference on Europe following the successful conclusion of the accession negotiations in the early hours of 23 June. When he tried to get the idea defeated in the National Executive Committee (NEC), Wilson was defeated by one vote, that of the prominent pro-European, Shirley Williams, who believed that all views should be heard. So the Conference duly took place on 17 July and Wilson made what Roy Jenkins described as a pedestrian speech which 'took him out of intellectual hailing distance with us. It was like watching someone being sold down the river into slavery, drifting away, depressed but unprotesting.'[28]

---

[27] Callaghan may have been shamefaced about the speech in later life. There is no mention of it in his memoirs.

[28] Roy Jenkins, *A Life at the Centre* (London: Macmillan, 1991), p. 320.

There was no vote at the Conference, but the anti-European mood was clear. On 21 July, in a debate in the House, Wilson sought to demonstrate that the terms the government had just finished negotiating with the Six were notably inferior to those which would have been secured by a Labour government. His claim lacked credibility, and all the more so as one after another, prominent former Ministers stood up to affirm that the terms negotiated by the Conservative government were ones they themselves would have accepted.

The terms themselves were reported to the House by Rippon on 23 June. As expected, New Zealand cheese exports to the EEC would be reduced to 20 per cent of their previous levels after five years. New Zealand butter exports would be no lower than 71 per cent of their previous levels even as late as 1977, and the expected price at which those exports were sold was expected to rise.

On the financial issues, the annual amount Britain would pay would start at 8.64 percent of the EEC budget in 1973, rising to 18.92 per cent in 1977. But a limitation would be applied for the next two years (1978 and 1979). Moreover, Britain, so Rippon claimed, could expect to receive payments from the EEC budget, with the result that the total net contribution would be around £100 million in 1973, rising to perhaps about £200 million in 1977.

'You do not haggle over the subscription when you are invited to climb into a lifeboat. You scramble aboard while there is still a seat for you.' That was the verdict of Geoffrey (Lord) Crowther in the House of Lords in July 1971. Crowther was a leading economist and his verdict has to form the backdrop of any analysis of whether the Heath government secured a good deal. Looked at without regard to the prevailing circumstances, it has to be said that they did not. Con O'Neill, the senior official involved in the negotiations, concluded that 'we bought a satisfactory arrangement for New Zealand dairy products by agreeing to a less than satisfactory one on Community finance'. O'Neill also believed that a mistake had been made in not trying harder to stop the adoption of a Common Fisheries Policy.[29] It was not, in O'Neill's view, that the United Kingdom had done less well for New Zealand than she might, but that the price of a good deal for New Zealand was that the UK was forced to pay more to the budget than would otherwise have been the case. To modern ears, that may seem an almost eccentric choice to have made. But it was not so then. On both sides of the House and in the country at large, affection for New Zealand was strong. New Zealanders had shed their blood in battle for the 'old country' and had sent vital food supplies in the lean post-war years.

---

[29] Sir Con O'Neill, *Britain's Entry into the European Community: Report on the Negotiations of 1970–1972* (London: Frank Cass, 2000), p. 347.

Heath was to have considerable trouble securing approval for British accession. Had he been thought to have ratted on New Zealand he would have had no chance at all. Nor had the British been blind to their dilemma. The government and its advisers believed that the magnetic pull of the European Community was so strong both politically and economically that, if they walked away from the negotiations, they would have to return to the table later on, with every likelihood of a worse deal. The negotiators knew that the financial deal would in all likelihood cost Britain dear. So much so that they sought and secured the endorsement of the Six to a statement by the European Commission which was written into the negotiating record. The Commission had argued that the British, in calculating their likely net contribution to the EEC budget by the end of the transition period, had underestimated the dynamic economic effects of membership and taken inadequate account of the benefits they would receive from the development of new, non-agricultural, EEC policies. Nonetheless, at British insistence, the Commission, in a paper of November 1970, accepted that 'Should unacceptable situations arise within the present Community, or an enlarged Community, the very survival of the Community would demand that the institutions find equitable solutions.' That statement was reproduced in the government's White Paper of July 1971 and became, as such, one of the conditions of Parliament's acceptance of the terms of accession. One of the Foreign Office's senior, and toughest, negotiators, John Robinson, described the Commission statement as a weapon which, if the button was pressed, would cause a nuclear explosion. Even he probably did not realize at the time that the button *would* be pressed, and that the fallout would be every bit as nuclear as he had predicted.[30]

The Heath government had brought home a deal. Could they get it through the House of Commons? Labour would oppose. Wilson's tactics would be to make the government's parliamentary majority as small as possible. He was not about to split his Party if he could help it. As *The Economist* (doubtless after talking to Wilson himself) put it, the Labour leader was 'picking his way along a path which leads neither into Europe, nor out of Europe, but towards the next General Election . . . He does not reckon he can bring the government down on Europe; and . . . he would prefer to have a whole Party at the end of the day rather than part of one . . . '[31]

---

[30] Author conversation with Sir Michael Butler, one of Robinson's colleagues.
[31] *The Economist*, 11 September 1971.

The key vote on membership was due in November 1971, and it was far from clear that Heath could carry the day with the votes of his own MPs alone. According to his Chief Whip, Francis Pym, there were about 26 hard-line opponents of membership on the Conservative benches and 19 whose support was uncertain. There were 281 who would vote in favour. The bleakest outlook was, therefore, that there might be 45 defectors. A more likely figure was 38. The government's overall majority was only 31. In that case, the Division could not be won without some Labour votes in favour of accession, or at least some Labour abstentions. Pym's bold advice to Heath (which Heath accepted with some hesitation) was that the number of Tory rebels would be exactly the same whether there was a three-line whip or a free vote and that the government should offer its MPs a free vote.

Wilson had, some months earlier, come close to offering Roy Jenkins and his fellow pro-Europeans a free vote on the Labour benches. But the Labour Party Conference in early October, instead of voting 3:1 against entry, as Wilson had anticipated, voted 5:1 against. So Wilson felt obliged for the sake of Party discipline to hold his MPs to a three-line whip. In doing so, he hardened the resolve of the pro-EEC Labour rebels. Sixty-nine of them voted with the government and 20 (including Tony Crosland) abstained. The government had a majority of 112.

The vote was but the start of a difficult few months. The Six had begun to negotiate a Common Fisheries Policy among themselves after the opening of their negotiations with Britain and the other applicants. This was a below-the-belt tactic which left the applicants scrambling to safeguard their existing fishing rights against the accomplished fact of a new Community regime. After the main accession negotiation was over, lengthy arguments between the applicant countries and the EEC continued. A complex deal was eventually done in the early hours of 12 December 1971. It gave Britain safeguards for its fishing industry, but not for an indefinite period. It was an unhappy introduction to one of the least successful, and most controversial, common policies of the Community.

A key argument in the debates over the six months following the successful November vote was over the issue of parliamentary sovereignty. In its White Paper on the legal implications of membership, the Labour government had said clearly that '*the constitutional innovation would lie in the acceptance in advance as part of the law of the United Kingdom of provisions to be made in the future by instruments issued by Community institutions—a situation for which there is no precedent in this country. However, these instruments, like ordinary delegated legislation, would derive their force under the law of the United Kingdom from the original enactment passed by Parliament.'*[32]

Enoch Powell was the most articulate exponent of the argument that this provision would fundamentally curtail Parliament's ability to legislate for the United Kingdom and thence undermine its sovereignty. Geoffrey Howe, Solicitor-General at the time, and therefore the Law Officer responsible for answering to the House on these matters, argued in his memoirs that 'the technical aspects had indeed been explained, in documents beginning with those published by the Wilson government in 1967. The electorate *had* endorsed the principle of membership. The final crucial stage could properly be entrusted to Parliament itself. For the very sovereignty of Parliament entitled that body to manage or deploy that sovereignty on behalf of the British people...'[33]

But, in reality, the endorsement of the British people in 1972 rested on the less than wholehearted wording of the Conservative General Election manifesto of two years earlier. Moreover, Heath himself had appeared to commit himself publicly to something more than a purely parliamentary process of approval. In a speech to the British Chamber of Commerce in Paris in May 1970, he had said that Britain would not join the EEC 'without the full-hearted consent of Parliament and the people'. This phrase was used to taunt Heath as the parliamentary debate on membership wound on. His claim that he had not had any thought of a public process of approval apart from the parliamentary one sat uneasily with the speech's implication of a direct vote by the electorate.

The European Communities Bill received its Second Reading in the House of Commons on 17 February 1972 in the dire circumstances of a lengthy coal miners' strike which, soon afterwards, compelled Heath to declare a national State of Emergency. The Second Reading vote was won by a narrow majority (309:301) which included the support of the Liberals. Heath himself had had to make the vote an issue of confidence, saying in his winding up speech that, if the Bill did not pass 'this Parliament cannot sensibly continue'.[34]

The Bill received its third reading, with a larger majority, in July and passed into law on 17 October 1972. In the same week, under Pompidou's chairmanship, the Six, together with the leaders of the three candidate countries, held their first summit meeting in Paris. On the agenda was the issue of economic and monetary union. The report which had been written by Luxembourg

---

[32] Cmnd. 3301, 1967.
[33] Geoffrey Howe, *Conflict of Loyalty* (London: Macmillan, 1994), p. 67.
[34] *Hansard*, 17 February 1972, cols. 752–3.

Prime Minister Pierre Werner in 1970 had recommended the 'total and irreversible convertibility of currencies, the elimination of margins of fluctuation in rates of exchange, the irreversible fixing of parity rates and the total liberation of movements of capital'. The Heath government were prepared to accept the recommendations of the report provided that they secured at the same time a date for the introduction of a regional policy which would offer the possibility of money coming to Britain to offset her expected large net contribution to the EEC budget. Heath secured the commitment.

Now often forgotten are the most politically adventurous bits of the Paris communiqué, though they were publicly promulgated at the time and give the lie to the modern contention that the EEC which Britain joined was intended purely to be a trading market. The two significant commitments were these: *'The Member States of the Community... affirm their intention to transform before the end of the present decade the whole complex of their relations into a European Union'* and *'The Heads of state or of Government reaffirm the determination of the enlarged Communities irreversibly to achieve the economic and monetary Union... The necessary decisions should be taken in the course of 1973 so as to allow the transition to the next stage of the economic and monetary Union on 1 January 1974, and with a view to its completion not later than 31 December 1980.'*

Thus, the United Kingdom was committed to goals which the Labour government had not opposed and which its Conservative successor now explicitly endorsed. Yet there was no evident majority in the House of Commons for either goal, and the public at large had not been asked to address these politically ambitious ideas. The public debate about membership revolved around the issues of cost, global influence, and, to an extent, sovereignty. Heath defended his acceptance of the goal of economic and monetary union on the basis that it did not commit the UK to anything beyond the second stage (freedom of capital movements). As to European Union, when asked about it in the House of Commons, Douglas-Home replied: 'This is something that has to be worked out in each sphere of the Community's activity over the years. Nobody was anxious at the conference to use labels like "confederation" or "federation" and therefore "union" is a word which will gradually become defined over the years.'[35]

The British were, therefore, relying on a step-by-step, experience-based approach to the future development of the Community. As matters turned out, they under-estimated the significance of political conclusions such as

---

[35] *Hansard*, 23 October 1972, col. 756.

those reached in Paris as building blocks of further integration. They over-estimated the extent to which the evolution of the EEC would be led by governments and did not appreciate either the proactive approach of the European Commission or the inbuilt dynamism of the Community method. By definition, laws agreed at European level subsumed or replaced national law, and the competence for the issues they covered became matters for the Community and no longer for national determination. The statement by the then Lord Chancellor, Lord Dilhorne, in 1962 (and repeated in 1967) that 'the vast majority of men and women in this country will never directly feel the impact of Community-made law at all' was incorrect.

Perhaps most importantly of all, it was reasonable to assume that once Britain joined the European Community, membership would become a fact of everyday life and that the existential argument would fade away. It did not. Had Britain, like all other Member States, enjoyed at least a few early years with clear financial and economic gains from membership, public and parlia-mentary opinion might have warmed to the project. But it did not. Instead, Britain was about to join the EEC because its alternative options had failed, because its own economy was struggling, and because the potential downsides of joining were outweighed by the political and economic downsides of not joining.

In the two months between the Paris summit and accession on 1 January 1973, the Heath government worked hard to prepare business and the public for membership. A 34-page brief called *Are You Ready?* detailed the basics of membership for the public and for businesses. Newspaper coupons and TV advertisements encouraged people to send for a copy and 615,000 were distributed, with 25 per cent of the demand coming from business and industry and 75 per cent from the wider public. Under the title *Fanfare for Europe*, a series of events, including concerts, was organized throughout the country. A 'The Three vs. The Six' football match at Wembley was watched by 36,500 people and was won 2–0 by the three candidate countries' players. It was by one of the accidents of history that the Minister who had to admit to Parliament that *Fanfare for Europe* had cost the taxpayer £350,000 was the Secretary of State for Education, a rising star in British politics named Margaret Thatcher.

On 1 January 1973, the United Kingdom became a member of the European Community. The year that was to be Heath's last full year as Prime Minister was also a problematic one for the global economy, for Anglo-US relations, and for the European club of which the UK was now a part.

5

Accession, Renegotiation, Referendum, 1973–1975

If *Fanfare for Europe* was, in Edward Heath's words, a 'high-spirited and good-natured introduction to Britain in Europe', it proved only a temporary respite from a harsher reality. Perhaps because they had been compelled to wait for so long in the European anteroom, British Ministers lost little time in manifesting an aspect of British performance inside the club that was to be enduring but hardly endearing. Britain, in the person of the Foreign Secretary, Alec Douglas-Home, took its place at its first meeting of the Council of Ministers in January 1973. Ireland and Denmark were the other new members of what was now a Community of Nine. In a referendum a few months previously, the Norwegian people had voted by a majority of 8 percent against membership. Douglas-Home, the most courteous of men, nonetheless chose his first meeting with his new colleagues to lecture them about the need to reform the procedures at their meetings and to spend more time on policy questions. This tactless intervention was promptly and predictably contradicted by the French Foreign Minister. Heath, meanwhile, was bemoaning to Jean Monnet the Council's 'terrible habit' of meeting late into the night. Instead of concentrating on the minor details of regulations, Heath was clear that the Council should focus on major questions of policy. The true position was somewhat different, and Michael Palliser, who had moved from the Paris Embassy to become Britain's first Permanent Representative to the EEC, tried to apply a corrective. At a time when the European Parliament was not directly elected and had very few powers, the Council of Ministers was, Palliser told the Prime Minister, required to be both legislature and executive, at once shaping policy and making law. As such, the Council was doing much of the work that in Britain and most other national systems was done by Cabinet, on the one hand, and Parliament on the other. For this reason, the Council found itself having to delve into detail and often to do so at length.[1]

[1] PREM 15/1527, TNA.

A more pertinent concern for many member governments was the development of specialist Councils. Foreign Ministers of the Community countries met in the General Affairs Council with, as its name implied, a general oversight of Community policy. But there were already specialist Councils of Ministers of Finance, Agriculture, and Transport. Within national governments, the ambition of Agriculture Ministers to spend more on farming was counterbalanced by the natural parsimony of finance ministries and by the requirements of other competing spending departments. Within the EEC, the European Commission, as the originator of all proposals, exercised oversight of the way the Community budget was spent. But agriculture dominated the work of the Commission and it was all too easy for Agriculture Ministers to hammer out agreements on agricultural prices in which the influence of powerful farming lobbies was more evident than that of a steadying hand from either the Commission or the Ministry of Finance back home.

This feature of Community life became more evident as the EEC increased its responsibilities. The Commission were the guardians of the European Treaties and had, under the Treaties, certain self-contained legal duties, such as the management of competition policy and the negotiation of international trade agreements. The enthusiasm for the goal of European Union that had been proclaimed by the EEC Heads of Government was just one of the incentives for the Commission to bring forward proposals for policy and legislative action in new fields of cooperation. The fact that there was an evident *need* for collective action in fields such as energy and the environment gave added impetus to the Commission's innate enthusiasm. For the smaller Member States, this was mostly welcome: Community rules, and Community policies, protected them from being dominated by the larger Member States. There was still a residual post-war nervousness about West Germany. France was also viewed with suspicion: since de Gaulle, French governments had jibbed at the kind of *communautaire* integration that gave increased power to the EEC institutions. For the smaller countries, the Commission, and the Treaty-based 'Community method' were their best safeguard against the dominance of the two big continental powers. Those same smaller Member States also hoped that the United Kingdom would in some ways hold the ring between France and Germany. In this they were to be largely disappointed.

In requiring the British government to agree to France's interpretation of the Luxembourg Compromise, Pompidou had rightly calculated that Britain would share France's reticence to allow more power to the European institutions. The supranational nature of the EEC had been something the UK had been obliged to accept as part of the price of membership. But in British eyes it was a price, not an advantage. The evidence of contemporary documents is that even Heath, the most *communautaire* of all Britain's Prime Ministers, saw the Commission as a bureaucracy that should be answerable to governments, and he both underestimated and resisted the unique and consciously independent role given to it under the Treaties. To an extent, the French shared that view, but they had a better appreciation of what lay within Commission competence and what did not. There was an early example. When the Ministers of the EEC began to take a close interest in foreign policy cooperation (known at the time as political cooperation) it was not surprising that Christopher Soames, whose Commission portfolio covered the EEC's external trade policy, sought to seize the opportunity. But Pompidou was having none of it. Pompidou and Soames bumped into each other in an Elysée corridor when Soames was calling on one of the President's advisers. Pompidou told Soames in no uncertain terms that foreign policy cooperation was for governments, not for the machinery of the Community. If Soames had been the British Foreign Minister, Pompidou told him, he would have been happy to see him handling the issue. But he was not, and it was not for the Commission to do so. According to Soames himself, Pompidou told him firmly: '*Retournez à vos places*'.[2]

Agricultural policy, on the other hand, was absolutely within the competence of the Commission under the Treaties, and at this point in the life of the Community it was considered entirely natural, for example, that the senior Commission official, the Director-General for Agriculture, should be a Frenchman. Where agriculture was concerned, the French had a strong *national* interest in being the most *communautaire* of members. The opposite was true for the United Kingdom, and differences over agriculture between France and Britain were bound to arise. Of all the EEC members, Britain was the largest importer of food from outside the Community and, through the levies and duties imposed on such imports, destined to be one of only two net contributors to the Community budget (the other being wealthy Germany). Ninety percent of the money so raised was then spent on agricultural support policies from which Britain derived relatively little benefit. Community farmers sold their produce at a price guaranteed by the Community. This of itsel' encouraged over-production, but that overproduction could in turn be 'so' into intervention' (as it was called) by the farmers to the Community ? guaranteed price. This policy was soon to give rise to the 'beef and b mountains', and the 'wine lake' of familiar notoriety. Moreover, if

---

[2] PREM 15/2243, TNA.

agricultural prices were lower than Community prices, the EEC surpluses were 'sold out of intervention' onto world markets at subsidized rates, thereby also undermining the struggling agriculture of developing countries.

As early as April 1973, the British government was placed on the back foot in the House of Commons when the former Labour Cabinet Minister and prominent critic of the EEC, Peter Shore, drew attention to the 'total lunacy' of the Common Agricultural Policy (CAP). Two hundred thousand tonnes of butter, sitting in frozen storage in various places around the continent, had just been sold by the Commission to the Soviet Union at dumped prices, representing a loss of £110 million. Was it not a disgrace, Shore asked, that this matter had not even been put to the Council of Ministers but had been 'handed over for a decision to a number of unenlightened despots who would speak in our name, without any mandate from the British people?' The most that the unfortunate junior Minister for Agriculture (Anthony Stodart) could say in reply was that this was 'one of the features of the agricultural policy which needs changing. We have always recognised that the Common Agricultural Policy has these weaknesses...'[3]

British pressure for a review of the CAP was therefore one early source of friction with the French government. Another was the issue of sterling. The currencies of the EEC member countries were in the so-called 'snake', an exchange rate band within which parities were managed. The 'snake' was a response to the unilateral economic measures taken by the Nixon government in the United States in 1971 when Nixon, without warning, cancelled the convertibility of the dollar against gold. The UK had briefly entered the 'snake' before accession but had soon been forced to leave because of the speculative pressures on the pound resulting in part from sterling's position as a reserve currency.

It was against the background of the US measures that the EEC Heads of Government had decided, at the Paris summit in October 1972, to commit themselves to economic and monetary union (EMU). Barely a month after UK accession to the EEC, in February 1973, the US dollar was devalued. With the UK outside the 'snake' the pound was not under immediate pressure. But the currencies in the snake were and Heath, on a visit to Bonn at the start of March, found himself in the middle of a financial crisis as German banks took in $2.7 billion in the course of one day. Both Heath and Chancellor Willy Brandt were quick to see that this was a moment when radical action needed to be taken at European level. For Heath, it was an historic moment. At a dinner

---

[3] *Hansard*, 11 April 1973, col. 1329.

in his honour in Schloss Gymnich on 1 March, Heath departed from the prepared text of his speech. Before very long, he said, the Community would be faced with the sort of situation with which free Europe had been faced in June 1940 when Churchill had offered the French common citizenship. There came a time when political leaders had to take great decisions and make a great leap and Europe was near, if not at, that point in relation to its monetary affairs.

In discussion after dinner, and again the following morning, Brandt and Heath discussed the idea of a Community float which would involve support for weak currencies such as the pound and the Italian lira, the pooling of reserves and the acceleration of other aspects of economic and monetary union such as harmonization of monetary policy, interest rate policy, and perhaps even fiscal policy. No conclusions were reached, though Heath suggested that Italy and the UK might have to join the float when they could, rather than from the start.[4]

That caveat contributed to killing the idea. When EEC Finance Ministers met in Brussels on 4 March, Anthony Barber, the Chancellor of the Exchequer, set conditions for British participation which led Jean Monnet to write to Heath complaining that, at a moment when France, Germany, and Great Britain needed to show to themselves and to the world that they were determined and able to solve their main problems together within the Community, Barber had given the impression that his conditions for participation had been put forward on a 'take it or leave it' basis. Heath responded, making the reasonable, and true, point that most of Britain's partners had also shown themselves not to be ready for such a far-reaching move.[5]

The opportunity passed, but within the Heath government, which was more open to the implications of economic and monetary union than any subsequent government until that of Tony Blair nearly thirty years later, work was set in train. Sir John Hunt, who was shortly to become Cabinet Secretary, supervised the work. His advice to the Prime Minister took it as read that full EMU was 'an essential element in complete political union in the Community and, achieved in the right way, would bring all the economic benefits which are expected to flow from completely free movement of goods, services, labour and capital within the Community'. But, Hunt warned, the road was a dangerous one and, if Community exchange rates were to be locked irrevocably, either economic performances (growth rates, rates of increase of wages, productivity, etc.) would need to converge to a much greater extent than

---

[4] PREM 15/1576, TNA.   [5] PREM 15/1494, TNA.

hitherto, or central provision must be made for imbalances to be offset by massive and speedy resource transfers. Failing that, equilibrium could only be restored by inflation in high performance countries and unemployment and stagnation in the low performance currencies. What the UK, and not just the UK, would need, therefore, was a package of measures to bring about economic convergence.[6]

So, here was another source of friction with the French. Christopher Soames, in his capacity as a European Commissioner, called on Pompidou on 21 March and was told very firmly that Britain must fix her parity. It was clear, so Soames told Heath a few days later, that Pompidou regarded this issue as the touchstone of Britain's commitment to the EEC. In general, Soames thought, the British were giving the impression in Brussels of hanging back. The government, Soames advised, should show greater awareness of the significance for its wider relations within the Community of the particular positions it took on individual issues.[7]

John Hunt was inclined to agree. As Britain completed its first 100 days of membership in early April 1973, Hunt thought that Britain had done well in securing senior jobs in the Commission (Soames was a vice-president, and the second British Commissioner, the former Labour Cabinet Minister, George Thomson, was responsible for creating a regional development policy), and the Whitehall coordination machinery was working efficiently. Other things had gone less well: the handling of the EMU issue, where Britain's terms were seen as having been pitched unacceptably high; the continued hostility of the anti-Marketeers; and the lack of convincing signs of readiness on the part of British industry to take advantage of membership. Britain was correct in its criticisms of the CAP but the issue had been made to look like an Anglo-French confrontation.

Hunt concluded his assessment with a swipe at the Foreign and Commonwealth Office (FCO). The FCO should concentrate, he told Heath, on advising other government departments on the negotiability of policies and on lobbying and presentation. Instead, they were all too ready to argue the merits of policy with the Home Departments and they felt that they should have a coordinating role, a job which ought, Hunt advised (not surprisingly), to be left to the Cabinet Office.[8]

The question raised by Hunt was a persistent one. When I became involved in European Community policy in the Foreign Office in 1983, the arrangements for policy decisions on EEC matters were still those that had been set in

---

[6] Ibid.   [7] PREM 15/1498, TNA.   [8] PREM 15/1529, TNA.

place ten years earlier. The Foreign Secretary was the senior Minister with overall responsibility for EEC policy. He chaired the relevant Cabinet sub-committee where issues could be resolved at ministerial level. Coordination between Whitehall departments was the responsibility of the European Secretariat within the Cabinet Office, which chaired its own subcommittees of officials from across Whitehall to thrash out policy recommendations. Senior Whitehall officials, together with the UK Permanent Representative to the EEC, met once a week under Cabinet Office chairmanship to take stock and to attempt to resolve issues that were still in dispute. In practice, there was a triumvirate of Cabinet Office, Foreign Office, and the UK Representation (UKRep) versus the rest. The UKRep (composed of staff drawn from across Whitehall) was, at this period, invariably headed by a Foreign Office official, the European Secretariat by a home civil servant, often from the Treasury. Outside the FCO, there was relatively little EEC expertise in Whitehall. Expertise did exist in the Ministry of Agriculture, the Treasury, and the Department of Trade and Industry, but tended to be heavily focused on the defence of departmental interests and not on the issues of strategy and negotiability that Hunt had identified. Hunt's prescription for the proper and limited role of the FCO was not practically feasible: there was no point in UKRep or the FCO focusing solely on the negotiability of policies, and not on their merits. At European level, the merit of a particular British policy or objective depended in practice on whether it was negotiable. Those officials in Whitehall who had no direct negotiating experience were all too inclined to insist on the merits of their departmental position without regard for the negotiating realities.

Policy on EEC issues was ultimately the responsibility of the ministerial committee chaired by the Foreign Secretary, and written correspondence between Whitehall departments, at official and ministerial level, was a fre-quent tool of debate and decision. Via the Whitehall messenger service (and a vacuum tube linking the FCO and 10 Downing Street), the system was quick and efficient. Much informal negotiation was done by telephone. But the Foreign Secretary's primacy on EEC issues did not mean that he could overrule his colleagues. Each Minister fought the departmental corner fer-ociously, and the divisions over Europe within both main Parties limited the degree to which Ministers were prepared to be flexible. The result was an accumulation of British positions which, once decided, could be changed only with difficulty. This contributed to the British having a reputation in Brussels for professionalism, but also for inflexibility. The British tended to treat all their policy stances as of equal and immutable importance. Prioritization was hard to achieve. Anyone working in the UK Representation in Brussels soon came to feel that negotiating with EEC partners was a lot more straightforward than negotiating with Whitehall.

Heath himself had earlier noted that many of the problems within the EEC arose from a 'we' and 'they' attitude, and had observed that 'we certainly have a long way to go to get over this in Britain'. Heath thought that the Community, and the Commission in particular, suffered from exactly the same problem, 'constantly barging ahead with regulations drawn up to suit themselves and then coming along, more of less with a take-it-or-leave-it attitude'. Heath's remedy was to 'muscle in on this machine now in a big way'. When Heath's views were passed onto Rippon, his response was that the answer lay in 'far more contacts with the Community at all levels'. He was confident that such contacts 'would give a rapidly increasing number of officials from home departments first-hand experience of dealing with the Community and so make a very effective contribution to the spread of European-mindedness throughout Whitehall'.[9] In the event, both tendencies persisted. Over the years, Whitehall engagement with the rest of the EEC became widespread, continuous, and expert, but real conceptual and policy differences between the UK and her partners, and domestic political pressures, always contrived to trouble the European landscape for successive British governments.

If there was one bilateral relationship within the EEC that was characterized by mutual suspicion and antagonism, it was the relationship between Britain and France. Each had for centuries been the traditional enemy of the other. French post-war resentment of the British was matched by innate British mistrust of French motives. Through all the British archives, there is one consistent theme: if there is trouble for Britain over any European matter, the French are almost invariably either the cause, or seen as the cause, of it. So, as Heath prepared for another visit to see Pompidou in May 1973, the British Embassy sent a paper to London revealingly entitled 'Living with the French'. The paper contained advice on tactics but also identified three areas of particular friction: the CAP, the issue of sterling, and a big difference over transatlantic relations. Pompidou would want to know that Heath shared his concept of defending the European personality against the Americans. Heath would, the Embassy suggested, want to promote the idea, which was common to most of the EEC countries apart from France, that Europe needed to define its relationship with the United States as a matter of political consultation leading to a common approach.[10]

---

[9] PREM 15/326 and 15/351, TNA.   [10] PREM 15/1554, TNA.

This last issue had taken on some urgency. On 23 April, with no prior warning or consultation, the American Secretary of State, Henry Kissinger, had made a major speech devoted to the importance of reaffirming and reconstituting the Atlantic Alliance in what Kissinger called 'the Year of Europe'.[11] The speech was intended both to appeal to Europe and to challenge it. The challenge posed by Kissinger was whether 'a unity forged by a common perception of danger can draw new purpose from shared positive aspirations ... to lay the basis of a new era of creativity in the West ... to deal with Atlantic problems comprehensively'. 'We can', Kissinger concluded, 'no longer afford to pursue national or regional self-interest without a unifying framework'. There should be a clear set of common objectives (what Kissinger called 'one ball of wax') which should be formulated in a new Atlantic Charter to be worked out by the time of President Nixon's planned visit to Europe towards the end of the year. Kissinger's initiative coincided with growing pressures on President Nixon as evidence of his direct involvement in the Watergate scandal began to emerge. Kissinger was, at the time, professing to believe that Nixon would ride out the storm. That was not the view of the American participants in the annual Bilderberg Conference that year, all of whom, according to Denis Greenhill, the Permanent Secretary of the Foreign Office, had maintained that 'the cumulative evidence, working on Mr Nixon's temperament, would in the end bring about a resignation'.[12]

Kissinger's speech also coincided with growing public rumours about the state of health of President Pompidou, of which there was increasing evidence in his appearance. Not until the President's death a year later was it revealed that he had been suffering, since 1972 at least, from multiple myeloma, a malignant and lethal cancer of the bone marrow. In 1973, no information was released and the health stories were played down. I was then serving in the British Embassy in Paris and vividly recall that Christopher Ewart-Biggs, the second in command in the Embassy, was convinced from the start that Pompidou was dying.[13]

It was against this troubled backdrop that Pompidou and Heath met in Paris on 21 and 22 May 1973. Their meeting was, as the British Embassy subsequently observed, more mutual explanation than negotiation. Heath was at pains to reassure Pompidou that the UK accepted the CAP, but the

---

[11] See *DBPO*, Series III, Vol. IV, *The Year of Europe: America, Europe and the Energy Crisis 1972-4* (London: Routledge, 2006), No. 70.

[12] PREM 15/1992, TNA.

[13] Christopher, who had fought in the Second World War and lost an eye in the Battle of El Alamein, would himself die in 1976; assassinated by the IRA.

President had to understand that the British public resented the fact that they were now paying a higher price for butter than they had before accession; all the more so when they saw butter surpluses being sold off cheaply to Russian communists.

Pompidou rejoined with what he called a 'very French point' about the importance of preserving the rural way of life. The small farmer formed part of a politically sensible and moderate social class and it was in the French national interest that this class be kept alive. Pompidou did not need to spell out that this same social class also contained the bulk of his own political supporters. He agreed about the absurdity of the Russian butter sales which were—in France—handled by a communist company. More fundamentally, and perhaps prophetically, Pompidou said that he, and the French more widely, did not believe that the future should lie in giant concerns. There was an increasing need to come back to a more modest rhythm. He intended to say to Nixon that even a relatively small (6–7 per cent) transfer of the French population from country to town would lead to the advent of a Socialist/Communist government in France.

On monetary matters, Heath explained that the efforts of the previous Labour government to defend the parity of sterling had been defeated by external speculation. Hence his government's decision to let the pound float and to protect the reserves. Now, the economy was growing, along with investment. He strongly supported the Community monetary system, regarded it as the basis of Community life and wished to return to it. But he had to choose the right moment.[14]

Of all this, Pompidou was understanding. The two men also edged closer together on the prospective European Regional Development Fund (ERDF). For Heath, as he explained, the regional fund was a necessary *quid pro quo* for British acceptance of the CAP. In that case, said Pompidou, clearly a solution must be found. He would be content if progress could be made at a reasonable rate.

The main issue where the French and British leaders diverged was over Europe's relationship with the United States. Heath, on his return to London, told Cabinet that, while his talks with Pompidou had been 'full and valuable', Pompidou had not been willing to take part in any discussion with the United States on European defence. Nor was the French President willing to coun-tenance any idea of a joint meeting between the US President and members of

---

[14] In so saying, Heath would certainly not have expected that the perceived 'right moment' would not arrive until 1990 and that the 'right moment' would then soon be widely seen as the wrong one.

the European Community. Pompidou had been similarly reluctant to contemplate the idea of a declaration of transatlantic principles. Heath had tried to
tempt him by suggesting that he (Pompidou) should draft the document
himself. But this ploy had failed.

Christopher Ewart-Biggs (a part-time novelist with a fluent pen) summed
up the French position in words which were sent to London over the signature
of the Ambassador, Sir Edward Tomkins. 'There is', said the despatch from
Paris, 'a magnificent effrontery in the double claim to be the *interlocuteur
priviligié* of Europe both with the Soviet Union and with the United States, in
one case because France is the most forthcoming of the Nine and in the other
because she is the least: to command the eastern front from the front and the
western one from the rear'.[15]

Heath was the most 'correct' of politicians, far removed from the skuldug-
gery and paranoia of the political world of President Nixon. Neither man was
at ease socially and there was therefore little by way of personal sentiment to
stand between Heath and his growing irritation with US policy as the year
1973 progressed. Heath attached importance to the UK's relationship with the
United States, but he also firmly believed that the economic and political
prominence of the European Community would change the balance in transatlantic relations. In June, he told President Lyndon Johnson's former
National Security Adviser, Walt Rostow, that the United States was no longer
number one, either militarily or in economic and trade matters. The USA had
allowed her nuclear superiority to be eroded. Now, with the enlarged
European Community on the stage, the USA could no longer deal with the
countries of Europe on the old basis. The Kennedy concept of the twin pillars
of Atlantic solidarity was a reality. But the EEC had no defence personality and
what Kissinger was proposing (a grand negotiation with Europe on the whole
range of relevant issues in a single forum) was not possible. So, in Heath's
opinion, the Kissinger initiative was flawed. Nor was it just the rhetoric and
terminology that could be faulted. If Kissinger had been floating the idea of a
Soviet–American Charter there would have been tremendous preparation and
exploration to see what could, or could not, be done. In future, the United
States was going to have to deal with Europe in the same way. He wished there
was more understanding in the United States of the facts of the situation.[16]

[15] PREM 15/1554, TNA. On the Heath–Pompidou meeting see also *DBPO*, Series III, Vol. IV, Nos.
98, 101, and 103.
[16] PREM 15/1542, TNA, and *DBPO*, Series III, Vol. IV, No. 133.

As the year progressed, so tempers on both sides of the Atlantic frayed. In November, Kissinger complained to the British Ambassador in Washington, Lord Cromer (a former Bank of England Governor) that the special relationship between the USA and the UK was collapsing. Britain's entry into the EEC should have raised Europe to the level of Britain. Instead, it had reduced Britain to the level of Europe. The USA had not hitherto treated Britain as a foreign country. Now it was different. The party was over. So far, the United States had refrained from public attacks on France for her attempts to build Europe on an anti-American basis, but that restraint could not continue. Nor could the French do what they were doing without the tacit help of the United Kingdom. The United Kingdom made it possible for France to pursue its policies. Britain no longer counted as a counterweight to France in Europe. France had made the cold-blooded assessment that it could drive the UK to share in the construction of Europe on the basis of coolness towards America, in the belief that the Americans would not retaliate. This was the worst decision since the city states of ancient Greece confronted Alexander.[17]

A few days later, US Press reports suggested that British official sources were 'biting' in their off-the-record attacks on Kissinger. It transpired that the official sources were in fact Heath himself, speaking at a supposedly off-the-record dinner with American journalists where he said that although 'people on the other side of the Atlantic seemed unable to understand it, the Europeans were at last getting their act together'.[18]

Much of this friction was caused by differing European and US responses to the Arab–Israeli war (the Yom Kippur war) in October 1973. The countries of the EEC were more even-handed as between Israel and the Arab world than were the Americans. They nonetheless found themselves criticized on both fronts. Kissinger berated the Europeans (including Britain, specifically) for failing to stand with the Americans. The Arab world blamed Europe for not bringing pressure to bear on the United States to be even-handed. The consequence of Arab dissatisfaction was a decision by the oil producers' cartel, OPEC, to reduce their oil production by 5 percent a month until the Israelis withdrew from occupied territories and the legal rights of the Palestinian people were recognized. Germany and the Netherlands were especially penalized by an Arab embargo on oil sales to countries thought to be hostile to Arab interests. Britain and France benefited from being seen as more balanced in their stance.

[17] PREM 15/2089, TNA.   [18] PREM 15/1989.

The scene was summed up at the end of November by Bernard Nossiter, the London correspondent of the *Washington Post*. It was an over-jaundiced view, but not very far from that of the British public of whom, in an opinion poll published at the same time, only 29 per cent thought that membership of the EEC was being helpful to Britain. Nossiter summarized the reasons. The timetable for European Union had been derailed, the second stage of EMU (due at the start of 1974) forgotten. The New Year present that Heath intended to give to the British public, a hefty fund for depressed areas such as Belfast and Glasgow, was disappearing since the French had linked it to progress on EMU and, anyway, intended to make little more than a token contribution, as did the Germans. The failure of the rest of her partners to help the Dutch (who were especially penalized by the Arab oil embargo) was a reminder that the big EEC members would always put their own interests first. Finally, Nossiter considered that a curious Gaullist streak of rancour had rubbed off on Heath. In that last observation, Kissinger agreed with him. His verdict was that Heath had 'actively sought to downgrade' the Anglo-US relationship.[19]

Heath and Pompidou met at Chequers in mid-November 1973. As the Private Secretary to the British Ambassador in Paris, I had a significant role in the preparation of these Chequers summits. At their first Chequers meeting, Pompidou—on the basis that he was going to the English countryside—arrived wearing a tweed suit. The Prime Minister—on the basis that the meeting was one of official business—greeted Pompidou at the airport wearing a grey business suit. At the first break in the ensuing talks at Chequers, both leaders retired briefly to their respective bedrooms and emerged, Pompidou wearing a grey business suit, Heath a tweed country suit. My task before each subsequent meeting was to ascertain what the President would be wearing so that sartorial sameness could be assured. Of the various responsibilities passed on to me by my predecessor in Paris, this was the only one that had any measurable impact on the course of Anglo-French relations.

The French and British Ministers at the Council in Brussels had already conveniently agreed that the best way to ensure the continued flow of oil, despite Dutch and German requests to the contrary, was to say as little as possible about mutual solidarity. Ten days later at Chequers, Heath and Pompidou contrived to agree both on the importance of moving towards a common European foreign policy and on the inadvisability of any intervention with the Arabs on behalf of their suffering EEC partners. Pompidou reasoned that the sole effect of such an intervention would be to provoke the

---

[19] Henry Kissinger, *Years of Renewal* (London: Weidenfeld & Nicolson, 1999).

Arabs into subjecting France and Britain to the same bad treatment they were meting out to other EEC countries. Heath agreed. The Foreign Office had been clear in its advice to 'resist short term or collaborative approaches' that might set at risk Britain's oil supplies.[20]

What, as a result, *was* set at risk were Heath's hopes of securing a decision on the introduction of a Regional Development Fund (ERDF). In response to the British refusal to help them, the Dutch threatened to block progress on issues of importance to Britain, such as the ERDF. When the European Council met in Copenhagen in mid-December, Community solidarity had started to unravel in the face of national pressures. Britain would make no move on energy solidarity without the ERDF. Others would make no move on the ERDF without solidarity on oil. It was, Heath wrote in his memoirs, 'the worst Summit I have ever experienced'.

Kissinger had proposed the establishment of an Energy Action Group to prepare a programme of collaboration in all areas of the energy crisis. Heath was not opposed, but Pompidou was; he saw it as an American attempt to make Europe dance to their tune. The German government supported the American initiative and declined to commit to the proposed Regional Development Fund to which Heath was so attached. In the aftermath of the Copenhagen summit, Douglas-Home blocked a resolution setting up a Community Energy Committee. The British government's policy was: no cooperation on energy policy without money for the ERDF. When Cabinet discussed the issue the prevailing view was that 'success in Community negotiations depended on being prepared to press with determination for national objectives'. Unless the government did so, Britain would never play an effective and decisive part in Community affairs or achieve benefits for the United Kingdom. Heath summed up that the establishment of the ERDF was the government's prime immediate objective within the Community and the government must be prepared to press the objective 'with the greatest determination'.[21]

And so the United Kingdom's first year as a member of the European Community ended in ill-tempered confrontation. The energy crisis had led to disarray and mutual recrimination. The smaller Member States had found themselves, probably for the first time since 1945, lined up with Germany against Britain and France. 'Were we quite blameless?', Michael Palliser asked in his annual review of the year from Brussels. 'Could we have played the hand

[20]   PREM 15/2093, TNA.
[21]   Cabinet of 20 December 1973, CC (73) 63rd Conclusions, CAB 128/53, TNA.

in some way differently, and even perhaps with more silence and discretion?'[22] The first year of Britain's membership had, Palliser observed, revealed one of the penalties of a policy of 'join now and negotiate later' especially when, unlike Denmark and Ireland, there was no measurable financial gain from membership and a potential source of gain, the ERDF, had got nowhere. The Treasury, moreover, were warning that the net gain from the ERDF would go only a small way towards offsetting the cost of membership.

The first year of membership also revealed a wider fact of EEC life—one that is even more evident in the EU of the present day: the absence of solidarity in the face of severe economic and political pressures. Heath shared with Brandt and Pompidou the idea that the three largest member countries should provide leadership but, as Palliser pointed out, 'all too often in 1973 it had looked as if the three partners could manage one or other variant of a *ménage à deux*, but not a *ménage à trois*'.

For Heath, the opportunity to learn from that first year was not to arise. On 7 February 1974, in the face of a national coal strike, he decided to seek a dissolution of Parliament and to fight a General Election on the issue of 'Who governs Britain?' The answer of the electorate was a hung Parliament with a minority Labour government under Harold Wilson.

Heath never again held office. He is entitled to the accolade of being the most committedly European of all Britain's modern Prime Ministers, and his place in history is assured by his achievement in taking the UK into the EEC. Yet his record as Prime Minister suggests that, like his successors, he had little belief in a Europe of the institutions, as set out in the Treaty of Rome, and a strong belief in a Europe of nations, led by the large Member States. Had he stayed in power he would, like Wilson and Thatcher, have been confronted with the harsh economic and political reality of the United Kingdom's excessive net contribution to the EEC budget. Judging by his hard-headedness over securing money from the Regional Development Fund, he might well have pursued the issue with more rigour than Harold Wilson. He would certainly *not* have done so with the aggressive brinkmanship of Margaret Thatcher. But the story of British accession and of Britain's first year as a member of the European Community shows the extent to which Heath had to contend with hostile opinion within his own Party and in the country at large. For his successor, Harold Wilson, that problem and its management were to define his last term as Britain's Prime Minister.

[22] PREM 15/2076, TNA.

Harold Wilson, it is said, had not expected to find himself as Prime Minister for the third time. Heath's 'Who governs Britain?' election had produced only one clear result: it would not be a government led by Heath. Labour had more seats than the Tories but no overall majority and a smaller share of the vote. Heath's attempts to strike a post-election deal with the Liberal Party leader, Jeremy Thorpe, came to nothing. A Labour minority government took office.

The new government was committed by its election manifesto (at ten pages long, one of the shortest ever) to renegotiate the terms of Britain's EEC membership. But, in setting its own exam paper, the Party had been careful to give itself maximum flexibility. So, for example, the goal of 'Resistance to proposals for EMU' was qualified by the words 'which would lead to increased unemployment'. Similarly, 'No harmonisation of VAT' was qualified by 'which would require Britain to tax necessities'. This was a manifesto written by politicians who had been in government before and knew the perils of over-commitment to specifics. One pledge, however, had not been ducked. In the event of a successful renegotiation, the people would decide the issue through a General Election or a 'Consultative Referendum'. If the renegotiation did not succeed, then the government would not regard the obligations of the Accession Treaty as binding (a curious formulation because the government could not simply wish away legal obligations entered into by Parliament), would explain to the British people why the new terms were unacceptable and would 'consult them on the advisability of negotiating Britain's withdrawal from the Communities'.[23]

Harold Wilson and Jim Callaghan (who, as Foreign Secretary, would lead the negotiations) were canny. Wilson was clear from the start in public that he would only take a decision on continued membership, and make a recom-mendation to the British people, in the light of the negotiations and their outcome. This required a bit of theatre and Callaghan was sufficient of a bruiser to play that part to perfection. As a start, Callaghan brought all Britain's Ambassadors in EEC countries to London, telling them that he could not say from the outset whether he would prefer the outcome to be that Britain should stay in the Community or leave it. He was agnostic. Thereafter, he visited Bonn and shocked his German interlocutors, who included Willy Brandt, by the extent of his scepticism. The German Press reported German government circles to have been 'alarmed by Callaghan's announcement that the Labour Government prefers cooperation in a loose

---

[23] Labour Party Manifesto, February 1974.

customs union to being closely bound in a political and economic European union'.[24]

At his first Council meeting with his fellow EEC Foreign Ministers Callaghan, according to Roy Hattersley, his Foreign Office ministerial deputy, sounded 'deeply antagonistic to Britain's continued Common Market membership'.[25] According to the *Financial Times*, Callaghan was 'blunt to the point of rudeness'.[26] When Michael Palliser, Britain's Permanent Representative to the EEC, took Callaghan to meet Ortoli, the Commission President, the British Foreign Secretary behaved with gratuitous and embarrassing roughness.[27]

In all of this, there was a degree of theatre. Nicholas Spreckley, working in the Department in the Foreign Office handling the negotiations, wrote an internal account of the renegotiation which was regarded as so sensitive that it remained hidden from public sight well after it would normally have been released under the thirty-year rule.[28] Spreckley's view was that, while nothing was made explicit, officials gained the early impression that Callaghan and Wilson wanted the negotiation to succeed.

One early key test was whether the new Labour government would insist that the renegotiation of the terms of British membership should include changes in the Treaty of Rome and the UK Accession Treaty. Palliser was clear from the outset in advising that a British demand for treaty change would be a critical threshold, involving an intergovernmental conference of all the Member States and unanimous agreement followed by Parliamentary ratification in each capital. One of the earliest positions taken by Callaghan and Wilson was that the government should *not* seek treaty change, a view that was endorsed by Cabinet at a point when the Eurosceptics failed to realize the significance of what they were agreeing to. This was the first clear signal to officials that the two men were negotiating for success.

From the outset, it had been clear that the French government would be the principal obstacle to a successful outcome. At the Council meeting where Callaghan played rough and tough, most of the other members were nuanced in response. Michel Jobert, who had graduated from Secretary General at the Elysée to become Foreign Minister, was the only one who was overtly hostile,

---

[24] PREM 16/92, TNA.

[25] Roy Hattersley, *Who Goes Home? Scenes from a Political Life* (London: Abacus 1995), p. 152.

[26] *Financial Times*, 2 April 1974.

[27] Conversation with the author. Cited in Stephen Wall, *The Official History of Britain and the European Community, Volume II* (London: Routledge, 2013), p. 520.

[28] The Spreckley Report was published by the FCO Historians in 2014: https://issuu.com/fcohistorians/docs/1_spreckley_report_-_part_1.

warning Callaghan that it was for Britain to adapt to the EEC and not for the EEC to adapt to Britain.

Jobert was reflecting President Pompidou's own hostility. Pompidou had never liked Wilson, and the message he was getting from his old friend, Edward Heath, was that the Labour minority government would not long survive and that Pompidou could afford to await the return to power of the Conservatives. But then, on 3 April 1974, Pompidou died. Despite the long-standing rumours about the President's health, his death took France and the rest of the world by surprise. In reality he had for months been failing, in acute pain, before the eyes of his close staff. But only at the meeting of the French Council of Ministers, six days before his death, did Pompidou say anything about his health. Even then, it was only because of his appearance, rather than what he said, that 'his Ministers watched him with pity as well as with their customary apprehension', as Christopher Ewart-Biggs described it.

Pompidou's funeral was attended by the Duke of Edinburgh (piloting an aircraft of the Queen's Flight) and by Wilson, Heath, and Thorpe. It was something of a working occasion. President Nixon, despite his Watergate troubles, was greeted enthusiastically by a French crowd and so far forgot the nature of the occasion that he proclaimed it 'a great day for France'.[29] A month later, Willy Brandt resigned as German Chancellor following a spy scandal. France had a new President in Valéry Giscard d'Estaing and Germany a new Chancellor in Helmut Schmidt. Both men, like Callaghan, were former Finance Ministers. Both were rather wary of grand pronouncements about the future of Europe. Both were preoccupied with problems around energy policy, inflation, and unemployment, and saw the British negotiation as a sideline, albeit an irritating one.

For the British negotiators, there were three sets of problems in bringing the renegotiation to a successful outcome. The first was that the trickiest issue (Britain's budget contribution) required the other Member States to accept that there was a problem, that it was as big as the British suggested and that they should accept to pay more into the European Community budget so that the UK could pay less. On these three conditions of success there was no early progress. Nor was there likely to be. For the second problem for the British government was the question in continental minds as to whether the Wilson government would survive. 'Giscard', as Christopher Ewart-Biggs advised London, 'would not want to help a Labour government, uncertain about

---

[29] I was in the Faubourg St Honoré, home of the Elysée Palace and of the British and US Embassies, and heard him say it.

Europe, to keep out a Conservative government committed to Europe'.[30] The third problem was summed up by Sir Nicholas ('Nicko') Henderson, Britain's Ambassador in Bonn. It was not just that the Germans were biding their time in the expectation of a fresh General Election in the UK, but that, for the Germans, as for the French, their mutual relationship was 'more important politically and economically to the two countries than the relationship of either of them with the United Kingdom, particularly in our present state of political instability and indifference towards Europe'. The Germans, according to Henderson, were anyway convinced that, unless irrationality prevailed, Britain was bound to stay in the EEC, 'if not out of any belief in the idea of Europe, at any rate from the hard headed calculation of where Britain's own national interest lay'.[31]

The challenges of the renegotiation for Wilson and Callaghan lay as much within the Cabinet, and even more within the National Executive Committee (NEC) of the Labour Party, as with other EEC members. But, against the background of new leaders in France and Germany, by mid-year Wilson was talking in conciliatory terms. He told the Belgian Prime Minister, Leo Tindemans, in late June 1974 that he had been surprised to find that so much change could be envisaged within the Community without the need to alter the Treaties. Fred Peart, the Minister of Agriculture, had found a large degree of flexibility among his EEC colleagues. The British people were starting to find the EEC more interesting and to welcome the signs of fresh thinking evident within it.[32]

Later on the same day, Wilson told the Danish Prime Minister, Poul Hartling, that the terms of accession agreed by Heath had been crippling. But, apart from the totally committed 'pros' and the totally committed 'antis', the largest single group of people in Britain would be in favour of remaining in the Community if the terms were right. It now looked, Wilson said, as if the British government could get all they needed by way of renegotiation without the need to alter either the Treaty of Rome or the Treaty of Accession. He expected the new French President to look at issues 'with a clear mind, uncluttered by ancestral voices from Colombey les Deux Églises'.[33]

In a meeting with Luxembourg Prime Minister, Gaston Thorn, Wilson said that he 'firmly believed that by the sensible and civilised processes of negotiation, the problems we had raised could be solved'. The image of the Community in Britain when Labour took office had, he added, been horrible. In some ways, the Community had become a music hall joke. Even the solidly

---

[30] PREM 16/97, TNA.   [31] PREM 16/73, TNA.   [32] PREM 16/11, TNA.   [33] Ibid.

pro-European British Press had been hard-pressed to find a good word to say about the EEC. But things had now changed, and there was a new and fresh atmosphere. If renegotiation was successful, and Britain secured the right terms, then she would play her full part in the Community.

Thorn asked whether another British government might engage in yet another referendum in the future. Wilson said the answer to that question was 'no'. He did not believe so. Once the British people had voted on the question, it would be settled for good.[34]

It was not just Wilson who was making emollient noises to Britain's EEC partners. Callaghan began to find himself criticized by the anti-Europeans in Cabinet for a perceived lack of toughness in his interventions in Brussels and for not making more of the issue of sovereignty. His was a difficult balancing act between keeping the sceptical Labour Party onside, convincing the other EEC governments that there was good reason to continue to negotiate with Britain, and satisfying the electorate at large.

The latter had their chance to express a view when, on 15 September, Wilson announced that there would be a General Election on 10 October. Cleverly, the manifesto did not remind the voters of the specific undertakings made in February but rested its case on three key points: the government had wasted no time before getting on with the negotiations, was negotiating toughly, and, whatever the outcome in Brussels, the decision on Britain's future would be taken in Britain by the British people. The manifesto thus portrayed Labour as the friend of the people, by contrast with the Conservative and Liberal Parties.

Labour won the election with a small overall majority, less because of its European promises than because of public reluctance to return to the industrial strife of the Heath years. The bill that the country would have to pay for Wilson's placatory stance towards the trade unions was not then apparent. Wilson left his senior ministerial team unchanged. Callaghan had Wilson's confidence in conducting the renegotiation because of his skill, his ability to straddle the left and right wings of the Party, and because Wilson did not want to be seen as too prominently implicated should the negotiations fail. There was, nonetheless, a difference between the two men. Wilson, with memories of the Macmillan and Heath accession negotiations, attached huge importance to agricultural issues such as butter imports from New Zealand. Callaghan, by contrast, correctly saw that the growing problem of Britain's contribution to the EEC budget was the predominant issue. Wilson was also acting tactically.

[34] Ibid.

The government needed to be able to tick all the boxes of its negotiating promises to the electorate. He saw how readily measurable in hard cash success or failure in delivering on the budget would be.

A key moment came at the annual Labour Party conference, which had been postponed to late November 1974 because of the General Election. The mood of the Conference on Europe was sour, with speech after speech from the floor demanding a fundamental renegotiation of the Treaty of Rome and the Treaty of Accession and calling on the government to tell the EEC 'where to get off'. The Conference mood was turned, however, by a speech by the German Chancellor, Helmut Schmidt. Schmidt and the Labour leaders were old friends and Schmidt had accepted Callaghan's invitation to speak. He did so in excellent English and with humour. He acknowledged the faults of the EEC, assured the delegates that Germany shared Britain's criticisms of the CAP and flattered them by saying how much Europe needed Britain. He pleaded with his British comrades, on grounds of Socialist solidarity, not to leave the Community. It was a *tour de force*. The threatened walkout did not materialize and Schmidt was warmly applauded.

Even more significant was the weekend that Schmidt then spent with Wilson, Callaghan, and Healey at Chequers. Schmidt put Wilson on the spot. At the forthcoming EEC summit in Paris, Wilson, he argued, needed to tell his partners, especially the French, clearly that his government would be willing to recommend continued membership to the British people if Britain could achieve favourable terms. So far, according to Schmidt, this had not been clear. If people on the continent felt that Britain did not really want to stay in the Community, then they might conclude that the best course was not to offer too many inducements to them to stay and simply to let them go.

Wilson's reply would have surprised many of those who had seen how he had had to duck and weave on Europe after the 1970 election defeat. But it was consistent with his strategy and tactics over many years. His position, Wilson told Schmidt, was what it had been since 1966. His view was the same as that of Macmillan. Like Macmillan, he believed that, on the right terms, membership was good for Britain and for Europe too. If, on the other hand, the terms of membership were crippling, he could not advise Parliament or the British people to stay in. But he saw no reason why the terms should be crippling.

Schmidt welcomed what Wilson had said but noted an important difference between Macmillan and the Prime Minister. Macmillan had been negotiating to see if acceptable membership terms were attainable. Today, Britain was a member of the Community and had signed and ratified a treaty. So, Britain's partners were inclined to ask what kind of partner Britain was when it sought to call in question the validity of a treaty it had freely ratified.

Wilson, in response, reminded Schmidt that, under the British constitution, no Parliament could bind its successor. Heath had signed a treaty without, as he had promised, the full-hearted consent of the British people. The Labour government were trying to tread a path between outright rejection of the Treaty and outright acceptance of the terms negotiated by Heath.

In discussion with officials after Schmidt had left Chequers, Britain's Ambassador to West Germany, Nicko Henderson, was struck by Wilson's caution over making too much of the budget issue in the negotiations. In Wilson's view, there was no possibility of getting hard cash in the short term. Yet he (Wilson) must be able to show the British people that he had got better terms than the Tories had done.

Henderson came away from the Chequers talks with no great feeling of optimism. But those in Number 10 close to the Prime Minister saw the Chequers weekend as a turning point, after which Wilson clearly wanted the UK to stay in the Community. In a telephone conversation with Callaghan soon after Schmidt's departure, Wilson said that he was feeling a good deal happier about the possibility of an acceptable outcome. Wilson then enumerated the various issues in the negotiation with reference to the government's manifesto commitments. For Callaghan, the Community budget and sovereignty were the main outstanding concerns. Wilson thought that, on sovereignty, it would be necessary to improve the arrangements for parliamentary scrutiny of possible Community developments and legislation before they occurred. For his part, Callaghan was sure the problem could be solved through some reaffirmation of the Luxembourg Compromise. Wilson reiterated his view that there was not much 'magic' in the budget issue. Callaghan should be looking for possible magic, particularly on the issue of sovereignty, so as to strengthen the case that would be made to the British people.[35]

On 9 December, Wilson flew to Paris for the EEC summit. He was not very well, suffering from some form of cardiac arrhythmia, and his mood was tetchy. He was uncharacteristically rough with his civil service advisers, accusing them of being too biased in favour of the EEC. The meeting the following day ran well into the night. Thanks to Schmidt, who promised Wilson that he would 'fix it', agreement was reached on the outline of a new corrective mechanism for the EEC budget. For the eight Member States, who would accept no exception to the rules of the EEC budget designed for Britain

---

[35] PREM 16/77, TNA.

alone, the face-saving formula was that the new corrective mechanism which would be established would be of general application and would be compatible with the system of Own Resources. At the same time, it would be designed to 'prevent during the period of convergence of the economies of the Member States the possible development of situations unacceptable for a Member State and incompatible with the smooth working of the Community'.[36]

For the eight other member governments, especially the French, it was vital to assert the rule that money raised for the European Community, notably through the levies and duties collected at the frontier with third countries (Own Resources) belonged to the Community. It was also vital to imply that any budgetary corrective would be temporary only. The mechanism had to be seen to be applicable to all in principle even though everyone knew that, in practice, it was designed for Britain alone. This formula was to govern the attitude of the Eight five years later when Margaret Thatcher insisted that what they saw as the Community's money was in fact 'hers' and she wanted it back.

In exchange for the budget formula, Wilson made three significant concessions. He agreed to a communiqué which said that 'the time has come to agree as soon as possible on an overall concept of European Union' and which commissioned the Belgian Prime Minister, Leo Tindemans, to prepare a report on the subject. Along with his fellow leaders, he affirmed that on EMU 'their will has not weakened and that their objective has not changed since the Paris Conference' (of October 1972). Wilson also agreed with the other Heads of Government that 'in order to improve the functioning of the Community they consider that it is necessary to renounce the practice which consists of making agreement on all questions conditional on the unanimous consent of the Member States, whatever their respective positions may be regarding the conclusions reached in Luxembourg on 28 January 1966'.

So Wilson had reaffirmed the commitments to European Union and to EMU made by Heath. And he had given a fair wind to the greater use of majority voting on European legislation while also hinting at a diminution in the force of the Luxembourg Compromise—the very plank on which the government would later make their case to the British people that important national interests could always be safeguarded.

On his return from Paris, Wilson was sarcastically congratulated by Heath on his commitment to EMU, to European Union, and to the renunciation of the Luxembourg Compromise. Wilson was unabashed. He and his fellow leaders had simply agreed to avoid over-use of the veto; European Union

[36] Communiqué of the Paris summit.

was a very desirable objective but meant what anyone wanted it to mean; and EMU was acceptable as a long-term objective. 'There is not a hope in hell—', Wilson told the House, '—I mean the Common Market...of EMU taking place in the near future'.[37]

In the new year of 1975, it looked as if, as in 1972, Britain would be faced by her partners with having to choose between a deal on the budget and a deal on access for New Zealand dairy exports. British officials were clear in their advice to Callaghan: the budget was the important thing to go for. Whatever his private feelings, Callaghan ruled that he would not accept a trade-off. The government must fight for a good outcome on both issues. In doing so, they must be ready to risk a breakdown in the negotiations at the Dublin summit in March.

As the date of the summit approached, Callaghan's assessment of the negotiations was that sufficient progress had been made on immediate agricultural issues, notably a beef regime in line with British interests. More broadly, a new Community trading agreement had been reached with the African, Caribbean, and Pacific (ACP) countries which suited the Commonwealth ACP members. The Community had adopted a liberal negotiating position for the forthcoming wider multilateral trade negotiations. That was as much, Callaghan concluded, as could be achieved on the CAP within the renegotiation. The government's position was also helped by the rise in world agricultural prices which meant lower Community farm subsidies and fewer consumer complaints about the adverse impact of EEC membership on food prices in British shops.

France and Germany were seen in London as the key to success or failure. German attitudes were not clear. Schmidt had contracted pneumonia and had been advised by his doctors not to go to Dublin. In Paris, Giscard's domestic position had strengthened. He had got the Gaullists under control and the Socialist and Communist opposition were divided. According to Britain's Ambassador in Paris, Edward Tomkins, all the signs were that the French would be very impatient of British demands and very obstinate. It was highly likely that the French would indeed seek to be accommodating over New Zealand at the price of being very unaccommodating over the budget. The British were, as was not unusual, in the doghouse with French public opinion and it would do Giscard good domestically to be seen to be defending the integrity of the Common Market 'against', as Tomkins put it, 'the seemingly endless British appetite for concessions and special treatment'.[38]

---

[37] *Hansard*, 16 December 1974, col. 1139.   [38] PREM 16/409, TNA.

The summit was due to start on 10 March 1975. On 6 March, Wilson told Cabinet that, if sufficient progress was made there to bring the renegotiation to an end, he and Callaghan would say no more in Dublin than that negotiations had gone as far as they could and that they would be reporting to Cabinet. On 18 March, Cabinet would review the situation and take a decision.[39] Wilson, Callaghan, and the delegation flew to Dublin by RAF Comet on 10 March.[40] The first day of the summit was difficult and no progress was made. Discussion continued over dinner and it was nearly midnight before the Heads of Government adjourned for coffee and brandy. The next day was Wilson's 59th birthday and, just after midnight, his EEC colleagues treated him to a chorus of 'Happy Birthday'.

Only late on the second day was agreement reached. Continued access to the Community for New Zealand dairy products was assured. There was a much longer wrangle over the corrective mechanism for the budget. Schmidt insisted on a ceiling on any budget rebate of 250 million units of account (roughly the equivalent of the same sum in US dollars). The British had put forward a mechanism which would have made them eligible for a budget rebate. The Germans proposed an alternative formula in which eligibility for a refund was linked to share of GNP and the balance of payments position of the country concerned. Wilson was warned by officials that this formula had been devised by the German Finance Ministry to ensure that the eligibility criteria would never be fulfilled. Wilson took no heed and decided to settle. It may be that he decided that he had secured enough to win the support of Cabinet and country. The officials who were with him believed him to be bored and unmotivated. In any event, the warning given by the officials was correct: Wilson had agreed to a mechanism which would never deliver any benefit to the UK.

If Wilson made a tactical calculation that the time had come to settle, he was probably characteristically shrewd. He reported on the Dublin summit to a mostly uncritical House of Commons. Even the new Leader of the Opposition, Margaret Thatcher, let him off lightly. The Continental Press expressed relief that the year of British blackmail was over. The satirical French newspaper, *Le Canard Enchaîné*, printed a cartoon showing Wilson in bed with the nubile figure of Marianne (France's female equivalent of Uncle Sam). Wilson's head is nestled on her ample bosom and, as the couple make love, Marianne is

---

[39] Cabinet of 6 March 1975, CC (75) 11th Conclusions, CAB 128/56, TNA.
[40] In general, Wilson preferred the turbo-prop Andover on the basis that, the longer he was in the air, the longer he would be free from anyone being able to contact him with fresh problems.

saying to him: '*Entrez ou sortez mon cher Wilson. Mais cessez ce va et vient ridicule*'.[41]

Cabinet, which met over two days to consider the outcome of the renegotiation, would not prove so straightforward. Wilson told his colleagues that he and Callaghan believed that the government's manifesto commitments for the negotiation 'had substantially been met'. Their recommendation was that the UK should remain a member of the EEC. Those members of the Cabinet who opposed membership (Michael Foot, Eric Varley, Peter Shore, John Silkin, Barbara Castle, Willie Ross, and Tony Benn) all spoke. Benn warned his colleagues that Cabinet was 'on the verge of a tragic decision'. By a majority of 16:7, Cabinet voted to accept the terms negotiated.[42] By the time Cabinet voted, public opinion had started to turn in favour of staying in the Community. In February staying in beat leaving by eight points in the opinion polls and that favourable trend must have been in Wilson's mind when, in Dublin, he decided to bring the negotiation to a close.

Since there had already been two General Elections in less than a year, it was clear that the issue would be put to a referendum. The date was set for early June 1975. The question was: 'Do you think the United Kingdom should stay in the European Community?', with boxes on the ballot paper for 'Yes' or 'No'. There were two main campaigning organizations: *Britain in Europe* and the bizarrely named *National Referendum Campaign*, arguing for the UK to leave. Both sides were given broadcasting time and a grant of £125,000 each. They were free to raise additional money themselves. *Britain in Europe* raised £1.3 million; their opponents a mere tenth of that sum. The government set up a Whitehall information unit, a fifteen-person phone bank led by a Foreign Office civil servant, to provide factual information to the public. The idea was criticized in Parliament as a case of government bias but over the weeks it took several hundred enquiries a day without incurring serious complaint.

Each side was allowed to send a campaign document to every household. In addition, the government sent its own—raising the accusation that the remain side had an unfair advantage. In their pamphlet, the government made no mention of the EEC's goals of political and monetary union, even though Heath had publicly signed up to them in 1972 and Wilson had reaffirmed the commitment during the renegotiation. The pamphlet correctly pointed out that the British Parliament retained the final right to repeal the Act which had

---

[41] *Canard Enchainé* of 12 March 1975: 'Come in or go out, my dear Wilson, but stop this ridiculous coming and going.'
[42] Cabinets of 17 and 18 March 1975, CC (75) 14th Conclusions, CAB 128/56, TNA.

taken Britain into the European Community. It said nothing about the fact that, once laws had been made at EEC level (albeit with British involvement in the formulation and approval of those laws) Parliament at Westminster could not change them. The pamphlet (placing heavy weight on the fragile base of the Luxembourg Compromise) also stated that 'no important new policy can be decided in Brussels or anywhere else without the consent of a British Minister answerable to a British Government British Parliament... These decisions can be taken only if all the members of the Council agree. The Minister representing Britain can veto any proposal for a new law or a new tax if he considers it to be against British interests...'[43]

For their part, the anti-campaign claimed that 'the Common Market sets out to merge Britain with France, Germany, Italy and other countries into a single nation', a claim that was widely perceived as absurd. Scare stories about Britons being forced to drink Euro-beer and eat Euro-bread also failed to land.

Wilson had given his divided Cabinet the right to campaign as they chose, even though a majority had approved the recommendation to stay in. So, leading members of the Cabinet were pitched against each other: with Roy Jenkins and Shirley Williams as leaders of *Britain in Europe* and Peter Shore, Tony Benn, Barbara Castle, and Michael Foot prominent on the other side.

By the end of May, the campaign to stay in was 34 points ahead in the opinion polls. The three main Party leaders: Wilson, Thatcher, and Thorpe, were all for staying. So was virtually all of the British Press.

Britain in Europe's leaders had a greater hold on public trust than did their opponents.[44] With the British economy lagging behind that of the other EEC countries, and with the Soviet Union widely seen as a serious threat, safety in numbers ruled the day. Cost of living issues loomed large but world agricultural prices had risen so EEC subsidies, and therefore shop prices, had fallen. The 'housewife', so-called at the time, proved to be more interested in Britain's voice and place in the world and in a secure future for her children.

Growing public support for continued EEC membership did not seep into the nooks and crannies of the Labour Party. The National Executive Committee (NEC) decided to support the 'No' campaign and threatened actively to campaign against the government. Once again, Wilson had to put his leadership on the line to force them to back down, but he could not prevent a one-day special Labour Party conference in London. Wilson knew what the

---

[43] *Britain's New Europe Deal*, PREM 16/407, TNA.
[44] A Harris Poll in April showed the pro-EEC Liberal leader, Jeremy Thorpe, to be the most respected campaigner at +29 while the anti-EEC leader of the Northern Ireland DUP was the least respected, at –59.

outcome would be and arranged for the conference backdrop to be a banner, constantly in view, which read: *Conference Advises—the People Decide.*

The Labour Party delegates voted by a majority of 2:1 against membership. Wilson himself had to intervene again to ensure that the NEC then stuck by their commitment not actively to campaign against their own government. Wilson's stance in the 1975 referendum campaign was quite presidential, but it was not neutral, indifferent, or disengaged. It was Wilson who wrote the foreword to the government's pamphlet that was sent to all electors, setting out clearly that the government were 'recommending to the British people that we should remain a member of the European Community' and 'asking you to vote in favour of remaining in the Community'. Wilson agreed to the establishment of a small informal ministerial campaign committee, under Callaghan's chairmanship, to coordinate the presentation of the government's case on a day-to-day basis. He addressed meetings every evening during the last two weeks of the campaign. He either participated in referendum-related TV interviews, or featured in a related TV news item, on twnty-five occasions, a total only exceeded on the 'pro' side by Roy Jenkins. At the same time, he had to intervene to keep the peace between warring Cabinet members (most notably Benn and Jenkins) who were on opposing sides. He had to be sufficiently above the turmoil to be able to heal the wounds in the Labour Party regardless of the outcome.[45] In the event, on 3 June, on a 64.5 per cent turnout, 67.2 per cent of the British people voted to stay; 32.8 per cent voted to leave. While support in Scotland lagged behind the rest of the UK, only Shetland and the Western Isles voted 'no'.

The outcome of the referendum was acclaimed. Wilson enjoined both Parliament and the country as a whole to follow the government's lead 'in placing past divisions behind us, and in working together to play a full and constructive part in all Community policies and activities'. For the Opposition, Margaret Thatcher, who had campaigned actively, joined 'in rejoicing over this excellent result'. Enoch Powell, one of the few anti-Marketeers who had achieved a marginally positive rating in the Harris Poll, struck a different note. He reminded the House of Commons of the words of the government's campaign pamphlet ('Our continued membership will depend on the continuing assent of Parliament'), adding that 'whether anyone likes the deduction or not...this result can be no more final than that of any single General Election'.[46]

---

[45] Wall, *Official History, Volume II*, pp. 586–8.   [46] *Hansard*, 9 June 1975.

Wilson was not, unlike Heath, a European of the heart. He faced, within his own Party, greater divisions over Europe than Heath had faced in his. But both men came to the same conclusion as to where the national interest lay and sought to have their view accepted by the British public. Wilson, in effect, appealed over the heads of the Labour Party to the British people—and succeeded. But both Heath and Wilson presented an interpretation of what membership entailed that was conditioned by the realities of British politics. As such, it was more an expression of hope for the kind of Community that Britain would find congenial than an accurate rendering of the reality as implied by the EEC Treaties or the true political trend as measured by the attitudes and aspirations of Britain's continental neighbours.

I thought at the time that membership of the EEC would become an established fact. We might grumble about it, as we grumbled about our own government, but it would become part of the accepted fabric of life. It did not take long for the grumbling to turn once again to opposition or for the divergence of view between Britain and her partners to widen.

6

The Years of the Tiger, 1975–1984

With the benefit of hindsight, the verdict of *The Times* on the referendum ('the United Kingdom is in Europe, virtually for good') looks closer to what has happened since than does that of the leading Labour anti-Marketeer, Tony Benn ('I have always said that the referendum would be binding. There can be no going back').[1] In practice, Benn and the other Labour opponents of EEC membership were to return to the charge after the briefest of pauses. But even without the pressure they would bring to bear from within, the freedom of movement of the Labour government was constrained by the more general European scepticism of the Labour Party, by the innate British distrust of institutional change, and by the weakness of the British economy. For the time being, the prospects for the economy were gloomy. Britain had a considerable trade deficit with the rest of the EEC. Unemployment was expected to rise to 1.5 million. Manufacturing productivity was poor, as were industrial relations.

Unsurprisingly, therefore, Callaghan's advice to Wilson, in the aftermath of the referendum victory, was to concentrate on the two areas of European activity where a Labour government could be positive: foreign policy and energy policy, the latter resulting from the discovery and exploitation of large oil resources in the North Sea. But the government recognized that continental pressure for institutional change would not go away. Some of the continental rhetoric around European unity would be just that, but for countries whose frontiers had collapsed like the walls of Jericho in the Second World War, political union represented a real safeguard. At the same time, Chancellor Schmidt was making clear his continued commitment to economic and monetary union. The British knew that EMU might be deferred, but it would not be stopped. As they looked at the problem of Britain's growing financial commitment to the EEC budget, minds began to turn to what conditions the UK could set for allowing progress towards Economic and Monetary Union. One obvious condition was some kind of economic support for countries such as Ireland and Italy which had poor, agricultural economies, and the United Kingdom which needed industrial regeneration.

[1] *The Times*, 7 June 1975.

It would soon fall to Callaghan to lead the country in navigating these issues. On 16 March 1976, Wilson (who was not yet 60) told his surprised Cabinet that he had decided to resign. Only the Queen, Callaghan, and Wilson's closest advisers were in the know. There was ingenious and interminable speculation at the time about Wilson's motives. The Press found it hard to believe that there was not some guilty secret waiting to be exposed. The reality was more banal. Wilson was tired. Of his 31 years in the House of Commons, 30 had been spent on the front bench. He had led the Labour Party for over 13 years, with over 11 years in Cabinet and nearly 8 in Downing Street. He had worked, he told his colleagues, at least 12 to 14 hours a day over a seven-day week. He had had, on average, to read at least 500 different documents each weekend and had undertaken over 100 engagements outside London each year. Wilson promised that once he left Downing Street 'I am not going to speak to the man on the bridge, and I am not going to spit on the deck', a promise to which he adhered.[2]

Three weeks after Wilson's announcement, Callaghan was elected Leader of the Labour Party, beating his nearest rival, Michael Foot, by 176 votes to 137. At 64, Callaghan was older than Wilson. Insofar as he had exhibited scepticism, or even hostility, towards the European project, his stance had been largely tactical. The Dutch Foreign Minister at the time described him as a 'lapsed heretic'. In reality he had never been either a heretic or a true believer. The unity and survival of the Labour Party were his primary concerns. But Callaghan, as Prime Minister, belied his reputation of artful dodger in a three-year, but ultimately unsuccessful, attempt to persuade his party, and the trade union movement on which it depended, to accept essential economic reforms and to come to terms with membership of the European Community.

Callaghan was a more clubbable colleague for his European opposite numbers than Wilson had been. He got on with the French President and was a personal, as well as political, friend of the German Chancellor, Helmut Schmidt. Like Wilson, he attached huge importance to the UK's relationship with the United States. He established a rapport with the Republican President, Gerald Ford, and devoted considerable personal attention to understanding the character and interests of his Democrat successor, Jimmy Carter, elected in 1976. The transatlantic tensions of the Heath period were put aside.

As far as European policy was concerned, Callaghan's tenure was marked by the difficulty of pursuing a positive European policy in the face of Labour Party scepticism, the problematic conduct of Britain's first term as President of

[2] CC (76) 10th Conclusions, 16 March 1976, CAB 128/58, TNA.

the Council in the EEC, the parlous state of the British economy, and Callaghan's unwillingness to join with Schmidt and Giscard d'Estaing in establishing the Exchange Rate Mechanism (ERM), the precursor of economic and monetary union. On top of all that, Callaghan was increasingly preoccupied by the financial burden that the UK would incur when, from 1978 onwards, she would become a full contributor to the EEC budget. Margaret Thatcher is famously remembered for demanding her 'money back', but it was Callaghan who first placed the issue on the agenda of his fellow European leaders.

A government that had convincingly won a referendum on EEC membership might have expected to sail in relatively calm domestic waters on European matters. But the EEC was seen by many in the Labour movement as a right-wing project that risked hindering the natural inclination of a socialist administration to manage its economy through state aids to industry and, if necessary, economic protectionism. Callaghan, and Denis Healey, his Chancellor of the Exchequer, found themselves at loggerheads with their own supporters in the trade union movement and more generally as they fought to control wages, prices, and inflation.

Friction over EEC issues was a constant of the Callaghan years, not least because of controversy within the Labour movement over the commitment of all EEC governments to move to the first direct elections to the European Parliament by mid-1978. Wilson had reserved the government's position pending the outcome of renegotiation but correctly interpreted the referendum result as committing the government to going ahead. But the whole idea of giving democratic legitimacy to a European institution was anathema to many in the Labour Party, compounded by the fact that the electoral arithmetic favoured the Tories and that a clear nod in favour of proportional representation had to be given by the government to the Liberal Party on whose votes they increasingly depended for survival. The issue was a running sore in relations between Britain and her European partners, only finally resolved following the Conservative victory in the 1979 General Election.

Britain's first six-month period as Chair of the Council of Ministers took place in the first half of 1977. Callaghan had chosen as his Foreign Secretary, Tony Crosland, one of the big beasts of the Labour Party, a rival to Callaghan for the leadership and the author of what was then seen as a radical rethinking of the role of the modern Labour Party, a book entitled *The Future of Socialism*. Crosland's first task as chair of the meetings of his fellow EEC foreign ministers was to address the issue of enlargement of the Community to Greece, Portugal, and, soon after, Spain.

Britain, under Thatcher, Major, and Blair, was to become the foremost champion of enlargement and was often suspected by her partners of favouring the widening of the European project in order to dilute it. But when the Labour government of 1976 first addressed the issue, their position was more nuanced. The candidates for membership (Greece, Portugal, and Spain) were all poor countries with agricultural economies that would add to the costs of the CAP. They would also, being poorer than the UK, compete for the very funds for regeneration that the British badly needed. So Callaghan's summing-up of an early Cabinet discussion in 1976 was one in which, he concluded, Cabinet, somewhat reluctantly, accepted that enlargement was inevitable. The government should not seek to hasten it, he said, but nor could they afford politically to seem obstructive. They should therefore move with the main body of Community opinion, neither in the van nor in the rear. Above all, Britain should take a *communautaire* attitude, though what that would mean in practice was not defined.[3]

In practice, not being politically obstructive soon came to mean being rather proactively in favour. All three of the candidate countries were emerging from periods of dictatorship. Both Spain and Portugal had endured long decades of Fascist government. Callaghan, as Foreign Secretary, had been active in giving material support to the Portuguese Socialist leader, Mario Soares, in his ultimately successful efforts to prevent the Communists taking power in Lisbon. It fell to Crosland, in the chair, to steer the Council to a reasonably positive response to the Portuguese application for membership. In this he was helped by overt French reluctance. Giscard was openly favourable to Greek accession, but Portuguese and Spanish entry would potentially create an influx of Mediterranean agricultural products. This in turn would arouse the French farmers whose champion was the Gaullist leader, Jacques Chirac, Giscard's main rival for the votes of the centre and the right.[4]

Before February was out, Crosland was dead, after suffering a stroke which today would probably have been treatable but was then inoperable. He was replaced as Foreign Secretary by his deputy at the Foreign Office, David Owen who, at the age of 38, became the youngest British Foreign Secretary since Anthony Eden. Owen was one of the Labour rebels who had defied their Party's three-line whip in 1971 and voted in favour of British accession to the EEC. Owen had remained something of a rebel, conspiring with Roy Jenkins

---

[3] CM (76) 9th Conclusions, 11 June 1976, CAB 128/59, TNA.
[4] Giscard famously instructed one of the (French) members of the *cabinet* of the Commission President to pass a message to his boss. The message was: '*On ne dit pas non au pays de Platon*' ('You cannot say no to the land of Plato').

to change the leadership of their Party. Owen had been dismayed, after a late night of plotting against his leader in 1968, to get a summons to see Wilson in Downing Street. He expected a carpeting. Instead, Wilson invited him to become Navy Minister in the Ministry of Defence. 'But, Prime Minister', Owen protested, 'I am one of your fiercest opponents'. 'Not any more you're not', Wilson replied.[5]

Callaghan's choice of Owen for Foreign Secretary reflected the fact that he was a fast-rising star. It was also partly done because the obvious senior candidate, Denis Healey, could not be spared from the Treasury and because all Prime Ministers like to be able to surprise the Press and public. Owen had given proof of his political skill as Health Minister and had the European experience the government needed in its EEC Presidency. Callaghan rightly thought that a young radical would be a shot in the arm for the Party and for the government. He had rather an avuncular relationship with his protégé and Owen (in his radical new policy towards the fraught issue of Rhodesia and majority rule) was to break the mould of convention and, in so doing, sow something of a whirlwind which shook the corridors of Foreign Office convention but exhilarated those of us who worked closely for him. During my career, I worked at close quarters with five Foreign Secretaries and three Prime Ministers. David Owen was not the easiest to work for but was the most original, exciting, and inspiring.

In their role as Presidency of the EEC, both Callaghan and Owen sought to provide effective and impartial chairmanship of the EEC meetings over which they presided. The same was not true of all British Ministers, some of whom imported their anti-European sentiments into the meetings and were thought by Britain's partners to have abused the role of the chair to try to favour British policy interests. At the end of the British Presidency, the German view of it was summed up by Britain's Ambassador in Bonn. The most precise description Sir Oliver Wright could come up with to characterize the German reaction to Britain's conduct was 'Good Riddance'. In German eyes, the British approach to a Community, which depended on give and take, was to take as much, and give as little, as possible. Some British Ministers had exhibited the opposite of the 'fair play' for which Britain was supposedly renowned. The Germans had come to believe that British Ministers had used their chairmanships, not to seek agreements, but to fuel anti-European sentiment at home.[6]

That anti-European sentiment was writ large in papers on Europe written at the time by the NEC of the Labour Party. Some of them were so negative,

⁵ Speech by Lord Owen, 2016.   ⁶ PREM 16/1625, TNA.

Callaghan told a special meeting of Cabinet in July, as to suggest that the ultimate objective of the Labour Party should be to leave the EEC altogether. At the request of Number 10, David Owen had written a paper on Britain's European strategy and had worked on it closely with Callaghan's own advisers. Owen recommended a positive, confederal approach to EEC membership, using both the institutional Treaty-based procedures and intergovernmental cooperation. This would give the Labour government a distinct stance before the next General Election.

Owen presented his paper at the Cabinet meeting. There were clear divisions of view. Some Cabinet members thought the NEC had been right to argue for the recovery of the sovereignty that had been transferred to the European Community. At the same time, the UK should use its best endeavours to align UK policies with those of a more loosely based Community. Others argued that the government must recognize that pure nationalism was unworkable. If the Labour Party failed in the superhuman task of achieving common ground between the NEC and the government before the next election, then there would be a violent spasm which would both lose the election and split the Party.

Callaghan summed up the meeting by recognizing that there were divisions within Cabinet that some felt were too wide to be bridged. But Cabinet had at least agreed that an effort must be made. It was clear that if the Labour movement decided to leave Europe then some ministers would leave both the government and the Party. The Cabinet must find ways of preventing that.[7]

Callaghan himself attempted to bridge the gap in a letter of September 1977 to Ron Hayward, the Secretary General of the Labour Party. Callaghan opened by arguing that, in measuring dissatisfaction with the EEC, insufficient weight was given to the coincidence of British accession with a five-fold increase in oil prices and the worst world recession in forty years. The solution to those aspects of EEC policies which did not work for Britain did not lie in leaving, but in reforming and changing the EEC from within. A British-led reform programme would include maintaining the authority of national governments and parliaments; democratic control of EEC business; common policies that recognized the need for national governments to attain their economic industrial and regional objectives; reform of the CAP; the development of a Community energy policy compatible with national interests; and enlargement. Callaghan claimed that the course he was proposing would 'enable a

---

[7] PREM 16/1639, TNA.

united Labour movement to offer the British people a programme of radical reform within an evolving European Community'. In advocating enlargement, Callaghan referred to the role the EEC could play in supporting democracy in the candidate countries, adding that 'the dangers which some foresee of an over-centralised, over-bureaucratised and over-harmonised Community will be far less with twelve Member States than with nine'.[8]

Callaghan's letter was widely publicized in the UK. In domestic terms, it was a skilful attempt to reconcile the Labour Party to EEC membership. In continental Europe, the letter provoked dismay. It looked like the manifesto of a government with no wholehearted commitment to the European project, minimalist in its ambitions and wanting to use enlargement to dilute the European project. Even when the letter's rationale was explained to other EEC colleagues, and they understood its motives, they nonetheless saw a government still struggling to come to terms with the realities and aspirations of the European project as other Member States conceived them. The incident passed but it exemplified an enduring aspect of the way successive British governments, Labour and Conservative, felt obliged to manage and present their European policies. Instead of giving a positive message of shared ambition and success they treated 'Europe' as a problem to be solved: the EEC was flawed but it could be reformed; Britain could and would stop the undesirable things that others wanted; 'Europe' might not be great but being outside would be worse. Quite often, under successive governments, the British conveyed the impression that they knew better than their EEC partners where the interests of those same partners lay.

It was in part because of the difficult domestic politics surrounding the EEC that Callaghan passed up what, as things turned out, was probably the last opportunity for the United Kingdom to form a privileged relationship with France and Germany as joint leaders of the Community.

EMU had not faded from the agenda. Indeed, it had found a new champion. Before his departure from office, Wilson had dangled in front of Roy Jenkins the prospect of being nominated as Britain's senior Commissioner in Brussels and of becoming Commission President. Jenkins was tempted. Had Callaghan, on becoming Prime Minister, offered Jenkins the Foreign Office, Jenkins would probably have accepted. But Callaghan did not make the offer. He and Callaghan were longstanding rivals. Jenkins was the leading Labour pro-European. He and Callaghan had both held the office of Home Secretary and Chancellor, and Jenkins had done so with a flair and distinction that Callaghan

---

[8] PREM 16/1630, TNA.

lacked. So, Jenkins had gone to Brussels as Britain's first, and only, Commission President.

In October 1977, Jenkins made a speech advancing the case for a great leap forward to full-scale monetary union. The speech was enthusiastically received in Italy and the smaller Member States and given a positive response by France and Germany. Jenkins' ideas were some years away from realization but an initiative for an Exchange Rate Mechanism (ERM), the precursor of the single currency, was soon to take shape in the mind of Helmut Schmidt.

Callaghan and Schmidt met in Bonn in March 1978. Schmidt was due to host a G7 summit in Bonn later in the year. Schmidt, naturally pessimistic and no great admirer of the US President, Jimmy Carter, was increasingly gloomy about achieving any transatlantic meeting of minds about the management of the global economy. Callaghan, by contrast, was determined 'not . . . to sit back and let the free world economies drift downwards' and had developed a five-point plan for a series of economic measures to be taken by different countries in different fields which, together, would form a package to be agreed at the Bonn meeting. The plan was very much of Callaghan's making, was valuable of itself, would help cement Anglo-US relations, and demonstrate both domestically and internationally that the British Labour government was an effective operator. Against this background, it is not surprising that Callaghan did not at first appreciate the full significance of what Schmidt called 'an exotic idea' which he outlined to Callaghan when the two met in Bonn. Schmidt would not, he said, go as far as Roy Jenkins wanted on EMU but he intended to propose that the Federal Republic of Germany (FRG) and certain other members of the Community should each put half their reserves into a new pool, the currencies of which would be fixed against a European Unit of Account. The Unit of Account would be the currency which operated vis-à-vis the dollar, and would be the sole unit of intervention. Countries in difficulties could borrow from the pool. Schmidt added that he intended to involve Giscard. But he had thus far told no one else (not even his own Finance Minister) and he asked Callaghan to treat the matter with similar secrecy.

Callaghan responded that he did not have the technical knowledge to respond immediately. On his return to London, he consulted a very small group of advisers. In the meantime, Giscard had been approached by Schmidt and, seeing its political significance, and against the advice of his own advisers, had enthusiastically signed up for the scheme. On the British side, there were divided views. John Hunt, the Cabinet Secretary, saw the danger of a two-tier Community if some Member States were in, and some outside, the scheme. Treasury advice was cautious and matched Callaghan's instinctive reservations. When Callaghan and his senior advisers met Schmidt in late April, Callaghan pointed out that, were the UK to join, it would have to do so at a lower exchange rate than the existing one since, given her trading position, the UK could not afford to commit to an uncompetitive rate. Within a year of a General Election, it was not politically feasible to tell the electorate that the government had taken the country back into the 'snake' with a 20 per cent devaluation. The Chancellor of the Exchequer, Denis Healey, added that a 1 per cent fall in the effective rate of the pound against the proposed basket of currencies would lead to a half per cent increase in the price index.

Callaghan's scepticism, which was briefed to the Press, soon cast him in the role of chief critic of Schmidt's scheme. It quickly became a Franco-German initiative which Britain was still free to join but not to influence. The risk that the UK's self-imposed exclusion would damage her standing in what might become a two-tier Community was understood in Whitehall but the parlous state of the British economy, and the state of Labour Party and public opinion, dictated the decision not to join. Callaghan pressed his fellow European leaders to undertake what he called parallel studies to determine the action needed to ensure greater economic convergence between the stronger and weaker member countries but, while the studies were commissioned, it soon became clear that France and Germany were only willing to contemplate practical economic help to Ireland and Italy, who were committed to joining the ERM, and not to the UK.

From the Opposition benches, Margaret Thatcher criticized Labour for putting Britain, which had been the victor in Europe, into the second division of European countries. But she was careful to make no commitment on behalf of a future Conservative government and her criticisms of the government were ones of tactics, not economic substance, and gave little indication of her own views which, both then and later, were very cautious on ERM membership.

In the end, in order to have a say in the policy debates around the scheme and its future evolution, the government made a deal with its partners: it would agree to the scheme going ahead within the institutional machinery of the Community provided Britain could be in the European Monetary System (EMS) but not the ERM. So, Britain could have a say in the operation of the scheme while being out of the ERM which was the scheme's whole *raison d'être*.

The fact that Callaghan took the decision he did was probably an inevitable one given the economic and political realities of the time. It was nonetheless a fateful decision in that the collaboration between Schmidt and Giscard, in leading and shaping the scheme, cemented the habit of Franco-German leadership of the EEC more generally. Other opportunities for Britain were to arise but successor British governments faced similar pressures and constraints to those that influenced Callaghan, with similar consequences.

Callaghan, as it happened, had more immediately pressing European worries. With the expiry of the post-accession transition period in which contributions were phased in, the excessive budget contribution, which the Heath and Wilson governments had always feared, was about to hit Britain. When Callaghan raised the issue with him, Schmidt was astonished to learn that Britain was already the second highest contributor to the EEC budget, with only Germany paying more. It was against this background that Callaghan had sought an agreement on resource transfers from the wealthier Member States as a condition of British participation in the ERM. His request had fallen on stony ground.

What the British had by then realized was that the budget problem needed to be approached from two angles: expenditure on the CAP (of very little benefit to the UK) needed to be decreased and expenditure on regional development (potentially of considerable value to the UK) needed to be introduced and increased. But even that would not be enough. Britain's gross contribution to the budget was too big to be alleviated by overall expenditure cuts and by increased expenditure in the UK. The problem needed to be solved on the revenue side of the budget as well.

The obvious way to achieve some alleviation of the British budget contribution on the revenue side of the budget was by modifying the Financial Mechanism agreed at the Dublin summit in 1975 so as to make it actually deliver a benefit to the United Kingdom. At the heart of the mechanism lay the principle that where a country with below average GNP made contributions to the EEC budget that were excessive in relation to its ability to pay as measured by its share of GNP, that country should have part of its contribution reimbursed. The mechanism was not due to be reviewed until 1981 but the British thought that the prospective enlargement of the EEC might provide an opening.

Callaghan used one of the big set-piece occasions of his calendar (the Lord Mayor's banquet at the Guildhall on 13 November 1978) to fire the first salvo in what was to become a six-year war between the UK and her European partners. The lack of equity in the EEC's finances must, Callaghan told his audience, be faced squarely in the interests of the Community as a whole. He was not, he said, arguing that every Member State must benefit equally from each and every Community policy. But the outcome of the Community's policies, taken as a whole, should reflect a balance which was satisfactory to all EEC members, not just some. Before Britain's accession, both the European Commission and the Member States had indicated that the balance of EEC spending would shift from agriculture to industrial and regional priorities. But that promised shift had not happened. The predominance of expenditure on the CAP meant that some of the wealthiest countries of the Community were also those who got the biggest share of Community spending. 'We cannot accept', Callaghan concluded, 'that Britain should become the largest net contributor to the Community Budget. If this situation were to remain uncorrected, it would do long-term damage to the Community as a whole as well as to Britain.'[9]

When Callaghan discussed the issue with the Cabinet Secretary in February 1979, Hunt told him that all the devices to achieve savings that officials had worked out would bring savings of only £400 million out of the £900 million total of the British annual net contribution. Hunt and Callaghan recognized that an opportunity for redress would occur at some time in the early 1980s because the Community's expenditure would bump up against the permitted ceiling of its so-called Own Resources. The ceiling could only be raised with the unanimous consent of the Member Governments, so Britain would have a veto and therefore a lever. But Callaghan doubted whether public opinion in the UK would wait that long. At some stage, the Community would have to be told in clear terms that the UK was not prepared to tolerate a situation in which countries with a below average GDP could be net contributors to the budget. Callaghan favoured a two-pronged approach. At the March European Council, he would focus on reducing CAP costs and, at the June meeting, he would concentrate on the budget.[10]

One of the debates at the March European Council in Paris was on the economic and social situation in the EEC. Callaghan used his intervention to highlight the wasteful use of resources in the CAP; the failure to develop policies to deal with unemployment and social problems in industrial areas; the Community's inability to meet its own objective of economic convergence; and, in Britain's case, 'the unacceptable position that is approaching when we become by far the largest net contributor to the Community's financial resources'. Callaghan's answer to the question whether the EEC's spending priorities were right, was that they were not. He set out his argument. The CAP absorbed 76 per cent of the budget. Two decades previously European agriculture had been relatively depressed. But it was not agriculture that was now

[9] PREM 16/2041, TNA.   [10] PREM 16/2036, TNA.

in crisis. The evils which now commanded the attention of European leaders were those of industrial unemployment and restructuring and the decline of the urban environment. But resources could not be spent on addressing those problems when 40 per cent of the budget went on storing food that the EEC did not need and then selling it to other countries at a loss. The butter surplus cost over £50 million a year to buy and store. There was 20 per cent over-production of sugar in the EEC, although other countries could produce it more cheaply. But the export earnings of poorer countries which depended on sugar exports were reduced because of the Community's policy of selling its surplus sugar at a loss on world markets, thus depressing world prices. And then, when the EEC had undercut the earnings of poorer countries, it offered them financial aid! In three or four years, the Community would be unable to waste money in that way because it would have hit its financial ceiling. Some Member States (by implication the UK) would be unwilling to see an increase in the ceiling when money was simply financing waste. 'Today', Callaghan continued,

'we are the second largest net contributor to the Community. By 1980, Britain will be the largest net contributor to the Community. This is not a tolerable situation when our net contributions are measured against our national income. I must earnestly and urgently ask the Community to face up to this problem ... The purpose of the European Community Treaty is to ensure harmonious development by reducing the differences between vari-ous regions and countries. That means convergence of our economies. The present financial arrangements are more likely to encourage them to grow further apart ... The overseas expenditure which has grown fastest ... is our financial contribution to the Community. We cannot accept that we should become, by a substantial sum, the largest net contributor to the Community Budget ...'[11]

For Callaghan, this powerful intervention was to be his European swan song. On 28 March, his government was defeated in the House of Commons by one vote in a confidence vote. A General Election was called. The winter of 1978/79 had been that of the now infamous 'winter of discontent', in which the Labour government's efforts to curb wage increases and thence inflation were defeated by the trade unions who formed the bedrock of Labour's support. Inflation as high as 17 percent and industrial disputes which left rubbish

[11] PREM 16/2943, TNA.

uncollected in the streets and bodies waiting for cremation or burial, dealt a mortal blow to the Callaghan government. His avuncularity looked like complacency. A party divided over economic, defence, and European policy was at the mercy of Margaret Thatcher: a revolution was needed and she would lead it.

Callaghan, like Wilson, was a European of the head, rather than the heart. In January 1978, Callaghan had asked Prime Minister Karamanlis of Greece what advantages he saw in the accession to the EEC for which he was pressing. Karamanlis replied that, by its history, its culture, and in many other ways, Greece was part of the European family. Membership would remove the temptation of dictatorship from which Greece had only recently emerged and would motivate the Greek people to exert themselves to catch up with the rest of the continent. In reply, Callaghan said that the EEC aroused no such emotions in the UK. The economic arguments were finely balanced and, while he himself accepted the political case for membership, the British people did not. Closer ties with India were more credible to the British than were close ties with Europe.[12]

The Labour Party in Opposition was soon to be riven on the subject of Europe and to become, for several years, openly in favour of leaving the Community. That made it easier for the Conservative government of Margaret Thatcher to present itself as the Party of Europe. But the reality was to be different. Margaret Thatcher would wage war on her European partners with a vehemence which would leave lasting scars on them and on the British body politic, opening up a fissure within her own Party and in the country whose tremors shake us still.

At the time of the General Election, I was working as a Private Secretary in the Foreign Secretary's office. One of the senior Private Secretaries working on foreign policy for the Prime Minister in 10 Downing Street was always a high-flyer from the FCO. In April 1979, it was Bryan Cartledge, a future Ambassador to the Soviet Union. A telephone hotline linked the two private offices and a red light shone on desks when one side of Downing Street called the other. The FCO secondee to Number 10 was the sole in-house foreign policy adviser to the Prime Minister and depended on the resources of the FCO to provide facts, advice, briefing, draft speeches, etc. We were in constant touch. One day, very soon after Mrs Thatcher's arrival in Downing Street, I picked up the hot-line phone to speak to Bryan. A female voice answered: 'What do you want?' With a presence of mind which can only have been born

---

[12] PREM 16/1624, TNA.

of complete panic I apparently said 'Oh, I'm very glad to have got you Prime Minister because I shall get an answer more quickly'. And, though I cannot recall what I wanted, I did indeed get the answer.

Thus was I exposed to the relatively soft breeze of what was otherwise a whirlwind which swept through Whitehall. The Iron Lady was not of course an unknown quantity. As 'Thatcher the milk snatcher' she had borne the unpopularity of the Heath government's decision to abolish free school milk, a health boost for post-war schoolchildren so revolting that to this day I cannot drink milk on its own. She was known to be firm-minded. But the public perception of Mrs Thatcher was tinged with a degree of patronizing and misogynistic amusement at her grocer's shop origins, her carefully elocuted accent, and her over-styled hair and clothes. Few in Whitehall, or her own Cabinet, were prepared for her single-minded determination, her instinctive challenge to conventional wisdom, and her unmatched directness in expressing her views.

A typical example is her comments on an early minute on fisheries policy from the new Foreign Secretary, Lord Carrington. Britain was at loggerheads with her European partners over the Common Fisheries Policy, an issue which the new government had inherited from its predecessor. Carrington had discussed the issue with the Minister of Agriculture and Fisheries, Peter Walker, and wrote to the Prime Minister to recommend the course of action the two men had agreed. Under previous Prime Ministers they might have expected some queries, perhaps the odd suggested change or, at the outside, a polite request to meet to address more serious concerns. That was not Thatcher's way. She planted her flag and took a stance. These are extracts from Carrington's minute, together with her marginalia:

"We agreed that our negotiating leverage on this issue is likely only to deteriorate as time goes by" [MT: "No"];
"I therefore firmly endorse Peter Walker's recommendation that we should seek a settlement of the CFP within the next few months". [MT: "No"];
"If you can agree to an approach along the lines of Peter Walker's minute [MT: "No"], I would propose that he gives Mr Gundelach [the EEC Commissioner responsible for Fisheries] an indication of the way we are thinking". [MT: "No"];
"We must remember our pledges" [MT: "Yes, they are contrary to everything in this minute"].[13]

13 PREM 19/233, TNA.

Like Heath before her, Thatcher represented a break with the Conservative Party's patrician, public school past. Unlike Heath and her other predecessors, she was not a natural seeker of consensus. She moved the Conservative Party to the right and succeeded in making that the centre ground of British politics in part because of Labour's swing to the left once Callaghan had left its leadership. She was socially illiberal and Section 28 of the Local Government Act haunts her reputation to this day for its demonization of homosexual people. She came to office with virtually no overseas experience. She had no natural sympathy for the African liberation movements of South Africa and Zimbabwe (then Rhodesia). She forbade any ministerial contact with Nelson Mandela's ANC, regarding it as a terrorist organization. She had no real understanding of the motivating power of the ideals which underpinned the European Community and she treated concepts such as European Union as if they were the dangerous products of romantic wishful thinking.

Mrs Thatcher's attitudes to the European Community went through different stages during her eleven-year occupancy of Downing Street, and beyond. She had been a teenager in the Second World War and the Anglo-American relationship was for her closer and more robust than any European relationship. She formed no close political relationship with any other European leader. Giscard d'Estaing patronized her intolerably and she disliked him intensely. With Giscard's successor, François Mitterrand, she got on better but she shared the general Whitehall suspicion of French motives. She liked the German socialist, Helmut Schmidt, who spoke excellent English and whose economic policies were much closer to hers than they had been to those of the Labour government. Schmidt's Conservative successor, Helmut Kohl, might have been a natural ally, especially on economic matters after Mitterrand took French economic policy in a direction of which both the British and German governments disapproved. But there was no mutual empathy. Her comment to Charles Powell, her Foreign Office Private Secretary, that Kohl 'is very German, isn't he?' was not just an observation but a clear signal of her limited view of the relationship as a whole. Britain came to envy, and complain about, the Franco-German relationship as the motor of Europe. But personal and political attitudes on the English side of the Channel under the Wilson, Callaghan, and Thatcher governments were in large part to blame for driving France and Germany into each other's embrace.

Thatcher, as Leader of the Opposition, had campaigned vigorously for the UK to stay in the EEC. Yet Callaghan had been warned that he must watch his own Eurosceptic flank because she was also flirting with the anti-European wing in her own Party. Sir Michael Butler, then the senior FCO official working on European matters, and someone whom she held in high regard, recalled to me how, on an early visit to Rome after her election as Prime Minister, she had sat, whisky in hand in the British Ambassador's house in Rome, railing against the failings of the Community. Not only did she not understand the political importance of European Union to her partners, she made no tactical accommodations to it. She understood, and believed in, the importance of the EEC as an instrument of peace and prosperity and as a bastion of democracy when half of Europe was under Soviet tyranny. But, for her, integration meant practical steps towards economic liberalization and a degree of foreign policy cooperation, provided that they were led and conducted by national governments.

The first five years of Thatcher's premiership were consumed by arguments with Britain's partners over the future of the Common Fisheries Policy, the CAP, and, above all, Britain's budgetary contribution. Thatcher started as she meant to continue. After the almost constant tension between the Wilson and Callaghan governments and the other EEC governments, Whitehall civil servants were expecting fairer weather under the Conservatives. The signs that, instead, Whitehall was facing what senior FCO official John Fretwell later called 'a tiger unleashed' were not long in coming. Advised by John Hunt that Helmut Schmidt's forthcoming visit within days of the election was but one example of a well-established pattern of two bilateral meetings a year with each of France and Germany, she countered that there were too many such meetings. She declined the opportunity to attend the signature of the Greek Accession Treaty. She was quickly clear in directing that the budget situation was unfair and unjust and must be remedied fast: the calculation of budgetary contributions should be directly related to a country's GDP.

Despite her reservations, Thatcher's first overseas visitor was Schmidt. At a dinner in his honour, she described what she called her own European philosophy. It was, she said, 'founded in the belief that the variety of our distinct nation states, which we must always cherish, is enriched by a common purpose; that the view of free Europe is stronger when we pursue our ideals together'. She went on to describe what that meant: the offer of peace, prosperity, liberty, and democracy to all within the Community; a Europe in which freedom meant also free enterprise, fair competition, and the chance for every citizen to take his own decisions and to develop his own talents.

There was nothing in this to which Schmidt could not subscribe but it was a far cry from the German aspirations of a genuine political union in which the relationship between the Union (as represented by its institutions) and the Member States would be increasingly federal. Of course, each Member State had a vested national interest in their vision of Europe's future. For the smaller Member States, a European Union with a strong supranational centre was a protection against the resurgence of a nationalist Germany. For Italy, it was easier to have faith in strong European institutions than in its own national democratic structures. As for Germany, I do not believe that we in Whitehall really understood in the early 1980s the full import of Germany's championing of European political union. At the time, all western governments paid lip service to the goal of German reunification. But virtually no one predicted the death of the Soviet empire that was in fact to occur at the end of the 1980s and which allowed reunification to happen. Few thought that German unification would happen in their lifetimes. The private view of the British and French governments was that German unification was to be feared rather than hoped for: a resurgent, dominant Germany was seen as an economic threat and a political risk. For Germany, and especially for Schmidt's successor, Helmut Kohl, by contrast, the goal of reunification was a potent aspiration. So, when German leaders spoke of European Union, they did so because they recognized the fears (in both West and East) that reunification would provoke. Kohl also feared that a reunified Germany which was not anchored firmly in the West could be tempted into a dangerous neutrality. The only safe space in which German reunification could happen, therefore, was that of a European Union with strong, powerful institutions which would contain and even constrain those of the nation state. So when German Chancellors proclaimed the goal of European Union, we in Britain thought of it as a misguided idealism and did not link German EEC policy as closely as we should have to their aspirations for reunification.

Even had we done so, however, a correct analysis would almost certainly not have made the Thatcher government any more sympathetic to German policy. When German reunification did become an imminent reality, Margaret Thatcher, alone among Western leaders, opposed it and only came to terms with it once it was an accomplished fact.

Asked at his joint Press conference with her whether he had found Mrs Thatcher more conciliatory than Callaghan, Schmidt could only respond: 'fairly conciliatory'. The German Press accurately commented that the two leaders had talked past each other, albeit cordially. Schmidt himself was quoted as saying that he detected no change in basic British attitudes.[14]

In arguing the British case on the EEC budget, Thatcher had to persuade her partners that Britain had a case to make, namely that the issue had not been

---

[14] PREM 19/53 and 58, TNA.

adequately dealt with in the renegotiation; that, in reopening it, Britain was not asking to get back precisely what it put in (the so-called '*juste retour*'); and, above all, that the UK's partners should pay more so that the UK could pay less. Mrs Thatcher went about the task with characteristic vigour and persistence. She was not one to sweeten any pill or to mince words or to spare the sensibilities of others. She had already shocked her new Foreign Secretary, Lord Carrington, and his deputy in the House of Commons (also a Cabinet minister), Ian Gilmour, by telling them that 'she was prepared to take the fisheries issue down to the roots of the UK's membership of the EEC'. Now, at her first European Council, in Strasbourg in June, her first intervention was, according to Commission President Roy Jenkins, 'quite good'. But when she opened up on the budget 'she immediately became shrill, and even more so in her quickly following second intervention'. She managed to get into an argument with Schmidt, on whose support she would depend to get anywhere with the French. When she made to intervene for a third time, Jenkins wisely and helpfully cut her off, and proposed that the Commission should make a study of the facts and propose remedies. This was agreed.[15]

By the autumn, Thatcher was in full cry, with visits planned to several European capitals prior to the next European summit in Dublin at the end of November. She was also looking at ways with which to strengthen her leverage, asking Carrington for a paper on 'the threats which could, if necessary, be used to get our way. This will cover, not just ways of turning off the tap [of money] (where the Chancellor of the Exchequer [Geoffrey Howe] is already looking at the legalities) but the range of possibilities for blocking progress in other areas of Community activities (new expenditure, CAP prices and the 1% VAT ceiling etc.)'.[16]

The effect this was having on one of the UK's oldest friends, Helmut Schmidt, was vividly voiced in a private conversation between Schmidt and Britain's Ambassador in Bonn, Oliver Wright, in September. The Wrights had invited Schmidt to dinner in honour of the sculptor Henry Moore, who had lent one of his works on long-term display to the Chancellor's office. Sitting with Wright on a sofa, Schmidt reflected on how the British trade unions had brought down Heath and then Callaghan. How Mrs Thatcher dealt with them would be decisive and he wanted her to succeed. She had made a very good start and he admired her for it. The remedy lay in Britain's hands and it would take Mrs Thatcher ten years to achieve all she needed.

[15] Roy Jenkins, *European Diary 1977–1981* (London: William Collins, 1989).
[16] PREM 19/54, TNA.

Schmidt then turned to the issue of the EEC budget and of Britain's contribution to it. He quite understood the British position: the situation needed a remedy. But the British government should at all costs avoid giving the impression that it was engaged in a second renegotiation. Britain's performance, in the seven years since she had joined the Community, had disappointed all her friends, including those closest to the UK, the Dutch. He, and, he thought, all Britain's partners, had looked forward to Britain's entry to give a new impulse and sense of direction to the Community, and a new political dimension. But what had happened? The UK had given little or no such impetus. It had no vision of what it wanted the Community to be. Instead, the British had spent six years or more haggling like Italians for a little bit here and a little bit there. This was no way for a country like Britain to act. What if Britain's contribution did amount to £1 billion? No one could convince him that this was a make or break sum and that Britain would be sunk if she did not get it. Compared with the UK's real problems, the issue was insignificant. And, compared with the real problems facing Europe and the world, it was a distraction. Where was the UK's sense of pride? Wherever one looked in the Community, Schmidt continued, it was not Britain who had used her wisdom and experience to point in a new direction or come up with answers to European or world problems. The UK seemed to have lost confidence in itself and to have turned inward on itself. Schmidt cited Britain's half-in-half-out attitude to the EMS as a good example of Britain putting herself on the sidelines of the Community and, in so doing, making her partners indifferent to whether she stayed in or left. Now, with a second renegotiation on the budget, even a new Conservative administration, on which so many hopes had been placed, was in danger of following the old negative paths. It was a dreadful thing to observe Britain uncommitted, unsure of itself, depriving itself of the opportunity of shaping events. But events would happen and would shape themselves without Britain. A big psychological heave was needed to get the UK out of its state of introspection.[17]

Mrs Thatcher would certainly have seen the report of Schmidt's views and he in any case reverted to them when the two met at the end of October. At that meeting, they again talked past each other. Schmidt urged Thatcher to avoid a clash with France. When the Commission had reported on the budget problem, France, Britain, and Germany should get together to solve it. Britain had a legitimate grievance. A solution must be found, but its handling and presentation were crucial. For Thatcher, it was simple: in the end, the problem

[17] PREM 19/762, TNA.

came down to finding the money. Those who were getting it at present would want to go on getting it. She would look closely at the legal position in regard to unilaterally withholding the UK budget contribution. Schmidt, somewhat wearily, urged her to look at the various means which might be used to help solve the issue.[18]

Thatcher, 'the tiger unleashed' of John Fretwell's description, landed with a snarl at the Dublin summit in November 1979. The advice Thatcher was getting both from Roy Jenkins, as Commission President, and from Christopher Soames, a former European Commissioner and now a member of her Cabinet, was that she could expect to make some progress at Dublin but not to settle the issue. That was not her way. According to Ian Gilmour, Carrington's Foreign Office deputy in the House of Commons, 'she lived down to all Peter Carrington's worst fears. After giving a shrill exposition of the British case ("I am not asking for anybody else's money, I just want my money back") at the first afternoon session of the Council, she again harangued her colleagues for almost the whole of a working dinner which took some four hours. Schmidt feigned sleep. Giscard sat back contentedly watching her weaken her own position, and the others became increasingly unconvinced of the validity of the British case.'

A breakdown loomed and, once again, Roy Jenkins rode to the rescue with a proposed postponement to the next summit. Through gritted teeth, Thatcher agreed to approach the next meeting in a spirit of compromise. But in the months before the next summit in Luxembourg in April 1980, there was no meeting of minds. At the summit itself, the eight other EEC members put forward a proposal for a rebate for Britain over a two- or three-year period, but the amounts were not enough to satisfy Thatcher and she had anyway decided that she would not be bought off by short-term palliatives: there had to be a solution that dealt with the problem for as long as the problem itself lasted.

The meeting ended in acrimonious failure and Giscard and Schmidt were adamant that they would not discuss the issue again at the next European Council meeting in Venice. Carrington and Gilmour were given a mandate to try to find a way through. They did so, at what became a mammoth eighteen-hour session of the Council of Foreign Ministers, ending in the early hours of 30 May. The two Ministers secured a three-year agreement: not as much as the British wanted but a better offer than had been on the table in Luxembourg.

Carrington and Gilmour arrived, sleepless and exhausted, at Chequers to report to the Prime Minister. Ian Gilmour recounted their reception in his

---

[18] PREM 19/55, TNA.

memoirs. 'Had we been bailiffs arriving to take possession of the furniture, or even Ted Heath paying a social call in company with Jacques Delors [a future Commission President who became Thatcher's *bête noire*], we would probably have been more cordially received', he recalled. Thatcher berated the two senior Ministers for failing to defend British interests. She was in the middle of a seminar and commuted between the seminar room and the room in which Carrington and Gilmour were seated, returning only to denounce them more vehemently. They were offered nothing to eat or drink. Both men offered to resign. No, said the Prime Minister, she would resign. Gilmour reckoned that there was in all between two and two and a half hours of 'an interminable barrage of irrelevance' from Thatcher as she harangued them 'like a firework whose fuse has been lit'. One of those present at Chequers was a Treasury official named Rachel Lomax. Gilmour assumed she was there 'to ensure that the wet Foreign Office was seen off by the dry Thatcherites'. But Lomax proved to be something of an ally, politely pointing out to the Prime Minister where she had failed to understand aspects of the agreement.

Gilmour's conclusion from the episode was that Thatcher's objection 'was to the fact of the agreement, not to its terms. This was not because we had succeeded where she had failed. It was because, to her, the grievance was more valuable than its removal.'[19] Throughout the period of the fraught negotiation between the British government and its partners, Thatcher's Press Secretary, Bernard Ingham, played up the drama of the confrontation. The government were waging an unpopular battle for economic reform at home. Inflation remained stubbornly high and unemployment had increased. Much of the economic establishment in Britain thought the government were pursuing a policy doomed to fail. The government's popularity was low. A number of Thatcher's more traditionally Conservative Ministers were waiting for her to fail. It suited Thatcher to have the EEC as a whipping boy and it has to be said that Britain's partners, even without being goaded by Thatcher's intemperance, fell all too readily into the role. They too had their own economic difficulties and every one of them had a vested national interest in resisting the British case. Her tactics and language made it easier for them to wrap in the flag of European principle and virtuous solidarity what was in fact an entirely self-interested reluctance to pay more so that Britain could pay less.

Carrington and Gilmour's deal carried the day. They secured the approval of Geoffrey Howe, the Chancellor, and beat Ingham at his own game by pre-

---

[19] Ian Gilmour, *Dancing with Dogma: Britain under Thatcherism* (London: Simon & Schuster, 1992).

emptively briefing the British Press that the deal they had secured represented a major triumph for the Prime Minister. When Cabinet discussed the deal there was an overwhelming majority in favour of settling rather than facing what some called 'a new and dangerous situation...[with] profound consequences at least for our membership of the Community and perhaps for the future of the Community itself'.[20]

Roy Jenkins, who had little personal animus against the Prime Minister, and indeed found some aspects of her character such as her lack of pomposity or stuffiness attractive, nonetheless concluded that the new settlement was only cosmetically different from the one Thatcher had turned down at Luxembourg and that all the intervening drama and turmoil had been the result of her stubbornness.[21]

In the lull of more than a year that followed the agreement, and before the argument over the British rebate resumed in earnest, quarrels nonetheless continued, notably with the French over the CAP and the CFP. The French were ever ready to question Britain's commitment to the EEC, not least because it suited them to present their national interest as synonymous with that of the Community as a whole. But Thatcher herself took several occasions to spell out in public her own commitment to the success of the European project. In September 1980, in Bordeaux, she spoke at a meeting of the Franco-British Council. The Council had been set up by the French and British governments at the time of accession and the Prime Minister's speech was the most pro-European of her time in office. She began by citing the French influences that had so penetrated English life that they now formed an indissoluble part of British culture. Past rivalries had given way to common interests. In a world of super-powers and super-weapons, it was no longer possible for even the greatest European nation to stand wholly on its own. That was why the countries who were, or aspired to be, members of the EEC had resolved to pool their resources to preserve and strengthen liberty. The EEC was perhaps the most original and practical concept to be brought forth by the European genius since the American and French revolutions. As her own name implied, Thatcher continued, she was more interested in construction than demolition. She wanted to build a solid and weatherproof structure to resist the storms which lay ahead. She went on to conjure up the prospect of promoting trade, political, cultural, and human contacts between the two halves of what should be one continent, i.e. reaching out to the countries

[20] CC (80) 21st Conclusions, 2 June 1980, CAB 128/67, TNA.
[21] Jenkins, *European Diary*, p. 606.

under Soviet rule which had shared in the European experience for centuries past. In the past, she concluded, politicians had worked mainly within their own nations, seeking to win the support of their people. That support remained the basis of all political achievement. But national institutions were no longer sufficient on their own and it was the task of politicians to construct other institutions which would bring their nations together for their mutual benefit.

Giscard d'Estaing had declined to be present and sent his Prime Minister, Raymond Barre, instead. Barre's response was notably ungracious, and was commented on as such by French journalists. His theme was that Britain was an island and that France, by contrast, belonged to the continent. He vaunted France as the champion of the European Community and implied that that accomplishment was under attack from the UK.[22]

Just a few weeks later, Mrs Thatcher gave an interview to German television. It was forty years since the German air raid on Coventry that had destroyed the cathedral and the interviewer asked whether her teenage memories of that event coloured her view of Germany. She replied that they did not. The UK was totally dedicated to keeping the peace in Europe and it was inconceivable that the nations of Western Europe would ever again quarrel so seriously as to lead to war. The UK's future was inextricably bound up with the Common Market. Britain's trade and foreign policy cooperation were bound up with Europe. Withdrawal would be 'so damaging to jobs and employment'. As practical problems such as the budget issue were solved, so British public opinion would turn.[23]

If Giscard was never on good terms with Thatcher, that problem would soon be solved by his defeat at the hands of François Mitterrand in the Presidential election of April/May 1981. The odds were (just) in favour of Giscard being re-elected, and Thatcher lost a £5 bet with Ian Gilmour who, alone among Ministers and the Paris Embassy, correctly predicted that Mitterrand would win. Mitterrand consolidated his position when, in June, his Socialist Party secured a landslide victory in the elections to the National Assembly.

July 1981 saw the start of the second British Presidency of the Community, the first under a Conservative government. The search for a lasting settlement of the budget problem was high on the British list of priorities and Britain's continental partners were correspondingly wary. Mitterrand held the characteristic French view that Britain was out to achieve the *juste retour*: to get back

---

[22] PREM 19/239, TNA.   [23] PREM 19/471, TNA.

financially exactly what she contributed and, when they met in September, Mitterrand told Thatcher that he was hostile to the idea, which would make a nullity of the European Community. In fact, Thatcher and Howe, her Chancellor, had agreed that their aim should be to make Britain a small net contributor—rather than the largest, or second largest after West Germany. So she told Mitterrand firmly that her policy was certainly not that of the *juste retour*. Her goal was to get to a point where the budget allowed resources to flow from the richer to the poorer members. Countries such as Ireland, Greece, and Italy must be seen to benefit from membership, whilst those countries which were the richest per head should not be the beneficiaries of the budget as they were now. Without an equitable system, conflicts would ensue. She stressed the importance she attached to the Community. It had locked together countries that in the past had fought each other. Such hostilities must never happen again. The Community was playing a vital role in bringing much of Europe closer together.

Mitterrand responded positively to what Thatcher had said. She and he were, he commented, both politicians who knew what could and could not be done. Although, on some questions, his point of view and hers differed, her overall approach was just what he would have hoped for.[24]

Throughout this period, one of the tokens by which Britain's continental partners measured her European commitment was her willingness to join the ERM. The issue was later to become a political dividing line between Thatcher and others in her government but at this stage there was no division between Howe and Thatcher; neither believed that the economic case for joining was strong enough. Her economics adviser, Alan Walters, was even more forthright in his view. Within the ERM, he argued, exchange rates and the adjustment of parities were determined by the most enormous argy-bargy. It was not difficult, for example, to imagine a bargain being struck for turkeys (whose import the UK had banned on spurious health grounds) against sterling. If, Walters continued, the EMS showed signs of being a genuine central bank, depoliticized and running the European money supply with sensible rules for stability etc., then he would take a different view. But the EMS in its existing form was riven with political bargaining and was simply an extension of the usual acrimonious Brussels debate. The government would do better to let the exchange rate float more or less freely and to concentrate on putting Britain's own economic house in order.[25]

[24] PREM 19/456, TNA.   [25] PREM 19/743, TNA.

A few days later, Walters was even more forthright. He would, he said, be much more favourable to the EMS if it was a step on the road to a true central bank for Europe, which would have one currency and a unified fiscal and monetary system. But he did not believe that monetary and fiscal union would ever be achieved in Europe or that there was any chance of a proper central bank, depoliticized and independent of governments, running European monetary policy. Almost forty years later, the Eurozone is aspiring to the goal Walters described, albeit with some way to go to achieve a unified fiscal policy.

In the run-up to the December meeting of the European Council in London, the British government devised a new proposal for dealing with the budget problem. It was designed to benefit the UK and Germany as the two net contributors, while exempting the poorer Member States from contributing to the refund from which the UK would benefit. The French would be among those who would have to contribute to the British rebate. In his Presidential campaign against Giscard, Mitterrand had argued that Giscard had conceded too much to the UK in the 1980 agreement. So now, as President, Mitterrand was prepared to do *something* for the UK, but only on the basis of a temporary, degressive scheme which would not extend beyond 1984. There was thus no basis for an agreement in London and the summit ended in failure, albeit, as *Le Figaro* put it, an '*échec à l'amiable*'. It was left to Carrington, at the last meeting of EEC Foreign Ministers under the UK Presidency, to get agreement that the Commission would come up with fresh proposals in 1982.

The new year brought no change in the positions of the different protagonists and British minds turned once again to the issue of leverage. The annual meetings of EEC Agriculture Ministers, at which EEC agricultural prices were set, were mammoth set-pieces of the European calendar, with sessions lasting days and nights until compromise was reached. In theory, under the EEC Treaty, decisions could be taken by majority vote but, in practice, consensus was always the rule and the British government decided to make their agreement to an agricultural package conditional on parallel agreement to a new budget settlement. The Agriculture Council met for two days and nights in mid-March without agreement. Then, on 2 April, the Argentine military dictatorship invaded the Falkland Islands and Britain declared war and dispatched a naval force to try to recapture their territory. Lord Carrington took responsibility for the failures that had allowed the capture of the Falklands to take place and resigned. He was succeeded as Foreign Secretary by Francis Pym who had previously been Defence Secretary. Carrington had been loyal to Thatcher but also candid and unintimidated. She liked him. In appointing

Pym, she later wrote, she had 'exchanged an amusing Whig for a gloomy one' and that she and Pym 'disagreed on the direction of policy, in our approach to government and indeed about life in general'. Pym for his part was a believer in consensus politics and, coming fresh to the budget issue, could quickly see that the linkage which Britain was making between a budget rebate and agricultural prices would make it harder to secure sustained support from her partners for the sanctions against Argentina that the Community had just agreed.

The issue came to a head on 18 May. The British refused to agree the agricultural package on grounds of its excessive cost. This was, Peter Walker formally told the other nine Member States, a very important national interest for the UK. He invoked the Luxembourg Compromise. According to the doctrine established by the French (a doctrine whose acceptance had been a condition of French agreement to British accession) this should have been enough to prevent a vote being taken. Instead, with the exception of Greece and Denmark, the other Member States (France included) voted the UK down in the Agriculture Council. The essence of the Luxembourg Compromise was that it was up to the country which invoked it to determine when an issue constituted a 'very important national interest'. Now, the French redefined the circumstances in which the Luxembourg Compromise could be invoked. The French Agriculture Minister, Edith Cresson, told the Council that the purpose of the Compromise was to ensure that nothing was imposed on any one Member State if its vital interests were at stake. That had never been contested. But it had never been intended that it should allow one Member State to paralyse the normal functioning of the Community and fundamentally change its rules.[26]

Inside the British government, the reaction to this humiliation was one of anger. Thatcher herself was afraid the whole issue of Europe would be reopened within the Conservative Party. But, while Peter Walker, the Agriculture Minister, was apocalyptic, Pym was calm and persuaded Thatcher and other Cabinet members not to be rushed into an immediate response. The British task force had landed on the Falklands on 21 May and the government could not afford to fight on too many fronts. The agricultural price fixing was an accomplished fact. On Pym's recommendation, the British government accepted a more modest refund for 1982 than they would other-wise have done. The Luxembourg Compromise survived, though it was never again formally invoked by British Ministers (by contrast with German

[26] PREM 19/740, TNA.

Ministers who denied the validity of the Luxembourg Compromise even while invoking it when it suited their national interest).

Much as Thatcher held reservations about Pym, she could not afford to lose another Foreign Secretary and she was persuaded by him that, since the ad hoc refunds so far received by the UK amounted to around 66 per cent of Britain's net contribution, that was a reasonable sum to aim for in the longer-term provided, and the condition was vital for her, that any agreement should have no time limit.[27]

Before the end of October, Thatcher had a new German opposite number. Schmidt's coalition collapsed in September and Helmut Kohl, leader of the CDU, formed a coalition with Schmidt's old coalition partners, the FDP, led by Foreign Minister Hans Dietrich Genscher. Thatcher had hosted Kohl in London when both were in Opposition. Their parties were sister parties. 'You have met Kohl', Pym advised Thatcher on the eve of Kohl's first visit to London as German Chancellor. 'He is a nice man. He was never impressive in opposition but I see no reason why he should not develop into a very good Chancellor of the committee chairman, rather than the national leader, type. In any case, I see every reason to build him up rather than write him down . . . You will want to make the most of his and our common belief in conservative values, including the family . . .'[28]

Pym's prediction that Kohl would be a 'very good Chancellor' was closer to the mark than his dismissal, as 'the committee chairman type', of the man who was to reunite Germany and take his country into the European single currency. At their first meeting, Kohl and Thatcher saw eye to eye on their world view but Thatcher told Cabinet that 'Kohl wanted to be seen to be getting on well with everyone but did not wish to negotiate seriously about contentious issues before the German elections in March 1983'. Despite this downbeat assessment, when Kohl came to Chequers in February 1983, at the start of the German EEC Presidency, he seemed ready to help over the budget. Following a convincing win in the German elections in early March 1983, Kohl was as good as his word. A summit under Kohl's chairmanship agreed that the budget settlement for 1982 would be paid in 1983, and so debate could begin about future arrangements. Needless to say, this optimism was short-lived. The UK was expecting a refund of over 1,300 million ecus for 1983, representing 66 per cent of the UK's likely net contribution of 2 billion ecus. Instead, according to reports reaching London, the German Presidency were planning to propose a refund of only 400 million ecus. But before the next

[27] PREM 19/742, TNA.   [28] PREM 19/765, TNA.

round of argument could be joined, Mrs Thatcher had called a General Election. The government's economic policies were beginning to bear fruit. Victory in the Falklands had given the Prime Minister herself a big popular boost. The Labour Party, now led by the left-wing veteran, Michael Foot, was committed to withdrawal from the European Community and to unilateral nuclear disarmament. A number of senior Labour figures, led by Roy Jenkins (back in London after his Brussels stint) and former Cabinet Ministers Shirley Williams, David Owen, and Bill Rogers had split from Labour to form a Social Democratic Party (the SDP). Michael Foot had prevaricated over the Falklands War and Labour policies, including on the economy, did not resonate with the public. The SDP made few inroads in the election but highlighted the leftward drift of the Labour Party itself. In the election, Labour lost 52 seats and the Conservatives gained 38. The Conservative overall majority increased to 143.

The first casualty of Mrs Thatcher's success was Francis Pym, whose personality, realism, and moderation ensured his dismissal. Geoffrey Howe moved from the Treasury to the Foreign Office. As Chancellor, he had been hardline on EEC budget matters, presenting himself as an advocate of withholding Britain's budget contribution as a lever in the negotiations despite the clear illegality of doing so. Once at the Foreign Office, his stance would soften and his attempts to moderate the combative instincts of his leader would come to make his advice suspect in her eyes. Mrs Thatcher's own verdict was that Howe 'fell under the spell of the Foreign Office, where compromise and negotiation were ends in themselves. This magnified his faults and smothered his virtues.'[29] As someone who saw a lot of Howe on EEC matters and who served as his Private Secretary in his last year at the FCO, I can bear witness to the other side of the medal: his brain power, his conscientiousness, his realism, and, above all, his belief in the persuasive power of reasoned argument. Those qualities were to stand him in good stead with his fellow European Foreign Ministers and to contribute significantly to the eventual success of the British budget campaign, a success for which Thatcher gave him little credit.

Thatcher's election victory strengthened Britain's negotiating hand to the extent that she had a clear five years ahead of her. It did not lead to any detectable softening in continental attitudes. The British government continued to argue both for reform of the CAP and for a new budget mechanism. On CAP reform, the British proposal was simple in concept: the rate of growth in EEC agricultural spending should be markedly lower than the rate of

[29] Margaret Thatcher, *The Downing Street Years* (London: HarperCollins, 1993), p. 309.

growth of the Community's Own Resources. In other words, agricultural spending should be kept within the ceiling of the available budgetary resources. This eminently sensible idea commended itself to no other Member State. Most of Britain's partners saw the solution to the budget shortage as lying with an increase in the Own Resources ceiling.

On the budget, Britain was proposing a scheme based on the principle of relative prosperity. If a Member State's GNP per head was less than 90 percent of the Community average, its net contribution would be zero. Above that percentage, the extent of any member's net contribution would rise gradually with relative prosperity. As to how the net contribution should be measured, in British minds one part of the calculation would be based on the fact that the UK, in particular, received too little from the EEC budget while the other would be based on measuring the excessive burden (in the UK's case) of paying customs and levies collected at the external frontier into the EEC coffers. In theory, the scheme would apply to any Member State that met the criteria. In practice, it was designed by the British, for the British. Not surprisingly, all aspects of the British proposal were badly received by her partners. But the British government did make one significant concession. Hitherto, Thatcher had been resolutely opposed to any increase in the ceiling on the revenue the European Community could raise. But, in November 1983 she allowed Howe to tell the House of Commons that the UK would agree to an increase provided the growth of agricultural spending was curbed and the financial burdens of the budget were fairly shared.

So, the British government faced the European Council in Athens in December 1983 with some hope of making progress. In the event it was, according to Thatcher, a fiasco. She had relatively little time for Andreas Papandreou, the Greek Prime Minister who chaired the meeting, describing him as more skilful at securing Community subsidies for Greece than at running a meeting. That was unfair: the real problem for the British was Mitterrand who, contrary to expectations, was not prepared to consider anything except a short-term, modest, ad hoc arrangement to meet Britain's budget problem.

On the second and last morning of the summit, Thatcher and Mitterrand met against a background of Press comment on the Anglo-French row which, Mitterrand told her, smacked of a return to the Hundred Years War. Thatcher did not share the joke. The situation was, she replied, much more serious than just a disagreement between France and Britain. The Council had run away from the fundamental problems. She found it particularly difficult to understand Mitterrand's position because he and she had both appointed personal representatives who had been in discussion in order to avoid surprises. Jacques Delors, the French Finance Minister (for whom Thatcher at that time had considerable respect) had produced proposals on budgetary control which she supported, but she had been alone in doing so. (At this point in the discussion Mitterrand's right hand man, Jacques Attali, gave the President a whispered explanation of what was in the paper submitted by his Finance Minister.)

Officials in London were mystified by Mitterrand's behaviour. So too were French officials. One explanation was that Mitterrand did not want to settle the issue on the eve of the French Presidency of the EEC but to take the reins in his own hands. This did not mean, so Britain's Ambassador in Paris, John Fretwell, advised, that Mitterrand would agree to a long-term deal at an acceptable level. He had, however, just appointed a close and trusted associate, Roland Dumas, as his Europe Minister. Thatcher quickly invited Dumas to visit London.

Dumas came to London early in 1984. He was a man of considerable charm. Thatcher warmed to him, not least in thanking him 'for the most beautiful orchids which you sent me after our meeting the other day'. She had found her talks with Dumas 'most valuable' and sent him her best wishes 'for the daunting task which you have undertaken'.[30] But there was still a big gap between French and British positions. On the eve of a European Council in Brussels in March, under Mitterrand's presidency, the French piled on the pressure. According to Fretwell 'the French now see the European Council as essentially a contest with the UK over budget refunds ... Mitterrand ... would like a success but probably reckons that the alternative strategy of isolating and pillorying the UK would go down quite well in France'. As if on cue, the French, alone among EEC governments, fired a shot across British bows by refusing to adopt the regulation authorizing the payment of the UK's agreed 1983 refund.[31]

The summit duly failed but not because of Mitterrand. 'Well, what can I say? So near and yet so far. What a pity', was Thatcher's verdict at her post-summit Press conference. There had, she believed, been moments when agreement seemed to be in sight. But the Irish had had problems over proposed controls on milk production and the Germans had had problems over their role in limiting the UK's budget contribution. And, as Michael Butler, Britain's Permanent Representative to the EEC saw it, some of the leaders had not understood the issues they were supposed to be discussing and had not thought through the consequences.

[30] PREM 19/1240/1, TNA.   [31] PREM 19/1227, TNA.

Between March and the final European Council under French Presidency at the end of June, intensive discussions took place privately between British and French officials and between Dumas and Howe. Howe's relationship and negotiations with Dumas played as big a part in the eventual agreement as did Thatcher's robustness. Both sides were edging to a compromise, but there was still a big gap. The British were prepared to accept that they should not be compensated for the money they collected for the EEC in the form of levies and duties. But they should be compensated for the gap between their other contribution to the budget (a notional share of VAT revenue) and the expenditure in the UK that they got from the budget. The British also accepted that they would not be compensated for the whole of this VAT share/expenditure share gap. They wanted to be compensated to the tune of 70 per cent. Mitterrand, it was believed, would not agree to so high a percentage. At last, so the British thought, they had got agreement on a scheme which would endure, replacing the ad hoc temporary refunds of recent years. But then, on the eve of the Council Dumas wrote to Howe proposing three more years of ad hoc refunds followed by a system based on only 60 per cent of the VAT share/ expenditure share gap. The two British officials leading the negotiations (David Williamson from the Cabinet Office and Robin Renwick from the FCO) told their French opposite number, Guy Legras, that no negotiations could be conducted on that basis. The percentage figure was too low. More importantly, the system had to be a lasting one. Britain would accept no more temporary fixes. Privately, Legras agreed with them.

To Mrs Thatcher's frustration, the budget was not discussed at the first session of the European Council in Paris on the afternoon of 25 June 1984. The meeting adjourned for separate dinners for the Heads of Government and for Foreign Ministers. The Foreign Ministers were tasked with discussing the budget and reporting back. The Heads of Government, drinking their postprandial coffee on the terrace of the Hôtellerie du Bas-Bréau near Barbizon, could see the Foreign Ministers taking their coffee on a neighbouring terrace and assumed they had done their work. It transpired that they had scarcely dealt with the issue and Mitterrand, not best pleased, sent them back to work. When they emerged, shortly before midnight, they had not reached agreement but had 'clarified points of difference'. Cheysson (not the most accomplished of France's Foreign Ministers) had suggested that the UK might get back between 50 per cent and 60 per cent of her budget contribution as measured by the VAT share/expenditure share gap.

Thatcher was livid. 'How dare they treat Britain in this way?', she fumed privately. 'Have they forgotten that we saved all their skins in the war?' she asked. She sent three officials (Williamson, Renwick, and Michael Butler, the UK Permanent Representative to the EEC) to negotiate through the night with Legras.

When the European Council met the following morning, it was still far from clear that a basis for agreement existed. In mid-morning, Mitterrand interrupted the plenary session for bilateral consultations, known, given the largely Roman Catholic origins of the Community, as 'confessionals'. In his first meeting with Thatcher and Howe, Mitterrand would not be drawn beyond a willingness to compensate more than 60 per cent of the gap. Howe and Thatcher then saw Kohl who said that 65 per cent was his upper limit. Dumas separately told Howe that Mitterrand would not go up to the 70 per cent compensation rate that the British were seeking. Thatcher and Mitterrand met again. She would accept one more year of ad hoc refunds before the new, lasting, mechanism kicked in. The President said that he would go to 65 per cent in order to settle. Other delegations were prepared to go to somewhere between 60 per cent and 65 per cent. None was prepared to go as far as 70 per cent.

There were a number of rooms off the main meeting room and Thatcher told Howe, Butler, and Williamson that she wanted a private word with them. When they got into the room, they all sat in silence until, after a time, Thatcher said: 'It's time to settle'.

Thatcher saw Mitterrand again. She told him that she was ready to settle but that it would be helpful to her to have 66 per cent (the same percentage as in the 30 May 1980 agreement reached by Carrington and Gilmour). Mitterrand suggested that she raise the point when the plenary meeting resumed.

When the full Council met, the French tabled a paper which had been agreed with the British, save that the French had gone back on one earlier undertaking. At the Brussels European Council in March, the French and British had agreed on a text saying that any increase in the UK's net budget contribution resulting from Portuguese and Spanish accession would be subject to the corrective mechanism. Now, three months later, the paper tabled by the French said the opposite. Thatcher objected strenuously and got her way. She also told her fellow leaders that it would be absurd to deny her 'my one percentage point'. Mitterrand supported her: 'Of course, Madam Prime Minister, you must have it', he said. Among the delegations, probably only the French and British had worked out that that single percentage point would be worth about £15 million a year to the UK.

Mrs Thatcher did not claim a great victory. She told Cabinet that it was 'a very reasonable settlement'. The Elysée described the outcome as being one of 'neither conqueror nor conquered'. Chancellor Kohl's reported comment that it was 'a very respectable settlement' seemed to be the general continental view.[32]

In an interview in 2009, Jacques Attali claimed that Thatcher had suffered a defeat at Fontainebleau since, he asserted, she was demanding a 100 per cent cashback deal. The truth lies elsewhere, as this account shows. Thatcher did compromise on the amount of rebate she was prepared to settle for. What she consistently resisted were the attempts of her partners to fob her off with a few more ad hoc, year on year refunds, of diminishing amounts and finite duration. Her great achievement was to secure a rebate which endured despite regular attempts by the European Commission and the UK's partners to dilute or terminate it.

Thatcher's tactics are more questionable. Her successor, John Major, demonstrated that it is possible to be both steely on substance and unaggressive in manner. For Thatcher, the steel and the aggression were inseparable. Major was astute at reading the body language of his fellow leaders and at putting himself mentally in their negotiating shoes so as to understand the constraints under which they were operating. That was not Thatcher's way. She would probably regard it as a compliment that she is best remembered on the continent for her demand for 'my money back'. But the phrase, apart from being confrontational of itself, laid her open to the unjustified charge that she was seeking the *juste retour* which was an anathema to her partners as being contrary to the whole conception of the Own Resources system and to Community solidarity. That in turn made it easier for her partners to attack her for being un-*communautaire* and to present themselves as staunch defenders of the Community interest when in fact all they were really defending was their own national exchequers.

None of that detracts from her achievement. Had the excessive British budget contribution not been resolved, the question of Britain's continued membership of the EEC would have risen up the domestic political scale to potentially existential levels. In the event, it did leave a legacy. It left Mrs Thatcher feeling that her fellow EEC leaders were untrustworthy and that every issue was a potential confrontation. It established in the minds of the British Press and public the notion of the EEC as a 'win or lose' battleground. Despite all that, there remained two issues on which Mrs Thatcher would show herself as something of a European pioneer. The first of them was her greatest single European achievement: the creation of the European Single Market.

[32] PREM 19/1222, TNA.

7

No, No, No

Thatcher Defiant, 1984–1990

Margaret Thatcher had focused single-mindedly on the UK budget rebate for five years. But that was not her sole European objective. She was ambitious for the European Community but her ambition was essentially practical and framed by her own domestic ambitions and policies. She believed in the EEC as a vehicle for peace through shared democratic principles and economic policies. She was prepared to accept the integration inherent in achieving those shared policies provided it took place within the legal framework to which the UK had committed itself in the Treaty of Rome. She and her Ministers therefore accepted that the legal competence of the EEC institutions would grow as more common policies were agreed at European level. For her, that organic growth had to be conditioned by what was in the national interest as she saw it. In turn, that accumulation of practically focused policies would constitute as much 'European Union' as was sensible or desirable. She had no wish, or tolerance, for the declared ambitions of other Member States for a European political union in which powers would be ceded to the European Commission and European Parliament by a new treaty.

Thatcher had faced up to this challenge during the German EEC Presidency in the second half of 1983. The German Foreign Minister, Hans-Dietrich Genscher, and his Italian opposite number, Emilio Colombo, had been working for more than two years on what they hoped would be a solemn European Act of Union. This was exactly the kind of initiative of which Thatcher was suspicious and impatient. At the same time, as she confessed in her autobiography, she 'could not quarrel with everything'. So the British concentrated on two main objectives. The first was to avoid the document being called an 'Act', which smacked too much of law in British minds. Under instructions from Number 10, Foreign Office negotiators therefore strove to avoid European Union being defined, as the Italians and Germans wanted, as a goal. In this, the British were following a well-worn path. My father-in-law, a young diplomat in the post-war British Embassy in Rome had accompanied his Ambassador in 1950 when the latter, on instructions from London, called on the Italian

Foreign Minister to persuade him of the ill-advised nature of the proposed Coal and Steel Community. The Minister, Count Sforza, listened politely. At the end of the Ambassador's reasoned case, Sforza smiled tolerantly. 'My dear Ambassador', he said. 'There are times at the opera when you should enjoy the music and not worry about the words.'[1]

We British worried intensely about 'the words'. With no overarching written constitution, the words of Parliamentary Acts were all we (and the courts which interpreted them) had to rely on. At one level, we were right to do so. The document eventually agreed by EEC Heads of Government in Stuttgart in the autumn of 1983 became, at British insistence, a 'Declaration', albeit a 'Solemn' one, rather than an Act. And the British achieved their second objective: European Union was defined as a process. 'European Union' said the Declaration, 'is being achieved by deepening and broadening the scope of European activities so that they coherently cover, albeit on a variety of legal bases, a growing proportion of Member States' mutual relations and of their external relations'. The government confidently told the House of Lords in a memorandum that the Solemn Declaration consisted 'for the most part either of statements of current practice or the expressions of hope for the future'. Those expressions of hope were, in reality, expressions of intent and even commitment: to speaking with one voice in foreign policy, to a significantly greater role for the European Parliament, to improved harmonization of social security systems, to action on the road to EMU, and to strengthened cooperation among judicial authorities. The Solemn Declaration may not have been a legal Act, but it was the political foundation on which much subsequent legally binding European action was built.

Thatcher had been persuaded by the Foreign Office to make some accommodation to the ambitions of her European partners. But she saw the Foreign Office tendency to compromise as both an inherent weakness in its *déformation professionelle* and a ploy to increase FCO influence in Whitehall. It is true that many senior officials of the time were scarred by Britain's failure in the 1950s to judge correctly the trend of European politics: the European train had left the station and we had been left forlornly on the platform. Officials were perhaps over-preoccupied with not making the same mistakes again. But a large part of Foreign Office thinking at the time was also rooted in Britain's centuries-old need to avoid being the victim of continental

---

[1] Author conversation with the late Norman Reddaway. Cited in Stephen Wall, *A Stranger in Europe: Britain and the EU from Thatcher to Blair* (Oxford: Oxford University Press, 2008), pp. 47–8.

encroachment. The battle of the budget had pitted Britain against the rest and had contributed to cementing a relationship between Kohl and Mitterrand in opposition to the UK, even though by political background and economic persuasion, Kohl and Thatcher should have been the two natural allies.

Foreign Secretary Geoffrey Howe, and the officials he led, believed that an enlarged Community of twelve (once Portugal and Spain joined, which they did in 1986) would pose problems of governance. Enlargement would turn France into a significant net contributor to the EEC budget. The three large Member States had global economic interests not matched by the others. There was thus an opportunity for trilateral collaboration which should not be missed but could only be seized if the UK was willing to make some accommodation to the political aims of France and Germany. But Thatcher did not believe in such an institutionalized relationship. Her economic policies were far removed from those of Mitterrand. Politically, she was far removed from Kohl's European ambitions and, as she was to demonstrate over the issue of German reunification, she disputed the French notion that the way to prevent German domination was through strong European institutions that would bind Germany into the European family. Thatcher's view was that the best way of constraining Germany was through strong nation states ready to stand up for their interests. Getting the Prime Minister past her instincts and prejudices onto common ground with the FCO's view of how best to secure UK objectives was a constant struggle. By the end of her time in office, the struggle had turned into a standoff in which she fundamentally distrusted the advice she was receiving. But, in 1984, there was still scope for constructive engagement and common purpose.

Now largely lost to view, the most comprehensive statement of European policy ever made by a British government was made by Margaret Thatcher. It took the form of a blue-covered booklet called *Europe—the Future*, which Mrs Thatcher issued to her EEC fellow leaders at the Fontainebleau European Council in 1984. The booklet was written by officials but was agreed to in both principle and detail by the Prime Minister. It is a mark of its relevance that Tony Blair quoted it to good effect in the House of Commons in 2004 when he was under attack from the Conservative Opposition for 'selling out' Britain's traditional defence stance for the sake of European compromise. To boos and general heckling from the Opposition benches, Blair set out the case for a greater European role in the common defence. When the tumult sub-sided, he revealed that the words he had just spoken were not his but those of the canonized fallen leader, Margaret Thatcher. The punctured Opposition subsided like a balloon.

At the heart of the pamphlet was the case for a genuine single market in Europe. Of course, this was a British national interest since Britain had liberalized its economy under Thatcher and wanted to benefit from similarly open markets on the continent. But the British could hardly be accused of being non-*communautaire*. The establishment of a common market was one of the founding principles laid down in the Treaty of Rome. Yet, nearly thirty years later, barriers to free trade persisted. Mutual recognition of professional qualifications was unknown, so that anyone wanting to move from one EEC country to another had to prove their compliance with that country's domestic provisions before they could practise. Social security systems were unharmonized. Tour buses crossing from one EEC country to another had to stop at each frontier for passport inspections and to be assessed for local VAT and to have the fuel they were carrying measured and taxed. Trucks carrying goods had to complete up to forty different documents for inspection at every frontier. Impediments to trade, such as Germany's refusal to allow beer imports (on spurious health grounds) were common. Change was urgently needed and Mrs Thatcher had the backing of Jacques Delors, newly appointed as President of the Commission. As French Finance Minister, he had restored sense and discipline to Mitterrand's muddled and failed economic prescriptions and Thatcher had supported his appointment.

At Fontainebleau in 1984, the Heads of Government had set up two committees. One was a Committee on A People's Europe whose terms of reference related to making the EEC more relevant to its citizens in ways which ranged from the abolition of frontier formalities for people, and the creation of a single document for the movement of goods, to the development of a European flag, the adoption of a European anthem and the formation of a European sports team. Not surprisingly, the European flag and anthem did not commend themselves to the Prime Minister. The second committee (which became much more significant) consisted of the personal representatives of the Heads of Government. Its remit was to make suggestions 'for the improvement of the operation of European cooperation in both the Community field and that of political, or any other cooperation'. It was to work 'on the lines of the Spaak committee'. In other words, its remit was to be as far-reaching as its members could agree to make it.

July 1984 had seen the start of the Irish Presidency who, naturally and correctly, proposed one of their own, Senator James Dooge, as the committee's chairman. Kohl had been determined that he would appoint as chairman a former German President, Karl Carstens, and he was angry and sulky when the Irish refused to be bullied into submission. Some EEC governments did send personal representatives to sit on the committee. For example, Mitterrand sent Edgar Faure, a former Prime Minister. This had both the advantage and disadvantage of his being unconstrained by the policy of his own government. He could speak his mind freely. Equally, the French government would not be bound by what he said. No such freedom could be entertained in London, and Mrs Thatcher's personal representative was the Minister of State in the FCO responsible for EEC policy, Malcolm Rifkind, a pro-European rising star among younger Ministers.

Within a very few weeks of the Dooge Committee's formation, Thatcher was beginning to get alarmed at its direction of travel. Proposals had been made to give the European Parliament responsibilities on the revenue side of the budget, to place restrictions on the use of the Luxembourg Compromise, and, worst of all, to have a new European treaty. One argument for a new Treaty was that more use of Qualified Majority Voting (QMV) would prevent protectionist Member States from blocking progress on the very liberalizing measures the British favoured. The Foreign Office advised Number 10 that 'this would be of major concern to the UK given the implications for sovereignty' but that, in any event, a number of other Member States were certain to shoot down the idea. With this latter argument Thatcher (correctly as it turned out) had little truck. 'I have seen this advice many times', she commented tartly, 'and watched those who were against just fade away when the argument got tough, leaving us alone to fight their cause'.[2]

The issue of majority voting was to dominate British consideration of the Committee's work. FCO officials were worried that the UK could be outvoted on proposals the government opposed. Rifkind put the counterargument succinctly in a departmental minute: 'If we are to be able to pick and choose', he wrote, 'blocking proposals which we do not like ... then others will have the same ability. [The Department's] conclusion might be reversed: full application of the majority provisions of the Treaties would result in votes against our interests in a significant minority of cases but (with the ultimate safeguard of the Luxembourg Compromise) that is a price worth paying for the equally significant number of cases in which decisions would be taken which suit our interests and which would not otherwise have been achieved.' Votes which might be against British interests in the short term, Rifkind argued, could, in the longer term, achieve the Single Market which the UK wanted. Did the UK want improved decision-taking or not? If it did not, then what the UK would be doing was 'the positive presentation of a determination not to budge on the

[2] PREM 19/1478, TNA.

real questions at issue'. But Rifkind's own conclusion was that the UK *did* want change for, without it, decisions in the European Community would become harder and harder to take at all, especially after enlargement.[3]

Rifkind was not permitted to turn his astute analysis into a change in his instructions. In the Dooge Committee, only Denmark and Greece joined with the UK in opposing the greater use of majority voting. So, at the start of 1985, the Foreign Secretary, Geoffrey Howe, was complaining to the Commission President about the lack of progress on achieving a genuine European internal market, while also arguing that the best way of achieving it was not through majority voting but by making better use of the existing rules, e.g. by countries abstaining on issues requiring unanimity. At the European Council in March 1985 (which approved the terms of Spanish and Portuguese membership at the cost of a huge bribe for Greece and others in the form of so-called Integrated Mediterranean Programmes) Thatcher poured scorn on 'the way in which directives spewed forth from Brussels'. At the same time, while reaffirming her commitment to the unanimity rule, she proclaimed herself as an enthusiast for the common market for which the UK would continue to work hard.

Alongside the argument about majority voting ran a linked argument about European political union. In a speech in 1984, Kohl had called for a united states of Europe. In an interview with the *Sunday Express* a little later in the year, Thatcher was uncompromising in her response. She believed, she said, in a Europe of separate countries, cooperating together in a common market. 'I do not believe', she went on, 'in a federal Europe and I think to compare it to the United States is absolutely ridiculous.' To those who talked about a two-speed Europe (with Britain implicitly in the slow lane) her response was: 'Let me tell you what I mean [by a two-speed Europe]. Those who pay more are in the top group and those who pay less are not. It is absolutely ridiculous to expect a change in the Treaty...'[4]

Howe took a somewhat different view, reinforced by advice from Britain's Ambassador in Bonn, Julian Bullard, who reported that at the heart of Kohl's high-flown ideas lay a desire to strengthen transatlantic and Western European solidarity. Britain, so Howe argued, could at least meet Kohl in his desire to formalize political cooperation (foreign policy coordination) in the shape of a new formal and binding document. Thatcher was persuaded to agree. A British text setting out the proposed obligations of Member States in the field of foreign policy was produced and Thatcher gave a copy in confidence to Kohl when the two met at Chequers in May 1985. Kohl responded positively and both leaders agreed that there should be discussions between their respective officials. Kohl gave Bullard a lift back to Bonn on his aeroplane and Bullard described him as being in high spirits 'rhapsodising about Chequers'. He had had a good day and had agreed with Mrs Thatcher on most points, the one exception being the European Parliament, whose powers Kohl was intent on increasing.[5]

A copy of the UK draft was given to Mitterrand on a similar basis and both men were asked to let the Prime Minister have their views before the document was circulated to other EEC colleagues. Despite reminders, answers came there none.

The European Council was due to meet in Milan in the last week of June 1985. As senior officials walked across Downing Street to the usual pre-summit briefing with the Prime Minister, they received the news that the French and Germans had circulated a brand new Treaty of European Union. On close examination, it transpired that the French and Germans had taken the British foreign policy text, verbatim, and had added a heading to the effect that this new text, together with the existing treaties, constituted European Union. This was, as Thatcher crisply observed, the kind of behaviour that would get you thrown out of a London club. She was angry and, to judge by the way the issue still rankled when he came to write his memoirs ten years later, Howe was even more hurt and irate. No explanation, let alone apology, was ever forthcoming. On a personal level, it was an egregious act of discourtesy which reflects badly on the characters of both men. As a piece of diplomacy, it was amateurish and crude. The other Member States could see that the Franco-German draft was a straight crib from the British text and quickly dismissed it as being nowhere close to a true treaty of European Union.

The most plausible explanation for this Franco-German behaviour came from the German Ambassador in The Hague, in a private conversation with his UK opposite number. It was, the German said, politically impossible for Germany to be seen accepting Britain as wresting the leadership of Europe from France and Germany.[6] Perhaps too, there had been less of a meeting of minds at Chequers than had appeared. A meeting record of the time showed Kohl telling Mitterrand that he had not come away from Chequers with a good impression and that Thatcher 'was moving away from Europe'.[7]

---

[5] PREM 19/1507, TNA.   [6] PREM 19/1492, TNA.
[7] Charles Moore, *Margaret Thatcher, Volume Two, Everything She Wants* (London: Allen Lane, 2015), pp. 397–8.

After this inauspicious prelude, the Milan European Council proved to be something of a humiliation for the British. A majority of the Member States clearly wanted Treaty change and the Italian Presidency, under Prime Minister Bettino Craxi, were keen to deliver it. To do so required a decision by the Heads of Government to set up an Intergovernmental Conference (IGC) of the Member States to conduct the negotiations. Thatcher was opposed. Since decisions at the European Council had hitherto been taken by consensus, the British delegation assumed the same would be true on this occasion. But the Treaty of Rome provided for procedural decisions to be taken by simple majority vote and the Italian Presidency used this provision for the decision to call the Conference. When Thatcher saw which way the wind was blowing, it would have been open to her to rally to the majority. In her memoirs, she accused Howe of being willing to concede an IGC rather than go down fighting. So, go down fighting she did. Her EEC partners had got used to her abrasiveness, and wise to the fact that she had generally done her homework better than they had. They had lost out over the budget deal. Here was an opportunity for a counter-coup, and they took it. Thatcher was outsmarted and outvoted and there was now nothing she could do to prevent the IGC from taking place. As she marched resolutely to her post-summit Press conference her officials urged her not to rule out taking part in the IGC. 'The other view prevailed, and we must go to that IGC', she told the Press. Later that same evening, she gave vent to her irritation in an interview with Paul Reynolds of the BBC, telling him: 'We shall go to the IGC. You can only get a treaty amendment by unanimous agreement of all national Parliaments. I think, therefore, the IGC will fail.'[8]

The British had been out-manoeuvred and senior officials were seriously worried that, once again, Britain was at risk of marginalizing herself at a decisive moment. Thatcher, too, seems to have been conscious of this. She agreed that officials should attend the IGC negotiating sessions, but they should make it clear that they had no instructions, that they would listen to the arguments and suggestions and that the Prime Minister would then take a view.

For a Whitehall which abhorred any absence of a fully worked-out policy on each and every proposal, however trivial, this approach was agonizing. But it proved to be smart tactics. Officials believed that in reality the Germans, and the French even more so, were a good deal less ambitious for change than their rhetoric had suggested. Indeed, their perfidy over the British text on foreign

[8] PREM 19/1492, TNA.

policy cooperation had proved that they were prepared to pretend that a substantive, but hardly revolutionary, text formalizing foreign policy cooperation was an all-singing-all-dancing Treaty of European Union. EEC partners who were accustomed to allowing the British to shoot down proposals, while claiming that they were suitably outraged by Britain's lack of European commitment, were forced from cover.

This did not mean that the British were disengaged. They were active with other delegations behind the scenes and, as the Luxembourg European Council in December 1985 drew near, had whittled down the number of Treaty articles where they were under pressure to concede majority voting. The Prime Minister had agreed to allow a move to qualified majority voting on a number of treaty articles necessary to achieve progress on trade in goods and services. She would make no such concession on taxation matters. Economic and Monetary Union also proved to be a difficult issue. Thatcher had inherited the commitment to EMU made by her predecessor as Tory leader, Ted Heath, at the Paris summit of October 1972. She could scarcely disown it. There was considerable pressure from other Member States to establish a formal treaty commitment to EMU. Kohl was caught between the pressure of his coalition partners, the FPD, to agree to the goal and pressure from the Bundesbank not to. In the end, he sought to persuade Thatcher to accept a new title in the EEC Treaty: *Co-operation in Economic and Monetary Policy (Economic and Monetary Union)*.

Thatcher had been warned by her Chancellor of the Exchequer, Nigel Lawson, of the risks of being sucked into EMU. But Kohl told her that he was opposed to EMU, that the text was harmless and meaningless and that the requirement for further treaty change before EMU could happen was a further protection. She accepted the text. To get the opening of the European market she so wanted, Thatcher was obliged to compromise, as she herself put it a few days later in the House of Commons: 'We wanted something from our European partners, and they wanted something from us. It seemed a reasonable compromise.' The reasonable compromise, which enabled the Single European Act (SEA) to be agreed in Luxembourg was acceptance of more majority voting as the price of opening up continental markets to free trade in goods and services, freedom of capital movements, and free movement of people. The wording on EMU also seemed like a reasonable compromise at the time. In practice, the text gave Jacques Delors the basis for pressing forward with plans for EMU which, for him, was always an essential component of a true single market.

The European single market is probably the EU's biggest single achievement and it would not have happened, when it happened, had Mrs Thatcher not pressed it onto the agenda of her more protectionist colleagues and then made the compromise that turned aspiration into reality. It is today sometimes suggested that Mrs Thatcher was misled by her officials about the import of what she was agreeing to. She herself never made that claim. David Williamson, her senior Cabinet Office official adviser on Europe, later recalled standing at the foot of the Downing Street staircase waiting for the Prime Minister to come down to a pre-Luxembourg meeting about the draft treaty text. She had it in her hand. It was voluminous. 'I've read every word', she said. And she had.

What is true is that, in two respects, subsequent interpretation of the Single European Act (SEA) went beyond what officials believed it, at the time, to entail. Article 8a of the SEA defined the internal market as 'an area without internal frontiers in which free movement of goods, persons, services and capital is ensured in accordance with the provisions of this Treaty'. The phrase 'in accordance with the provisions of this Treaty' meant, so the British argued, that there could be no discrimination based on nationality between workers *of the Member States*, [my italics]. The UK had, to make doubly sure, secured a General Declaration, appended to the SEA, which asserted that 'nothing in these provisions shall affect the right of Member States to take such measures as they consider necessary for the purpose of controlling immigration from third countries'. At the time, the Commission and other Member States did not acquiesce in the British view that freedom of movement was confined to EEC nationals. Over time, rulings of the European Court of Justice (ECJ) favoured their interpretation which was that, once a citizen of *any* country had satisfied the EEC's entry requirements at the first Community frontier they crossed, they were free to travel anywhere in the Community free of further frontier controls. This was the principle enshrined in the Schengen Treaty to which five of the Member States had committed themselves earlier in 1985. The UK was eventually able to use the negotiation of the Amsterdam Treaty in 1997 to secure a provision permitting it to maintain passport controls at the frontier. The newly elected government of Tony Blair completed the negotiation of that Treaty, but the concession had already been secured before the General Election of May that year by the then British Europe Minister, David Davis.

The second issue where the UK's safeguards proved inadequate was EEC/EU social policy. The Treaty of Rome provided only for close cooperation, not harmonization, between Member States in the social field. The SEA extended that provision by giving the Commission the right to propose legislation 'encouraging improvements, especially in the working environment, as regards the health and safety of workers'. The British secured a qualification requiring such measures to avoid placing burdens on small and medium firms. In practice, 'health and safety' gave room for wide interpretation and the Commission found majority support among the Member States for measures, such as the Working Time Directive, which went beyond the British conception of what health and safety meant and beyond what they believed necessary for the functioning of a single market.

The Single European Act had a contested passage through the House of Commons. The Labour Party, just beginning to emerge from its years of opposition to EEC membership, opposed the measure on the grounds that the removal of customs barriers would open the British economy to the excesses of market capitalism.[9] There was some opposition too from seventeen Conservative backbenchers, some of them already carrying the torch of hostility to the entire European project. But, with Thatcher's support for the project not in doubt, the Tory rebellion was limited.

The Single European Act had to be ratified by the Parliaments of all the Member States. The UK acted early but the Act as a whole did not enter into force in the EEC until July 1987. By that time, Mrs Thatcher had won another General Election. Her new Secretary of State for Trade and Industry, David (Lord) Young, set about raising the awareness of British business to the opportunities of the single market through a three-month campaign of television advertising, fronted by, among others, a young Alan Sugar. By the end of the campaign, business awareness had risen from 3 per cent to 97 per cent. At the same time, public support for EEC membership also rose to around 66 per cent according to opinion polls, a high point not again reached in the UK.

The British government had won a significant and lasting budget rebate and pioneered the opening of a genuine EEC-wide marketplace. Reform of the CAP remained unfinished business and renewed pressure on the EEC's financial ceiling provided an opportunity to press for cuts in farm subsidies. Once again, Britain and France were pitched against each other. Mitterrand had lost his majority in the French National Assembly and was now in an uneasy cohabitation with the Gaullist leader, Jacques Chirac, as French Prime Minister. Chirac had been France's Agriculture Minister and much of his electoral support came from rural France. I saw quite a lot of Mitterrand when I worked for John Major and quite a lot of Chirac (by then President)

---

[9] Martin Westlake, *Kinnock: The Biography* (London: Little, Brown and Company, 2001), p. 484.

when I worked for Tony Blair. Mitterrand was intellectual, dry, aloof. Functionaries such as me were beneath his gaze. At meetings of the European Council, he would spend much of the time writing postcards which were intermittently gathered up by a smartly uniformed military officer. The President might then turn his attention to the proceedings.

Chirac was as tall as Mitterrand was short and as clubbable as Mitterrand was reserved. Chirac was a man of the people, never happier than being photographed with a peasant and a cow at a country fair. Once he knew who you were, he would come up to you at a meeting and greet you warmly. Unlike Giscard d'Estaing who, when entertaining at the Elysée, had himself served first, Chirac would, as host, be served last. He was a good trencherman and always drank beer rather than wine. He was shrewd, friendly, and approachable—but he could also be rough and tough when he chose. As French Prime Minister, he was not going to allow Thatcher's reforming zeal on agricultural spending to go unchallenged. President Mitterrand could claim to be in favour of CAP reform, safe in the knowledge that Prime Minister Chirac would fight the French corner.

In 1987, Chirac was pressing for an oils and fats tax: basically a protectionist measure against agricultural imports into the EEC from third countries. Thatcher was opposed. CAP spending, Chirac argued, was compulsory under the EEC Treaty and Thatcher's attempts to curb it were in direct contravention of legal obligations. Maybe, he argued, all other expenditure should be curbed. Or maybe the UK's Treaty of Accession should be renegotiated. Thatcher held firm. The 'compulsory' nature of the spending was a technicality relating to the budget powers of the European Parliament. It had nothing to do with the levels of spending, which were for the Member States to determine. France, said Chirac, would never allow the CAP to be undermined. Britain, said Thatcher, would never allow an oils and fats tax. That measure required unanimity. She prevailed. But battle was soon rejoined. Reportedly accused by Chirac of acting like 'a housewife', Thatcher told *Der Spiegel* that it was a pity that more politicians didn't act like housewives: 'Housewives of the world unite...I am such a passionate believer in the Community that I accept all the accusations of being a troublemaker. No, I am not awkward; I just want the EEC to work...'

A European Council discussion on agricultural reform in December 1987 ended in failure. In February 1987, at a special summit on agriculture, Thatcher and the Dutch Prime Minister, Ruud Lubbers, sought to toughen up the language of a text on budgetary discipline in the face of a combined onslaught from Kohl and Chirac. After two days of hectoring and bullying from the German and French leaders, Lubbers decided he could take no more. Thatcher faced the risk that eleven Member States would adopt a text without Britain. An accommodation was reached.

Howe, who, as Thatcher's Foreign Secretary was the only person at her side at European summits, was beginning to chafe at what he called privately the UK's self-marginalization. But what was for him 'self-marginalization' was, for Thatcher, standing up for important interests, and even principles, and not caving into the bullying of others or even the tendency of the majority. She was incapable of being tough without talking tough. Straight talking had been her stock-in-trade and was one of the reasons why the British electorate kept returning her to Downing Street. As time went on, her antennae, as David Owen put it, stopped receiving and were only broadcasting. She became more adamant, less exposed to independent and challenging advice and less tolerant of it. She was nice to her subordinate staff but could be harsh and publicly humiliating to her Ministers. It became more habitual for them to complain behind her back than to speak up in her presence.

In September 1988, Mrs Thatcher set out her views of Europe in what became a famous—some would say notorious—speech at the College of Europe in Bruges. She had been persuaded by Howe that this was a good moment to make a speech, setting the seal on the reforms Britain had secured in the EEC, looking forward to the single market and bringing Britain's economic success to the attention of a wider European audience. Almost my last act, as Head of the Foreign Office European Department, before taking up a post as Geoffrey Howe's Private Secretary, was to write the first outline of the speech. Our draft was a worthy, if workaday, statement of Britain's vision of a liberalized European Community. It sought to contrast the world of the 1950s in which the European Community was founded with the world of the 1980s. Then, the priorities had been survival, security, and sufficiency of supply. Now, in the 1980s, we had gone from agricultural insufficiency to over-sufficiency. In general, we needed liberalization, not harmonization. It urged a step by step approach on the basis that, however far we in the EEC wanted to go, we could only go one step at a time.

Soon after we had sent our outline to Number 10, Mrs Thatcher gave a long interview on Jimmy Young's Radio 2 programme, then one of the most listened to shows on the BBC. Jimmy Young was a household name, popular and populist. He devoted much of his interview with Mrs Thatcher to Europe and he put the critical case persistently, focusing on remarks by the Commission President, Jacques Delors, who had suggested that the nation state was soon to be subsumed in a wider, federal Europe. Thatcher responded vigorously, clearly enjoying the cut and thrust of a good argument. She made plain her support for the EEC project as she conceived it: political and economic cooperation between nation states in a framework where they could be stronger by acting together than alone. Hers was a practical view and she had no truck with ideas of Political Union or a single currency and a European Central Bank. She was a realist and her job was to make sure that realism prevailed.

It was in no sense an anti-European performance. Indeed, she was answering the anti-European case put by Young. But she did it in terms which were uniquely British. At the time, Delors' aspiration to see the Commission become a quasi-government, more laws being made at European than at national level, and more power ceded to the European Parliament at the expense of national parliaments, was regarded among other EEC governments as wholly unexceptionable. It was an ambition they shared, or purported to share. But Young was expressing a view which was representative of much of his audience and Thatcher responded in terms that were directed to that same audience.

After the Jimmy Young interview, the FCO submitted a slightly amended outline of the speech. In submitting it to the Foreign Secretary, John Kerr, the senior official handling European policy, observed: 'Though the Jimmy Young Show shows that the No 10 market for constructive language on the Community may still be poor, we can delay no longer...We are most likely to produce a constructive outcome if we play on two firmly held Prime Ministerial views – the need for an enterprise Europe and the maintenance of European defence efforts'.

Whatever chances the FCO draft might have had of finding favour in Downing Street were almost certainly blown away by the speech made by Jacques Delors at the TUC conference in September 1988 in which he called for European-level collective bargaining. The fact of the speech, let alone its content, was a red rag to Mrs Thatcher. It is not clear that Delors himself appreciated that appearing as a friend in the camp of the enemy would be seen as a calculatedly hostile act.

So the version of the draft speech that was sent back across Downing Street to the FCO bore no relationship to the Foreign Office draft and was much closer to the tone and content of what the Prime Minister had said to Jimmy Young. It was almost wholly the work of Margaret Thatcher's Private Secretary, Charles Powell. But the views and sentiments were hers. The Foreign Office sought a few changes to the text. Howe commented that he agreed with the speech's argument that a stronger Europe did not mean the creation of a new European super state, but he also argued that it did, and would, require some sacrifice of political independence and of the rights of national parliaments: that was inherent in the Treaties. Howe thought the draft tended to view the world as though the UK had not adhered to any of those same European treaties. A few of Howe's suggested changes were accepted but the speech as delivered was a perfect expression of Thatcher's views. It sent shockwaves around Europe.

The speech started with a joke. Inviting her to make a speech about Europe was, said Mrs Thatcher, rather like inviting Genghis Khan to speak about the virtues of peaceful co-existence. But Europe was not the creation of the Treaty of Rome, or the property of any one group or institution. The British, she pointed out, were of Celtic, Saxon, and Danish origin. They had, to use a favourite European term, been 'restructured' under the Normans and Angevins. Europe's belief in personal liberty was, said Thatcher, based on the 'idea of Christendom with its recognition of the unique and spiritual nature of the individual'. She added, even more controversially, that the 'story of how Europeans explored and colonised and – yes without apology – civilised much of the world is an extraordinary tale of talent, skill and courage'. She vaunted Britain's role in saving Europe: 'Over the centuries, we have fought and died for her freedom, fought to prevent Europe from falling under the dominance of a single power. Had it not been for that, Europe would have been unified long before now – but not in liberty or justice.'

Then came one of the statements which constitute the most powerful and, at the time most controversial, bits of the speech. 'The European Community', said Thatcher, 'is one manifestation of that European identity. It is not the only one. We must never forget that east of the iron curtain people who once enjoyed a full share of European culture, freedom and identity have been cut off from their roots. We shall always look on Warsaw, Prague and Budapest as great European cities.'

Mrs Thatcher went on to make clear that the UK, under her leadership, was committed to her membership of the European Community. The British record, she said was one of 'nearly 2000 years of British involvement in Europe, cooperation with Europe and contribution to Europe, a contribution which is today as strong as ever. The European Community belongs to all its members. It must reflect the traditions and aspirations of all its members. And let me be quite clear. Britain does not dream of some cosy, isolated existence on the fringes of Europe. Our destiny is in Europe, as part of the Community... The Community is not an end in itself...The European Community is a practical means by which Europe can ensure the future prosperity and security of its people...Success goes to the countries which encourage individual initiative and enterprise, rather than those which attempt to diminish them.'

Mrs Thatcher then set out her prescription for a liberal, non-protectionist, enterprise-friendly Community. To try to suppress nationhood and concentrate it instead at the centre of a European conglomerate would be highly dangerous. 'Working together', she asserted, 'does not require power to be centralised in Brussels, or decisions to be taken by an appointed bureaucracy. Indeed, it is ironic that, just when those countries such as the Soviet Union, which have tried to run everything from the centre, are learning that success depends on dispersing power away from the centre, there are some in the Community who want to move in the opposite direction. We have not successfully rolled back the frontiers of the state in Britain, only to see them re-imposed at European level with a European super state exercising a new dominance from Brussels. Certainly, we want to see Europe more united and with a greater sense of common purpose. But it must be in a way which preserves traditions, parliamentary powers and sense of national pride in one's own country.' Her approach, Thatcher told her audience, did not require new documents. What were needed were decisions on the next steps forward rather than the distraction of utopian goals. For, 'Utopia never comes. We know we should not like it if it did. Let Europe be a family of nations...doing more together but realising our national identity no less than our common European endeavour'. She had spoken of the importance of NATO. 'Let us have a Europe', she said, 'which preserves that Atlantic community – that Europe on both sides of the Atlantic – which is our noblest inheritance and our greatest strength'.[10]

Thatcher's speech was welcomed in Washington. President Reagan's National Security Adviser, Colin Powell, briefed President Reagan that 'Thatcher's assertiveness in advancing her vision of East-West and Alliance relations generates hostility from our European allies'. All her points were, said Powell, welcome to the USA but her speech had been viewed in Europe 'as another attempt by Thatcher to dictate the extent and limits to a united Europe'. The US Secretary of State, George Schultz, wrote to her with 'admiration and respect' for her 'clear, compelling and convincing' prescription for the EEC.[11]

Thatcher's Press Secretary, Bernard Ingham, had spun the speech so as to give it maximum favourable exposure in the tabloid media. On the continent,

---

[10] For the text of the speech see: https//www.margaretthatcher.org/document/107332.
[11] https://www.margaretthatcher.org/archive/1988 CAC6.

it was greeted with dismay. Her attack on the centralizing ambitions of the European Commission was regarded as profound heresy: a deliberate attack on the principles of integration to which every other Member State paid lip service. Almost more shocking was her suggestion that Europe was more than the European Community and that it encompassed the countries of eastern and central Europe—with the implication that they might one day be members of the Community. This too was a heresy.

At the time, and subsequently, the Bruges speech became a rallying point for Eurosceptic Conservative politicians who, unlike their leader, were indeed opposed to Britain's EEC membership. That it should be so treated was not Thatcher's intention.

I re-read the speech for the first time in many years when I was working for Tony Blair in Downing Street in the early 2000s. Blair asked me one day to produce a copy for him to read. When he had done so, he spoke out loud the thought that had come to my mind on re-reading it: that it was a good, and far from extreme, speech. Indeed, today, it represents a view of the European Union to which probably all its Member States could subscribe. But beneath the words, there had been a significant shift in Thatcher's attitudes. The trend of EEC policy as conceived and fostered by Jacques Delors was increasingly alien to her thinking and she was not disposed to accept it.

Thatcher had supported Delors' initial appointment as Commission President in 1984. Her favoured candidate for the job at the time was Etienne (Stevie) Davignon, the Belgian Commission member responsible for industrial policy. He was a rigorous operator whom she admired. But, at a time when the Commission President was appointed by a consensus of the EEC Heads of Government, Davignon was unacceptable to Chancellor Kohl. Davignon had been especially rigorous in managing the restructuring of the EEC steel industry and the German government, despite its European rhetoric, was one of the more protectionist EEC members. Davignon had not been forgiven for his exercise of the European, at the expense of the German national, interest.

Claude Cheysson, the French Foreign Minister, was, with Delors, one of two possible French candidates for the job. Cheysson had been a thorn in British flesh over the budget issue, and Thatcher told Roland Dumas, Mitterrand's closest confidant, that, to save him the embarrassment of having to ask her, she would 'tell him that Cheysson would not make a good President'. Dumas replied that she 'was right in her comments on possible French candidates'.[12]

---

[12] PREM 19/1220, TNA.

Thatcher had skilfully traded her support for Delors' candidacy so as to secure Mitterrand's support for a candidate of her own. The Frenchman, Emile Noel, had been Secretary General of the Commission from its outset and was due to retire. Thatcher persuaded Mitterrand to agree to support, as his successor, her closest and most trusted official adviser on Europe, David Williamson. Williamson was to experience an uneasy tenure under Delors but is remembered fondly in Brussels for the decent, clever, honest, and honourable man he was.

By the end of the British Presidency in the second half of 1986, relations between Thatcher and Delors had begun to deteriorate. The London European Council chaired by Thatcher in December 1986 focused on targets for completion of the single market. After it was over, Thatcher and Delors appeared together for the traditional Press conference. Thatcher hogged the limelight and Delors sat silently beside her. When eventually invited to speak, he refused to do so. 'I had no idea you were the strong silent type', Thatcher observed, to general laughter.

A few days later, Thatcher flew to Strasbourg to address the European Parliament at the end of the British Presidency. This required a workmanlike speech on what had been achieved in the six months, and I and others had produced a draft of suitable worthiness which the Prime Minister duly delivered. Delors then stood up and, in effect, denounced the British Presidency. Thatcher was livid. At the end of the debate, she demanded a right of reply and electrified the European Parliament with a House of Commons performance which was feisty and combative. The grown-ups then adjourned for lunch, where the Prime Minister and Delors were compelled to sit next to each other. David Williamson, still then her adviser, was also present. He commented afterwards that, in his relations with the Prime Minister, Delors had contrived to perform like a sports car in reverse: by his attack on her in the Assembly he had gone from 60 mph to zero in eight seconds.

There were to be deeper reasons for the mutual disaffection. The first was the way in which Delors, who had denounced the Single European Act as tame and timid, then misused it (in British eyes) to promote an agenda of social harmonization disguised as measures on health and safety at work. More significantly, Delors was intent on carrying forward the work on EMU for which the Single European Act had created an opening.

In June 1988, at a European Council in Hanover, Thatcher agreed to the establishment of a committee, chaired by Delors, to examine the issue of EMU. In her autobiography, Thatcher glossed over why she had agreed to the establishment of the committee, an act which was viewed with dismay by her Chancellor of the Exchequer, Nigel Lawson. She appointed as her representative on the committee the Governor of the Bank of England, Robin Leigh-Pemberton. Leigh-Pemberton was not the man, either by temperament or inclination, to stand up to Delors. Knowing that the Chairman of the German Bundesbank, Karl-Otto Poehl, had considerable reservations about the wisdom of a European single currency, Thatcher hoped that he would deter Kohl from going ahead. In this she was mistaken.

Thatcher took little interest in the work of the committee and Leigh-Pemberton received almost no guidance from Downing Street. My own belief is that Thatcher was to some extent influenced by what had happened when the French and British had purloined the British text on foreign policy cooperation and proclaimed it as an all-singing and dancing treaty of European Union. Indeed, asked by the Press after her Bruges speech about her views on EMU, and a European Central Bank in particular, she had said: 'I neither want nor expect ever to see such a bank in my lifetime nor, if I am twanging a harp, for quite a long time afterwards. *What I suspect they will attempt to do is to call something a European Central Bank*' [my italics].

Whatever Thatcher's expectations, by early 1989 the Delors committee had come up with a report which comprised a complete plan for progress to EMU in three stages. In Stage One, all Member States would join the ERM. There would then be a transitional Stage Two, culminating in Stage Three in which exchange rates would be fixed and a European Central Bank established.

The proposal that all Member States should join the ERM in Stage One put further pressure on the Prime Minister on a question that preoccupied the government and Whitehall increasingly during 1989. British membership of the ERM had been urged on the new Conservative government by Helmut Schmidt when it came into office in 1979. The issue was examined on a number of occasions. Thatcher, and indeed Howe during his time as Chancellor, believed that the economic risks of membership outweighed the advantages, not least because of the exposure of sterling as a reserve currency. The government's formula: that it would join 'when the time is right', had, by 1989, become something of a mantra and it was well known that both Lawson, as Chancellor, and Howe, as Foreign Secretary, were increasingly in favour of joining. The economic arguments were credible. The ERM, with the German Deutschmark at its core, provided a spine of discipline. Lawson was convinced that ERM membership would reduce exchange rate fluctuations and would bolster the government's anti-inflationary policy.

Thatcher, powerfully supported by her economic adviser, Alan Walters, remained adamantly opposed and decreasingly open to argument on the subject.

The issue came to a head in June 1989. The European Council was due to meet and Thatcher and Howe were to fly to Madrid on Sunday, 25 June. Attempts by Howe and Lawson to get Thatcher to address and discuss the issue of ERM membership had been resisted strenuously. On the Saturday, twenty-four hours before leaving for Madrid, Geoffrey Howe asked me, as his Private Secretary, to seek a meeting for him and Lawson with the Prime Minister to discuss what should be said about Britain's ERM policy at the summit. Initially, Thatcher's Private Secretary, Charles Powell, told me that Thatcher would not see them. I persisted, making it clear, as Howe had instructed me, that this was too important an issue for the PM to refuse to see her two most senior Ministers.

A meeting was held between the three on Sunday morning. Howe and Lawson threatened to resign if Thatcher refused to set a date for the UK's membership of the ERM. Thatcher did not respond and the meeting broke up in silence.

En route to Madrid, the Prime Minister, instead of having the Foreign Secretary sit with her as usual, stayed ensconced with her own staff while Howe and his team were placed in a different section of the RAF aircraft, separated by a curtain which was very deliberately closed by one of Thatcher's staff every time the movement of the plane threatened to open it. None of the usual discussion took place about the conduct of the meeting the next day. When we arrived in Madrid, I travelled in a car with Charles Powell, who was monosyllabic. Our Ambassador to Spain had arranged an informal dinner at his house for the Prime Minister and the delegation. She did not show up. Instead, she stayed in her hotel and had supper in her room.

The following morning, the Prime Minister gave Howe no indication as to what she was going to say at the meeting. In the event, she did not suggest a date by which the UK would join the ERM but she departed from the usual formula and did enough to convince both Howe and the other Heads of Government that there had been a substantive change in her position.

At lunchtime, there was a delegation meeting. The Prime Minister was due to go to Austria for a summer break. Austria was a candidate for EEC membership. At one point in the meeting, Thatcher turned to Powell: 'Remind me to tell the Austrians not to join', she said.

Thatcher's treatment, both of the ERM as an issue, and of Howe as a colleague, was led by emotion as well as reason. So was her action in removing

Howe from the Foreign Office in a reshuffle a few weeks later. Howe had been Foreign Secretary for six years. In principle, a change was not unreasonable. Relations between the two people who had worked together to effect the Thatcher revolution had deteriorated. Yet Thatcher, before Madrid, had told her Chief Whip that she planned no change at the FCO. After Madrid, she changed her mind. It was an act of revenge and was handled as such. Howe considered resignation. She offered him the role of Leader of the House of Commons. Howe asked for, and secured, the title of Deputy Prime Minister, only for her Press Secretary to tell the Press that the title was meaningless. Howe eventually resigned from his new post fifteen months later. Her personal treatment of him in the intervening period was sometimes abusive and certainly humiliating.

By the end of 1989, opinion in the EEC (against British opposition) was moving towards holding another intergovernmental conference (IGC): this time to discuss EMU. To that agenda was soon to be added the topic of Political Union. Meanwhile, the collapse of the Soviet Union at the end of 1989, and German reunification in 1990, were redrawing the map of Europe. The collapse of the Soviet Union was, of course, welcome to Thatcher. She was the first western leader to establish a constructive working relationship with President Gorbachev. Claims that are sometimes made that the collapse of the Soviet Union, and the consequential liberation of central Europe, can be credited to Reagan, Thatcher, and Pope John Paul II are wide of the mark. Revolutions are generally made from inside. The greatest credit for the peaceful nature of the revolution goes to Gorbachev and his Foreign Minister, Shevardnadze, who were determined that the horrors Russia and her satellites had suffered under Stalin would never again be repeated. But Thatcher was one of the first to recognize that Gorbachev was a quite different, and reformist, Soviet leader and she was rightly seen in the countries of eastern and central Europe as a champion and role model. She had, as she herself claimed, been one of those in the West 'who were prepared to defend liberty and who kept alive their [the people of Soviet-controlled Europe's] hope that one day eastern Europe too would enjoy freedom'.[13]

The reunification of Germany was a different matter. It had long been British policy to support the goal of a reunited Germany, but in the expect-ation that it would not happen on any foreseeable timescale. Thatcher, a teenager in the Second World War, shared the suspicions of Germany that were widespread among Britons of her generation given the experience of two

---

[13] Margaret Thatcher, *The Downing Street Years* (London: HarperCollins, 1993), p. 859.

world wars. Together with President Mitterrand, she feared that a united Germany would dominate Europe. In part encouraged by the rhetoric of Mitterrand, who described the Germans to her as a people who had never known where their borders lay, she resisted the notion that reunification was inevitable and desirable. But East Germany as a viable state collapsed and the intervention of the Bonn government became an irresistible necessity which Thatcher was obliged to accept. When one of Thatcher's most loyal Ministers, Nicholas Ridley, gave an interview to the *Spectator* in which he denounced EMU as a German racket, German behaviour as 'absolutely intolerable' and predicted that Kohl 'would soon be trying to take over everything', his views were seen as echoing those of his leader. Only reluctantly did she accept Ridley's resignation, forced by the storm provoked by the interview.

Over German reunification, Thatcher had positioned herself, in the words of President George H. Bush as an 'anchor to windward', i.e. perceived as adrift from mainstream opinion. Over EMU and Political Union, the gap between Thatcher and the rest of the EEC was also widening. Lawson resigned as Chancellor in October 1989, to be replaced by John Major who, only three months earlier, had been promoted to Foreign Secretary. Major, aided by Douglas Hurd, his successor at the Foreign Office, succeeded in persuading Thatcher to allow the UK to join the ERM in October 1990. She did so with reluctance. The original argument advanced by Lawson for joining (to combat inflation) was by then made more compelling because of the inflationary policies Lawson had pursued following her 1987 election victory. The Thatcher economic record was becoming tarnished. There was a Cabinet majority for joining the ERM and, if Thatcher was going to argue against economic and monetary *union*, she needed to demonstrate that the UK had a clear basis on which to press for the alternative course of *cooperation*. Joining the ERM was part of that process.

So too was a proposal which had been put forward in July by the Chancellor of the Exchequer, John Major, for a common currency, the so-called 'hard ecu'. This was to be a new international currency which would coexist besides the national currencies of the twelve EEC Member States. This new ecu would never be devalued. It would always be as strong as any other European currency. The idea was to try to bridge the gap between British opposition to a single currency and the desire of other EEC Member States to progress towards such a single currency. Under the British scheme, there was a possibility of the common currency evolving into a single currency. It was a clever proposal and a sensible one. Had it been adopted, much of the controversial history and track record of the single currency might have been avoided. But it was, for Britain's partners, too little too late. It was regarded as a spoiler and given scant serious attention.

Accordingly, at a European Council in Rome on 27 and 28 October 1990, Thatcher came under pressure to agree to a start date for the second phase of EMU. She resisted. For the first time in the life of the EEC, a delegation (the British), refused to agree to the conclusions as drafted by the Presidency and formally reserved its position both on EMU and on political union.

Geoffrey Howe resigned from the government on 1 November 1990. In his autobiography, Howe describes his dismay at how, as soon as she was out of the Rome conference room, Thatcher 'hardened her position on EMU. The Community, she said, was on the way to "cloud cuckoo land". The British Parliament would "never agree to a single currency". We should "veto the very idea", and any subsequent treaty, because "we shall block things which are not in Britain's interests".'[14]

Howe was already contemplating resignation, but decided to await the Prime Minister's statement to Parliament on the European Council on 30 October. His account of Thatcher's statement suggests that, once the carefully prepared statement had been made, 'she let herself go as she had never before been heard in public' on Europe. Her statement itself was forthright, but reasoned. She had 'reserved the United Kingdom's position on, for example, extension of the Community's powers into new areas, greater powers for the European Parliament in the legislative sphere, defining European citizenship, and a common foreign and security policy. All these are areas for discussion at the intergovernmental conference, rather than to be settled in advance.'

On EMU, she had 'stressed that we would be ready to move beyond the present position to the creation of a European monetary fund and a common Community currency which I have called a hard ecu. But we would not be prepared to agree to set a date for starting the next stage of economic and monetary union before there is any agreement on what that stage should comprise. And I again emphasised that we would not be prepared to have a single currency imposed upon us, nor to surrender the use of the pound sterling as our currency. The hard ecu would be a parallel currency, not a single currency. If, as time went by, people and Governments chose to use it widely, it could evolve towards a single currency. But our national currency would remain unless a decision to abolish it were freely taken by future generations of Parliament and people. A single currency is not the policy of this Government . . .'

[14] Geoffrey Howe, *Conflict of Loyalty* (London: Macmillan, 1984), p. 643.

In the subsequent debate, the Prime Minister was characteristically feisty:

'It is our purpose to retain the power and influence of this House, rather than denude it of many of its powers...

'Yes, the Commission wants to increase its powers. Yes, it is a non-elected body...The President of the Commission, Mr Delors, said at a press conference the other day that he wanted the European Parliament to be the democratic body of the Community, he wanted the Commission to be the Executive and he wanted the Council of Ministers to be the Senate. No. No. No...

'What is the point of trying to get elected to Parliament only to hand over sterling and the powers of this House to Europe...?

'...Several countries in the Community are highly protectionist. The Common Agricultural Policy is a protectionist policy, but we will try to reduce the protectionism, first because it would help the third world, secondly because it would mean that we would not have export subsidies – and thereby take business away from other countries – and thirdly because in this country we believe in open trade...

'This Government have no intention of abolishing the pound sterling. If the hard ecu were to evolve and much greater use were made of it, that would be a discussion for future Parliaments and generations. That decision could be taken only once. It should not be taken in the current atmosphere, but only after the greatest possible consideration...We are more stable and influential with sterling, and it is an expression of our sovereignty. The Government believe in the pound sterling.

'There are some things for which there was majority voting within the Community when we went in, and we accepted that; and for the specific objective of achieving the Single European Act only, there have been more matters. Now there is an attempt to get far more things passed by majority voting. That means we would have more laws imposed on us, even if the House was flatly against them...We should be very slow to add to any majority competence on the part of the Community.

'...It is very ironic indeed that, at a time when eastern Europe is striving for greater democracy, the Commission should be striving to extinguish democracy and to put more and more power into its own hands, or into the hands of non-elected bodies.

'...I accept that many in the European Community would like to have their version of economic and monetary union, which would lead to passing powers away from national Parliaments to a non-elected body – in fact to a central board of bankers – to majority voting and to the giving of more legislative power to the European Parliament. That is their version, but it is not the version that we have accepted. The Single European Act defined economic and monetary union as "Cooperation in Economic and Monetary policy". That is all you need, in my view...I am pretty certain that most people in this country would prefer to continue to use sterling. If, by their choice, I was wrong, there would come a time when we would have to address the question. However, that would not be for us but for future generations in the House.'

In response to questions, Mrs Thatcher said that she thought many of her European colleagues would say that 'there is no way in which there can be a single currency until all economies are in the same state of development, the same state of prosperity and in a Europe with one economy right across it. I do not think that there is any possibility of that stage being reached for a very long time. To take a single currency long before that has happened would be to weaken it and not to strengthen it.' There would, she said, 'have to be enormous transfers of money from one country to another...If we have a single currency or a locked currency, the differences come out substantially in unemployment or vast movements of people from one country to another. Many people who talk about a single currency have never considered its full implications.'

One of Thatcher's questioners was David Owen, former Foreign Secretary and, before that, pro-European Labour rebel. Owen had been part of the radical centre group of senior Labour figures who had broken with the Labour Party to form the SDP in the 1980s, in part because of Labour's anti-EEC policies. Owen had become leader of the SDP after Roy Jenkins lost his parliamentary seat in the 1987 General Election. A majority of the SDP had then voted for merger with the Liberal Party (which became the Liberal Democrat Party as we know it today). Owen, who opposed merger, and a small minority of the SDP, had continued alone but the Party had finally been wound up earlier in 1990. Now, Owen asked in the House whether it was 'not perfectly clear that what was being attempted at Rome was a bounce which led only one way – to a single federal united states of Europe?'

Thatcher agreed. 'That', she said, 'is precisely the stance we took. It is the stance we have taken on many previous occasions. The European monetary system to which we belong is designed for twelve sovereign states, in cooperation with one another, to come to an exchange rate mechanism. What is being proposed now – economic and monetary union – is the back door to a federal Europe, which we totally and utterly reject. We prefer greater economic and monetary cooperation, which can be achieved by keeping our sovereignty.'

Challenged by a Labour MP that her European performance was one in which 'she squawks and makes a noise at the beginning but always comes round and gives way in the end', Thatcher retorted: 'That is what they said when I was negotiating for a better budget deal for Britain... They found out differently.'[15]

It was all too much for Geoffrey Howe. He resigned on 1 November. In his resignation statement in the House on 13 November, Howe said: 'The tragedy is – and it is for me personally, for my party, for our whole people and for my Right Hon. Friend herself, a very real tragedy – that the Prime Minister's perceived attitude towards Europe is running increasingly serious risks for the future of our nation. It risks minimising our influence and maximising our chances of being once again shut out. We have paid heavily in the past for late starts and squandered opportunities in Europe. We dare not let that happen again. If we detach ourselves completely, as a party or a nation, from the middle ground of Europe, the effects will be incalculable and very hard ever to correct.'[16]

Howe's resignation statement triggered a challenge to Thatcher's leadership of the Conservative Party. By the end of November, she too was gone.

Was Geoffrey Howe right in his analysis and his predictions? As far as the Conservative Party was concerned, he was. There was already a significant anti-European segment in the Conservative Party, and growing anti-European sentiment in the Conservative-leaning Press. Ennobled after her resignation, Lady Thatcher became, in the House of Lords, a focus of Conservative Eurosceptic discontent. In time, she became the instigator and rallying point of opposition to the European policies of her chosen successor, John Major. Anti-Europeanism became a token of loyalty to her as the fallen leader. As John Major himself said to me when I worked for him: 'I am standing astride a crack in the Conservative Party that is getting wider by the day.'

Sir Nicholas Henderson, successively British Ambassador in Warsaw, Bonn, Paris and Washington, played a brilliant part in influencing the US government and American public opinion during the Falklands war. He recognized all of Margaret Thatcher's qualities of leadership and indomitable courage. I dedicated my first book on the EEC to him. When he had read it, he said that

---

[15] *Hansard*, 30 October 1990, vol. 178, cols. 871–80.
[16] *Hansard*, 13 November 1990, vol. 180, cols. 461–5.

he thought that our failure to be wholehearted members of the European Union could be laid primarily at Thatcher's door.

In 1987, Britain's Ambassador in Bonn, Julian Bullard, wrote a letter to the FCO which vividly expressed what many of us working on European issues at the time also felt. 'Here we have', he wrote, 'a Prime Minister in her ninth year in office, with vast international experience, including more than twenty-five European summits, presiding over a country whose economy, thanks largely to her, is turning out enviable statistics . . . You would think, wouldn't you, that in these circumstances Britain would be giving a lead in Europe and the Continentals would be following. But is this happening? I think not. Why not? Because we don't seem to be interested in any particular objective except the internal market in which Smarties can be sold in the same packet everywhere from Copenhagen to Constantia . . . What I think is missing: Vision.'

By contrast, Bullard continued, the pattern of the Franco-German relationship had been 'for the two Heads of Government to plant flags far ahead of their respective front lines, towards which the troops then valiantly struggle . . . I would plead that at least more thought should be given to the style of British policy in Europe. The plain speaking of the House of Commons does not translate well into Continental languages, especially in countries that live by coalition and compromise. Chancellor Kohl once said to me that in any political argument one should bear in mind, not only the current battle, but the next. And not everything unquantifiable is unimportant.'[17]

Two questions arise in my mind. The first is whether Thatcher was in substance, as opposed to style, significantly different from other British leaders. She certainly argued Britain's corner more stridently than any British Prime Minister before or since. To an extent, she made Britain's place in the EEC a 'corner' by so doing. If Thatcher had been capable of changing her style, she would not have been the leader she was. That style undoubtedly discombobulated diplomats like me whose job was both to represent British interests and avoid turbulence in doing so. Under Thatcher, few issues of importance could be glossed. On the other hand, she put Britain on the map as never before. A visit to Washington by Prime Minister Jim Callaghan rated a few lines in the *New York Times*. The first visit of Thatcher as Prime Minister, for which I was the gofer late in 1979, dominated the headlines and the TV news. Her address to both Houses of Congress electrified the audience. I spent the first ten years of my Foreign Office career doing my bit to represent a country in visible decline: widely seen as the sick man of Europe. All that changed with Thatcher.

[17] Wall, *A Stranger in Europe*, pp. 76–7.

On substance, it is harder to argue that her policies were significantly different from those of her predecessors, Wilson, Heath and Callaghan. Both Wilson and Heath were committed on paper to EMU. But they thought its realization was far distant. Even Heath saw it more as an aspiration than a commitment and, in the event, funked the bold move to monetary integration that he and Willy Brandt had imagined soon after Heath became Prime Minister.

As for her immediate successor, John Major did make one very significant shift. Thatcher wanted to oppose a single currency outright. Major accepted the legal advice he received that, in such a situation, eleven Member States would make a treaty of their own, outside the EEC framework, giving the UK no opportunity to influence its content. Hence the opt-out for the UK that was to be at the heart of the Maastricht Treaty. But Thatcher, herself, had she remained in office, would very probably have come to the same conclusion, just as she had reluctantly shifted her stance on majority voting in order to secure the single market. And it is striking, that in the House of Commons session that triggered Howe's departure, on two occasions Thatcher did not rule out a single currency for ever but said that it would be for future generations of the House of Commons to decide.

On the key issues on which she fought, Thatcher was pursuing longstanding UK interests: a fair budget settlement, reform of the absurdly wasteful CAP, economic liberalization and the creation of a single market, anti-protectionist trade policies, openness to the countries of Eastern and Central Europe. On all those issues, apart from enlargement, Thatcher was pursuing the task started by Macmillan with the first application for membership: to redress the harm done to British interests by our failure to join the EEC at the outset and thus to shape its policies. She, like Wilson and Heath, was also paying the price for de Gaulle's ten-year-long veto of British membership. During that time the EEC policies (budget, CAP, protectionism) most damaging to British interests were set in place. They had become the *acquis communautaire*: in large part, the sum total of the vested interests of the founder members. To change that required more than even the radical Thatcher could accomplish.

Like her predecessors and successors, Thatcher also had to operate within the constraints of parliamentary and public support. Successive governments, from Macmillan onwards, had played down a fundamental fact of EEC membership: laws made in the EEC could not be changed by national parliaments. The gradual accretion of European competence through practical steps on product safety, common technical standards etc. did not arouse significant opposition and was justified by the practical benefits. By contrast, Treaty change, as was involved in the Single European Act and EMU, raised in stark terms the whole question of parliamentary sovereignty and was bound to reopen old arguments about the political and constitutional price of membership. No other Member State at the time faced that same argument so acutely. Against that background, even Tony Blair, the most European of Prime Ministers since Heath, was unable to fulfil his declared aim of taking the UK into the single currency.

The second question is harder to answer: was Thatcher more far sighted than her critics, such as Geoffrey Howe? She clearly foresaw the huge implications of a single currency, political and economic. That is why her successor, John Major, and Gordon Brown as Chancellor of the Exchequer under Blair, placed such emphasis on the need for economic convergence as a prior condition of a successful single currency. The inherent loss of control over exchange and interest rates removed two of the levers of economic management open to national governments. Thatcher foresaw the implications of those constraints on national action in terms of unemployment, and that to forestall that unemployment would require large fiscal transfers from the rich to the poor members of the Eurozone. Some on the continent saw it too but the Germans, in particular, refused to countenance fiscal transfers as an instrument of Eurozone management. To an extent, crisis in the Eurozone has forced that concession on them but, by general consent, too little too late.

One by-product of that tension within the Eurozone has been the rise of nationalist, anti-EU sentiment. That possibility was implicit in Thatcher's scepticism about the political realism of federal ambitions in a Community of separate nation states. She accepted that there might be an osmotic process: a common currency might, given the consent of parliaments and people, evolve into a single currency. But, in her view it could not successfully be forced. In that, her judgement has proved to be prescient. The general view at the time was that expressed in Bullard's letter to the FCO: if the French and Germans planted a flag, others would follow and the march to a federal future would continue. In reality, the single currency, as set out in the Maastricht Treaty, was a compromise between France, which would accept German reunification provided Germany was tightly and indefinitely bound into European structures; and a Germany which reluctantly agreed those terms as the price of French acceptance of reunification. It was at heart a bilateral political deal turned into EU form. Today, no Member State inside the Eurozone wishes to leave: the price of staying in is lower than the cost of leaving. But, given what they know now, few of the present Eurozone members regard the single currency, as constructed at Maastricht, as wise in how it was conceived or executed.

It is futile to argue that, had Britain been in at the beginning, the single currency would have been designed differently. It was as politically inconceivable for a British government to embrace the single currency in the 1990s as it had been for the British government of the day to embrace the Coal and Steel Community in the 1950s. Nonetheless, the course that Thatcher set hardened the fault lines between Britain and her European partners. It was the ambition of her successor, John Major, to put Britain at the heart of Europe. That hope was to prove to be all too forlorn.

8

One Foot In and One Foot Out, 1990–1997

The most fraught negotiation in the life of any Foreign Secretary takes place less than a hundred yards from his own grand office, overlooking Horse Guards Parade and St James's Park. That negotiation is the annual set-to with the Chief Secretary of the Treasury, guardian of the government's purse strings and scourge of departmental budgets.

In 1988, I accompanied the then Foreign Secretary, Sir Geoffrey Howe, to do battle with a youngish John Major (Chief Secretary in his first Cabinet post) over the FCO budget. Officials of the two departments had been arguing about it for weeks.

Howe was the government's most senior Cabinet member. John Major treated him accordingly: he was friendly (as was his nature) and polite. And, in his charming, good-natured way, extremely tough. The secret of being a successful Chief Secretary is to know the budget of the Department, whose pleas for more cash you are obliged to deny, better than the Departmental Minister whose budget you are attempting to cut down to size. In that respect, Major had met his match. Howe had not been a successful commercial barrister for nothing. He was master of his brief.

The Foreign Secretary enjoyed the use of a magnificent 'grace and favour' stately home in the Kent countryside, called Chevening. It also happened to be conveniently close to Howe's constituency. The Howes went there at every available weekend. At one point in the to and fro of argument, Howe said ingratiatingly to Major: 'If you give me this point, I'll invite you to Chevening.' 'If', said John Major, 'you don't agree with what I am asking, you may not have a Chevening to invite me to'.

Thus did I meet the politician who, a year or so later, was to become my boss in the Foreign Office and subsequently in 10 Downing Street. He was charming, warm, quite without pomposity. Contrary to his public image as a 'grey' politician, in private he was sharp and witty. He came from a family which fell on hard times. He left school without taking A-levels and did not go to university. He secured a job in the Standard Chartered Bank and was posted to Nigeria. Badly hurt in a car crash, he spent nine months in hospital in Lagos. During that time, he read. Prominent among the books he read were the novels of Anthony Trollope, on whose work he is expert. Many of us would argue that there could be no better education: in the richness of the English language, in the understanding of human nature and motivations and in the excitement, intrigue, highs and lows of political life.

Back in the UK, Major entered local politics in Lambeth, on the Conservative side. One of his Labour opponents was Ken Livingstone, the future Mayor of London.[1]

John Major's appointment to succeed Geoffrey Howe as Foreign Secretary in the July 1989 Cabinet reshuffle was as much of a surprise to the rest of the political establishment as it was to him. Thatcher wanted someone 'who thinks as I do', as she told him. That was not always to be the case, even in the early days. But, if John Major did not always think as Thatcher did, he always knew how she would think. That was why, when, just three months later, Lawson resigned as Chancellor in October 1989, she did not hesitate to move Major to the Treasury in his place. It was Major who convinced her to appoint Douglas Hurd, rather than her favourite, Cecil Parkinson, to succeed him at the FCO. And it was Major, albeit with Hurd's support, who persuaded her, finally, to accept that the UK should join the Exchange Rate Mechanism (ERM). Of the three candidates to succeed her when she fell from power in 1990 (Heseltine, Hurd, and Major), Major was her clear and open favourite, though once he was in office, and she was out of it, she came to treat him to levels of hostility and overt opposition which far surpassed the similar treatment that Heath had meted out to her.

I had quickly learned, while working for Major in his brief time at the FCO, that he was sensitive about his relative lack of formal schooling, especially in a department that still drew its senior staff from private schools and Oxbridge. But it would have been a rash official who assumed that lack of higher education meant lack of high intelligence. Major was not just a quick study, he was acutely tuned to assessing the character and motivations of the politicians from other governments with whom he had to deal. He was methodical in his approach to decision making, often drawing a line down the middle of a page and writing the pros and cons of courses of action on either side. His judgement was good. He swiftly decided that a proposal to sell Hawk trainer aircraft to Iraq's Saddam Hussein—heavily touted by the Arabists in the FCO—was not an acceptable proposition given Saddam's

---

[1] During Major's time at Number 10, Livingstone was a backbench Labour MP. If he had a question on the Order Paper for PM's Questions, instead of deploying the usual trick of trying to catch Major out, he would sometimes call Downing Street to say what it was he wanted to find out about.

persecution of many of his own citizens. That plan had sat undecided in the Foreign Secretary's in-tray for months before Major's arrival.

John Major's views on the EEC were those of a pragmatic Conservative. He had voted in the 1975 referendum in favour of continued membership. There had been times subsequently when his enthusiasm had waned but his consistent opinion was that the UK had made a decision to be a member and had to make a success of that commitment. He did not share Thatcher's intolerance of the ambitions of other Member States, even when he did not go along with them. He was not as easily riled by the machinations which characterize European negotiating. He had no animus against Germany and was personally and politically at ease with German reunification.

Mending fences with the German Chancellor was an early priority. Helmut Kohl, as a Conservative politician, wanted a good relationship with his British sister Party. Given how poor the personal chemistry between Kohl and Thatcher had been, an improvement was not difficult. But Major worked hard at it. He was a good listener and a good reader of the body language of others. He did not find it difficult to warm to Kohl's homespun but heartfelt accounts of his European philosophy and politics. Kohl had been a child in the war, with teenage memories of the devastating human consequences of the eventual German collapse. He did not take it for granted that Germany would remain democratically committed to the West. In his mind, there was a lurking risk of Germany drifting into a dangerous neutrality. Kohl believed fervently that the European Community was, both for Germany and her European partners, a safe space in which reunification could be accepted and managed: tied into rules made at European level.

A crucial part of that 'tying in' was Germany's bilateral relationship with France. Franco-German reconciliation had been at the heart of Churchill's call for a United States of Europe in 1946. That reconciliation had been cemented formally and practically by Chancellor Adenauer and President de Gaulle in the treaty signed immediately after de Gaulle's first veto of Britain's application for EEC membership. It had been reinforced by the cooperation between Schmidt and Giscard d'Estaing in establishing the ERM, and further consolidated in a seemingly unlikely partnership between Kohl and Mitterrand. That partnership was unlikely because of the very different political backgrounds and economic policies of the two leaders. But the institutionalization of frequent and intense contacts between France and Germany at all levels of politics, officialdom, and wider society had been one of the ingenious parts of the Franco-German treaty. The leaders of the two countries were locked into arrangements which compelled cooperation. Had Callaghan been able to join in pioneering the ERM, and had Britain been able to share and support a big vision of European union, it is just conceivable that the duo could have been a trio. But Thatcher had never warmed to the idea when it had been put to her by the Foreign Office. She preferred, not to cuddle up, but to stand up, to Germany. On top of that, Mitterrand and Kohl had been driven into each other's confidence and solidarity by their shared impatience of Margaret Thatcher's fight for 'her money back' and by her restrictive view of the limits of European integration.

Personally, Mitterrand had been as dismayed as Thatcher by the prospect of German reunification. For France, three times overrun by Germany in less than a century, apprehension about German power and motives was instinctive. At the time of German reunification, the French media reflected that anxiety in a way which was almost totally absent from British coverage. Would the new Germany be dangerously neutral or would it, conversely, become the one European superpower, dominant over all the other Member States? Reporting to London in May 1991, Britain's Ambassador in Paris, Sir Ewen Fergusson, wrote: 'It has become axiomatic in Paris that, over the medium term, a united Germany threatens to evolve into a European superpower. This unease over Germany translates into an almost obsessive anxiety to contain them within reinforced European structures . . . The clearest example is their determination to press quickly ahead with EMU as a means of getting a handle on German monetary policy before their economy recovers its former vigour and lest Kohl's Europeanist policies be replaced with more assertive nationalist ones.'[2]

When Kohl had assured Thatcher that he, like her, did not want to see a single currency come into being, he was not being disingenuous. But the fall of the Berlin Wall radically changed the political dynamic: Kohl was prepared to accept a single currency as the price of French acquiescence in Germany's reunification. In the Commission President, Jacques Delors, the two leaders found a skilled architect to turn their commitment to a single currency into reality. Germany, as a federal country, had few reservations about the transfer of powers to the European institutions that Delors advocated.

For the Germans, those institutions included the European Parliament. For them, the growth of a powerful European Parliament was a democratic imperative. In this, they did meet some French resistance. Mitterrand held the European Parliament in almost complete contempt, regularly asking John

---

[2] Stephen Wall, *A Stranger in Europe: Britain and the EU from Thatcher to Blair* (Oxford: Oxford University Press, 2008), p. 117.

Major whether anyone anywhere could name as many as five Members. But here too, the French were prepared to make limited concessions. At the time, in Britain, the idea that national identity and sovereignty were vested in Parliament at Westminster was taken for granted. Parliament's role and powers embodied a national view of the kind of country we were. In France, the National Assembly had no such resonance. For the duration of their appointment, French Ministers did not sit as members of the Assembly. The French Prime Minister was answerable before the Assembly; the French President was remote from it. So, for the French, what powers to cede to the European Parliament was a matter of negotiation. For the British, the issue raised intractable questions of existential democratic principle.

Of the European issues facing Major as he crossed the Downing Street threshold, mending fences was one priority. Major's views on substance were not far from those of Thatcher. But a stance on Europe which had exacerbated a split in the Conservative Party and led Britain's partners to an instinctive aversion to British ideas no matter what their merits, had to be addressed. Major not only cultivated Kohl from the outset; he chose Germany as the site of his first big speech on his European policy. That speech is an exemplar of the difference of approach between Thatcher and Major. On substance, it was close to Thatcher: Europe should develop by evolution, not by some treaty-based revolution; Britain was playing her part in the transformation of Europe, but not to the detriment of her ties with the United States or the Commonwealth; there were limits to what a European common foreign and security policy could accomplish; NATO must remain paramount. As far as EMU was concerned, Major thought 'it best to reserve judgement...We cannot accept its imposition'. Cooperation was the way forward for members of the EEC. Europe was made up of nation states. It was important 'to strike the right balance between closer cooperation and a proper respect for national institutions and traditions'. Then came the phrase, John Major's own addition to the draft presented to him by officials, that caught the headlines: 'My aims for Britain in the Community can be simply stated. I want us where we belong. At the very heart of Europe. Working with our partners in building the future.'[3]

'At the heart of Europe' was certainly intended to imply 'no longer at the throat of Europe' but it did not mean that Britain was suddenly going to change its previous stance and adopt that of the majority of its continental

[3] Sarah Hogg and Jonathan Hill, *Too Close to Call: Power and Politics—John Major in No. 10* (London: Little, Brown and Company, 1995), p. 79.

partners. Some, notably within the Conservative Party, chose to interpret it as a commitment to continental-style integration, and the phrase immediately became an albatross around Major's neck.

Major would have to attend his first European Council as Prime Minister in December 1990. The Italian Presidency had already succeeded, in October, in launching the promised intergovernmental conference (IGC) on the subject of EMU. They sought a similar leap forward towards political union, embracing co-decision on EEC laws for the European Parliament, i.e. a move towards equal legislative power with the Council of Ministers. They also wanted to bring the Western European Union (WEU) within the scope of the EEC Treaty. Since the WEU Treaty committed its members to a strict mutual defence guarantee, this represented a massive increase in the powers of the European Commission and in the obligations placed on Member States.

Saddam Hussein of Iraq had invaded and occupied Kuwait during the summer of 1990. Under UN authority, the United States and the UK were building support for an international coalition of forces to liberate Kuwait. Among EEC member countries there were huge disparities between both military capacity and serious commitment where the use of force was concerned. The Italian proposals smacked of the worst kind of grandstanding, but grandstanding with real and dangerous consequences on two counts: the first, a massive increase in powers which would pass from the nation state to the EEC institutions; and the second, a recipe for duplication of effort (since Europe's collective defence was assured through NATO) with resultant muddle and ineffectiveness. Given that the first duty of any British government was, and is, the defence of the realm the idea (as it was seen in London) of shedding responsibility and authority in that way was inconceivable.

Rather than adopt Thatcher's habit of digging in against all comers, and fighting every jot and comma of the European Council draft conclusions, Major preferred to let others put what he called their 'favourite dishes' on the menu so long as British ones (rather plainer fare than was to continental taste) were there as well. Unanimity would be required to conclude the IGC, so the UK's position was safeguarded.

Thus the issues of economic and monetary, and political, union were running in tandem. Major's stance on EMU was not ideological. He realized that, while Britain could block a treaty made under EEC rules requiring unanimity, she could not stop eleven other countries making a treaty on their own. So the idea of an opt-out for the United Kingdom was soon in British minds. But, just as important, was Major's wish to keep open the option of joining a single currency at a later date. A single currency was not his wish but he recognized that it might be successful. In the meantime, as he told President Mitterrand early in 1991, the British Parliament would not vote for membership and the credibility of a single currency would depend on adequate economic convergence between the prospective members. That convergence was lacking.

Major's more conciliatory language, and his friendly relations with Kohl, in particular, but also with Mitterrand, led to an effort on the part of all three governments to find common ground. But the main game remained a Franco-German one. Both governments knew that the balance of power was shifting in Germany's favour. France could no longer count on being the senior partner. At the same time, Germany was still interested in disguising its potential strength, Kohl telling Major that he knew that Nicholas Ridley's excoriation of Germany had gone wider than Ridley himself and that his views were shared, not least in some French quarters. So the pressure for an accommodation between France and Germany around the nature of a single currency was far stronger than any pressure on either of them to accommodate the British government—which did not want a single currency at all.

The British were also out on a limb in resisting, not just the proposed evolution towards a European defence identity, but also attempts to bring cooperation on migration matters and the fight against cross-border crime within the jurisdiction of the European Community, as opposed to the continuing national authority of the Member States. On top of all that, the French Prime Minister, Michel Rocard, was pressing for a European system of social organization. The example of capitalism in Latin America, he told Major, showed how dangerous capitalism could be unless social institutions were in place. This rang very loud alarm bells in the already Eurosceptic brain of Michael Howard, the Employment Secretary, who warned Major of the risk that other member states would ultimately be willing to accept extensions of Community competence and qualified majority voting (QMV) in areas such as the collective and industrial rights of workers. This would undermine the achievements of the Thatcher revolution.

In the arcane world of European Community negotiation, the argument between the British view and that of a majority of her partners centred around whether the EEC should be a tree or a temple. The Dutch, Belgians, Italians, and the Commission wanted the EEC to be a tree: a single structure in which, ultimately, all issues would be subject to the competence of the Community. So, the Commission would have the sole right of legislative initiative, the European Parliament would play a part of increasing power, and the ultimate arbiter of the law would be the European Court of Justice.

The French had reservations, notably about the power of the European Parliament. Their view of defence cooperation was also rooted in policy rather than ideology. The French argument was that it should be inconceivable that a country such as Austria should aspire to join the EEC while remaining neutral. By joining the EEC, they should be obliged to take on obligations within an EEC defence structure. Moreover, in French minds, if there was a clear division between European union, on the one hand, and European defence on the other, then the Germans might accept the first and pass on the second, thereby drifting into the dangerous neutrality that was the stuff of French nightmares.

To the British, on the other hand, if the WEU were brought into the EEC, as was suggested, then some would gain automatic membership of a defence alliance by virtue of EEC membership while others, who might have a better claim on grounds of defence capability, would only be eligible for second class membership.

As a result, the British were the architects of the view that the European Community should be a temple, albeit a temple in which they themselves would hardly qualify as ardent worshippers. Drawings were made which showed a Greek or Roman temple with three pillars: a Community pillar encompassing all the policies and law-making governed by the Treaty of Rome and the Single European Act; a pillar covering foreign policy and security cooperation; and a pillar covering Justice and Home Affairs. The issues dealt with under the first pillar would safeguard the existing powers of the European Commission and European Parliament. The second and third pillars would not necessarily exclude roles for the Commission and Parliament but, ultimately, decisions would remain under the control of the Member States acting intergovernmentally.

The EEC Presidency, in the first half of 1991, was held by Luxembourg. Smaller EEC Member States often provide the best Presidencies. It matters to them to be seen to do a good job. They pull in their best people from around the world. They lack the swagger of the larger countries. The Luxembourg Presidency in 1985 had steered the Single European Act to agreement. Now, before the end of their Presidency in June 1991, they tabled a draft treaty which respected the 'pillared' approach favoured by the UK. The UK did, however, have some objections: to the proposed 'federal goal' of the EEC, and to proposals for European Union citizenship and for social policy, including decision making by QMV. But on the whole, Whitehall was reassured. The Netherlands assumed the Presidency in July. The traditional torpor of August descended on the European Community.

At the *rentrée* (back to school), at the beginning of September 1991, the Dutch circulated the draft treaty. Around the puzzled, and in Britain's case, dismayed, capitals of Europe, officials looked for the Luxembourg treaty language—language that was not just produced on a Presidency whim, but as the result of months of discussion. It had disappeared and, in its place, the Dutch proposed a new text which removed the pillared structure, gave the Commission competence in foreign policy matters, significantly enlarged the powers of the European Parliament and extended Commission competence over all aspects of employment.

Two weeks later, Major told the Dutch Prime Minister, Ruud Lubbers, that he would not bang the table, but nor would he accept the new text. It was not clear how others would react. The Germans claimed to like the text, hoping that by planting a flag in the opposite corner to the Luxembourgers, the Dutch could end up with something half way between. But the Luxembourg Foreign Minister, Jacques Poos, led the attack on the Dutch text when Foreign Ministers met to discuss it. The Italians followed. The German Foreign Minister both commended the text and consigned it to oblivion by declaring that it clearly would not run. So far so good, for London. But Kohl wanted to see irreversible progress towards European Union, not least to justify Germany's agreement to a single currency. And, in Paris, Mitterrand, who was mired in domestic problems, wanted to be seen as the President who had locked Germany into a Europe that was still recognizably of French design. The net result was that it was the British who would end up with the most 'red lines' in the negotiation.

The European Council was due to meet in Maastricht in the Netherlands early in December 1991. Shortly before that, Major took the unusual step of arranging a debate in Parliament in which he set out in detail his objectives for the summit. As had become the norm with British governments, there was a series of negatives: No federalism. No commitment to a single currency. No Social Chapter. No Community competence in foreign or home affairs or defence. But Major did also set out a view of the EEC, and Britain's place in it, which encapsulates the position of Prime Ministers from Macmillan to Cameron. 'There are', he said, 'in truth, only three ways of dealing with the Community: we can leave it, and no doubt we would survive, but we would be diminished in influence and prosperity; we can stay in it grudgingly, in which case others will lead it; or we can play a leading role in it, and that is the right policy. It does not mean accepting every idea that is marketed with a European label. It does mean trying to build the sort of Europe that we believe in...'[4]

The Maastricht Treaty negotiations lasted from Monday morning, 9 December until the early hours of Wednesday. Major won his points, but not without argument. He made clear from the outset that the UK would not be forced into a single currency. Kohl argued that a single currency, the Community's most important decision since the Treaty of Rome, must be irreversible. Mitterrand supported him, also contending that there could be no permanent opt-outs. On the proposal for a Social Chapter in the new Treaty, Britain would not accept the Treaty with such a Chapter. France would not accept the Treaty without it.

Britain's partners knew that the UK proposed to opt out of the single currency. They had not expected the fully worked-up, detailed text which, at Major's insistence, was only tabled by the British delegation in the middle of the second day. Nigel Wicks, the Treasury's senior official handling EMU, made clear it was not negotiable.[5] Had it been tabled earlier, it would have been nibbled and niggled to death. As it was, acceptance of it by others became the price the other Member States had to pay for British acquiescence in the Treaty they wanted.

The issue of the Social Chapter was more problematic. Britain wanted no part of it. The obvious solution lay in another opt-out for the UK. But even the opt-out from the single currency would have to be sold hard to sceptical Tory backbenchers. Major did not want to have to defend another opt-out.

Work had been done in the Department of Employment on a text which officials believed would safeguard the UK position. But that was not acceptable to their Secretary of State, Michael Howard. Both John Major, in his auto-biography, and Sarah Hogg and Jonathan Hill,[6] in their book on the Major government, gloss over Howard's role from London as the second day of the summit progressed. 'Throughout the day', according to Major, 'Sarah Hogg had been in touch with Michael Howard, who provided useful ammunition against seductive offers'.[7] What John Major does not say is that the 'ammu-nition' included Howard making it clear that concessions on the Social Chapter were, for him, a resigning matter. Major calculated that Ruud

[4] House of Commons Debate of 20 November 1991, *Hansard*, vol. 199, cols. 269–390.
[5] Nigel Wicks was held in such high regard by his EU colleagues that he went on to chair the EU Monetary Committee, despite the UK's absence from the single currency.
[6] Sarah Hogg headed the Number 10 Policy Unit. Hill (later a British member of the EU Commission) was senior political adviser.
[7] John Major, *The Autobiography* (London: HarperCollins, 1999), p. 285.

Lubbers, the Dutch Prime Minister who was chairing the summit, would not allow it to fail when overall agreement was in sight. After some anxious debate, Lubbers agreed that the Social Chapter would be agreed by the other eleven Member States in a separate protocol outside the Treaty. Britain would not be involved.

In the early hours of Wednesday morning, 11 December, a small group of us sat in John Major's hotel bedroom. What should be said to the Press? Someone suggested 'Game, Set and Match'. I remember thinking to myself 'Is this wise?' but I did not want to rain on the parade and I kept silent. The phrase was used and seized on by the British media. It worked with the tabloids and, by the same token, created ill-feeling among our EEC partners.

More significantly, at a time when IT was scarcely in its infancy within government, Sarah Hogg and Jonathan Hill ran an unprecedented media operation. A summary of what had been achieved was faxed to Number 10 and copies were couriered before dawn to the homes of every Cabinet Minister. The 'line to take' was there for every senior Minister to speak to as soon as they—and the *Today* programme and the like—awoke.

John Major returned to London to something of a triumph. The Press were enthusiastic, *The Times* headline ('Major wins all he asks for') reflecting the media mood. That afternoon, in the House of Commons, Major also had a rapturous welcome from his own back benches. He set out what had been achieved:

- A treaty on EMU, with a single currency by 1997 or 1999. There would be strict convergence criteria covering inflation, budget deficits, exchange rate stability, and long-term interest rates. The UK would have exactly the same option to join the single currency as other Member States and would be involved in all the relevant decisions but, unlike other governments, the UK had secured the right, set out in a binding protocol, to decide for itself whether or not to move to Stage 3 of the process: i.e. whether or not to adopt the single currency.
- A new legal framework for cooperation between Member States in foreign and security policy and in the fight against international crime. That cooperation would take place on an intergovernmental basis outside the Treaty of Rome. The European Commission would not have the sole right of initiative and the European Court of Justice would have no jurisdiction. Britain had resisted pressure for decisions in this area to be taken by QMV. Instead, there was a clause allowing the Council of

Ministers to decide, by unanimity, that certain implementing decisions could be taken by majority vote.

- On defence, a framework for cooperation in which the primacy of the Atlantic Alliance had been confirmed and an enhanced role given to the WEU.
- Britain had resisted pressure to grant the European Parliament a power of co-decision with the Council of Ministers on legislative proposals. Instead, there would be a new conciliation procedure in some areas. Here the European Parliament would have a blocking power in certain circumstances, but only by an absolute majority of the members.
- Britain was committed to a social dimension to the Community and had implemented all nineteen directives so far adopted. But it had not accepted the new Social Chapter which dealt with employment and labour laws which were best determined in the UK and in the House of Commons, and not imposed from outside.

On the eve of the summit, the Soviet Union, as the world had known it for generations, had collapsed and given way to a new Commonwealth of Independent States. Those events were, Major told the House, 'a salutary reminder that reform in the Community is not an end in itself'. He went on to set out a clear and simple objective, which was to mark him as the champion of enlargement to the newly democratized countries of eastern and central Europe: 'The Community's primary task', he said, 'must be to extend its own advantages of democracy, stability and prosperity to eastern Europe'. At British initiative, the Maastricht summit had committed the Community to its further enlargement, starting with the EFTA countries: 'When they, and in due course, the new democracies of eastern Europe are ready to join the Community, we shall be ready to welcome them.'[8]

The Maastricht Treaty required primary legislation before it could be ratified and, with a General Election due no later than May 1992, Major told the House that that could not be done in the remainder of the existing Parliament but would be a matter for the next one. At the time, it seemed like a statement of the obvious.

In early 1992, John Major sought a dissolution of Parliament, and a General Election was called for 10 April. His first task as Prime Minister in 1991 had been to fight a war in Iraq. His conduct of it, and his own style of leadership, had won him popular support in the UK. By abandoning the hated Poll Tax

[8] *Hansard*, 11 December 1991, vol. 200, cols. 859–78.

that had been one cause of Thatcher's downfall, he had brought his party back from the brink. He had resisted the calls from some of his team to call a 'khaki election', reasoning that the glow of victory in Iraq would soon fade under the glare of more day-to-day domestic issues. But now, on the eve of the General Election a reformed Labour Party, under the leadership of Neil Kinnock, was ahead in the polls.

Not only were Labour ahead in the polls, they were the firm favourites to win. Charles Clarke, a future Home Secretary, was then Kinnock's Chief of Staff. He and Major's Principal Private Secretary, Andrew Turnbull, were having the perfectly correct and normal conversations about a possible transition that take place in a closely fought election. But the sense that the Kinnocks were already measuring Number 10 for carpets and curtains was palpable.

John Major fought a very personal campaign, far from the focus-group style his political advisers wanted. Standing on a soapbox, he addressed noisy crowds without evident fear. About eight days before election day, Kinnock, waving his arms manically, addressed a Labour crowd in Sheffield. He seemed to take victory for granted. In fact, he was already beginning to sniff that the wind had turned. So had Major. I saw him in his Downing Street flat, each morning of the campaign, at about 7 a.m., to brief him on overnight news and to get his instructions before he set out for a day's campaigning. About a week before election day, he and the Conservative canvassers began to sense a change of mood on the doorsteps. Major began to believe that the Conservatives would be the largest party, though not necessarily with an overall majority.

As the polls closed and the first results came in, I received an anxious phone call from President Bush, wanting to know how his friend was faring. It was becoming clear that he was faring rather well. On the day, the Conservatives won, with an overall majority of 21, a huge reduction from the majority of 102 they had previously enjoyed, but something of a personal triumph nonetheless. Yet Major could already sense that his reduced majority would spell future problems. When I congratulated him on the psychological and real advantages of having secured his own mandate, he replied: 'You wait. This is where my troubles really begin.' He did not have long to wait.

The Maastricht Treaty legislation was soon introduced and passed its first and second readings in the House of Commons without serious difficulty though, ominously, twenty-two Conservative MPs, one more than the government's overall majority, voted against it. Then, on 2 June 1992, the Danish people voted against the Maastricht Treaty in a referendum. Within twenty-four hours, an Early Day Motion calling on the government to take a new approach to Europe had attracted sixty-nine signatures in the House of Commons. On the same day, Kinnock asked for a debate on the implications of the Danish vote before progress was made on the Bill. Major agreed. At the same time, in France, President Mitterrand announced that France too would hold a referendum on the Maastricht Treaty. Support, Mitterrand told Major, would not be overwhelming, but he was confident of carrying the Treaty with a margin of around 5 per cent.

The Danish result, followed by the promise of a referendum in France, began to put pressure on the pound within the ERM. This was compounded by a weakening dollar, money going into Deutschmarks in Germany, and rising German interest rates at a time when countries such as the UK needed low rates. The Italian lira came under severe pressure. These adverse pressures only helped stir Tory backbench sentiment against the Maastricht Treaty.

On 1 July 1992, the United Kingdom assumed the six-monthly Presidency of the European Community. On the morning of Wednesday, 16 September, Major chaired a meeting to consider how the UK, as Presidency, should handle the outcome of the French referendum on the Maastricht Treaty, which was to be held on the following Sunday, 20 September. The Cabinet Ministers present were Heseltine (Deputy Prime Minister), Hurd (Foreign Secretary), and Clarke (Home Secretary). It was clear that the Treaty might go down to defeat and, by this point, with UK parliamentary opinion increasingly hostile to the Maastricht Treaty, the not-so-silent hope of those in the room was that it would indeed be defeated. A Danish 'no' was not a terminal blow to the treaty. A French 'no' would be.

All these calculations were to be shattered by a massive run on the pound, the futile hikes in interest rates made by the Chancellor (Norman Lamont) in an effort to steady the currency, and the enforced departure of the pound from the ERM later in the day. The Italian lira was also forced out of the system.

The part played by the Bundesbank, and by Kohl himself, in this debacle is disputed to this day. There is no doubt that the aggressive pressure on the Germans that Lamont had brought to bear, at an informal meeting of EEC Finance Ministers in Bath shortly beforehand, had caused significant German anger. There had, though, also been unguarded public suggestions from the Bundesbank that the pound would have to be devalued. Had there been normal circumstances at the time, an agreed realignment within the system might have been possible. But realignments within the ERM had become rare and there was no question of France being able to sustain the uncertainty of a realignment in the week leading to the Maastricht referendum. Major's appeal to Kohl on that 'Black Wednesday' to persuade the Bundesbank to intervene strongly, received a non-committal response. Kohl, as I recall, pleaded the independence of the Bundesbank. The suspension of British membership of the ERM had become inevitable.

The impact of Britain's withdrawal from the ERM was game-changing. The effect on the government's popular standing was dramatic. The Conservatives' image as sound managers of the economy was gravely damaged. The fate of the Maastricht Treaty, and with it that of the government, now hung in the balance. On 24 September, in a specially recalled House of Commons, Major and his government took a pounding from the Labour Opposition under its new Leader, John Smith. Only weeks before Black Wednesday, the *Sunday Times* had carried a story reporting that Major had 'embarked on an economic strategy designed to see the British pound replace the German mark as the hardest and most trusty currency in the EEC'. Ambitious enough when it was made, the claim now rang especially hollow and Smith evoked it to denounce the government and its Prime Minister as 'fatally flawed by incredibility and incompetence'. Major was, Smith said, 'the devalued Prime Minister of a devalued Government'.

Major's defence was stalwart. He upheld the government's stance on EEC issues, rejecting the idea of the UK's future 'as being a sour, isolated country off the mainland of continental Europe'. The Maastricht Treaty had become 'a totem around which those in favour and those opposed to Europe are now dancing'. He did not believe 'that it would be proper for a British Prime Minister to agree a treaty, and then come back to the House of Commons to disown it'. But he recognized the fears in the UK that the European Community sought to intervene too intrusively in the country's national life: that things that had always been dealt with by individual states—and should so be dealt with—were instead being drawn within the control of the Community. What was needed, Major argued, was a settled order of what was for national action and what was for Community action. Clear criteria were needed by which Community proposals could be judged. When the government were satisfied that such a system had been put in place, and when it was clear that the Danes had a basis on which they could bring the Maastricht Treaty back to their electorate, then the Maastricht Bill would be brought back to the House of Commons.

In the aftermath of Black Wednesday, there was some demand from other Member States for a special meeting of the European Council. For the first, and so far only, time Birmingham was chosen as the host city for the summit, on 16 October 1992.

The main British aim for the summit was to address what they saw as the fault lines in the ERM. These included an issue first raised by Jim Callaghan in 1978. Under the ERM system, countries with a weak currency, liable to fall out of the mechanism, were obliged to intervene in support of their currency. No similar obligation fell on countries with a strong currency that was close to the top of the agreed band. The UK had hiked its interest rates in a desperate attempt to stay in the ERM. Germany had ignored the requests of Major and others to lower its interest rates. Major wanted a better balance of obligations within the system. But his attempt at reform of the ERM got short shrift from other Member States.

He had better luck on the subject of subsidiarity. The declaration issued from the summit explicitly recognized the importance of national identity. It acknowledged that the Community could only act where Member States had given it the power to do so under the Treaties. It stipulated that action at the Community level should happen only when necessary, that such action should take the lightest possible form, that there should be better consultation by the Commission before they made proposals; and it called for a greater role for national Parliaments in the work of the Community.

It was enough to paper over a few cracks. But the 'summit that never was', as it was dubbed, was memorable only for two extraneous circumstances. The first was the absence of Mitterrand for parts of the meeting, as he received care from his doctor for the prostate cancer that would eventually take his life. John Major, too, was absent from the chair for much of the time. During the morning of the one-day meeting, I took a call from Major's Principal Private Secretary, Alex Allan. The Chancellor, Norman Lamont, had been at a meeting of the so-called Star Chamber, the ministerial group formed to settle disputed departmental financial settlements. It appeared that Lamont had stormed out of the meeting. He had not returned to the Treasury and his Private Office, headed by a young Civil Servant named Jeremy Heywood, did not know where he had gone and could not find him. It seemed possible that he might have resigned. Eventually, the missing Chancellor was tracked down. He had not resigned. The Treasury heaved a sigh of relief knowing that, whatever the vagaries of the Chancellor's behaviour, the Department was safe in the hands of Heywood's calm and professional management.[9]

Major's troubles were not over. In early November, the government faced defeat at the hands of its own rebels. Major had promised Kinnock a so-called

---

[9] Jeremy Heywood (1961–2018) was to have a brilliant Civil Service career, ending as Cabinet Secretary.

paving debate on the Maastricht Treaty before consideration of the legislation was resumed. With Margaret Thatcher holding court in the House of Lords, and cajoling and bullying Conservative MPs to vote against their own government, it looked as if as many as fifty Tories might do just that. Major was ready to resign if the vote was lost. A last-minute deal was done with one Conservative backbencher, who was promised that passage of the Bill would not be completed at Third Reading until after the Danes had held a second referendum on the Maastricht Treaty. The government carried the day by three votes. The deal had been brokered by Heseltine. Major was a party to it. The Foreign Secretary, Douglas Hurd, was not. There was a tense meeting in the Cabinet Room the next day. Hurd had a keyring given to him by the Italian Prime Minister, Giulio Andreotti. Appropriately for an Italian gift, it featured a silver horse's head. Hurd sat twirling the horse's head in his hand, cross and agitated. Should the government back away from the deal? Major asked. That, Hurd argued, was not possible. The angry moment passed. Hurd was, as he wrote in his memoirs, 'cross for a couple of days'.

In the end, as Hurd noted in his memoirs, the two processes (Danish and British) came together, quite naturally, in May 1993. But Heseltine could not have known that at the time he struck his desperate deal. The ploy put the passage of the UK's legislation at the mercy of the Danish electorate though, had the Danes continued to resist the Maastricht Treaty, the Bill would not have passed anyway. In the meantime, other Member States, notably France and Germany, had little patience with the Danes. The last summit of the British Presidency, in Edinburgh in December 1992, would potentially be critical to Denmark's place in the EEC.

Edinburgh in mid-December tends to be cold, wet, and bleak. December 1992 was no exception. But, maybe because one of my maternal forebears was lady in waiting to Mary Queen of Scots, I also find the city, even in winter, dramatically beautiful. Nothing tears at the heartstrings like the skirl of bagpipes and the British Presidency, together with the City of Edinburgh, laid on all that and much more. The Queen generously lent her Edinburgh home, Holyrood Castle, for the summit. It was just big enough to allow conference and office space for the delegations of twelve countries. Politicians take delight in some of the minutiae of organization, and John Major had views about the allocation of offices, particularly insisting that the Commission President, Jacques Delors, should be allocated an office in the bedroom where Lord Darnley, lover of Mary Queen of Scots, had been assassinated. We had made a reconnaissance visit a few weeks before. We viewed the conference room and its plush faux-antique red leather chairs. One of the PM's party flung himself into one of the chairs: just, he explained, to make sure that it could support the bulk of the German Chancellor.[10]

John Major's qualities and ability are better recognized today than they were during his time in office. The conduct of the Edinburgh European Council showed him at his best. He readily mastered a brief. He read body language. He was tough on substance while being unthreatening in manner. He kept his cool. The British were well prepared, not least because Major had travelled to each of the EEC capitals beforehand. That was his job as President. He had to secure an outcome which all twelve Member Governments would accept. His task was complicated by the fact that the UK had several dogs in the fight, needing commitments on subsidiarity and on greater openness by the EEC institutions and an outcome on the future funding of the EEC to the end of the century that was not too costly but which also preserved the UK's hard-won abatement.

The summit lasted two long days and into the small hours. The trickiest issue of all was how to handle the Danish referendum vote against the Maastricht Treaty. In order to win round their public opinion, the Danes had proposed a number of opt-outs from the treaty, encompassing defence and security, citizenship, police and justice and the adoption of the euro. The large Member States, France and Germany especially, have an unattractive tendency to bully the small. Edinburgh was no exception. At lunch on the first day, Kohl and Mitterrand supported each other in threatening Denmark that it would not be allowed to hold up the rest of the Community. If Denmark separated itself from the rest of the EEC, Germany, said Kohl, would want to go further. Mitterrand agreed. France would continue with those who were willing.

This was part substance and part tactics. The French and Germans wanted to make Danish flesh creep so that they would feel pressured into coming back inside the tent. It was also a warning shot to the UK. John Major took issue with them. If, he said, the Danish government lost a second referendum, the remaining eleven could not simply go ahead and ratify the Maastricht Treaty regardless. It required ratification by the Parliaments of all the Member States. There would have to be a new negotiation. Nor would an agreement which excluded Denmark be acceptable to the British Parliament.

---

[10] At a later EU summit, the British delegation arrived in a small RAF aircraft. As we stood on the tarmac, two large Lufthansa jets touched town. 'Why', we asked ourselves, 'do the German delegation need two airplanes?' Major concluded that the second aircraft was probably bringing Helmut Kohl's lunch.

Major's warning, that the UK would not let Denmark stand alone, helped to focus minds on the solution which had been worked on for some weeks. It was largely the product of the ingenious mind of the Council of Ministers' legal adviser, Jean-Claude Piris. It incorporated the Danish opt-outs in a decision that would be legally binding on all Member Governments but would *not* require ratification by the Parliaments of the Member States.

The debate over the future financing of the EEC came down to two issues: who got what by way of Community funding; and the future of the British budget rebate—hard won at Fontainebleau by Thatcher. Britain's partners hoped to see the rebate reduced, if not abolished altogether. The Spanish Prime Minister, Felipe Gonzalez, was not a man for fine detail. A cohesion fund was to be established to help the four poorest Member States (Greece, Ireland, Portugal, and Spain), and Gonzalez focused on the total sum he expected to receive. He got a long way until Kohl, whose coffers would be bearing the biggest burden of the funding, had had enough and called time. As to the rebate, the British Presidency had been criticized in Brussels for tabling fifty pages of text on the future EU budget while leaving a blank where the figure for the British rebate was to be inserted. The tactic of not offering up a figure, which would have become target practice for all the other delegations, paid off. The final deal froze Community spending until 1995 and then allowed for gradual increases up to 1999. The British rebate was preserved unchanged.

The summit also agreed to open enlargement negotiations with the three candidate countries: Austria, Finland, and Sweden and, finally, it addressed the issue of the seats of EEC institutions. Argument about which country gets which EU institution in its capital is always the point at which European solidarity breaks down and a street brawl breaks out. The main victor of this one was Mitterrand. Under the provisions of the Treaty of Rome, Strasbourg had been set as the seat of the European Assembly, with eleven of the twelve monthly meetings being held there. The offices of the European Assembly were in Luxembourg and work between plenaries was centred in Brussels. This was (and remains) a recipe for wasting time, energy, and money. The members of the European Parliament (as it had become under the terms of the Single European Act) were inclined to rebel against the rules. Now Mitterrand achieved a binding reassertion of the original ruling.

Following the conclusion of the summit, we left Edinburgh in the early hours of the morning. As Major walked through the UK delegation office he was applauded by the civil service team. Edinburgh had been a *tour de force* of chairmanship. The Danes had been saved from exclusion, the European

Community had secure financing for the rest of the decade, and the UK rebate had been safeguarded. The Council had agreed on the financing of infrastructure projects throughout the Community in transport, energy, and telecommunications. The Community was on target to complete the single market in goods by the end of the year. The door had been opened to the accession of Austria, Finland, and Sweden as new members. The British Presidency, which had started with the humiliation of Black Wednesday, ended on a high note.

But the government's travails were far from over. The Maastricht Bill struggled through the House of Commons during the first half of 1993, with an opportunistic alliance of the Labour Party and Eurosceptic Conservatives constantly putting the government's majority at risk. In a particular act of extremist opposition, right wing Tories, who abhorred the Social Chapter that was in the Treaty, and who knew that their position was protected by the exclusion from it secured by Major, nonetheless conspired with Labour to support an amendment which would have imposed the Social Chapter. It was a measure of the anti-European infection within the Conservative Party that Conservative MPs were prepared to risk the survival of their own government for the sake of their obsession.

John Major and his senior colleagues decided that, if the vote was lost, they would move straight to a vote of confidence, linked to the passage of the Bill: the rebels would have to be ready to defeat their own government and trigger an immediate General Election. The rebels backed down. The government had a majority of thirty-nine. The Danes had won their referendum. The Maastricht Treaty was ratified. The European Community became the European Union. Although the start date for the single currency was, because of a further ERM crisis in 1993, deferred to 1999, the Maastricht Treaty set the EU on an irreversible road to economic and monetary union.

John Major's 1992 election majority of twenty-one was, even then, smaller than the number of Eurosceptic backbenchers in his own party. By-elections whittled down that majority still further. Growing disgruntlement is built in to the life cycle of governments. A new government starts with optimism. Those given ministerial posts are happy. Those not in ministerial posts can hope for recognition and promotion. Then come the ministerial reshuffles. Those dismissed become discontented backbenchers. Backbenchers hopeful of promotion become disillusioned when it is evident that they are not going to be chosen. Governments get tired, not just figuratively, but literally. The life of Ministers is one of stress, impossible hours, and very little, if any, respite. Adrenaline can mask exhaustion but it is a dangerous drug: addictive and potentially toxic. I believe that much of Thatcher's almost unhinged, and certainly damaging, behaviour towards John Major after she lost power can be explained by the withdrawal symptoms she felt acutely when the adrenaline of office was no longer pumping. She still needed the adrenaline 'fix' and fomenting revolt against her successor provided it. The Conservatives had been in power continuously since 1979. They were weary. Labour's leader, John Smith, had died suddenly of a heart attack in 1994. His successor, Tony Blair, was attractive, modern, the personification of a new generation and a reformed Labour Party brimming with new ideas. The Conservatives seemed shop worn, divided, riddled with petty but damaging scandals.

In the early 1990s, cows on British farms started staggering, falling over and dying in increasing numbers. They were suffering from Bovine Spongiform Encephalopathy (BSE), a fatal neurodegenerative disease. British farmers had been feeding to their cattle a mixture composed of mashed up infected animal parts from the abattoir. That was the source. No one knew how readily transmissible the disease was to humans, in the form of Creuzfeldt-Jakob disease (CJD), but a similar disease, scrapie, was already well known in sheep and had not crossed the species divide to other animals, let alone to humans. Since scrapie did not cross the species threshold, it was assumed that the same would be true of BSE. Measures to ban the use of animal feed consisting of animal bone meal had been put in place but had not been rigorously enforced. Moreover, reconstituted meat (often from the spinal cord of cows) was permitted as a 'meat' ingredient in beef burgers, sausages etc. The spinal cord is potentially one of the most infected, and infectious, part of the cow's anatomy. The extent and gravity of the threat became clear in 1996 when evidence came to light that BSE could, after all, be transmitted to other animals and to humans in the form of variant CJD. CJD was, and is, untreatable and invariably fatal. The frequent and unqualified public assurances by British Ministers that British beef was perfectly safe had been based on the assumption that no *evidence* of transmission was the same thing as no *risk* of transmission.

When the extent and gravity of BSE became unmistakable, Douglas Hogg, the Minister of Agriculture, warned Cabinet that the entire British herd might have to be destroyed. That analysis was rejected. Nor did the government take timely steps to inform the European Commission, who were responsible for the management and safety of the EU food market. Not surprisingly, the Commission, acting responsibly, imposed a global ban on exports of British beef. The EU's Standing Veterinary Committee extended the ban to cover by-products such as gelatine, tallow, and bull's semen. I was by then the UK Permanent Representative to the EU in Brussels. The UK's chief veterinary officer addressed a dinner of all of the EU's chief vets at my house, the first and only dinner I have hosted where bull's semen was a principal topic of dinner-table conversation. The British side argued that the extended ban was excessive. The others argued that, though the science was not clear, caution should prevail. The UK did not have a convincing counter argument to make to men (they were all men) who had to advise their governments on what risk to public health they could afford to take.

The extended ban remained in place. Opponents of the EU in the House of Commons declared war on Europe. Faced with the risk of a defeat, the government decided on a policy of non-cooperation: for so long as the ban persisted, the British government would veto any proposal for EU legislation that required unanimity. On 21 May 1996, Major announced the policy in terms designed to appease—and in practice encourage—the Eurosceptic and nationalistic reaction that was sweeping the Tory benches. 'A balanced proposal based on the best scientific advice has been ignored by a number of member states...I must tell the House that I regard such action as a wilful disregard of British interests and, in some cases, a breach of faith...We cannot continue business as usual within Europe when we are faced with the clear disregard by some of our partners of reason, of common sense and of Britain's national interests...'[11]

The Italian government held the EU Presidency. They were remarkably tolerant of the string of British vetoes that the new policy brought in its wake. But it was quickly apparent that the policy was both risible and unsustainable. The Home Secretary, the Eurosceptic Michael Howard, found himself vetoing a proposal that had been his idea in the first place. The Foreign Secretary, Malcolm Rifkind, found himself uncomfortably isolated at a Foreign Affairs Council where every single one of his colleagues spoke firmly of the unacceptability of the British position. From Brussels, I warned Number 10 privately that, if the policy continued, we could expect our partners to seek ways of retaliating. We would also lose the good will of the Commission. I cited Commission rulings on state aid cases. For example, Commission approval was necessary for the state aid the British government wished to provide to the Ford Motor Company (then the owners of Jaguar Cars) for a new production facility at Coventry. Decisions such as that were taken by the Commission on the advice of the responsible Commissioner. Ninety per cent of such a decision was based on evidence, 10 per cent on political judgement. That 10 per cent could spell the difference between success and failure.

[11] *Hansard*, 21 May 1996, vol. 278, cols. 99–101.

The British government started to realize that its stance was unsustainable. A large-scale cattle culling programme had already been agreed. The President of the Commission, Jacques Santer, played a key role in helping to build a ladder for the UK to climb down through a mixture of measures which would gradually restore confidence in British beef. Even then, the British resisted implementing the cull and only conceded in the face of EU pressure. The ban was partially lifted late in 1997 and fully lifted in 1999.

So far, some 178 people (most of them young) have died from CJD, linked to eating infected beef. That is far, and tragically, too many. It is, so far, fewer than was at one time feared, though there is no test for the risk of CJD, and evidence from other parts of the world suggests that it can be present for decades before manifesting itself in distressing, incurable and always fatal symptoms.

I had been for two years Britain's Ambassador to Portugal before moving to Brussels. The Embassy had been very successful in promoting the sale of beef cattle to Portugal. The Portuguese herd had to be culled in the wake of BSE. That was a real measure of the harm that had been done. If, as was alleged, our EU partners were motivated by malice and protectionism, how was it that the EU ban was lifted once the evidence so dictated, whereas an identical US ban remained in place, a ban which produced no similar accusations of bad faith from the British?

It was only following the election of the Labour government in 1997 that the entire EU ban was lifted. Even then, the French maintained it on their side of the Channel. They had mixed motives. Part of it was genuine apprehension. The French government had faced its own scandal: the accusation that blood, known to be infected by HIV, had been given by transfusion to haemophiliacs. Laurent Fabius, who had been Prime Minister at the time, was charged with manslaughter and brought to trial in 1999. But part of the continued French ban on British beef was undoubtedly motivated by traditional French protectionism. Part was also due to the habitual lack of bilateral cooperation by the government of Lionel Jospin, an old-school Socialist who had no time for New Labour and no time for Tony Blair, the charismatic young Labour Prime Minister who was the poster boy of a new Europe. The European Commission took the French government to the ECJ. The ECJ found against the French. The ban remained in place. The ECJ threatened the French with massive fines. The French backed down. I cited this case during the 2016 referendum campaign as an example of the safeguards provided by UK membership of a rules-based organization. The argument had no impact.

The BSE crisis passed, though its full long-term health impact is almost certainly not yet clear. EU membership remained a running sore within the Conservative Party. There was a fundamental difference of approach between the Major government and most of its continental partners, perfectly encapsulated in a speech made by Foreign Secretary Malcolm Rifkind in Bonn in February 1997. Rifkind, as Europe Minister in the Foreign Office just over a decade earlier, had been one of the leading young pro-Europeans. Now, in part, no doubt, with leadership ambitions in mind, Rifkind was cast in the role of sceptic. The British, he told his German audience, were disturbed by what they saw as a constant transfer of power in one direction only. 'They see all the footsteps leading into the cave and none of them coming out. So they doubt whether it is wise to go any further inside themselves. Where does it end? The conclusion that many draw is that, logically, the process will end in a European state.' Rifkind went on to put the blame for this state of affairs squarely onto the Germans for wanting what he called Maastricht II, III, IV, and V. Every German proposal consisted of a transfer of power from the Member States to the European institutions. Kohl, said Rifkind, might deny that he wanted a United States of Europe, but his proposals looked no different from such a United States of Europe. Kohl had talked about Europe as a convoy that should not be held back at the speed of the slowest ship. But a convoy that did not go at the pace of the slowest ship was not a convoy. In any event, the issue was not convoys; it was democracy itself.[12]

Rifkind's speech was striking for its metaphor of the EU as a cave with, by implication, a voracious and dangerous beast within it. His speech infuriated Kohl and its tone was certainly, and deliberately, provocative. Rifkind was taken to task by *Die Welt* for what they called his desperate electioneering, though whatever offence Rifkind may have caused was as nothing compared with the offensiveness of the *Frankfurter Allgemeine* newspaper in referring to the British Foreign Secretary as 'The Jew, Rifkind'. In any event, behind the rhetoric of the speech, lay generations of history and policy which defined the different approaches of the British and their partners. The British had swallowed hard and accepted the transfer of sovereignty implicit in the Treaty of Rome. They had spent the first ten years of their EEC membership in effect renegotiating the terms of that membership. They had then had to face up to a further transfer of sovereignty in the Single European Act, followed by another one in the Maastricht Treaty. Now, Germany and other partners were indeed pressing for Maastricht II: another new Treaty involving more majority voting;

---

[12] Wall, *A Stranger in Europe*, p. 159.

more co-decision with the European Parliament (i.e. more power for the EP at the expense of national governments); more steps towards common defence. For a country which could just about cope with the organic accretion of powers inherent in EU legislation adopted for practical purposes such as the creation of a single market, this was challenging. For Germany, all the new powers they were proposing went with the grain of their political and public opinion. For the UK, the opposite was the case, and especially for a Conservative government wrestling with internal strife on the subject of Europe.

The particular source of Rifkind's irritation in Bonn was that the EU, as had been prefigured in the Maastricht Treaty, was engaged on a new intergovern-mental conference. After lengthy prior discussion in a special working group, the IGC had opened in Turin in March, 1996 under Italian chairmanship. The Italian Foreign Minister at the time was Susan Agnelli, a member of the prominent Italian family that owned Fiat. Indeed, the meeting took place in the building which housed the one-time Fiat test track on its roof. Susan Agnelli was an unlikely Foreign Minister, not because she lacked ability, but because she was elegant, courteous, and refined and not at all enamoured of the macho muscle-flexing so beloved of her male colleagues. At the opening session of the IGC Rifkind spoke on behalf of the United Kingdom. He did so comprehensively. 'Thank you, Malcolm', said Susan Agnelli, in her perfect English. 'If everyone speaks at this opening session for as long as you have, all the allocated time for the entire conference will have been exhausted.' Her rebuke, delivered with smiling authority, proved to be a characteristic of her approach to chairing. She treated her fellow Foreign Ministers as if they were amusing, but wayward, children who could be permitted to appear for nursery tea but whose nonsense could not be long endured by serious grown-ups. Regrettably, the Italian government of which she was a member was short-lived.

The Major government did have its own positive agenda for the EU, especially in championing the cause of enlargement to eastern and central Europe. Enlargement would, Major believed, require greater flexibility and diversity, and recognition that identity rested in nations and national parlia-ments. If some Member States wished to move ahead of others in some areas, so be it. But they should not do so on an exclusive basis. He was opposed to a hard-core Europe in which there would be inner and outer circles.

These issues dominated the IGC. Two of Kohl's associates from the CDU, Wolfgang Schäuble and Karl Lamers, put forward a paper which advanced the case for a federal Europe with a hard core built around France and Germany.

French Prime Minister, Edouard Balladur, proposed that there should be two tiers of Member States. Proposals were made to 'collapse' one of the three pillars of the Maastricht temple (the one dealing with the fight against crime) by bringing much of that action within the framework of Community law. There were good grounds for doing so: the intergovernmental approach had not worked. But the proposal posed problems for the British who opposed increased Community competence. Similar reasons lay behind British reluctance to extend the mission of the EU to combating discrimination based on 'sex, racial or ethnic origin, religion or belief, disability, age or sexual orientation'. This was not Major emulating the narrow-mindedness of Thatcher: he had, after all been the Prime Minister who removed the bar on homosexual men serving in the British Civil Service. The objection was not to the principle of the protections but to the extension of competence to the European Union as their guardian. Proposals for a growing EU role in defence, which blurred the boundary with NATO, also worried the British government.

The Europe Minister, David Davis, was in overall charge of the negotiating team, but, on a week by week basis I, as the UK's Permanent Representative in Brussels, occupied the negotiating chair. Before each meeting, I received pages of instructions, each line cleared with Davis personally. I did suggest to the Foreign Office that they could save much time and effort by simply borrowing the tag line from Nancy Reagan's war on drugs in the United States. Why not, I asked, send me a one-line instruction: 'Just Say No'?

As the spring 1997 General Election approached, the Head of the European Secretariat in the Cabinet Office, Brian Bender, and I agreed that, in the event of a Conservative victory, we would have to ask John Major whether there was *anything* in the draft Amsterdam Treaty to which the government could agree. That moment never came. On the morning after New Labour's landslide victory, I was in the Cabinet Office at the weekly European coordination meeting that I attended from Brussels. John Major had just returned from the Palace after submitting his resignation. We heard his voice in the street, delivering the words he had rehearsed in front of me at lunch in Downing Street only a few weeks before: 'When the curtain falls, it is time to get off the stage'. It was a poignant moment. But Tony Blair had, only hours before, announced that 'a new dawn has broken, has it not?' It was time to face a new day.

9

New Dawn or More of the Same?

Blair and Europe, 1997–2007

I was the UK's Permanent Representative to the EU when New Labour were elected to government in 1997. I left Brussels in 2000 and worked in 10 Downing Street as Tony Blair's senior official adviser on EU issues until 2004.

Before the 1997 General Election, which swept New Labour into power with a majority unprecedented in modern British politics, I had never met Blair. Prominent members of the Shadow Cabinet, such as Robin Cook (Shadow Foreign Secretary) and Gordon Brown (Shadow Chancellor) had been to Brussels and had questioned me on European policy. Cook wanted to know just how low Britain had sunk in the estimation of our partners under Major's government. As a Civil Servant, I was not about to denigrate the government I was then serving. I replied that, whatever opinions people might hold, the United Kingdom was one of the large Member States with the votes and the power in the system to match.

Not long afterwards, travelling by train from Gatwick Airport early one Friday morning for the weekly meeting of senior officials on EU matters, I turned to an inside page of the *Financial Times*. 'EU Envoy to be sacked' ran the headline. I assumed that some Balkan scandal had overtaken one of the less self-evidently suitable candidate countries for EU membership. But the envoy in question turned out to be me.

In the event, Robin Cook and I got on well. To his Private Office in the FCO, he was a nightmare of disorganization. The Permanent Secretary during his time in the FCO, John Kerr, a fellow Scot, was at almost permanent logger-heads with him. From Brussels, I had a different perspective. Cook's initial view of me was the suspicion of a man who had never before been in government and had spent eighteen years in opposition. He assumed that the Civil Service had been infected by long obedience to a Conservative government and that I, appointed by John Major to Brussels, would likewise be an unregenerate Tory. This was not surprising: the New Labour government was the first I had worked for where almost none of the senior Ministers had ever before held ministerial office. Cook's first meeting with FCO officials took place just two days after his appointment. The new government needed to establish its policy on every aspect of the prospective European treaty then under negotiation. Officials had drafted a minute for him to send to the Prime Minister. Cook was surprised to discover that the minute reflected the Labour Party's election manifesto. It had not occurred to him that we, as officials, would have read it in preparation for a possible (and in this case almost certain) change of administration.

A voter in the 1997 General Election had to be at least in their mid-20s to remember a time when the Conservatives had not been in office. The recession of the late 1980s, the disasters of the Poll Tax and of Black Wednesday and a series of petty scandals surrounding the government, had gravely eroded public support. In 1992, John Major had won the General Election against the odds because the economy was improving, and he was trusted while his Labour opponent, probably unfairly, was not. But now, Labour had completed the reinvention that Neil Kinnock had started and they had done so under a youthful, attractive leader, Tony Blair, with the Kennedy-like stardust of Camelot about him. New Labour promised an appealing mix of the kind of stable economic management that people associated with the Conservatives, together with modernization: better schools, better health and social care and liberal social values, including for LGBT citizens who had been demonized under Thatcher. That some of these hopes would ultimately be disappointed was inevitable, but the fact that Tony Blair was comfortably able to win three consecutive election victories, even after the Iraq war, speaks volumes for the lasting appeal of his project. He was helped by a succession of three Tory leaders who followed John Major and who were in turn uninspiring, second rate, and a throwback to the Thatcher era. Only with the selection of David Cameron in 2005 did the Conservative Party find themselves a leader capable of turning what Theresa May famously called 'the nasty party' into a reformed and electable proposition.

Tony Blair had first campaigned to enter Parliament in 1983, when Labour's official policy was to leave the EEC. He went along with the policy, though his heart was not in it. And, on the doorstep, he discovered that the policy of 'leave' did not resonate with voters either. He was a supporter of the pro-European changes in Labour policy that the new leader, Kinnock, introduced following Labour's massive 1983 defeat. Blair was entirely at ease with Britain's membership of the European Union. Indeed, membership of the progressive club that the EU represented, formed an important part of the identity of New Labour. There was, however, relatively little sign of that in Labour's election campaign in 1997.

Despite their massive opinion poll lead, the New Labour leadership could not quite believe that it would turn into votes on the day. Blair could only win if he attracted voters who had previously voted Conservative. He had travelled to Australia to meet Rupert Murdoch and Murdoch had switched the support of his papers, *The Sun* notably, from Conservative to Labour. When that happened, sitting in Brussels, I thought straightaway that there would be a price to pay in terms of just how pro-European a Labour government would turn out to be. The Labour election manifesto gave substance to my fears: 'We will stand up for Britain's interests in Europe after the shambles of the last six years, but, more than that, we will lead a campaign for reform in Europe. Europe isn't working in the way this country and Europe need. But to lead means to be involved, to be constructive, to be capable of getting our own way.'

In this language, there was no suggestion that the European Union represented a strong force for peace and prosperity, something to be celebrated. 'Europe' was, instead, presented as something other; a problem to be addressed. Later in the text, the manifesto contained language that could have been written in Conservative Party HQ: 'Our vision of Europe is of an alliance of independent nations choosing to cooperate to achieve the goals they cannot achieve alone. We oppose a European federal super state.' Blair himself went further, writing in *The Sun* on 22 April 1997: 'Let me make my position on Europe absolutely clear. I will have no truck with a European super state. If there are moves to create that dragon, I will slay it.'

The Labour manifesto itself borrowed language almost word for word from John Major in arguing that 'there are only three options for Britain in Europe. The first is to come out. The second is to stay in, but on the sidelines. The third is to stay in, but in a leading role'. An increasing number of Conservatives, according to the manifesto, overtly or covertly favoured coming out. The manifesto then set out the case for staying in, in words that were almost exactly replicated by Cameron and his team in the 2016 referendum: 'Withdrawal would be disastrous for Britain. It would put millions of jobs at risk. It would dry up inward investment. It would destroy our clout in international trade negotiations. It would relegate Britain from the premier division of nations.' Nowhere in the manifesto, or in Blair's one foreign policy speech during the campaign on 21 April 1997, was there any mention of the fact that the European Union is a pooling of sovereignty, let alone a vision for the European Union that acknowledged the desire of other Member States for closer union. Indeed, Blair's speech read like a toned down version of Margaret Thatcher's Bruges speech some nine years earlier: 'There is a good deal of unease about the pace and direction of integration in many continental countries, not just in Britain. And if there were a desire for a super state, we would not hesitate to stop it in its tracks. We want a Europe where national identities are not submerged and where countries cooperate together, not a giant and unmanageable super state run from the centre.'

Blair's agenda for reform was almost identical to that of the Conservative government: single market, CAP reform, tackling unemployment and creating flexible labour markets, making a reality of foreign policy cooperation. John Major had made a speech in Brussels on exactly those themes as recently as February, 1997. Blair was open to more majority voting provided it was in British interests and so long as a veto was retained for essential national interests. His policy on a single currency was similarly Majorite: 'There must be genuine sustainable convergence...We will have no truck with a fudged single currency. However, to rule out membership forever would destroy any influence we have over the process. Therefore, we will keep our options open.' The one substantive difference between Labour and the Conservatives was that Labour would sign up to the Social Chapter but, even here, Blair justified it on the grounds that 'we can use our membership of the Social Chapter to bring about change across Europe'.

That the European policies of the two parties, as presented to the electorate, were barely distinguishable was confirmed by the closing lines of Blair's speech: 'The issue between the parties is not the position on EMU. Our position and the formal position of the Conservatives are the same. The real issue is one of leadership and clarity. John Major's agonies over the single currency illustrate the real dividing line in Europe. It is not federalist or anti-federalist – neither of us wants a federal super state. We agree on the single market. We agree on our attitude to the single currency and the referendum [both parties had promised a referendum on the issue of EMU membership]. The real dividing line is between success and failure. The fundamental differences lie in party management, attitude and leadership.'[1]

In reality, Blair felt more at home in the EU than any of his predecessors, except Heath. His positive attitude was instinctive, but was reinforced by the fact that he did not have to watch his back within his own party, as Wilson and Callaghan had been obliged to do. There were no longer anti-European big beasts within Labour. The reverse was true within a Conservative party that became more Eurosceptic following its election defeat and that chose new leaders, starting with William Hague, to match. For the time being—and for

[1] Stephen Wall, *A Stranger in Europe: Britain and the EU from Thatcher to Blair* (Oxford: Oxford University Press, 2008), pp. 162–3.

much of Blair's period in office—that anti-Europeanism looked to the public as yet another instance of the Conservative Party being out of touch. When Hague ran the 2001 General Election on a campaign of 'twelve days to save the pound', a poll for the *Daily Telegraph* recorded 66 per cent of those questioned as describing Hague as 'a bit of a wally'.[2]

Despite their huge electoral victory, and a majority in the House of Commons of 179, the new government were nervous of public opinion which, while not necessarily anti-European, was hostile to Brussels. Blair himself was an instinctive believer in the intergovernmental, rather than the Community, method. Never having been in government, he had had no exposure to decision making in the EU. So, the pattern of EU legislating, in which the European Commission had, by Treaty, the sole right of initiative, was unknown to him. So too, the navigation of the balance of power between the Council of Ministers and the Commission, or the complex three-way power play between those two institutions and the European Parliament. In the British system, the government was composed of elected politicians answerable to the people. For Blair, the governance of the EU needed to be similar. The European Council brought together the Heads of Government of the EU. They should take the decisions, and be seen by the electorate to be doing so.

Blair's view of the Commission was that it should behave like the Civil Service and be answerable to the elected politicians. He understood that the Commission had certain powers, and came to see that they could be useful in curbing the protectionism of individual Member States. But, at the outset, and for some time afterwards, he did not 'get' that most Member States (and certainly the smaller ones) regarded the independent role and power of the Commission as essential safeguards. And he had little regard for the European Parliament, not least because quite a high proportion of the Labour Members (62 of the British total of 87) were more 'old' than 'new' Labour in their attitudes. At the end of the British Presidency of the EU, in June 1998, I accompanied Blair when he made the traditional end-of-Presidency speech to the European Parliament in Strasbourg. He did it with the consummate ability that was typical of him and dealt brilliantly with sometimes hostile questioning. He left to general applause. But, as we left the building, it was clear from Blair's private comment to me that, while he had taken the occasion seriously, it had not altered his low regard for the EP as an institution.

[2] Roger Liddle, *The Europe Dilemma: Britain and the Drama of EU Integration* (London: I. B. Tauris, 2014), p. 279.

Blair arrived in Downing Street having done a deal with Gordon Brown about the conduct of government. Accounts vary as to how firm a commitment Blair had made to Brown that he would make way for him as Prime Minister in due course. Brown behaved as if a firm promise had been made. Blair never admitted to having done so. Blair had, however, given Brown a very wide field of responsibility as Chancellor of the Exchequer, extending well beyond the management of the country's economy and into domestic policy more widely. From the start, there were tensions in the relationship, though those tensions did not mutate into hostility during the first few months. By contrast, there were, from the beginning, overtly competitive relations between Brown and Robin Cook. Their origin was probably lost in the mists of their Celtic origins but the two men were jealous of each other and their acolytes fed mutually disobliging stories to the political correspondents of British newspapers.

In this internecine struggle, Brown had the advantage. He was one of the early originators of the reform project that became New Labour, hence his belief that he had a natural claim to the leadership of the Party . Cook, on the other hand, was not part of the inner circle. His cleverness, and his track record in opposition, made him a natural choice as Foreign Secretary, but he was not trusted by Blair and his close associates. There were three preeminent members of that inner circle. Peter Mandelson, who was appointed to the Cabinet Office, had no seat in Cabinet but had Blair's ear at all times. Anji Hunter had been at Blair's side for years and guarded his back fiercely. Alastair Campbell, Blair's Press Secretary, was a *Daily Mirror* journalist and a stalwart Labour supporter. He masterminded the marketing of Blair's public persona brilliantly and ruthlessly. He was both frightening and fun in equal measure. For a time, he had the political journalists eating out of his hand. In the last year of the Major government, the political correspondents relayed uncritically most of the anti-Tory stories that Campbell fed them. The pattern endured for some time in government as well. Eventually, the worm turned. Campbell made himself almost as much the story as his boss was. His personal war against the BBC during the Iraq crisis of 2003 took him to the brink of emotional meltdown, and he left Downing Street. But, in the early years, the inner circle were a formidable team, backed by a former FCO Civil Servant, Jonathan Powell, who became Blair's Chief of Staff.

As Civil Servants, those of us working on EU policy, in the UK Representation in Brussels, in my case, and in the European Secretariat of the Cabinet Office and the FCO, had no initial inkling of the complex, and always unconventional, workings of the Blair government machine. Blair had dragged the Labour Party into the late twentieth century. He believed that only he and his immediate Number 10 team were competent to direct and manage policy.

Because Blair himself had no prior ministerial experience, he had no concept of departmental boundaries. Because so few of his Cabinet team had any prior ministerial experience, they had little concept of how much distinct authority they could wield and Blair had limited faith in their effectiveness unless he himself kept his eye firmly on the ball. If Blair took to an individual Civil Servant, as he did to Brian Bender, who headed the European Secretariat, then he would place his trust in them as professionals who could turn his instructions into action. Yet successive Cabinet Secretaries were kept at arm's length.

An early victim of this exclusionary approach was the Foreign Secretary. Robin Cook arrived in the FCO, determined to implement an ethical foreign policy. He was not the first Labour Foreign Secretary to aim for such an approach: human rights had been at the core of David Owen's tenure in the job. Owen had not found it easy: the nastiest governments were often the more powerful or, as in the case of apartheid South Africa, essential interlocutors on issues such as Rhodesia, which dominated Owen's time in office. But Owen had at least been able to count on the backing of his Prime Minister, Jim Callaghan. In Cook's case, no sooner had he briefed the Press on his new approach than Campbell briefed against him. The new policy was severely winged before it could take flight.

There were similar disparities of view over the Social Chapter. The exclusion of the UK from the Social Chapter that Major had secured at Maastricht, had given the Labour Party the pretext it needed to oppose the eponymous Treaty outright, in an attempt to bring down the Conservative government. Both Kinnock and John Smith, as Labour leaders, had pledged to sign up to the Chapter, once Labour were again in government. The Blair government was about to do so as the negotiations on the Amsterdam Treaty entered their final weeks in June 1997. Accordingly, at his first meeting with his EU counterparts, the new FCO Europe Minister, Doug Henderson, made a strong statement on the topic.[3] It had been penned by Robin Cook who hailed the Social Chapter as a historic step, a democratic response to the wishes of the British people.

---

[3] Joyce Quin, who had been Shadow Europe Minister, found herself appointed a junior Minister in the Home Office. She replaced Henderson as Europe Minister after just over a year, but was only permitted to stay in the job for twelve months, as one of a total of eight Europe Ministers appointed during Blair's ten years in office.

Henceforth, he claimed, Britain would be working with other Member States as a partner, not as an opponent.[4]

For Cook, the Social Chapter represented a core part of Labour policy. For Blair, it was an unwelcome commitment he had inherited from John Smith. Cook would have described himself, proudly, as a Socialist. Blair disliked traditional socialism. Inside Blair's Downing Street, the words Trades Union Congress (TUC) were seldom spoken. Whenever a new measure which might extend the rights of workers was bruited, the first response in Number 10 was to ask what the Confederation of British Industry (CBI) would think.

In the first days of the new government, these contradictions and tensions were unknown to me, but I soon had an insight into them. Blair had accepted the Cabinet Secretary's advice on the machinery of government in agreeing to have a Cabinet sub-committee to oversee EU policy, chaired by the Foreign Secretary. Peter Mandelson was a Member. I was invited to attend in my role as the UK Permanent Representative to the EU. At the first such meeting Mandelson raised the question as to whether the new government should stick to its Opposition pledge to see QMV extended to areas of social and industrial policy. Cook, in the chair, and Clare Short (Secretary of State for International Development) opposed Mandelson's idea. I was asked for my view. I said that, in Brussels, Britain's partners were asking themselves whether the new British government was really different from its Conservative predecessor, or whether it was only the rhetoric that had changed. If the new government went back on its promises, our partners would conclude that British policy remained much the same as under the old government. I was sitting next to Mandelson, whom I had not previously met. As I finished speaking, he whispered in my ear 'That is blackmail'.

I was due to meet Mandelson when the committee finished. We adjourned to his office. I explained that I saw it as my job to explain the realities as I saw them. Mandelson agreed but made it clear that, if I had such advice, I was to give it privately to him or to the Prime Minister. Despite that caution, I quickly found that Cook was a very skilful operator on the Brussels scene. I can think of only two senior Ministers in my five years in Brussels whose interventions in Council meetings were so interesting, original, and well argued, as to induce their colleagues to put down their copies of Le Monde or the Financial Times and to pay close attention to what was being said. One was the Conservative Chancellor, Kenneth Clarke, in ECOFIN (the Council of Finance Ministers), and the other was Robin Cook in the General Affairs Council. Cook had the

---

[4] Wall, A Stranger in Europe, p. 165.

great skill of being a quick study. He would read a brief, absorb it, think about it and make himself a few notes. He had a formidable memory. When he spoke, he reflected the official briefing but supplemented it with his own reading and knowledge. He also proved, during the UK Presidency of the EU in 1998, to be an excellent chair.

I was not privy to other aspects of Cook's conduct of his office. For whatever reason, prominent FCO officials made no secret of their distaste for him. He lost his job as Foreign Secretary following the 2001 General Election. He was appointed Leader of the House of Commons and instituted notable reforms. He was the only member of the Cabinet to resign in protest at the decision to invade Iraq in 2003.

If the personal rivalries and policy disagreements which later characterized relations between Blair and Brown were not in evidence in the early months, what was apparent was the new government's grasp of the emerging 24-hour media. President Kennedy said of Churchill that, in the Second World War, 'he mobilised the English language and sent it into battle'. Blair mobilized the English language in the cause of selling the New Labour project. He came across as new, fresh, clever but approachable. He articulated a vision for Britain that acknowledged and valued the reforming achievements of Thatcher while consciously reaching out to those who felt disinherited by her revolution. A more traditional Labour government might have attempted to revive or shore up the old industries on which jobs had depended. New Labour perceived that economic success, in a world where manufacturing had largely moved to emerging economies with cheap labour at their disposal, depended on education, in particular on the skills which would in turn feed the inventiveness that would enable the UK to compete and prosper.

For much of the Blair/Brown era this combination of economic prudence and competitive innovation was highly successful. The high ranking of British universities in global league tables is one witness to it. Gordon Brown's gradual abandonment of his own prudent fiscal rules contributed to the economic woes of 2008. But, in 1997, the government's most pressing economic and political decision, after its bold innovation in making the Bank of England independent in its management of monetary policy, was whether to sign up to the single currency.

In the run-up to the election, Blair had been notably cautious. In a first policy discussion in Number 10 (from which Robin Cook was deliberately excluded) Blair remained cautious. The official assessment he received from Nigel Wicks of the Treasury suggested that there were no insuperable obstacles to membership, though Wicks expressed concern about the performance of the Italian economy. The start date of the single currency had already been postponed from 1997 to 1999. Wicks 'forecast with great prescience that problems would arise if the Member States with a historic tendency to inflation could not live within a framework of monetary policy that would effectively be the same as the Bundesbank's'.[5]

Blair believed that it would be easier to win a referendum on membership of the single currency if it were already up and running successfully. Then, and since, it has been argued that the new government should have capitalized on its popularity to hold an early referendum on EMU, perhaps asking the electorate to authorize the government to join at a time of its own choosing. But, as we now all know, referendums are unpredictable and popular governments can lose them even when their overall standing remains high. The new government were to find this in September 1997 when the referendum on devolution in Wales was won by a margin of fewer than 7,000 votes and just 1 per cent.

Blair and his team knew that their European commitment would be judged by their attitude to the single currency. But they were under no immediate pressure from partners. Blair's first meeting with his EU colleagues was at an informal summit in late May 1997, under Dutch Presidency at the North Sea resort of Noordwijk. It was my first encounter with the Blair magic. If Leonardo di Caprio had walked straight off the *Titanic* onto the Noordwijk beach his reception would not have been more rapturous. Blair was the new, young star and older Heads of Government swarmed like wasps round honey, lapping up the glamour and the (as yet untested) sense that Blair represented a new hope for the progress of the European project.

A few weeks later, in Amsterdam, Blair had his first serious exposure to EU negotiations, in the European Council that was called to discuss and conclude the negotiations on what became the Amsterdam Treaty. Blair brought a new style to EU negotiations. The trend under his predecessors had been to dig in on those issues where unanimity was required and where a significant British interest was considered to be at stake. The tone had varied, from the strident under Thatcher, to the charming, but equally adamant, under Major. Blair rarely deployed those tactics. He sought to prevail by persuasion and, again unlike his predecessors, who had left the drafting wheezes to officials, he was keen to get involved in looking for accommodating solutions.

That did not mean that there were no red lines. There were. But there were no red faces of anger round the negotiating table (save for a moment when

[5] Liddle, *The Europe Dilemma*, p. 76.

Helmut Kohl looked as if he was about to punch Aznar, the Spanish Prime Minister). The new British government were prepared to see action against crime and terrorism brought within the purview of the Community treaties, the purely intergovernmental route having failed to deliver. But they maintained the insistence of their Tory predecessors on preserving the UK's right to maintain its own system of frontier controls. As Blair later told the House of Commons, the new government 'maintained, as we said we would, the veto on matters of foreign policy, defence, treaty change, Community finances and tax' and had 'prevented the extension of qualified majority voting in areas where it might cause damage'. Blair took credit, in reporting to Parliament, for putting jobs on top of the European agenda and, 'for the first time in a decade, setting a positive agenda for Europe, namely completion of the single market, CAP reform, enlargement and a more effective common foreign and security policy'.

Not much of that was, in reality, new, and Blair was still feeling his way on aspects of the Amsterdam Treaty which were to prove more substantial building blocks of future EU evolution than was apparent at the time. These included defence cooperation, the creation of a 'High Representative' for EU foreign policy, and the introduction of legislative co-decision between the Council of Ministers and the European Parliament—an innovation that, over time, changed the balance of power between the institutions.

There was one other innovation in the Treaty, which the Conservatives had opposed on the ground that it was beyond the competence of the EU. This was the provision that empowered the EU 'to take appropriate action to combat discrimination based on sex, racial or ethnic origin, religion or belief, disability, age or sexual orientation'. The new clause has, since its introduction, been the basis of significant progress on fundamental human rights.

The new Labour government were anxious to demonstrate that they were stout defenders of the UK national interest.[6] I spent much of the Amsterdam European Council locked, on Blair's instruction, in negotiation with the Secretary General of the Commission on an obscure, but sensitive, fisheries issue: quota hopping.[7] I emerged from this negotiation with my reputation enhanced but, in truth, I could take no credit. I was extremely fortunate that the Secretary General at the time was David Williamson, who as a senior

---

[6] The late Sir Michael Palliser, Permanent Under-Secretary at the FCO from 1975–1982, would never allow FCO submissions to describe Ministers as 'anxious'. Officials might be anxious. Ministers always had to be seen to be 'keen'.

[7] The practice of obtaining the right to catch part of a country's national quota for fish in EU waters by buying licences from its fishermen.

Whitehall official, and later head of the European Secretariat in the Cabinet Office under Thatcher, had forgotten more on the subject than most people had ever known in the first place. It was David who gave Blair his success on this issue, and it was Blair's own performance more generally that established his competence domestically and his authority within the EU. In the House of Commons, the Leader of the Opposition described the outcome of Amsterdam as 'not a triumph but a travesty'. That was uncharacteristically niggardly and, as Blair retorted, little more than 'a good try' on the part of John Major in his first, and last, weeks in the role.[8]

Iraq became the defining issue of Blair's premiership. The issue of membership of the single currency has dominated assessments of his European policy. The Blair government's policy on membership of the single currency is not easy to pin down. In the run-up to the 1997 General Election, Blair had been more sceptical than Brown, fearing the political fallout if Labour embraced the single currency. The single currency was not then in existence, its start date having been postponed to January 1999. Blair was intent on fostering his relationship with the Murdoch Press. According to Ed Balls, Gordon Brown's closest adviser in Opposition, and later in government, Blair wanted Brown to use a speech in New York in February, 1997 to convey a sense of caution. John Sergeant (then of the BBC and later, like Balls, an unlikely star of *Strictly Come Dancing*) accompanied Brown and the plan was for Brown to tell Sergeant in an interview that there were 'formidable obstacles' to joining the single currency, at least in the first wave. In the event, Brown could not bring himself to use those words and Sergeant left empty handed. To forestall a story that the Labour Opposition was in a dither on the issue, the so-called five tests for judging the issue were swiftly devised. Balls acknowledges that he saw the five tests as a potential help in persuading Brown of his view that joining the single currency was a mistake, but at the time their main intent was to demonstrate that the decision, when it came, would be based on sound economic criteria and not on politics alone.[9]

Blair's reservations appear to have continued in the months following his election victory, and agreement was reached that Brown would seek to put an end to the constant speculation on the issue. Quite who was in the loop of agreeing exactly what would be said by the Chancellor on the subject is obscure but, in late October 1997, Brown told Phil Webster of *The Times* that the UK would definitely not join in the first wave of members in 1999 and

---

[8] *Hansard*, 18 June 1997, vol. 296, cols. 313–30.
[9] Ed Balls, *Speaking Out: Lessons in Life and Politics* (London: Arrow, 2017), pp. 160–2.

that it was highly unlikely that the UK would join in the lifetime of the Parliament. The first Blair knew of the interview was when its contents were broadcast to the world from the Red Lion pub in Whitehall by Charlie Whelan, Brown's spokesman. It was a presentational mess. It was also a failure of communication and coordination between the Downing Street neighbours that was an early portent of worse to come.

For the time being, the situation was rescued by a statement to Parliament by Brown which was clear on one point: barring some fundamental or unforeseen change in economic circumstances, making a decision during the first term of the new government was not realistic. Business and the country as a whole were invited to plan on that basis. For the rest, the statement was a masterpiece of ambiguity in which positive tone disguised a long list of caveats. 'If', said the Chancellor, 'a single currency would be good for jobs, British business and future prosperity, it is right in principle to join...I therefore conclude on the question of principle that if, in the end, the single currency is successful and the economic case is clear and unambiguous, the Government believe that Britain should be part of it'. The statement also raised the importance of the five tests as the determinant of an eventual decision: 'Applying those five economic tests leads the Government to the following clear conclusions. British membership of a single currency in 1999 could not meet the tests, and therefore is not in the country's interests. There is no proper convergence between the British economy and other European economies now, and to try to join now would be to accept a monetary policy that would suit other European economies but not our own...'[10]

Brown's statement held the line until the single currency became a fact of life in January 1999 (launched at a special meeting of EU Finance Ministers from which Gordon Brown absented himself, Hogmanay in Scotland being a higher priority). Preparatory work had been undertaken in the meantime and, in February 1999, Blair announced a 'national changeover plan' to Parliament. 'Our intention is clear', he said. 'Britain should join a successful single currency, provided the economic conditions are met. Our membership is conditional; it is not inevitable. Both intention and conditions are genuine...What we announce today is not a change of policy: it is a change of gear.' The government wanted to keep open the option of making a decision to join early in the next Parliament and the time had come to step up practical preparations.

[10] *Hansard*, 27 October 1997, vol. 299, cols. 583-606.

The statement was warmly received by supporters of membership of the single currency. The former Conservative Chancellor, Kenneth Clarke, welcomed 'the marked change of tone represented by today's statement'. Sir Edward Heath, the Father of the House, agreed. 'No single market in the world has more than one currency', he argued. 'We cannot carry on in a single market if we go for multiple currencies. That simply is not feasible.'[11]

In the debate, former Conservative Deputy Prime Minister, Michael Heseltine, called for an all-party grouping to lead public opinion on the matter. The result was the *Britain in Europe* campaign. It was supported by the Prime Minister and Chancellor, the leader of the Liberal Democrat party, and by Clarke and Heseltine, and chaired by Sir Colin Marshall of British Airways. It was doomed from the start. Gordon Brown was determined to have control of the whole single currency policy. He resented the fact that Blair had made the changeover statement to the House. He thought Blair was trying to undermine him. By the time I started to work for Blair in Number 10 in 2000 cooperation across Downing Street on EU matters had become problematic. So intense was Brown's insistence on control that *Britain in Europe* was given no scope to make the case for the single currency. No Minister dared speak out on the subject and Robin Cook, who was a strong advocate, incurred the displeasure of both Number 10 and Number 11 for doing so. He was instructed by Alastair Campbell to back off. The single currency was an issue for the second term, not the first.

I had had some experience of Gordon Brown in Brussels. He was invariably moody and uncommunicative. 'Good morning Chancellor' was rarely greeted with a response. He never once asked my advice on substance or tactics. During the UK Presidency in 1998, under pressure from the British popular Press, he reversed the government's policy (unchanged since the Conservative government) of supporting the EU plan to abolish duty-free sales within the EU, e.g. on cross-Channel ferries. He arrived one morning for an ECOFIN meeting, having given his Treasury officials no forewarning of the change. Nor did he inform Mario Monti, the Commissioner responsible for the issue. From the chair, he tried to get his fellow Finance Ministers to reverse the established policy. They declined. He tried to sum up in favour of his own position. They repeated their united opposition. He tried once again to sum up in his own favour. The other Finance Ministers looked perplexed—and refused to budge.

This was characteristic of Brown's behaviour. Every meeting of ECOFIN was preceded by a story given by the Treasury to the British Press of the battle

---

[11] *Hansard*, 23 February 1999, vol. 326, cols. 179–96.

Brown was going to Brussels to win. The relationship between the planted story and the reality was often tenuous. Brown was pro-European to the extent that he recognized the crucial British economic interests that are dependent on EU membership. But he had no patience with the institutional structures and diplomatic norms of EU life. He may conceivably have believed that showing that he was fighting for Britain at every turn would prove that Britain was delivering good value for the UK voter. In practice, he reinforced he image of the EU as the enemy, and latched onto the fact that a Eurosceptic stance would ingratiate him with the likes of Rupert Murdoch or Paul Dacre, the editor of the *Daily Mail*.

When I was back in London, and heading up the European Secretariat, my job was to try to achieve consensus on EU policies across Whitehall. I had been used to the process when head of the European department in the FCO in the 1980s. Arguments with the Treasury were then frequent and heated. But they were open and candid and policy debate was refreshingly vigorous. In 2000, I found a situation where there was little dialogue and unwilling cooperation. If Number 10 asked the Treasury for a paper on an issue, as often as not it was refused. The issue of tax harmonization was one where the Labour government had maintained the fierce opposition to majority voting that had characterized the Thatcher and Major governments. In this, they had the support of the Irish government, whose economic miracle was fuelled, in part, by corporate tax rates which undercut those of other EU countries. The German government, the biggest net contributor in the EU, was starting to argue that it was unfair to expect them to give massive Structural Fund subsidies to Ireland, while facing unfair competition over inward investment. I wrote to the Treasury. I was not disputing the policy of adamant resistance to any change to the EU voting rules on tax matters. But what was the answer to the German argument? I received no answer. Instead, the senior Treasury official responsible for these issues approached me furtively in the street one day. 'Your letter raised a very good point', he said, 'but I am not allowed to answer it.'

In the General Election of 2001, Labour scored another massive victory, incurring a net loss of only five seats compared with 1997. Robin Cook was replaced as Foreign Secretary by Jack Straw, who had been Home Secretary in the first term. Straw had been a Special Adviser to Barbara Castle in the Wilson government of 1974 and had shared her opposition to EEC membership. But as Home Secretary, he had played a constructive role in the EU's work on issues of crime and terrorism and brought a similar positive pragmatism to European matters in his new role.

Tony Blair made it plain to me, as to others who worked for him, that he was committed to taking the UK into the euro in his second term. It formed part of his strong commitment to British leadership of the EU. That claim to leadership had been dented by the decision not to enter the single currency from the outset. Seeking compensatory initiatives, Blair had shifted the British government's traditional stance on defence, to the extent of agreeing with President Chirac a bilateral initiative on defence cooperation that was also a blueprint for the EU, giving the EU an autonomous peacekeeping capacity but without conflicting with the NATO commitment to mutual defence. Blair had also initiated the so-called Lisbon strategy, an agenda of economic reform intended to make the EU the most dynamic and socially inclusive economy in the world by 2010. Bilaterally, the government, under his leadership, had also embarked on a programme of 'step change' to reboot Britain's bilateral relationships with her EU partners. These were serious and positive initiatives but they could not compensate for Britain's absence from the single currency or mask the fact that the fundamentals of the government's attitude to the EU were firmly grounded in traditional attitudes.

I was intimately involved in the one big speech on Europe that Blair made in the UK early in the second term. It was made at Birmingham University at the opening of their European Research Institute on 23 November 2001. Re-reading it today, what is striking is how conventional it was in its argument. It is not the speech of a Prime Minister made against a background of public support for the European project; rather the reverse. The anti-EU propaganda of the Murdoch Press was constant, and both reflected and augmented public scepticism. Much of Blair's speech was an account of how and why the UK had failed to join the EEC at the creation and was then compelled by reality to do so. In making the positive case for leadership in Europe, Blair used a series of negative arguments, mostly about the risks of non-engagement. Europe, as Blair described it in the speech, was a success, but a flawed success. British leadership was needed because only through leadership could the necessary changes be achieved. There was an appeal to democratic solidarity in the wake of 9/11 and Britain, in Blair's view, was the bridge between the USA and Europe. But the speech was mostly about the traditional British goals of liberal economics, open markets, and inward investment. As John Major had done, Blair warned that 'Britain has no economic future outside Europe'.

The speech was made shortly before the European Council at Laeken in Belgium which was to agree a Declaration that in turn led to the Convention which drafted the European Constitutional Treaty. It does show Blair as interested in institutional reform. But the EU institution that Blair wanted to strengthen was the European Council, i.e. to further the role of Heads of Government in setting the direction of the EU, implicitly diminishing the role of the Commission and European Parliament, and certainly placing himself in opposition to those Member States who still saw the vocation of the EU as being a federal one. Much of Blair's support for the Convention, in large part the brainchild of the Belgian Prime Minister, Guy Verhofstadt, was rooted in our belief in London that the Convention would be a two-way process, with as much emphasis on limiting the powers of 'Brussels' as enhancing them. Blair had stressed the point in Birmingham when he criticized 'unnecessary inter- ference in what ought properly to be national, regional or local decisions. That is why I remain attracted to ways of strengthening national Parliamentary control over excess bureaucracy, over-regulation and unnecessarily centralis- ing proposals.'

In parallel with this approach, preparatory work on EMU continued. In 2002 and early 2003, in the European Secretariat, we prepared scenarios showing what needed to be done, and by when, if Britain was to meet the membership criteria so as to be inside the currency before the next General Election. Under the direction of the Cabinet Secretary, we also began work on the organization and administration of a referendum.

The Treasury, meanwhile, were engaged on a massive analysis of each of the five tests: the basis on which a decision would be taken on whether to join the currency. I was in touch with the Treasury Permanent Secretary, Gus O'Donnell, who had been Press Officer to John Major and was therefore an old friend and colleague. The strong sense I got from O'Donnell was that, from an economic perspective the criteria could be considered as met. The decision, in his view, was essentially a political one.

At various points in this period, Jonathan Powell (Blair's Chief of Staff) asked Blair: 'What about Gordon?' Blair would reply: 'You leave Gordon to me.' We assumed the two men were talking. As it turned out, they were not. When the analysis of the five tests was produced (in eighteen documents, standing over a metre high when stacked) Blair, Brown and a small group of officials met for them to be presented. Brown was accompanied by Ed Balls, his principal political adviser and, by common and accurate repute, the only person in the Treasury capable of extracting decisions from his master.

Until shortly before this moment, I had been convinced that we were motoring determinedly towards the single currency. Blair had spoken to me with conviction of his strength of purpose on the issue. He spoke similarly to business groupings. One day, in the spring of 2003, in a telephone conversa- tion with John Major, my former boss, I told him that our preparations were in full swing. 'Stephen', Major replied, 'what makes you think for a moment that Gordon will allow Tony to go into the euro?' The scales fell from my eyes. I knew of Brown's intense ambition to take the keys to 10 Downing Street. I was not then aware of just how bad relations had become, let alone of the virulent anti-Blair Press briefings conducted from the Chancellor's office. But it was obvious to me, after speaking to Major, that, if Blair tried to conduct a referendum on joining the euro without Brown's agreement, the Chancellor would resign and lead the campaign to defeat the proposal. That was a risk that Blair could not afford to take.

Later in the day of that phone conversation with Major, Peter Hyman, one of Blair's most able and agreeable political advisers, came into my room. Hyman had spoken to me of how a referendum on the euro would be won 'on the back of the Baghdad bounce', the mistakenly assumed success and popularity of the invasion of Iraq. Now, I said to him that I would take a bet that we would not be joining the single currency. Peter took the bet.

When the meetings with Brown took place, it was evident that Major had been right. For Brown, the conclusion of the tests was that the conditions for joining were not established. Blair disputed that conclusion. He at least wanted to get to a position where the government's stance was one of 'when' rather than 'if' the UK would join the single currency. Eventually, officials were asked to leave the Prime Minister's study and the argument was pursued between Blair and Brown alone. There were raised voices. According to Ed Balls' account, Brown returned to the Treasury thinking he might have been sacked. He had not, and Balls and Jeremy Heywood were tasked with trying to reach agreement on the statement that would be made to Parliament. After an all-night session, Heywood secured a few changes. The question of who would make the statement remained open. Then, word came from the Chancellor's office that if the Prime Minister made the statement, Brown would resign. Blair backed down.

Blair had one last throw. Each Cabinet Minister was given the opportunity to read the assessments of the five tests prior to a Cabinet discussion. The result was predictable: most members were in favour of membership but were not willing to press for an immediate commitment.

Brown's statement to the House of Commons on 9 June 2013 concluded, after a lengthy exposition of the economic background, that 'the financial services test is met. We have still to meet the two tests of sustainable convergence and flexibility. Subject to the achievement of sustainable convergence and sufficient flexibility, the tests for investment and employment would be met.'

Michael Howard, the Leader of the Opposition, had something of an open goal: 'Today's statement is...a result of the frantic efforts by the Chancellor and the Prime Minister to cover up their differences. After all, that is why the five tests were thought up in the first place...written on the back of an envelope in the back of a taxi to fix the damage done by the Chancellor's spin doctor in the back of the Red Lion pub. It was a four-pint briefing, which led to a five-point plan that has just given us a six-year run-around...The Prime Minister will pay any price to do down his Chancellor. There they sit, united in rivalry, each determined to frustrate the other, to scheme against the other and to do the other down...'[12]

Brown told the House that he was announcing major reforms that would assist in achieving the sustainable and durable convergence that would enable Britain to succeed within the euro zone. A small, informal committee was set up under Blair's chairmanship, to review progress. To my recollection, it met only twice. The Prime Minister would ask a question. Brown would sit in brooding silence. A brave official might hazard an answer. The committee died, along with the euro ambitions of the Prime Minister.

The day after Brown's statement to the House of Commons, he and Blair gave a joint press conference in Number 10 in an attempt to put on a show of unity. They announced a road show: they would travel round the United Kingdom to debate with the public the issues surrounding euro membership.

This was the first I had heard of the plan, although it would surely fall to the European Secretariat to organize it. I approached Jonathan Powell, the Chief of Staff, asking what he wanted me to do since we had, so far, made no preparations for implementing what had just been announced. 'Don't be daft', was Powell's reply, 'of course there isn't going to be a road show.'

Accordingly, we did no work on the subject. From time to time, journalists would ask the FCO about the state of progress. In Gilbert and Sullivan's operetta, *The Mikado*, the victims of the Mikado's wrath are saved from execution on the grounds that, once the Mikado has spoken, his orders can be considered to have been carried out already. The FCO were reduced to replies of a similar nature.

The subject of euro membership rates one paragraph in Blair's autobiography.[13] In it, Blair denies that the decision not to enter the euro had anything to do with Brown's opposition. His disagreement with Brown was, he says, all to do with positioning: the government should appear positive on the subject, even if in reality it was not going to join.

That assessment does not chime with what I witnessed. Nor can it be easily reconciled with the impression that Blair gave to me and others that membership of the euro was a high priority for him personally. In any event, it is curious that a policy which consumed so much time, energy, and political and personal capital should be dismissed in a single paragraph as largely inconsequential.

Iraq was, of course, Blair's overwhelming preoccupation at the time, and became the defining issue of his premiership. It was a turning point in his domestic standing. It was also a turning point in his relations with his EU partners.

To his credit, Blair saw more clearly than others that 9/11 would fundamentally change the way the United States viewed the world, and the way the world needed to view a terrorist threat driven by ideology, and intent on mass destruction of civilian life. The way he gripped the issue, travelling the world as the self-appointed convener of righteous opposition to the new evil, inevitably aroused the jealousy of those such as President Chirac who believed (with justification) that they knew a good deal more about the Middle East than Blair did. More significantly, Blair signed up to President Bush's agenda of war against Saddam Hussein as early as the summer of 2002. From then on, he became the advocate of Bush's policy to his fellow EU leaders. He took US policy to Europe. He never thought, or sought, to construct a common European policy that he could take to the United States.

In this, he met the strenuous opposition of President Chirac. Chirac was not a man of unalloyed probity or highly principled motives. But his argument on Iraq was logical: his personal experience as a subaltern in the French army in the Algerian war had taught him that war was always brutal and tragic. An intervention in support of the Shia majority in Iraq might well place the Shia in control, but a Shia majority was not the same thing as democracy. There would be thousands and thousands of deaths. And there was no basis in international law for an invasion. War should always be a matter of last resort. While the UN Inspectorate were still engaged in seeking out any weapons of mass destruction being developed by Saddam Hussein, and in the absence of clear evidence that he had such weapons, war was not justifiable. Blair had no time for any of those arguments.

The German Chancellor, Schröder, was different. He was not initially opposed to the war, telling Blair that, while Germany, for constitutional reasons, could play no part in a military operation, it could provide some logistical support. But, faced with a national election in Germany, and the growing unpopularity of the prospective war, Schröder hardened his position to the point that he and Chirac became the leaders of a group within the EU resisting the British position. To his side, Blair recruited Prime Ministers Aznar of Spain and Berlusconi of Italy, already allies in the campaign for an economically liberal Europe. The Portuguese Prime Minister, Durâo Barroso, joined them. The new states of eastern and central Europe by and large followed suit. The EU was split down the middle and a 'letter of the Eight', siding with the UK and the US, in opposition to the group led by France and Germany, provoked a huge sense of relief in Number 10 and equal fury in the Elysée.

Blair failed to secure the authority of the UN Security Council for war against Saddam Hussein. His Attorney General, Peter Goldsmith, concluded (after consulting American, but not French, lawyers) that the UN Security Council resolutions from 1991 provided continuing legal authority for action. Cabinet agreed. Parliament voted for war, but against the opposition of an unprecedented number of Labour MPs.

On the eve of war, on 17 February 2003, a special meeting of the European Council was convened in Brussels, with the UN Secretary General, Kofi Annan in attendance. It papered over the cracks in the EU with a statement which had something in it for both sides of the dispute. At the end of the meeting, Chirac spoke. Nobody, he said, had at any point in the meeting talked of death. If an invasion went ahead there would be thousands of deaths.

Some two weeks later, President Chirac explained on French television that when a US/UK draft resolution authorizing war came to the vote in the UN Security Council that night it would be defeated, either because it could not command the necessary nine votes in favour *or* because it would be voted against (i.e. vetoed) by one of the Permanent Members, of whom France was one. Whatever the circumstances (i.e. whatever the procedure that prevailed) the position of France in the Security Council that evening would be against war because the circumstances justifying a war did not exist.

I was walking down the main Number 10 corridor the following morning when Blair and Campbell, who understood precisely what Chirac had said, took the decision to brief the media that Chirac had declared that in no circumstances would France ever support war against Saddam Hussein. Soon afterwards, I received a phone call from former Minister, Joyce Quin. Did the Prime Minister and Campbell know, she asked, that the account that was being attributed to them in the media was not what Chirac had actually said? They did.

After the invasion, and when it was already clear that Chirac's predictions were being proved correct, an attempt was made to patch up relations. We flew to Paris in June. Blair and Chirac met alone. Chirac told Blair that the enlarged European Union which would shortly include some of the countries of eastern and central Europe (Hungary, Poland, the Czech Republic, Slovenia, Slovakia), the Baltic States (Estonia, Latvia, and Lithuania) and Cyprus and Malta, would be ungovernable. The answer was for the three largest countries (France, Germany, and the UK) to run the show. A meeting of the three leaders was set up for September, in Germany, and Blair was determined to make the new trilateralism work, despite the risks. The principal risk was to the UK's relations with the other Member States and, in particular, to Blair's relations with the Heads of Government of Italy and Spain (Berlusconi and Aznar) who had supported Blair over Iraq, at the cost of considerable popular opposition. Blair was aware of those risks, and of the grave doubts of the Foreign Office as to the workability of the initiative, given the offence it risked causing to other Member States. But Blair had striven to establish a close relationship with Schröder. There had been times when Schröder's irritation with Chirac had worked to UK advantage, but never for long enough to do more than dent the close bilateral relations between the French and German governments. Iraq had caused bad blood between Schröder and Blair, and overt hostility between Blair and Chirac. The attractions of a reconciliation seemed to make the risks worth taking.

The meeting itself was a success, despite continued differences over Iraq. Three-way consultation was established. Most of the other Member States reluctantly accepted that reconciliation between the three largest Member States was a necessary step. Neither Spain nor Italy saw it that way. Berlusconi was more mortified than angry. Aznar was angry and his political relationship with Blair did not recover. Nor did the new trilateralism last long. The habit of Franco-German collaboration was too entrenched for a third party to break into the charmed circle. When I and my Number 10 colleague, Nigel Sheinwald, went to Paris for the first trilateral meeting, we found that the French and Germans had been meeting beforehand to agree the joint stance they would take with the British. On the British side, Blair, weakened domestically by Iraq, could not afford to spend political capital in persuading individual Ministers to make the policy compromises that successful trilateralism required.

The Italian six months' Presidency of the EU had just got under way when the September 2003 meeting of Blair, Chirac, and Schröder took place. The Italians were charged with running the intergovernmental conference that was to turn the recently concluded Convention into a European Constitutional Treaty. Despite the British government's best hopes and intentions, the Convention had turned into a damage-limitation exercise as far as the UK was concerned, its integrationist thrust being more than the government could readily swallow. Despite his unhappiness at Blair's trilateral gambit, Berlusconi was a faithful ally in not pressing the UK on its 'red lines'. But Berlusconi was uninterested in detail and only focused as the European Council under his chairmanship drew near. When the Council met in October, it quickly became clear that in no circumstances were Chirac and Schröder prepared to allow progress to be made on Berlusconi's watch. Blair was the reluctant witness to the brutal political mugging that Chirac and Schröder meted out to Berlusconi. No reasons were given to Berlusconi. He was simply told that no agreement would be reached under his chairmanship.

In the following year, while the Irish Presidency, with consummate professionalism, moved the IGC to an agreement on a European Constitutional Treaty better suited to British taste, Chirac and Schröder sought to impose their will in another field. The President of the European Commission, Romano Prodi, was coming to the end of his term. Chirac and Schröder decided between them that his successor should be the Belgian Prime Minister, Guy Verhofstadt. Verhofstadt was an attractive young leader, a modern federalist who saw closer integration as a vehicle for economic reform and modernization in the EU. At one level, his ideas were appealing to the UK which, in the so-called Lisbon Agenda of 2000, had set the ambition of making the EU the world's most competitive economy by 2010. But an overtly federalist politician, who was clever to boot, was not one who appealed to Blair as Commission President or could readily be sold to the British media and public.

Under the treaty changes agreed by the EU at Nice in 2000, the President of the Commission was, for the first time, to be chosen by a majority vote: no one country would be able to exercise a veto, as John Major had over the Belgian candidate in 1994. Once Blair had decided against Verhofstadt (and it must be said that he initially gave somewhat ambiguous signals to Verhofstadt and to Schröder, which raised hopes that he might support the Belgian), he and Berlusconi combined to put together a coalition of votes to defeat France and Germany and their chosen candidate. In his stead, Blair and Berlusconi championed the cause of Durâo Barroso, the Portuguese Prime Minister, who shared Blair's approach to economic liberalization. In order to further Barroso's cause, Berlusconi and Blair first put forward the name of Chris Patten, the British EU Commissioner for external affairs who had been a huge success in the job and was admirably qualified. Chirac duly rejected it, thereby opening the way for Barroso to appear as a compromise. Barroso got the job, 'the first time that the twin-engine motor of Europe had been stalled in respect of such a big issue', as Blair himself put it. By his own admission, his relationship with Schröder never recovered.[14] In any event, even before her election victory in Germany in 2005, Blair had begun to find Angela Merkel more congenial company, both politically and as a person.

Three successive British Prime Ministers can lay claim to two huge contributions to the success of the European project: the campaign for economic liberalization and reform, and enlargement. Thatcher had proclaimed the goal of enlargement in her Bruges speech of 1998. John Major had taken up the cause when many (including the French) were, to say the least, lukewarm. In one conversation with Major, President Mitterrand had confidently predicted that none of the newly liberated states of eastern Europe would join before 2010. That was less an objective assessment than an expression of intent. Blair picked up the baton. Negotiations with the candidate countries began under the British Presidency in 1998 and the first wave of enlargement took place in 2004.

At the outset of the negotiations it had not been thought that all ten of the candidate countries would join together at the same time. Each country had to meet the political and economic criteria for membership laid down by the EU and the negotiating process was about establishing their ability to accept the existing EU rules, and the period of transition each would need before taking on the full obligations of membership. It was accepted that they would need large-scale assistance from the EU Structural Funds and, in many cases, expert advice on transforming their national civic institutions, after more than four decades of corruption under Soviet rule.

Much of the early focus was on Poland, Hungary, the Czech Republic, and Slovakia, and it soon became apparent that Poland's state of readiness was less advanced than that of the other central Europeans. But for Germany, for evident historical and geographical reasons, the idea that Poland might not be part of the first wave of acceding countries was unacceptable. The German argument was accepted and, almost by accident, all the ten candidates became bundled together in what became known as the 'regatta' approach and all joined the EU together in May 2004.

Under the transitional arrangements for the new entrants, full freedom of movement for their citizens was not guaranteed until 2011. Of the existing

[14] Ibid., p. 537.

Member States, only the UK, Ireland, and Sweden decided to grant full freedom of movement from the outset. When I asked my German opposite number in Schröder's office why Germany, as one of the champions of enlargement, was not doing the same, he replied that German demographic projections suggested that the country would not need the immigrant labour that the new members could provide until the end of the transition period.

Blair was not oblivious to the political implications of large-scale immigration. Far from it. Soon after the 2001 General Election, he identified immigration as perhaps the most volatile issue in British politics. But it was then seen as an issue of migration from outside Europe, not from within. Assessments were made of the number that might come to the UK from the new Member States. They seriously underestimated the actual figures, in part because estimates of a large influx from the Iberian peninsula following Spanish and Portuguese accession in the mid 1980s had not been realized, and it was thought that that pattern would be repeated. The overriding political consideration in 2004 was the geopolitical one, namely the importance of embedding democracy in countries which had been denied it since the Second World War. Britain had been their champion and was eager to maintain that position.

Blair's support was not confined to the ten countries who joined in 2004. Following their support for the NATO intervention in Kosovo in 1999, which had been led by the US and the UK, Blair had promised both Bulgaria and Romania that he would champion their claims to accession. He prevailed, and both countries joined the EU in 2007. The relative ease with which Blair persuaded his EU colleagues to open negotiations with countries that were far from ready to accept the obligations of membership was a measure of the extent to which the objective criteria for judging the suitability of candidate countries had to give way to the politics. Few would claim that Romania and Bulgaria were ready by 2007.

Blair also championed the right of Turkey to apply to join the EU and, in doing so, overcame the opposition of France and Germany. Popular feeling against Turkish accession ran deep in both countries. The large Turkish population in Germany was seen as ill-assimilated. In France, secular country though it is, Catholic religious sentiment against a country, also secular but with a majority Moslem population, was strong. In both countries, the fear of migration from a country with a larger population even than Germany was also a factor. Moreover, Turkey, as a Member State, would be entitled to more MEPs than any other Member. There was fear that Turkey would wield disproportionate power. A large, poor country, with a culture that many saw as alien, was not an attractive proposition to France or Germany.

Blair saw it differently. For a start, there was a question of principle. Before the UK had joined the EEC, the original six members had signed an Association Agreement with Turkey which recognized the country as part of Europe with a right to apply for full membership in due time. If there was ever an argument to be had about whether Turkey was a European country, that argument had been settled by the terms of the Association Agreement. More importantly, Blair saw (as did the Bush government in the United States) the advantages of having a western-looking country (a longstanding member of NATO) as a pivot of influence between Europe and the Arab world. Its government, under Prime Minister Erdogan, was committed to the reforms necessary to adapt Turkey for membership. Blair did not argue that Turkey was ready to join and always accepted that there would have to be a long transitional arrangement in respect of freedom of movement. But the pace of reform and of economic growth gave reason to think that the Turkish aspiration to be an EU member could and should be met.

The hopes of 2005 have faded, if not disappeared. The lack of enthusiasm for Turkey on the part of some in the EU played a part, but the internal dynamic of what has become the Erdogan regime, played an even bigger one. The ability of Turkey to play off Russia against the United States, or to hold the EU in thrall to its ability to turn off—or on—the migrant tap from Syria and beyond crudely illustrates the problem of Turkey, but also why the possibility of Turkish accession cannot be abandoned as a long-term possibility.

It was another decision of Blair's, taken at Easter 2004, that, in my view, also played a part, alongside that of EU immigration, in setting the UK on the road that led to the 2016 referendum. The European Constitutional Treaty was close to conclusion. Its title alone was a red rag to the right-wing media in the UK and to the Conservative Party's new leader, the Eurosceptic Michael Howard. Jack Straw, the Foreign Secretary, had argued a year earlier in favour of a referendum on the Constitutional Treaty. His reasoning was that, when the legislation to implement the Constitutional Treaty came before Parliament, there would be a majority in the House of Lords for an amendment requiring a referendum before ratification could happen. The government could invoke the Parliament Act to overturn that vote, but only after the statutory year laid down in the Act. The government would be out of time to do this by the likely date of the next General Election in 2005. So, the government would go into the election on the back foot, while the Conservatives would be able to wrap themselves in the Union flag as champions of the people. Even if the government won the election, they would probably have to concede the referendum. So, Straw concluded, better to jump than wait to be pushed.

Blair was unpersuaded. He argued to Straw that, once a referendum was promised, it would dominate politics to the exclusion of all else. Persuading Labour voters to turn out to vote on the minutiae of a treaty which was, in substance, less important than the Single European Act or the Maastricht Treaty would be a lost cause.

There the matter rested. I was Blair's senior official adviser on EU issues but I would not have known that the referendum argument had come back on the agenda in the spring of 2004 had Straw not been kind enough to give me a copy of the personal minute on the subject that he had sent to the Prime Minister. After reading it, I sent Blair a minute saying that I could not better his own arguments against a referendum and asking whether he might assess public reaction to the Constitutional Treaty, once finalized, before reaching a decision. I got the minute back after Blair had announced the decision to hold a referendum, with a note saying that he agreed with me but that politics had had to prevail.

Blair's account in his memoirs of the reasoning behind the decision follows the logic of Straw's argument. Blair also hints at the pressure he was under to offer a date for his own departure and to hand over to Brown. The Murdoch Press might well have used the referendum issue to begin pressing for an early handover, though Brown himself declined to get involved in Straw's lobbying. But the promise of a referendum was a fateful step. It opened up the expectation of a popular vote on Europe. When the Constitutional Treaty eventually failed, defeated in referendums in France and Netherlands, and was replaced with the more modest Lisbon Treaty, the offer of a referendum was withdrawn. The argument made by the government was that there was no longer anything of substance warranting a referendum. But there had been nothing of substance in the Constitutional Treaty to warrant a referendum either. People who had little interest in the substance believed that politicians had made a promise and that politicians had, perfidiously, withdrawn that promise. This was fertile ground for the emerging political force represented by Nigel Farage and his party, UKIP.

Britain's position as the closest friend of the new Member States (all of whose leaders had English as their first foreign language) had stood the Blair government in good stead during the negotiations on the Constitutional Treaty. But it was tested when negotiations began under Luxembourg's EU Presidency in 2005 on a new financial settlement for the EU, taking account of the costs of enlargement, including the need of the new countries for economic support. The budget rebate, successfully won by Thatcher at Fontainebleau and safeguarded by Major at Edinburgh, now came under severe attack from all sides. The French began early with the argument that the rebate meant that the UK would not be paying its fair share of the costs of enlargement. This was a highly questionable proposition, but the Treasury refused to engage on the merits of the British case (that we would continue to pay a fair share under the financing formula as it stood) and simply dug in on a position of no compromise. So, Britain was quickly put on the back foot with the new Member States, and was soon accused of being the good friend who had become the bad friend.

The British position was not helped by a further, if well meaning, British initiative. The Structural Funds were the EU's main vehicle for supporting the poorer regions of the EU. And the emphasis was on regions, rather than countries. Thus, relatively wealthy countries such as the UK, France, and Italy secured financial support for areas such as Cornwall, the Highlands and Islands, Wales, and the North East and North West. The British argued that, instead of this arrangement, the budget should be deployed to help the less prosperous *countries*, while the wealthier countries took care of their own regions. In other words, the criterion for eligibility should be the relative poverty of the applicant country, rather than that of its regions. Other beneficiary Member States objected. That was hardly surprising. More surprising were the objections of the countries (the new members) who had most to gain. But the psychology of their objection was sound. They reasoned that, so long as the wealthier Member States had a dog in the fight for regional support, then they would continue to support the entire Structural Fund project. If they did not, what motive would they have to continue to sign cheques to the benefit of others?

By the end of the Luxembourg Presidency in June 2005, the UK was the sole opponent of the budget package put together by the Luxembourg Prime Minister, Jean-Claude Juncker. Juncker, one of the younger members of the European Council, was nonetheless an EU veteran. As both Prime Minister and Finance Minister of Luxembourg, he had long been immersed in the detail. He had had several run-ins with Gordon Brown, not least in fighting to retain Luxembourg's tax system which made it a haven for tax avoidance. He and Blair had taken an instant dislike to each other. Blair refused to settle. But he wisely used the British Presidency in the second half of the year to reach a settlement that was very little different from that offered by Juncker. Holding the Presidency made him master of the timetable, gave him a unique position for negotiating to advantage with other Member States, and made it easier to justify compromise and to stand up to the unflagging opposition of Gordon Brown. Britain sacrificed a portion of the rebate to contribute to the costs of enlargement. Blair won short-term opprobrium but made the right call in terms of the UK's strategic interests.

At the start of the UK Presidency, Blair spoke at the European Parliament on 23 June 2005. He wrote most of the speech itself. It was memorable. Blair saw the defeat of the European Constitution in referendums in France and Netherlands, not as a rejection of a text, but as the expression of a wider and deeper popular discontent with the state of affairs in Europe. This, in his view, was not a crisis of political institutions, but of political leadership. In an era of profound upheaval and change, moderate people must give leadership. If they did not, then the extremes would gain traction on the political process. It was already happening both nationally and on a European scale. 'I have sat', Blair continued, 'through Council conclusions after Council conclusions describing how we are "reconnecting to the people of Europe". Are we? It is time to give ourselves a reality check. To receive the wake-up call. The people are blowing the trumpets round the city walls. Are we listening? Have we the political will to go out to meet them so that they regard our leadership as part of the solution, not the problem?'

It was a speech that won the audience. Yet, by the end of the British Presidency six months later, it was regretted by many as a rallying cry that had had no follow-up. But what might that follow-up have been? At home, Blair had to deal with the aftermath of the 7/7 terrorist attacks in London. Within the EU, the budget negotiation dominated the Presidency. Such negotiations pitch government against government in battles that are much more about relative national advantage than about the common Community interest. And Blair's own vision was anyway, as he told an Oxford audience almost a year later, one of 'ever closer union among freely cooperating sovereign governments'.[15] That was not a proposition that commanded wide support in the EU, even as the goals of the EU's founders increasingly fell short of being realized.

In his Oxford speech, his European valedictory, Blair claimed that his vision was the same as that of the EU founders. But it was not. Their vision was not of ever closer union among governments, but among peoples. Nor was it one of 'sovereign governments' 'freely cooperating'. Or, at least, if that was true of the impetus behind the European project, it was not true of the structures the founders had set in place to realize their vision. Their vision was of shared

[15] European Studies Centre Lecture, St Antony's College, Oxford, 2 February 2006.

sovereignty, and shared sovereignty implied a diminution of national sovereignty as the price of greater collective power and influence. The British had accepted that price, albeit reluctantly and while deluding themselves about the extent and significance of what they had signed up to. Every piece of EEC/EU legislation reminded them of the reality, as competence in new areas of policy became the purview of the European Commission and as the role of the House of Commons diminished. Treaty changes were an even more potent reminder, which was why successive British governments resisted them or fought to limit their scope.

For most of Britain's partners, for all of the period up to the early 2000s, the goal of a European Union which followed the path laid out by the founders was one they believed in. Most were willing to go further than the British towards attaining something that would recognizably be an economic and political union. The single currency was, and is, the most potent expression of that ambition. Blair did not follow in their footsteps. Instead, he followed in the footsteps of Heath, Wilson, Callaghan, Thatcher, and Major. Lacking any significant opposition to Europe on his own benches, and with large majorities throughout his time in government, he was not as hemmed in as Major or Wilson and Callaghan had been. He was much more at home as a European than Thatcher. He did not share her mixture of anger and contempt for his partners. But, to win power, he had hitched his wagon to Rupert Murdoch's anti-European star, just as Gordon Brown hitched his to Murdoch and to Paul Dacre at the *Daily Mail*. Attempts to explain the EU to the British were fitful and partial. If the language of battle was abandoned, that of reform took its place. Either way, the EU was faulty and needed fixing.

Blair was right to see, and to say, that the EU was no longer resonating with public opinion on the continent. The EU appeared to be delivering texts, not jobs. As an advocate of economic reform he, like Thatcher and Major, was often ahead of his fellow leaders. But, in fairness to them, their preoccupation with institutional reform was not just a pretext for ducking the harder issues. The institutional changes were intended to enhance collective governance, to increase democratic accountability and to make it easier for governments to embrace reform under the umbrella of a common agenda.

As to Blair himself. Was he a man of hidden depths or hidden shallows, as one of my erstwhile Number 10 colleagues once asked me? His depths were those of a charismatic leader who could conceive and articulate a vision and persuade people, both his own party and the British public, to follow. He was a strategist and tactician of a high order. On our way to a meeting with Berlusconi, when he and Blair were plotting against Chirac and Schröder, I ventured to suggest a way of dealing with the Italian Prime Minister.

'Stephen', Blair replied, 'I haven't got where I have today without knowing how to do this stuff'. He said it nicely. It was not a put-down, and it was true. The other side of the coin was that, compared with Major and Thatcher, he was not intellectually interested in the issues on which I advised him. Both his predecessors would read the documents supporting a policy submission. Blair rarely did so. But if I told him that I thought he needed to read ten of the proposed Articles in a draft EU Treaty, he would do so at speed, master the implications immediately and leave me running to keep up as he thought through the implications for British policy and tactics.

As a man, Blair was invariably courteous and good to work for. Perhaps, if I had pressed, I would have had with him the kind of in-depth discussion that would have exposed some of the contradictions in our European policy. But those contradictions were themselves the product of domestic constraints: those of an increasingly Eurosceptic media and a personally hostile Chancellor of the Exchequer. I made my own errors of judgement, not foreseeing the travails of the Eurozone or the extent to which immigration into the UK from the rest of the EU would increase, compared with what had happened in the 1980s.

Of all the politicians I worked for, Blair was the one who had most confidence in the rightness of his own judgement. That confidence, and his charisma, swept his government and Parliament to war.[16] On Europe, he had an innate conviction of the importance of British membership of the European Union. He articulated it persuasively because it came from his own experience and beliefs and his speeches, for all the work that I and others put into them, always ended up as being his own work and words, and were invariably the better for it. He had an earlier and clearer, understanding than many of his fellow EU leaders of the ways in which the EU was failing to meet the needs and expectations of its citizens. Like all his predecessors, he was constrained by the difficulty, in UK politics, of marrying far-reaching practical reforms with equally imaginative institutional advances.

As I left Downing Street, Blair commented to me that I must be disappointed by the limits to what had been achieved, and so I was. Had I remained, my disappointment would have been still greater. For Tony Blair's successor, Gordon Brown, was a man who 'believed that a social democratic case for Europe was too radical a message for a Labour Prime Minister to communicate to a public that was sceptical of the EU'.[17]

---

[16] An interesting analysis of charisma and hubris is in David Owen's book *In Sickness and in Power: Illness in Heads of Government during the Last Hundred Years* (London: Methuen, 2018), 'Part III: The Intoxication of Power, Bush, Blair and the War in Iraq', pp. 253–322.

[17] Andrew Wood in Andrew Adonis, *Prime Ministers on Europe: Half In Half Out* (London: Biteback Publishing, 2018), p. 218.

10

Brown and Cameron

Opening the Door Marked 'Exit', 2007–2016

It is a truth universally acknowledged that Gordon Brown saved Britain by keeping the UK out of the euro. But is it a truth? While the acknowledgement may be near-universal, and Britain certainly escaped the worst implications of the euro crisis of 2010/2011, one outcome of the decision to stay out was the referendum of 2016. Of course, to join the euro in the first place, a referendum would have had to be held: both main parties were committed to that. Winning such a referendum, even with a united Prime Minister and Chancellor behind it, would have been very problematic. But had Britain joined, then no government, Labour or Conservative, could have offered a referendum on remaining or leaving without posing a near-existential risk to the UK economy.

In his book *Britain: Leading, Not Leaving*, Brown records a conversation with Tony Blair in 2003. 'We can't join the euro. Is that what you said?', Brown reports Blair as asking. 'We can't join the euro', Brown replies. 'You can't say that', Blair retorts. But Brown argues that he can 'say that' because 'if the economic test was not met, and it was not in Britain's interest, I was clear that we should not join . . . I was of the view that we did not need to be in the Euro to be at the heart of Europe. Getting the balance right between autonomy and cooperation, I believe, should not require us to join in for the sake of joining.'[1]

Brown's book, written before the 2016 referendum, in support of the argument for remaining in the EU, is erudite in its historical analysis of the UK's relations with her European partners. Brown is alive to the failure of Britain's post-war Labour government 'to distinguish between the temporary state of Europe – its debts, devastation and divisions – and its long term prospects'.[2] He gives credit to Harold Macmillan for reassessing the UK's place in the world after Suez. He regards Labour's period of hostility to the EEC as a mistake. But the lessons that Brown draws are not radically different from

---

[1] Gordon Brown, *Britain: Leading, Not Leaving* (Selkirk: Deerpark Press, 2016), pp. 204–5.
[2] Ibid., p. 35.

those of his predecessors: the UK must engage in a world where interdependence has replaced simple independence. In Brown's world view, that engagement is very much on his own terms.

Like Blair, Brown saw the importance of a pro-EU stance in rehabilitating the Labour Party in the eyes of the British electorate. Thatcher's latter-day extremism, over the EU and the Poll Tax, had alienated much of that electorate. John Major had sought to redress the balance but had been held to ransom by the uncompromising anti-EU die-hards in his own Party. Labour would not make the same mistakes. But Brown's view of the European Union was no less unsympathetic to the vision of its founders than that of any of his predecessors, and the brutality of his personal style underlined the uncompromising content of his policies. If interdependence, rather than solitary independence, lay at the heart of Brown's world view, there was only one moment of his premiership, in October 2008, when Brown rose powerfully to the occasion. At the height of the banking crisis, President Sarkozy of France invited Brown to attend a summit of Eurozone Heads of Government. It was Brown who persuaded them to follow his approach, which combined recapitalization of the banks with guarantees for interbank lending. Following that meeting, Brown led the international response which culminated in the formation of the G20 group of countries.

That was the apotheosis of what Stewart Wood, Brown's EU adviser in both the Treasury and Number 10, has called his 'muscular intergovernmentalism'.[3] For the rest, Brown had no time for the EU institutions, especially the Commission and the European Parliament. For him, seeing off a Commission-led initiative for an EU savings tax (designed to prevent tax evasion) during his time as Chancellor was a triumph. He claimed it as a victory, not just on the detail, but for a wholly different approach: 'Coming just after the turn of the century, it represented the beginnings of a more general shift in outlook. First, we saw decision-making firmly grounded in intergovernmental negotiation and compromise – a top-down European Commission diktat was rejected ... In short, the savings tax decision demonstrated a United Europe of States at work rather than a United States of Europe.'[4]

Brown's claim that, as Chancellor, he had turned a 14:1 majority against him into 14 governments who had been persuaded of the rightness of his approach does not accord with my recollection. There was a months-long hard

---

[3] Stewart Wood, writing in Andrew Adonis, *Half In Half Out: Prime Ministers on Europe* (London: Biteback Publishing, 2018), p. 213.
[4] Brown, *Britain: Leading, Not Leaving*, p. 151.

battle, with Brown in a minority, and the eventual outcome owed most to the fact that unanimity was the prevailing rule for EU tax issues: without reluctant compromise in the direction of the UK, there would have been no outcome. Moreover, Brown's assertion of the triumph of inter-governmentalism assumes that its superiority over the traditional Community method is self-evident. Many in the EU, both then and now, would dispute that view.

The pattern of muscular inter-governmentalism of Brown's premiership was established during his time at the Treasury. I described in the previous chapter Brown's approach as Chancellor to the issue of EU duty-free sales. It was not a one-off. Both as Chancellor and as Prime Minister, Brown's conception of cooperation with Britain's EU partners was viewed exclusively through the lens of what could be achieved, or prevented, to UK advantage; and to the personal political advantage of Brown himself. If EU Finance Ministers were to meet on a Monday, the British Press (usually the *Financial Times*) would be briefed for the weekend or Monday papers that the Chancellor was going to Brussels to fight off some dastardly anti-British continental plot. It initially caused bewilderment among Brown's fellow Finance Ministers. What was this impending crisis of which they had had no inkling? Once they realized that the 'crisis' was usually entirely spurious, and designed to make Brown appear as a giant among pygmies, it simply caused irritation. But the spurious nature of the spats did not deter the Chancellor. He 'would march straight into the Press conference and proclaim victory, for a deal that had been sorted out between officials weeks earlier'.[5]

This pattern continued at Number 10. The Prime Minister would board Eurostar for a European Council in Brussels, open the brief for the first time, latch onto some subject (where agreement might already have been reached) and order his officials to turn it into a new argument that he could be seen to win.

While it may have been true, as Brown argued in his 2016 book, that the dominance of the European Commission was in decline during his time in government (and the organization, and travails, of the euro contributed to that) that decline was not something which other EU Heads of Government saw as a positive development. Their preoccupation with the EU Constitutional Treaty and, following its demise, the Lisbon Treaty, was seen by Brown as a diversion; irrelevant to the needs of Europe's citizens. He had a point, in that neither Treaty addressed the day-to-day concerns of the EU's citizens. But the Constitutional Treaty was not simply an EU predilection for

---

[5] Ibid., p. 208.

institutions at the expense of pragmatic policy. The whole point was to equip the Union with the legal framework in which decisions in common could be taken on important practical matters. The fact that the Constitutional Treaty ended up as neither fish nor fowl, disliked by constitutionalists and pragmatists in equal measure, was at least partly due to the UK's vigorous engagement as the naysayer to significant political and legal integration. Brown had no sympathy for that integrationist approach. He regarded Blair's cooperation over the Constitutional Treaty as a deviation from hard-headed economic analysis of what was in the public interest. Despite disagreeing with it, Brown did not meddle in Blair's decision to offer a referendum on the Treaty, but his own behaviour undoubtedly contributed to that decision being taken in the first place. In his obsessive quest to unseat Blair, Brown assiduously cultivated the right-wing, anti-European Press. Fear that Murdoch, in particular, might openly support a challenge from Brown was a factor in pushing Blair towards offering a referendum to which he was otherwise averse.

Apart from these political factors, Brown had little time for the human relations side of diplomacy. On an airplane to Berlin early in his time at Number 10, the new Prime Minister berated his officials for arranging a 'getting-to-know-you' meeting with Chancellor Angela Merkel. He saw it as a waste of his time.[6] Yet, Brown did manage to establish a good working relationship with Merkel, based on mutual respect for each other's intellect. Where there were ideas to be exchanged, Brown would engage with commitment. His was a very transactional approach.

Nonetheless, Brown's instinctive sympathies, and actual experience, lay far more with Democratic Party politics in the United States than with European politics. Geographically, mainland Europe was closer than the United States, but for Brown, the Atlantic was, psychologically 'the pond': closer to his thinking and interests. In fairness, it would have been hard for him to rebuild the 'bridge' between the USA and Europe, which both he and Blair believed the UK to be, but which Blair had sabotaged by his Iraq policy. Britain's natural allies in the EU had suffered the adverse domestic consequences of their alliance with the UK over Iraq. The banking crisis of 2008 was seen in continental Europe to be of Anglo-Saxon origin.

In any case, the waters of globalization that Blair and Brown had navigated with skill were increasingly choppy. In the wake of the banking crisis, and of Brown's gradual abandonment of his own fiscal prudence, the domestic economic winds were no longer set fair. The opposition Conservative case

---

[6] Wood in Adonis, *Half In Half Out*, p. 207.

for reduced government expenditure was met with contempt by Brown, but found an echo in the statements of his own Chancellor, Alistair Darling: government expenditure would have to be reined in. Large-scale immigration from the new EU Member States was undoubtedly positive for the economy but did not appear so to those who measured the immigrants' access to jobs, housing, and benefits against their own struggles to make ends meet. Britons were generally relieved to be outside the euro, but the UK remained a member of the EU, and the growing problems of the Eurozone and its perceived dysfunctionality exacerbated the innate scepticism which had always been part of British public opinion.

Speaking at the Edinburgh International Book Festival, in August 2019, Gordon Brown blamed David Cameron for losing the 2016 referendum: 'They didn't put a positive case for Europe and that's why we're in this position', he argued.[7] But, as Stewart Wood acknowledges, 'there may be an understandable view that there is not much to see in Gordon's time as PM with regards to an evolving view of Europe'.[8] What Roger Liddle, another skilled New Labour observer of the period, has called 'the Brown interlude' was just that as far as the UK and the EU were concerned. Brown, with a largely pro-EU Party behind him, had not been able to bring himself to champion the EU as it really was. His mantra of 'leading, not leaving' had been, in various versions, the slogan of a succession of British Prime Ministers. As far as 'leading' was concerned, the Single Market did indeed owe its existence to the UK under Margaret Thatcher. Much of EU financial regulation was designed in the City of London. The EU's external policies in trade and aid were increasingly open thanks to British expertise and influence. But the UK was outside the EU's central project: the euro. Two Labour Prime Ministers, with large pro-EU parliamentary majorities behind them, failed to make a persuasive case for the EU, and for one main reason. The EU that British leaders presented to the public was not the EU that the UK had actually joined but an airbrushed version that did not represent the reality. When the reality presented itself, in the form of further political integration via Treaty change, the UK usually resisted. At best, the British approach was a 'no, unless', compared with the 'yes, if' of most of Britain's partners. The claims of successive British governments to be the leaders in the EU rang hollow when what they were leading was habitually a rearguard action. The message that was conveyed by British politicians was that the EU was a problem but that they could fix it. The message of the Eurosceptics, in the Conservative Party and in the right-wing

---

[7] *The Times*, 27 August 2019.   [8] Wood in Adonis, *Half In Half Out*, p. 197.

Press, was that Europe was indeed a problem and that it could only be fixed by drastic action to regain 'lost' sovereignty.

In May 2010, the task of managing this troublesome burden fell on the shoulders of a new Prime Minister, David Cameron. Cameron was no enthusiast for the EU. He was something of a sceptic and that had helped him to the leadership of his Party at the young age of 39 in 2006.

The nature and extent of Cameron's version of Euroscepticism comes through loud and clear in his autobiography.[9] He was never one of those, such as Bill Cash, Daniel Hannan, or John Redwood, for whom taking the UK out of the EU represented their life's work. But he had cheered at Thatcher's Bruges speech, while also believing that both she and John Major had practised a kind of 'doublespeak'. In Thatcher's case, she had taken the UK into the ERM, despite the view she had expressed at Bruges. For his part, Major had criticized the euro while, at the same time, wanting the UK to be 'at the heart of Europe'. Cameron sought unambiguous clarity. The UK had signed up for the 'ever closer union' prescribed by the Treaty of Rome, but had never really wanted to live by the legal and policy consequences. Cameron wanted to 'get it across, once and for all, that the UK was not only travelling at a different speed, but that we had a different destination in mind altogether. "Yes" to the trade and cooperation, but "no"—indeed "never"—to political union, currency union or immigration union'.[10]

So, Cameron was not in sympathy with the members of his Party, such as Bill Cash, who had a lifetime of obsessive anti-Europeanism behind them. Equally, he knew that his immediate predecessors, all Eurosceptics of varying hues, had failed to defeat Labour. One of them, Hague, had fought the 2001 election on the slogan 'Three weeks to save the pound' and had found that those three weeks were not enough to save the Conservative Party from ignominious defeat. Cameron knew that the Party could not flourish if it was defined by a narrow Euroscepticism. At the same time, to win the leadership of his party he had to defeat his two opponents, David Davis and Liam Fox, both prominent sceptics. Davis was easily outclassed by Cameron in public debate but the leadership election took place under rules introduced by William Hague, which placed the final decision on the new leader with the Party membership. And that membership, natural readers of the anti-European newspapers that supported the Conservative Party (notably the *Daily Telegraph*, *Daily Mail*, and *Daily Express*), were increasingly averse to what they saw as the inroads of the EU into the nooks and crannies of national

---

[9] David Cameron, *For the Record* (London: William Collins, 2019).   [10] Ibid., p. 628.

life. Cameron promised his party voters that, if elected, he would withdraw the Conservative Members of the European Parliament from the European People's Party (the EPP). The EPP was the grouping within the European Parliament to which the German ruling CDU, and other centre-right parties, belonged. Cameron has denied that the promise was made for tactical reasons, or that it tilted the leadership election in his favour. Be that as it may, he failed to appreciate the consequences. The withdrawal of the Conservatives offended the German Chancellor, Angela Merkel, whose CDU should have been a natural ally of the British Conservatives. It also cut the Conservatives out of one of the key agents of influence in the European Parliament in terms of committee chair and rapporteur appointments, the organization of business, and the backroom deals on which all Parliaments thrive. The Conservatives did set up their own new group inside the EP: the European Conservatives and Reformists (ECR), together with the Czech and Polish Conservative parties. But those parties were illiberal on the social issues where Cameron wanted to signal moderation and reform domestically. His was an opportunistic move which tainted the Conservative brand and for which Cameron would pay a price as Prime Minister in terms of loss of European influence, both in general and at two key moments in his premiership.

That Cameron thought little of the implications of taking his party out of the EPP, is not surprising. He had had no prior immersion in EU politics or policy save through the lens of British politics. The significance of the European Parliament within the EU, or of the EPP within the Parliament, would have been unknown to him. His view beyond British shores was more global than European. He wanted his party to stop 'banging on about Europe'. His first foreign policy speech as Prime Minister, at the Lord Mayor's Banquet in November 2010, gave a good flavour of his approach. The speech contained no world vision of the kind that Blair had given. That was not what Cameron did, or sought to do. Instead, it was a coherent, sensible, moderate, but workaday view of the UK's global interests and how they should be advanced and managed.

The last thing Cameron wanted, or expected, was that his leadership would be defined by Europe. But, in the state of public opinion in the UK, there was already a clue as to what would transpire. In various forms, and subject to different conditions, all three main parties felt it necessary to enter the 2010 General Election campaign offering referendums on the EU. The Conservative manifesto reflected the uneasy state of opinion within the Party. A Conservative government would, it said, be positive members of the EU 'but we are clear that there should be no further extension of the EU's power over the UK without the British people's consent. We will ensure that by law no future Government can hand over areas of power to the EU or join the Euro without a referendum of the British people. We will work to bring back key powers over legal rights, criminal justice and social employment legislation to the UK.' The manifesto described the Labour government's ratification of the Lisbon Treaty without the consent of the British people as 'a betrayal of this country's democratic traditions'.

The Lisbon Treaty had been the final outcome of the negotiation that had initially produced the EU Constitutional Treaty, a Treaty that had expired under the combined weight of French and Dutch rejection in referendums in 2005. The failure of the Constitutional Treaty lay in the displeasure it gave to both sides of the European argument. To pro-Europeans, it flattered to deceive: pretending to be a genuine constitution, with all that implied for a sense of statehood, while in fact being an international treaty between sovereign governments like its predecessors. For sceptics, the very use of the word 'Constitution' was enough to condemn it as an assault on the survival of the nation state. The Lisbon Treaty, which was in negotiation in the last days of Blair's premiership, was more modest in content and intention. Nonetheless, Brown strove from stage right to raise objections. Blair ignored him. On his arrival in Downing Street, Brown dithered over whether to accept the Treaty negotiated by his predecessor. In exchange for some face-saving formulae, Brown agreed to sign up. But he arrived late for the formal signature ceremony in Lisbon, signing on his own just as every other EU Head was leaving, and creating a sense of disorganization in Downing Street that dogged his entire time as Prime Minister.

Blair had promised a referendum on the Constitutional Treaty. The Lisbon Treaty was in no sense a constitution and the referendum undertaking had accordingly been withdrawn. It cannot be said that the issue made huge public waves, but it did rankle. People who did not take an especial interest in the EU nonetheless felt that a promise of a referendum had been made and a promise had been broken. Cameron's response in Opposition was to oppose the Treaty in Parliament and to promise that if, but only if, it had not been ratified by the time of the next election, an incoming Conservative government would resile from it. This was a sensible proviso: no government could resile from a Treaty that had already been ratified without being in breach of international and EU law and of a fundamental basis of all international dealings: *pacta sunt servanda*.[11] But Cameron's refusal to undertake to reverse the Treaty, even if it was in force, displeased a significant section of his supporters.

The May 2010 General Election gave the Conservatives 307 seats, a lead of 49 over Labour, but not an absolute majority. The election had taken place in an atmosphere of dire national economic necessity. Cameron could have formed a minority government but it would have been at the constant mercy of opportunistic alliances between the Opposition parties and of black-mail from its own backbenchers, especially the Eurosceptics. Nonetheless, in offering coalition talks with the Liberal Democrats, Cameron made a bold and farsighted move which produced the UK's first coalition government of modern times. As the only consistently pro-European mainstream party in British politics, the Liberal Democrats could be expected to act as a restraining influence on Conservative hard line tendencies. But the Lib Dems had their own troubles, especially with anti-EU sentiment in the West Country from which they drew much of their support. So, whereas the Conservative mani-festo had promised that 'any proposed future Treaty that transferred areas of power, or competences, would be subject to a referendum—a "referendum lock"', the Lib Dems had gone at least as far, promising 'an in/out referendum the next time the British Government signs up to fundamental changes in the relationship between the UK and the EU'. Of course, what 'fundamental changes' might mean was left undefined.

Against that background, it was relatively easy for the future partners to find common ground on a European passage in the coalition agreement that promised more constraints on Britain's European engagement than had been offered by any previous government. There would be:

- No further transfer of sovereignty of powers during the course of the Parliament;
- The EU's existing competences would be 'examined';
- The application of the Working Time Directive in the UK would be limited;
- Any proposed future treaty that transferred areas of power, or compe-tences, would be subject to a referendum;
- The 1972 European Communities Act would be amended so that the use of any *passerelle* would require primary legislation;[12]

---

[11] Agreements must be observed.

[12] The *passerelle* is a clause in an EU Treaty that allows the alteration of a legislative procedure without formal amendment of the governing Treaty.

- The case for a UK Sovereignty Bill (to make it clear that ultimate authority remained with Parliament) would be examined;
- Britain would not join, or prepare to join, the euro during the Parliament;
- The EU budget should in future only focus on those areas where the EU could add value;
- The government would press for the European Parliament to have only one seat, in Brussels;
- Forthcoming EU legislation on criminal justice matters would be dealt with on a case-by-case (and by implication, restrictive) basis;
- The government would support the further enlargement of the EU.

So, out of eleven coalition undertakings on the EU, ten were negative and only one was positive. The coalition made good on most of its promises, while putting some water in its wine where the manifesto bumped up against practical reality. In particular, the European Union Act (2011) implemented the 'referendum lock' by requiring a referendum before a UK government could agree to a proposed change to the EU Treaties that moved a power or an area of policy from the UK to the EU. In addition, the new law stipulated that all types of EU Treaty change would require approval by Act of Parliament. Parliament would also need to approve, by Act, any agreement to use the *passerelle* provisions of the EU Treaties. A schedule to the Act listed those articles in the EU Treaties which would trigger a referendum in the event of a proposal to give up the national veto in that particular area. But, that schedule apart, Ministers gave themselves some leeway by enabling them to decide whether any other Treaty change would, in their view, transfer power or competence from the UK to the EU.

No other Member State had so limited its government's power to agree changes to EU law. But, of particular interest in the light of subsequent developments, was the government's public statement of what the new Act would not do: it would *not* lead to a referendum on EU membership. 'The government believes', said the statement, 'that membership of the EU is in the UK's national interest. We intend to champion vigorously the interests of the UK and play an active role in the EU. We believe the EU needs to change to do things better, and we are confident in Britain's ability to move it in the right direction.'[13]

On the issue of criminal justice matters, the new government was able to fulfil its manifesto pledge by virtue of an existing right to opt in or out of EU

[13] http://www.legislation.gov.uk/ukpga/2011/12/contents/enacted.

legislation. This included the right, negotiated by the Labour government, to opt out of all 130 security and justice laws adopted before the Lisbon Treaty (which introduced majority voting in the field). Under Theresa May's leadership as Home Secretary, the government opted out of the existing 130 laws but pragmatically then opted back into 35 of them, which included the European Arrest Warrant. This partial opt-in required the unanimous consent of the other Member States, which the government secured. It also required the government to stand up to those of its backbenchers who regarded the Arrest Warrant as an unacceptable infringement of national sovereignty.

On the issue of EU competences, the Foreign Office and Cabinet Office led an exhaustive Whitehall trawl of EU measures lasting from 2012 until 2014 and spanning the tenures of William Hague and Philip Hammond at the FCO. The final report covered 'everything deriving from EU law that affects what happens in the UK'.[14] On the Single Market, most respondents, from across all the relevant interests, supported the existing balance of competences on the free movement of goods, services, and financial services. As far as free movement of people was concerned, the report found 'considerable differences in opinion', some seeing free movement as broadly positive while others highlighted pressure on public services, housing, and employment. On economic and monetary policy, the balance of competences was thought to be 'mainly consistent with the UK's national interest'. There was strong support for the EU's competition, state aid, and consumer protection policies as being 'vital to the realisation of the Single Market, to making markets work well and to minimising the burden on business'. Similarly, on trade and investment, stakeholders believed that the balance of competences allowed the UK to achieve results that were in the national interest. On economic and monetary policy, given the UK's opt-out from the euro, the balance of competences was thought to be 'mainly consistent with the UK's national interest'. Only on social and employment policy were views fragmented. Some respondents believed that the EU should have no competence in the area at all. But a more common view (especially from business groups) was that EU competence was justified insofar as it supported the Single Market and a level playing field for competition. However, potential costs and burdens for business remained a concern. For those on the Conservative benches who had hoped that the review would spark a bonfire of the EU vanities, the outcome was a considerable disappointment.

---

[14] Command Paper 8415, 2014.

The overall picture of the coalition that gradually emerged was of a government led by three men, Cameron, Osborne, and Clegg, who were young, socially liberal, and in tune with an enterprise Britain seeking to recover from the economic crash of 2008. But that recovery required, as they saw it, an almost unprecedented and consistent prescription of austerity in order to reduce the UK's huge indebtedness (94 per cent of its GDP in 2010). So, those sectors of the population worst hit were inevitably those most dependent on the public services, which were most adversely affected. Two years into the Parliament, there was, as Clegg later recalled 'precious little evidence that our economic strategy was working – growth was flat and tax receipts were down'. Just when a competent and optimistic budget was required, the Chancellor, George Osborne, delivered the 'omnishambles' budget which, apart from applying VAT to Cornish pasties, also reduced the top rate of income tax from 50 per cent to 40 per cent: widely seen as a sop to the rich at the expense of the poor.

This groundswell of discontent was fertile territory for backbench unhappiness. Many of Cameron's own MPs had not forgiven him for failing to deliver an all-out win against an opponent (Gordon Brown) who had been widely seen as the UK's worst post-war Prime Minister. The reviving fortunes of the UK Independence Party (UKIP) added existential anxiety to their unease. UKIP came second in the 2009 European elections, fared less well in the 2010 General Election but made notable gains at the expense of the Conservatives in the 2012 local elections. The party provided a ready-made and skilfully wielded receptacle for a wide range of discontents. It began to unnerve the Conservative Party and gave a more broadly-based appeal to the Eurosceptic arguments of Conservative MPs who might otherwise have been considered marginal. At the same time, the travails of the Eurozone both reinforced the argument that the EU was flailing, if not failing, and forced Cameron into concessions to support the Euro members which played badly with his own backbenchers.

The start of the Eurozone crisis more or less coincided with the UK's General Election in 2010. As Sir Ivan Rogers has recalled, 'as the Eurozone crisis intensified, it became necessary to make urgent institutional changes to shore up monetary union and prevent disaster'. Those institutional changes required the unanimous agreement of all EU Member States, whether inside the zone or not. The result, in UK domestic terms, was that 'in Westminster, the passage of legislation specifically designed to cauterise Eurozone wounds and address Eurozone needs, inflamed Conservative opinion'.[15] So Cameron, who had hoped to prevail with his own brand of muscular Conservatism, based on impeding further integration, on sound economic management, and on advancing the completion of the Single Market, increasingly found himself, as Clegg put it, 'trying to manage the constant rage of the Tory Party'.[16]

In the autumn of 2011, a House of Commons motion in favour of an In/Out referendum on EU membership was defeated by 483 votes to 111. But the Government had had to lean hard on their backbenchers to keep them in line and, even so, 81 Conservative MPs voted in favour, despite a three-line whip.

At the European Council in December 2011, yet another Treaty amendment was in prospect. What was proposed was a fiscal compact to update and strengthen the economic obligations first incorporated in the Eurozone Stability and Growth Pact. The fiscal compact would not apply directly to the UK but aspects of it would affect the interests of the City and Cameron wanted safeguards. For the first time in Britain's EU membership, the government's senior representative in Brussels, the UK Permanent Representative to the EU, was not a Foreign Office nominee but a Treasury official, Jon Cunliffe, who had been Gordon Brown's closest adviser on EU matters. Cunliffe was acutely conscious of one of the conceptual flaws in the Euro project: monetary policy was in the hands of the European Central Bank, while fiscal policy remained in the hands of national governments. It was widely thought that this dichotomy would have to be addressed, and corrected, in the form of a significant treaty change requiring the agreement of all EU Member States, including those such as the UK who were not part of the Euro project. Just as the unanimity requirement in 1984 had given Thatcher the leverage to secure the rebate, so it was believed that the expected big treaty negotiation would give Cameron the leverage he needed to secure essential British interests. The Treasury devised a series of proposals designed to safeguard the position of the City, as the price of British acquiescence. They were not insignificant but, in the words of Ivan Rogers, 'the document consisted of several pages of dense prose on Treasury, Bank of England and financial sector issues … Had the document been made public, one would have struggled in vain to explain to an average voter why they should care about any of it …'[17]

Cameron had largely overcome Angela Merkel's initial reservations about him and he hoped that she would support what he wanted. He shared what he

[15] Rogers in Adonis, *Half In Half Out*, pp. 223–4. Ivan Rogers was the UK government's EU Sherpa from 2011–2013 and UK Permanent Representative to the EU from 2013– 2017.

[16] Anthony Seldon, *Cameron at 10: The Verdict* (London: William Collins, 2016), p. 168.

[17] Rogers in Adonis, *Half In Half Out*, p. 226.

had in mind with her. But, in an echo of what Kohl and Mitterrand had done to Margaret Thatcher a quarter of a century earlier, Merkel and President Sarkozy of France came to a Franco-German agreement at a meeting of the EPP leaders from which, by virtue of his self-exclusion, Cameron was absent. When the European Council met, Cameron's proposed safeguards met with no support. With due solemnity, Cameron exercised his veto. The proposed Fiscal Compact Treaty could not therefore go ahead. But then, as previously arranged between them (and as Cunliffe had warned), Merkel and Sarkozy proposed, and the remaining Member States agreed, that they would make a separate intergovernmental treaty outside the framework of the EU Treaties. Had the changes on the table been as far-reaching as London had originally expected, the manoeuvre might have been harder to pull off. But the final document was more modest, making it easier for Cameron to be bypassed. Clegg, back in London, had been kept in the loop. But the final drama happened in the early hours and a text message to him telling what was afoot went unseen. Angrily, he told Andrew Marr on BBC television two days later that 'there's nothing bulldog about Britain hovering somewhere in the mid-Atlantic and not standing tall on Europe and not being taken seriously in Washington'.[18] Clegg was conspicuously absent from the front bench when Cameron made his statement to Parliament on Monday, 12 December.

Of course, the sceptics in the Conservative ranks were delighted with the 'veto' and treated their leader as if he was now one of them. But, in reality, Cameron's veto had failed to prevent action by the other Member States and had signalled Britain's peripherality to the vital interests of the majority of EU members. A Prime Minister who had hoped to take Europe out of the headlines and to forge alliances had failed on both counts. Cameron had in effect been forced to sign up to the traditional EU discourse of British Ministers on European matters: Europe was a battleground and he had fought a heroic resistance. By the time of the 2015 General Election, with an In/Out referendum on EU membership in the offing, the Conservative manifesto would proclaim as a badge of honour the fact that 'Our Prime Minister vetoed a new EU Treaty that would have damaged Britain's interests – the first time in history that a British Prime Minister has done so.' Thus, in the pantheon of Tory Euroscepticism, Cameron was claiming the place of honour hitherto occupied by Margaret Thatcher.

In all, Cameron would fight four other big EU battles during his time in office: for budget constraint; to ensure that the UK took no part in Eurozone

---

[18] BBC *Andrew Marr Show*, 11 December 2011.

budget bailouts; to prevent the appointment of Jean-Claude Juncker as Commission President; and, most importantly, to secure a deal that would keep the UK inside the European Union. During the course of these negotiations, he maintained a sound working relationship with Chancellor Angela Merkel, though his head-on style of negotiation contrasted with her more sidelong approach. Their respective domestic politics were different. The Eurosceptic *Alternative für Deutschland* (AfD) was not yet a significant threat in a country where there was still a pro-European consensus across most of the political spectrum. Insofar as there was an EU issue in Germany, it related to the Eurozone where the German government's domestic constraints, both as regards bailout money for Greece and bold measures to safeguard the Eurozone as a whole, put it in an uncomfortable position: hated in Greece for its perceived Prussian brutality; criticized in much of the rest of Europe for doing too little too late.

Cameron's financial negotiations were a success: he secured Britain's non-participation in Eurozone bailouts. He achieved, in February 2013, a cut of 32 billion euros (3.3 per cent) in the EU's seven-year budget settlement. But it is a measure of Cameron's domestic problems that, as the negotiations on the budget got under way, in the autumn of 2012, he suffered a defeat in the House of Commons when an unholy alliance of fifty-three Conservative rebels, and the Labour Party, rejected his proposal for a real-terms freeze in the EU budget and, instead, voted for a cash freeze or cut. Needless to say, when (with Merkel's backing) Cameron managed to deliver on the tougher mandate forced on him by the House of Commons, he was teased by the Opposition leader, Ed Miliband, for his 'oversight' in not thanking both the Opposition and his own rebels for 'giving him such a strong hand'. In truth, what Cameron achieved was, as former Foreign Secretary Malcolm Rifkind, put it, 'the most important reform of the EU budget since Margaret Thatcher in Fontainebleau in 1984'. Cameron was also on strong ground in arguing that it was the Opposition, when in government, who held responsibility for the increase in the UK's budget contribution, despite the overall cut he had achieved: 'The last government gave away almost half our rebate. This has had a long-term and continuing effect . . . because when the European Union spends money on structural funds and cohesion payments in Eastern Europe, for example, the UK no longer gets a rebate on this money.'[19]

Sadly, for Cameron, his success had little public impact. Nor, like its Labour predecessor, did Cameron's government do nearly enough to point up the

---

[19] *Hansard*, 11 February 2013, vol. 558, cols. 571–4.

huge security, prosperity, and human rights dividend represented by the peaceful democratization of the countries of eastern and central Europe which successive British governments had championed. In strategic terms, they remained far away countries of which most people knew nothing. What people did know was that the EU was costing them more because of enlargement and was bringing with it a large increase in work-seeking migrants.

Cameron's budget battle had been successful because, although he could have vetoed the entire package (which required unanimity) he forged an alliance with other like-minded Member States, including Germany and Netherlands. In this instance, his potential veto could not have been bypassed. That gave him leverage. He had no such leverage where the election of the Commission President was concerned.

Until the 1993 Maastricht Treaty, the President of the Commission was chosen by the EU Heads of Government by unanimity. The European Parliament had no role. Under the terms of the Maastricht Treaty, the European Parliament won the right to be consulted on the choice of President and to veto the Commission as a whole. This gave the Parliament a *de facto* right of veto over the President, a right that was formally recognized in the Amsterdam Treaty of 1999. The Nice Treaty of 2003 changed the procedure by which the President was chosen by the European Council from unanimity to qualified majority voting. The United Kingdom had only once held the Presidency of the Commission, in the person of Roy Jenkins (1977–1981). But the UK had played an interventionist role in the choice of two other Commission Presidents.

In 1994, Kohl and Mitterrand had reached a bilateral agreement to support the candidacy of the Belgian Prime Minister, Jean-Luc Dehaene. It had been thought that Ruud Lubbers, the Dutch Prime Minister, would be the favourite but he had incurred Kohl's enmity because of a difference over aspects of German reunification. John Major was under pressure from the British right-wing Press to oppose Dehaene, who was admirably qualified but, being Belgian, could easily be caricatured as a dyed-in-the wool federalist. Major rightly resented the attempted Franco-German stitch-up and the unpleasant German Press criticisms of Lubbers that the German government had fostered. Support for Lubbers fell away under the pressure of Franco-German bullying. The Dutch withdrew their candidacy and John Major was alone in vetoing Dehaene's appointment. The Luxembourg Prime Minister, Jacques Santer, was appointed as a compromise candidate.

In 2004, The French President and German Chancellor (Chirac and Schröder) tried to foist another Belgian, Prime Minister Guy Verhofstadt, on the EU but met their match in the combined opposition of Blair and Italian Prime Minister Silvio Berlusconi. Their candidate, the Portuguese Prime Minister, José-Manuel Durão Barroso, got the job.

The procedure for choosing the Commission President was again changed by the Lisbon Treaty in 2009. The EU treaties now stipulated that:

> *Taking into account the elections to the European Parliament, and after having held appropriate consultations, the European Council, acting by a qualified majority, shall propose to the European Parliament a candidate for President of the Commission.*

In 2013, with European Parliament elections due in 2014, the President of the European Parliament, the German socialist, Martin Schulz, proposed that European political parties should fight those elections on platforms which included named lead candidates for the post of Commission President. His own group, the Party of European Socialists, duly named Schulz as their lead candidate (*Spitzenkandidat*, in German). The European People's Party followed suit, choosing the Luxembourg Prime Minister, Jean-Claude Juncker, over his French rival, Michel Barnier. Merkel herself made no effort to use German influence within the EPP to promote an alternative candidate to Juncker. Had the British Conservatives still been part of the EPP, it is likely that Cameron and Merkel could have steered the group towards a different nominee.

The EPP emerged from the EP elections as the largest Party grouping and the Parliament backed Juncker for the job of Commission President. In doing so, they managed to create an assumption that this was now the procedure required by the Lisbon Treaty. In fact, the procedure under the Treaties required the European Council to take account of the EP election results, not to follow them unquestioningly.

Few, if any, EU leaders thought Juncker the right person for the job. He had been a successful Luxembourg Prime Minister and Finance Minister but was not seen as someone who could provide dynamic leadership or public inspiration. He had had a bad relationship with both Blair and Brown, and Cameron was clear, from before the EP elections, that Juncker was the wrong man for the post. After the EP elections, Cameron went into action in an effort to stop Juncker. His arguments resonated with Merkel. At an informal dinner of EU Heads in Brussels on 27 May 2014, called to discuss appointments to top jobs, Merkel said that she favoured a wider slate of candidates for the job of Commission President, including female ones. She told the Press as much immediately after the meeting and, across the EU, it was assumed that Juncker's candidature was dead. But Merkel then ran into a political firestorm at home, involving huge Press criticism. In Germany, the European Parliament has always had far greater salience than it does in the UK and the *Spitzenkandidat* idea (virtually unheard of in Britain) had played a prominent part in the European Parliament election campaign inside Germany. Merkel took fright, as did the Dutch and Swedish leaders, despite their sympathy for Cameron's view. She backed down and came out publicly in support of Juncker.

Cameron persisted in his campaign for another month, by which time only the Hungarian Prime Minister, Viktor Orbán, was still supporting him. At the European Council on 26/27 June, Cameron used two arguments with his colleagues. One was that, if the European Council caved in to the European Parliament, there would be a power shift from the Council to the Parliament which would be irreversible. The second was that the election of a convinced federalist would play badly in the UK and increase the changes of a vote in favour of leaving in the promised EU referendum (then thought likely to be held in 2017). Despite being in a minority of two, Cameron insisted on a vote being taken. All but Cameron and Orbán voted in favour of Juncker.

Back home, in Parliament, Cameron defended his decision to go down to public defeat. 'I firmly believe', he told the House of Commons, 'that it should be for the European Council – the elected Heads of national Governments – to propose the President of the Commission. It should not be for the European Parliament to try and dictate that choice to the Council. That is a point of principle on which I was not prepared to budge... I believe that it was a bad day for Europe because the decision of the Council risks undermining the position of national Governments, and it risks undermining the power of national Parliaments by handing further power to the European Parliament.'

The Labour Opposition had itself also been against Juncker's appointment. But for Ed Miliband, it was the Prime Minister's 'combination of threats, insults and disengagement' that had produced the humiliating defeat.

That was par for the course for an Opposition reaction. But Miliband made a further, more prescient, observation. 'All the time', said Miliband, 'this is driven by a party whose centre of gravity is drifting towards exit... Does he not agree that his problem is the gap between what people behind him are demanding and what sensible European reform amounts to?' Of course, the Prime Minister did not agree. But Miliband had hit the nail on the head. Cameron was being driven by the growing Euroscepticism of his Party, and by the success of UKIP in offering an alternative to voters for whom dissatisfaction over Europe was a proxy for disgruntlement on a whole range of issues besides.[20]

UKIP became, over time, a refuge for disaffected Labour voters too, but at this stage its inroads were mostly, and most dramatically, being made into the Conservative Party. In the European Elections in May 2014, UKIP topped the poll, achieving 27.5 per cent of the vote and 24 seats. The Lib Dems lost all but one of their 12 seats and the Conservatives were forced into third place, after UKIP and Labour. Later in the year, two Tories (Douglas Carswell and Mark Reckless) defected to UKIP and won the subsequent by-elections in their constituencies. A poll by Lord Ashcroft showed that 57 per cent of UKIP voters believed that the Conservative Party, from which they had defected, would have a better chance of winning the next General Election with Boris Johnson, rather than Cameron, as the Tory leader. Thirty-five per cent of them would be more likely to return to the Tory fold were Johnson to be in charge.[21]

The decision of the Cameron government to offer an In/Out referendum on EU membership had been taken in mid to late 2012. But Cameron had begun to entertain the idea at the start of that year. Throughout his time at Number 10, with the help of journalist Daniel Finkelstein, Cameron recorded his thoughts on a monthly basis. In January 2012, he put onto tape his view that 'Europe is changing and Britain is changing in its relation to Europe because of the creation of the Euro and a multi-speed Europe...At some stage, altering Britain's relationship with the European Union in some regards and then putting it to a referendum I think would be good Conservative policy for the next Parliament.'[22]

Cameron has contested the view that he opted for a referendum to stem the erosion of popular support for the Conservatives and the rise of UKIP. It seems most likely that a range of factors was involved. Cameron's own feelings about UK membership of the EU were ones of avowed exceptionalism. He wanted to secure a place for the UK inside the EU but dancing to a different tune from that of the majority. So, in any event, he was facing the prospect of a significant renegotiation of the terms of British membership. No political leader can make the kind of distinction between party and national interest that the rest of us make, so, for Cameron, promoting a different model of EU membership and lancing the boil of Tory Euroscepticism were inseparable. He undoubtedly hoped to halt the rise of UKIP, and the dissent within his own

[20] *Hansard*, 30 June 2014, vol. 583, col. 599.
[21] Ashcroft poll cited in Seldon, *Cameron at 10*, p. 385.
[22] Cameron, *For the Record*, pp. 339–40.

Party, by conceding an In/Out referendum on the UK's membership of the EU, but his own view of the UK national interest was anyway leading him in that direction.

As is now well known, George Osborne was the one member of the inner circle who opposed the idea, accurately predicting the difficulty of securing a victory for staying in the EU. When the decision to call a referendum was taken, Cameron asked the three other politicians in the room how they would vote once the referendum took place. Oliver Letwin was for Leave, Osborne was for Remain, and Hague was for Remain if the terms were right. That, said Cameron, was his view too: he would want to remain if the terms were right.

Against that background, Cameron's speech in January 2013, promising a referendum on EU membership after the next General Election in 2015, remains something of a puzzle. Cameron was generally, in the words of one of his team, 'all over' the drafting of his speeches. In the case of this one, probably the most important of his political life, that was not the case. It was not that he was indifferent. His team knew the arguments he wanted to make and he trusted his Chief of Staff, Ed Llewellyn, to reflect them faithfully and accurately in the draft text. But it may be in part for that reason, and because the speech was under construction for weeks, that it contained what may have been a significant tactical error.

The first two parts described what was wrong with the European Union and what was needed to reform it. The third part was, at heart, the first round in the referendum battle: a powerful statement of all the reasons why the UK should remain a member of the European Union, almost regardless of what reforms were—or were not—achievable.[23]

Cameron's speech started with a classic British explanation of the UK's approach to EU membership. Britain was 'an argumentative and rather strong-minded member of the family of European nations', her psychology shaped by geography: an island nation, 'independent, forthright, passionate in defence of our sovereignty'. Because of that, Britain came to the European Union 'with a frame of mind that is more practical than emotional. For us, the European Union is a means to an end – prosperity, stability, the anchor of freedom and democracy both within Europe and beyond her shores – not an end in itself'.

Cameron then posed the rhetorical question: 'Why raise questions about Britain's role when support in Britain is already so thin?' His answer was that

[23] Bloomberg speech of 23 January 2013, https://www.gov.uk/government/speeches.eu-speech-at-bloomberg.

there were three major challenges: the problems of the Eurozone were driving fundamental change in Europe; there was a crisis of competitiveness, as other nations 'soar ahead'; and there was a gap—a gap that was growing dramatically—between the EU and its citizens. This gap, Cameron argued, was felt particularly acutely in Britain. If the challenges he had outlined were not addressed, 'the danger is that Europe will fail and the British people will drift towards the exit'.

The challenges, as Cameron described them, were, firstly that countries such as the UK, forever outside the Eurozone, needed safeguards to ensure that their access to the Single Market was in no way compromised. The second challenge lay in the failure of competitiveness and the third lay 'in a growing frustration that the EU is seen as something that is done to people rather than acting on their behalf'. He saw this frustration acted out in the streets of Athens, Madrid, and Rome, in the parliaments of Berlin, Helsinki, and The Hague and 'yes, of course, we are seeing this frustration with the EU very dramatically in Britain'. What was needed was fundamental, far-reaching change and Cameron set out his vision, built on five principles.

The first principle was competitiveness. This should be rooted in the completion of the Single Market, but also in exempting the smallest companies from more EU Directives, creating a leaner, less bureaucratic Union with fewer 'expensive peripheral European institutions', fewer iterations of the Council of Ministers, a smaller Commission, a tougher approach to curbing spending and shutting down programmes that had not worked.

The second principle was flexibility. The structures of the EU must reflect its diversity, accommodating the fact that some of the Member States were contemplating much closer economic and political integration, while many others, including Britain, 'would never embrace that goal'. There should not be a one-size fits all approach, given that seventeen EU members were part of the Eurozone and ten were not. The 'weary caravan of metaphors' about two-speed Europe, fast and slow lanes, and of countries missing trains and buses, should be consigned to a permanent siding. He called for 'flexible, willing cooperation' and denied that this would unravel the EU: 'Far from unravelling the EU, this will in fact bind its Members more closely because such flexible, willing cooperation is a much stronger glue than compulsion from the centre'. Cameron then made a proposal that would be one of his key demands: the UK should be freed from the EU Treaty objective of 'ever closer union among the peoples of Europe'. Instead, he advocated 'a flexible union of free Member States who share treaties and institutions and pursue together the ideal of cooperation... This vision of flexibility and cooperation is not the same as those who want to build an ever-closer union – but it is just as valid.'

Cameron's third principle was that 'power must be able to flow back to Member States, not just away from them. This was promised by European leaders at Laeken a decade ago. It was put in the Treaty. But the promise has never really been fulfilled.' The EU should examine what it should do and what it should stop doing. He cited the UK examination of EU competences as a model. 'We cannot harmonise everything', he said, citing the working hours of British hospital doctors as an example of where the rules should be set in the UK and not in Brussels. There needed to be an examination of 'whether the balance is right in so many areas where the European Union has legislated, including on the environment, social affairs and crime. Nothing should be off the table.'

Cameron's fourth principle was democratic accountability. He did not believe in a single European demos, but in national parliaments as 'the true source of real democratic legitimacy and accountability in the EU ... Those are the Parliaments which instil proper resect – even fear – into national leaders.' The European Parliament, directly elected, did not get a mention.

The fifth principle was fairness: 'whatever new arrangements are enacted for the Eurozone, they must work fairly for those inside it and out... It is a vital interest for us to protect the integrity and fairness of the single market for all its members.'

Turning to what all this meant for Britain, Cameron argued that public disillusionment with the EU was at an all-time high: 'People feel that the EU is heading in a direction that they never signed up to...Put simply, many ask "why can't we just have what we voted to join - a common market?"' The result of 'Treaty after Treaty changing the balance between Member States and the EU'—of referendums 'promised – but not delivered', of the travails of the euro and concern about what the deeper integration of the Eurozone would mean for a country which was not going into the Euro, was that 'democratic consent for the EU in Britain is now wafer thin'. Cameron acknowledged the contention that pointing this out put a question mark over Britain's place in the EU but argued that 'the question mark is already there and ignoring it won't make it go away. In fact, quite the reverse. Those who refuse to contemplate consulting the British people would, in my view, make more likely our eventual exit.'

So, Cameron concluded, he was in favour of a referendum: not while the EU was in flux and not before 'we have had a chance to put the relationship right'. He would negotiate the necessary changes.

Sarah Hogg, who headed John Major's Downing Street Policy Unit, and was a journalist by background, used to argue that it is all too easy for a speech to circulate like an aircraft, not quite knowing the best way to land. Cameron had his landing, a suitable peroration: 'It is time for the British people to have their say. It is time to settle this European question in British politics. I say to the British people: this will be your decision.'

He could have ended the speech there. But he chose to go in with the opening arguments of a campaign for Remain. He began with a warning that 'proponents of both sides of the argument will need to avoid exaggerating their claims' and went on to make a number of key points:

- Britain had more power and influence when acting together with others;
- The UK could leave the EU but could not, of course, leave Europe. It would remain for many years the UK's biggest market and the UK would remain tied by a complex web of legal commitments;
- Hundreds of thousands of British people took for granted their right to work, live or retire in any other EU country;
- Decisions made in the EU would continue to have a profound effect on the UK. But, outside, the UK would have lost its remaining vetoes and voice in those decisions;
- Continued access to the Single Market was vital for British businesses and British jobs;
- Since 2004, Britain had been the destination for one in five of all inward investments into Europe. Being part of the Single Market had been key to that success;
- Norway and Switzerland were not good models for a UK relationship with the EU;
- Not getting all the UK wanted did not mean that the UK should leave, not if the benefits of staying and working together were greater;
- There was no doubt that the UK was more powerful in Washington, Beijing, and Delhi as a result of being a powerful player in the EU;
- Leaving the EU would be a one-way ticket, not a return.

Lest there be any doubt, Cameron concluded by nailing his colours firmly to the mast: 'I know', he said, 'that there will be those who say the vision I have outlined will be impossible to achieve. That there is no way our partners will cooperate. That the British people have set themselves on a path to an inevitable exit. And that if we aren't comfortable being in the EU after 40 years, we never will be. But I refuse to take such a defeatist attitude...I believe we can achieve a new settlement for Britain . . . I believe something very deeply. That Britain's national interest is best served in a flexible, adaptable and open European Union and that such a European Union is best with Britain in it . . . '

Cameron would later say that he ruled nothing out, i.e. he was prepared to contemplate leaving the EU. But the Bloomberg speech gave the impression of a man who had made up his mind that, however unsatisfactory the EU might be, Britain's overwhelming interest was to remain part of it. That was in stark contrast to the tactics of Callaghan and Wilson in 1974/75, when their position was that they would only decide what recommendation to make once the renegotiation of the terms of UK membership had been completed. Even then, they kept themselves at some distance from the fray when the referendum campaign got under way. Cameron, by contrast, came close to saying that EU membership was of overriding importance to the UK, a sure way of devaluing his negotiating credentials both with his own Eurosceptics and with the EU partners from whom he would have to wring concessions.

The Conservative Party manifesto for the May 2015 General Election, was rather lighter than Cameron's Bloomberg speech had been on the merits of EU membership, concentrating on those aspects of membership that the Conservative government would reject and on those demands it would make of its EU partners: 'Yes to the Single Market. Yes, to turbo-charging free trade. Yes, to working together where we are stronger together than alone. Yes, to a family of nation states . . . whose interests are guaranteed whether inside the Euro or out. No to "ever closer union". No to a constant flow of power to Brussels. No to unnecessary interference. And no, of course, to the Euro, to participation in Eurozone bail-outs or notions like a European Army . . . We will protect our economy from any further integration of the Eurozone . . . We will not let the integration of the Eurozone jeopardise the integrity of the Single Market or in any way disadvantage the UK. We will reclaim powers from Brussels . . . And we want an end to our commitment to "ever closer union" as enshrined in the Treaty to which every EU country has to sign up.'

The manifesto also undertook to scrap the Human Rights Act, the law passed under the Blair Labour government, which incorporated the provisions of the European Convention on Human Rights into directly applicable UK law. Most readers of this commitment would have assumed that the Convention was the work of the EU. But it was part of the separate European Convention, adopted by the larger grouping of the Council of Europe, of which Britain was a principal founder member.

The manifesto promised a referendum before the end of 2017 and, on the back of his surprise victory in the General Election, Cameron returned to his

Bloomberg theme in a speech at the start of his renegotiation, in November 2015. He repeated the three themes of the earlier speech (the problems of the Eurozone, the crisis of European competitiveness, and the lack of EU democratic accountability). To those three, he added a new fourth challenge. The mass migration of Syrian refugees to mainland Europe had precipitated huge domestic political turmoil in many EU countries. Britain, Cameron pointed out, was not part of the Schengen open borders agreement within the EU, so was not directly affected. Nonetheless, he claimed, 'we do need some additional measures to address wider abuses of the right to free movement within Europe and to reduce the very high flow of people coming to Britain from across Europe'.

The issue of EU migration was already at the core of UKIP's appeal. By linking the issue of legitimate EU migration with the separate, and much graver problem, of mass refugee migration, Cameron handed a gift to his opponents. In the public mind, mass refugee migration and normal EU migration could be magnified into one huge problem.

There were, Cameron continued, four objectives for the renegotiation of the terms of UK membership of the EU on which he was embarking.

- Objective 1 was to protect the single market for Britain and others outside the Eurozone. This must mean a set of binding principles that guaranteed fairness between euro and non-euro countries.
- Objective 2 was to write competitiveness into the DNA of the whole EU. This included cutting the total burden on business.
- Objective 3 was to exempt Britain from an 'ever closer union' and bolster national parliaments through legally binding and irreversible changes.
- Objective 4 was to tackle abuses of the right to free movement and enable the UK to control migration from the EU. The precise form of those changes would be for the renegotiation but, if agreement was to be reached, it must be on a basis that was legally binding and irreversible and, where necessary, had force in the EU Treaties.

The Prime Minister had, he told his audience, 'every confidence' that an agreement that worked for Britain and her EU partners could be reached. If and when such an agreement was reached, he would campaign for it heart and soul. 'But,' he cautioned, 'if we can't reach such an agreement, and if Britain's concerns were to be met with a deaf ear, which I do not believe will happen, then we will have to think again about whether this European Union is right for us. As I have said before, I rule nothing out.'

As he had done in 2013, Cameron then used the rest of his speech to explain the inadequacy for the UK of the available alternatives to EU membership and why Britain's absence from the EU would 'permanently change our ability to get things done in the world. We have every right to do that as a sovereign nation. But we should do so with our eyes open . . . I say to those thinking about voting to leave. Think very carefully because this choice cannot be undone . . . '[24]

The Chatham House speech was the starting gun for the renegotiation. Cameron hoped that it might be completed by the mid-December meeting of the European Council, but the other leaders had more important preoccupations, notably the refugee crisis. This was particularly true for Angela Merkel. Her decision in September to open the German border to Syrian refugees who had been denied asylum in Hungary led to an influx which totalled some quarter of a million by the end of the year. So, the negotiation continued into the new year before it was eventually concluded late in February 2016.

The problem with the deal that Cameron secured during two days of intensive discussion was not that it was a bad deal for those who were sceptical about EU membership but that it had been heavily trailed and was therefore discounted by the Press, some of it already so determined on Britain leaving the EU that even a total victory would not have been enough to satisfy them. Cameron had sought a 'fundamental' change in Britain's relationship with the rest of the EU. On BBC radio immediately after the deal was done, Chancellor George Osborne described the outcome as 'substantial', before hastily adding the word 'fundamental' as well. 'Substantial' was nearer the mark. In substantive terms, the agreements on migration issues and on the relationship between Euro 'ins' and 'outs' were the most significant.

In a very competitive EU, the danger of the Eurozone adopting measures that could discriminate against non-members (and most notably the City of London) was a real one. The eventual agreement protecting UK financial interests had been hard to secure. The original document produced by the Commission had set alarm bells ringing in the European Central Bank and in Paris, where there were fears that it would allow the UK to put a brake on the Eurozone countries. The document as finally agreed asserted explicitly the rights of the Eurozone to integrate further, while protecting the Single Market rights of non-euro countries. In addition, a country such as Britain, if it felt that the rules were being unfairly skewed against the 'outs' (because the

---

[24] *The Future of Britain's Relationship with the EU* (speech given by David Cameron at Chatham House, London, on 10 November 2015).

Eurozone members constituted a qualified majority for voting purposes) would have the right to take the issue to the European Council. In other words, the UK did not have a right of veto but there would have to be a pause before such a measure was voted on and there would be a substantive procedure, led by the President of the European Council, to resolve the differences. These new measures would have the force of international law. At the next negotiation on EU Treaty amendment, they would be incorporated into the EU treaties. These agreements represented a significant (but not an absolute) safeguard for the UK.

On immigration issues, the agreed text allowed that non-discriminatory treatment of EU migrants could be subject to limitations on grounds of public policy, public security, or public health. 'Overriding reasons of public interest', quite widely defined, could also be used to restrict freedom of movement. Conditions could be imposed 'in relation to certain benefits to ensure that there is a real and effective degree of connection between the person concerned and the labour market of the Member State'. New proposals would be brought forward by the European Commission. These would not make it possible to stop payments to non-resident children of a benefit claimant, but they would enable a Member State to index those benefits to the standard of living of the Member State where the child lived.

More significantly, there would be an 'alert and safeguard' mechanism. Under this, a Member State could declare that 'an exceptional situation exists on a scale that affects essential aspects of its social security system, including the primary purpose of its in-work benefits system, or which leads to difficulties which are serious and liable to persist in its employment market or are putting serious pressure on the proper functioning of its public services'. In those circumstances, the Commission would be responsible for bringing forward a proposal, which would need the majority agreement of other Member States, to limit the access of European Union workers newly entering the labour market to in-work benefits for a total of up to four years. This limitation would be on a graduated scale, i.e. the benefits would gradually rise during the four-year period. The safeguard would be available for seven years. For their part, the Commission also said formally (and unprecedentedly) that they already considered 'the type of exceptional situation that the proposed safeguard mechanism is intended to cover exists in the UK today' and that the UK would be justified in triggering the mechanism 'in the full expectation of obtaining approval'.

Cameron also secured the so-called Red Card for national Parliaments. Under existing, so-called 'yellow card' procedures, if one third of the EU's national Parliaments opposed a proposed piece of EU legislation, then the Commission were obliged to pause and reconsider. Under the agreed new 'red card' procedure, where 55 per cent of the votes in national Parliaments amounted to a verdict that a proposed piece of legislation was objectionable on grounds of subsidiarity, the matter would be brought to the Council of Ministers where the members 'will discontinue the consideration of the draft legislative act in question unless the draft is amended to accommodate the concerns expressed...'. In addition, the European Council agreed to 'urge all EU institutions and Member States to strive for better regulation and to repeal unnecessary legislation', while the Commission itself (as the author of all EU legislation) undertook 'to establish a mechanism to review the body of existing EU legislation for its compliance with the principle of subsidiarity and proportionality...'

In one of the more bizarre texts ever adopted by a European Council, Cameron also secured his opt-out from the commitment of the Treaty of Rome to 'ever closer union among the peoples of Europe'. 'It is recognised', said the European leaders, 'that the United Kingdom, in the light of the specific situation it has under the Treaties, is not committed to further political integration into the European Union... The references in the Treaties and their preambles to the process of creating an ever closer union among the peoples of Europe do not offer a legal basis for extending the scope of any provision of the Treaties or of secondary legislation... They do not require that further competences be conferred upon the European Union or that the European Union must exercise its existing competences, or that competences conferred on the Union could not be reduced and thereby be returned to the Member States... The references to an ever closer union among the peoples are therefore compatible with different paths of integration being available for different Member States and do not compel all Member States to aim for a common destination... The Treaties allow an evolution towards a deeper degree of integration among the Member States that share such a vision of their common future, without this applying to other Member States...'[25]

One is left to wonder why the Cameron government wanted to remain in the EU at all when it was intent on resiling from the intent, and much of the content, of the original Treaties to which a Conservative government under Edward Heath had subscribed. Fortunately for the integrity of the EU, all these provisions would only take effect when the British government informed the

---

[25] EUCO 1/16 CO EUR 1, CONCL 1 of 19 February 2016.

rest of the EU that the UK had decided to remain a member of the European Union.

Despite his commitment and efforts, Cameron's deal was denounced as a damp squib by the right-wing media that constituted the usual base of his support. In the House of Commons, in a foretaste of the lukewarm support for remaining in the EU that the Leader of the Opposition would give during the referendum campaign, Jeremy Corbyn accused Cameron of failing to address the real issues facing the country. One of the other European socialist leaders had said to Corbyn: 'We are discussing the future of a continent and one English Tory has reduced it to the issue of taking away benefits from workers and children.' 'The reality', Corbyn continued, 'is that this entire negotiation has not been about the challenges facing our continent, or about the issues facing the people of Britain. Indeed, it has been a theatrical sideshow about trying to appease – or failing to appease – half of the Prime Minister's own Conservative party.'[26]

In approaching the tactics of the campaign, the government and *Britain Stronger in Europe* (the official Remain campaign headed by Will Straw, son of Labour Home Secretary and Foreign Secretary, Jack) were strongly influenced by polls which showed that a third of voters were for Remain and a third for Leave, with an undecided third in the middle. Focus group work suggested that the middle segment could be only persuaded to vote to remain by economic arguments related to their own jobs and family prosperity. The political case for Europe, on grounds of security and shared values in a dangerous world, was therefore made only once by Cameron in a major speech during the campaign. As with Osborne's threat that Brexit would provoke an immediate crisis and the need for an emergency budget, Cameron's speech was too easily dismissed as apocalyptic. It failed to resonate.

A huge number of different factors contributed to the eventual referendum outcome, some of them only tangentially linked to Britain's EU membership. A number of books by insiders and analysts tell the story.[27] One factor was that leadership of the Remain campaign lay formally with Will Straw's outfit, while strategy was being dictated from Downing Street. When Sweden held its referendum on whether to join the EU in 1994, and public opinion was veering towards a decision not to do so, the 'In' campaign took the decision to keep a marked distance from politicians and to have only people from other walks of life fronting the campaign. The UK referendum campaign, by contrast, was

---

[26] *Hansard*, 22 February 2016, vol. 606.
[27] See, for example, Craig Oliver, *Unleashing Demons* (London: Hodder & Stoughton, 2016).

dominated by politicians and the 'blue on blue' confrontations between prominent Conservatives were a natural magnet for media attention.

The Remain side had always known that immigration would be an issue but underestimated its salience until the Leave campaign, helped by disreputable advertising by the Brexit Party, succeeded in making it the central issue, crowding out the non-migration Remain arguments. The Remain side had no effective counter. There were some hints from the continent that Angela Merkel might be prepared to offer some further concessions on this issue but Cameron and his team decided that to ask for them would look like weakness on their part. They did not pursue the possible opening.

Craig Oliver, Cameron's Director of Politics and Communications gives a vivid account of one of the other key moments of the campaign: the visit to the UK of President Obama and his statement that a UK outside the EU would 'go to the back of the queue' in its search for a trade deal with the United States. Oliver believed at the time that 'the news is a dream. We couldn't have hoped for more'.[28] But Obama's comments backfired with voters who felt that the remarks were an insult to America's closest ally and, if anything, they helped the Leave campaign.[29] Some see it as a turning point in the fortunes of the Leave argument.

Cameron's reputation is overlaid by the ruins of his failed referendum campaign. He remains a hard figure to characterize. Some cannot get beyond the Eton and Oxford boy from a privileged background. But the perceived flashiness was tempered by his evident humanity and his experience of family tragedy. He was undoubtedly clever. Someone who worked closely with him says that, on any issue, however complex, Cameron never had to have its layers and ramifications explained to him: he 'got' them immediately. He was a hard worker. He took a box of work to his flat each evening and read thoroughly everything that was submitted to him. He took timely, clear, decisions. He saved the Conservative Party from being the 'nasty party' and showed, by the 2015 election result, that he could make inroads into what had been recent Labour territory. He may have been more interested in tactics than in strategy. Yet, as Seldon and Snowdon point out, 'if Cameron lacked principles, how do we explain his standing by Plan A on the economy, gay marriage and the decision to spend 0.7% of GNP on international development'?[30] None of those policies was popular with his own supporters. At one point in the

---

[28] Ibid., p. 198.

[29] Tim Shipman, *The Full Story of Brexit* (London: William Collins, 2017). Shipman's book is probably the most comprehensive and authoritative account of the Brexit campaign.

[30] Seldon, *Cameron at 10*, p. xxxiii.

campaign for Gay Marriage, a poll showed that 71 per cent of Conservative Party constituency chairs wanted Cameron to abandon it. I am one of many who have reason to be grateful that he did not.

At European meetings, Cameron was brilliant at knowing the subject, at concentrating while other leaders were lounging round the Council table, of texting his officials with the latest developments, getting their input and deploying deft responses. Yet, what also comes through loud and clear from Cameron's memoirs is that his view of the European Union was quintessentially English. He viewed the EU entirely through a domestic prism. His impatience with most aspects of the EU is palpable. He had a very UK-centric suspicion of the EU's institutions and of the motives of his partners. There is no sympathy for the existential crisis being suffered by the Eurozone in 2011 or the fact that his EU partners saw his Treasury-led demands as provocative game scoring while they were fighting for their lives. There is little evidence of him doing what John Major did: putting himself inside the mind of his fellow leaders and seeking to understand their motivations. At the heart of his view of Europe and of Britain's place in it lies a perhaps fatal paradox: he wanted to keep Britain inside the European Union but only on terms that would have so hollowed out our membership as to negate the solidarity that has to be an essential condition of that membership.

In the 1980s, retired politicians and civil servants looked back on the 1950s and asked themselves the question: why did we get it wrong in the misjudgements we made about the European project? Maybe Cameron at least deserves the perspective of distance before a definitive judgement can be made about what looks now to be a fateful error; a tragic mistake by a gifted political leader who was destroyed by the domestic monster he had set out to tame.

11

Brave New World?

What Next for the UK?

In a book called *A Stranger in Europe*, published in 2008, I wrote that 'there would be a huge loss to British interests if twenty-six [now twenty-seven] other countries were taking, without us, decisions on energy, environment, agriculture, trade, industry, foreign policy, and defence, when those decisions would in all cases bear directly on our national interest and, in most, have to be implemented in Britain simply because we would otherwise be unable to operate in the European market place'.[1]

That there is such a loss from the United Kingdom's departure from the European Union now seems obvious; whether it will be huge, we shall discover. Some of our chickens will come home to roost quite quickly in the form of the scope and conditions of whatever trade deal the UK is able to negotiate with the twenty-seven EU Member States. As they have done over the years since the 2016 referendum, our former partners will negotiate with little regard for the UK's interests, save where they coincide with their own, as they mostly do over trade in goods. Trade in services, and especially financial services, where the UK has had pre-eminence, is a prime field in which the twenty-seven will seek to redress the balance to their advantage. The closer our alignment with EU rules and terms of trade, the smoother the transition for the UK. But the precedents of Switzerland, or of the EEA countries such as Norway, are neither directly transferable to the UK case (politically or practically) nor anything like as beneficial as full membership. Even if we avoid the cliff-edge of the transition end-date, we are likely to find ourselves torn for a long time between the powerful magnetic pull of what has been by far our largest market and the domestic imperative of ensuring that Brexit is more than just a nominal reality. The risk for the UK is that we lose our privileged access to what has been our near-domestic market without finding even adequate (let alone equivalent) substitutes elsewhere. The speed and extent

---

[1] Stephen Wall, *A Stranger in Europe: Britain and the EU from Thatcher to Blair* (Oxford: Oxford University Press, 2008), p. 210.

of the adverse impact of Brexit on our economy will depend on what kind of trade deal can be done with the EU. It took fifteen years for successive British governments to get to grips with the new post-1945 European and global reality represented by the European Community, and a further twenty-three years to establish UK membership of the EEC on a basis which adequately met the UK national interest. History does not repeat itself but it does suggest that the reverse process will not be swift. We may divorce in haste but, even if we do not come to repent the action, we shall very probably learn to resent the self-inflicted harm that the divorce will entail.

It does therefore seem inevitable that the relative prosperity of the UK will diminish as a consequence of leaving the European Union (just as our relative prosperity suffered by comparison with the EEC members when we decided not to participate in their new project). We are giving up the unfettered access we have to the world's biggest market place; giving up the very market in goods and services we did more than any other EU member to design and create. Instead, we have to negotiate as an outside competitor for access to that market on terms which will be inferior to those we enjoy as of right now. And we shall have no say in shaping the future rules of that market. All this in the name of a so-called gain in sovereignty which will require us to accept the rules decided by our erstwhile partners if we want continued access to 'their' market.

It also seems to be inevitable that our global influence will diminish significantly when we are no longer part of the world's largest union of like-minded democracies, the world's biggest trading bloc, and the world's largest donor of international aid. We shall not have the national wealth, or strength in defence, to substitute for what we have lost. It may take time for all this to become apparent. Britain's decline as a global and economic power after 1945 happened slowly enough for us to grow accustomed to it. It took a revolutionary, Margaret Thatcher, to shake us out of our torpor. For all of the years since the end of the Second World War, the United Kingdom has sought to compensate for our decline in global importance by making ourselves the best friend of the United States. The 'special relationship' has been a greater reality for the UK than for the United States. It is more than likely that the British government, especially a Conservative one, will try to compensate for the loss of global political and economic influence occasioned by Brexit, by trying to give greater weight to the transatlantic relationship. When it comes to trade deals, the USA, who always play hardball, will seek to exploit our economic and political neediness to their advantage.

The European Union was, for almost half a century, the principal vehicle through which the United Kingdom exercised soft power in the world:

through the EU's commitment to shared democratic values, its trading power, and its role as the world's largest donor of development assistance. Now, when all the local and global issues which vitally affect our country are discussed by twenty-seven other governments, the UK is absent from the room. The telephone calls and email exchanges which buzzed between London and other EU capitals, as compromises were hammered out on EU policies and legislation are, for the UK, now past history. The generations of EU civil servants, who knew each other well as they negotiated in weekly Brussels working groups, no longer include those from the UK. British Ministers, who knew their continental counterparts at least as well as they knew their Cabinet colleagues, will now be relative strangers, and certainly outsiders. The British liberalizing influence, in the Commission, the Council of Ministers, and the European Parliament exists no more. We cannot afford to be absent from the management of those issues which affect our interests and we shall have to devise alternative strategies. In no circumstances will they be equivalent to the access by right that we enjoyed as EU members. We will have to maximize the remaining assets we have: our own democratic tradition, our language, our enterprise, our membership of the UN Security Council, of NATO and the G8. At a time of pressing demands for expenditure on essential public services, it may be hard for the claims of defence and diplomacy to make themselves heard. But both are critical to our long-term security and prosperity.

What Next for the EU?

The EU too will be the poorer, economically and politically, for the UK's absence. The absence of the UK will remove one of the principal foreign policy actors from the Union; one of the most effective advocates of a poverty-focused aid policy; one of the most vocal champions of free trade and a doughty campaigner for reform. There are other reasons, too, why the European Union itself may not go from strength to strength. It will survive because, as their response to Brexit has shown, its members still see great national advantage from membership, and the euro gives a compelling impetus to greater integration. But, the EU is less united politically than ever before in its history. Britain's departure has itself contributed to that. The threat of large-scale refugee migration continues to pose a near-existential threat. The disparate levels of democratic cohesion within the EU generally, and within the Eurozone, also continue to make it vulnerable. It may be that the EU will evolve into different circles of integration. But an inner circle would have to be built around countries that are naturally close economically and capable, and willing, to take the critical next steps towards fiscal integration. Thus far, even France and Germany struggle to find common purpose on the Eurozone's (and therefore the EU's) most essential requirements. Those who, not unreasonably, prescribe a small inner core, reminiscent of the original six members, cannot escape the fact that the Eurozone is indissoluble. So any inner core would in practice have to comprise all the Eurozone members. Given the size of the Eurozone, that becomes almost a contradiction in terms, at least in the short and medium term. Of course, different combinations of EU Member States will combine for different purposes, as they do already in practice on security issues. But there is no successful future for the EU without a successful Eurozone. The signs are that the necessary road to fiscal integration will be slow and painful.

The problems of the single currency have been rooted in the Maastricht Treaty which created it. That treaty represented a qualitative shift by comparison with anything else that had been done since the original Treaty of Rome. The Treaty of Rome was itself a balancing act between the continued existence, and *de facto* primacy, of the nation state and national governments, on the one hand, and the newly created supranational institutions and procedures of the European Community, on the other. The boldness of the enterprise, and the challenges it posed to statesmanship, were there from the beginning. Even with only six members, the early years were at times fraught. The strength of the project lay in the post-war political determination which underpinned it, in the historic act of reconciliation between France and Germany which made the whole thing possible and sustainable, and by a system of engagements to which the members bound themselves by law.

The goal of 'ever closer union' was ambitious, and from very early on, encompassed economic and monetary union. The Benelux members and Italy all championed the cause of a political union, as did Germany. The actual speed and steps were, in practice, set by the leaders of France and Germany, the undisputed motor force of the project. Thus, the European Monetary System and its Exchange Rate Mechanism were the brainchild of German Chancellor, Helmut Schmidt, wholeheartedly supported by French President Valéry Giscard d'Estaing (against the strong reservations of much of the French financial establishment). Those first steps were measured, deliberate, and limited, but they were taken within an ambitious political framework. In 1972, the Heads of Government of the EEC set the goal of economic and political union by 1980. They failed to reach it, but the failure did not invalidate the ambition or (despite British wishful thinking to the contrary) mean that the goal was unrealizable.

There was, however, a constant tension between the ambition of European rhetoric and the more mundane reality of day-to-day national self-interest. The early policies and practice of the EEC were designed to satisfy the needs of the original Member States: with an economic and industrial market which force-fed post-war economic recovery and an agricultural support system that was of special benefit to a France whose economy (and politics) were still rooted in the soil. When the United Kingdom and others eventually joined, the UK brought to the party a—not always welcome—dose of realism: pointing out, forcefully, that it made little sense to spend 90 per cent of a common budget on agricultural production which could not be consumed; or to have a supposed single market which largely existed only on paper. The British, of course, had their own internal tensions—more of which anon. But, however ambitious the ultimate declared goals of the European Community were, the steps taken towards that goal had to be, and were, ones that could be agreed by all the Heads of Government and implemented to the practical advantage, and with the political consent, of their electorates. That was the case up to and including the Single European Act which created the Single Market.

The argument that a single market should have a single currency was accepted by the majority of Member States. The ensuing Maastricht Treaty encapsulated the tried and tested belief that if the political leaders set an ambitious goal, then it could and would be reached. But a single currency, removing from the nation state its own control over exchange and interest rates, was a far more radical and demanding integration of economic policy than anything that had gone before, with equally far-reaching political implications.

German reunification was accepted by France on the condition that Germany agreed to be a part of a single currency scheme which bound her irrevocably into western European democratic structures. It is easy now to forget the nervousness that German reunification provoked: a fear either that Germany would become the dominant continental superpower, with all the warnings from history which that entailed; or, that she might drift into a dangerous neutrality, looking more towards the East than to the West. The German Chancellor shared some of those fears, overruled his own advisers and accepted to give up the Deutschmark in the cause of achieving a united Germany firmly bound to the West, and accepted as such by her partners.

Not surprisingly, the Maastricht Treaty was a flawed compromise, both politically and substantively. Some foresaw that a single currency could only work on the basis of genuine economic convergence between its members or, failing that, on the basis of a willingness by the wealthy member states to make large fiscal transfers to the poor. But the convergence was inadequate, fiscal transfers were explicitly ruled out and the conditions of membership were not rigorously applied. So, for the first time in its history, the European Union adopted a treaty that proclaimed the ends without providing the means to their fulfilment.

This massive challenge has been met and managed only through a series of crises and radical measures. That the challenge *has* been met, albeit often too little and almost too late, is one reason why I believe that the Eurozone will survive. But two consequences have been a loss of public confidence in the overall EU project (not helped by a succession of Treaties: Amsterdam, Nice, Constitution, Lisbon, of almost impenetrable irrelevance as far as EU citizens are concerned) and a serious weakening of the so-called Community method.

To bemoan the dilution of the Community method might seem like a sorry obsession on the part of someone too long immured in Brussels meeting rooms. But it goes to the heart of the EU project. As I have tried to bring out elsewhere in the book, successive British governments found the institutional balance inherent in the EU perverse and inconvenient. They fed the media caricature of an unelected bureaucracy (the European Commission) dictating to elected governments who knew best what their voters wanted. But it is of course precisely because each Member State has its own interests, and because those interests often diverge, that the Commission was given the twin responsibilities of being the sole author of new legislative proposals, and the guardian of the implementation of legislation once it had been agreed by elected Member Governments and the elected European Parliament.

The independent, supranational, role of the Commission lies at the heart of the Community method. But the Commission were given a notably reduced role in the Maastricht Treaty provisions on the single currency. They have had an important part to play in the successive Eurozone crises, as the facilitators, implementers, and sometimes enforcers, of decisions taken by the Member States, but those decisions have been taken inter-governmentally, denying the Commission their treaty-given responsibilities. The British government of David Cameron contributed to this state of affairs by vetoing a proposed amendment to the Lisbon Treaty and compelling the other Member States to adopt the Fiscal Compact as a separate intergovernmental treaty. The result is an unhappy mish-mash which has contributed to undermining the accepted authority of the Commission. This in turn has made it easier, for example, for Member States to dismiss Commission proposals for burden sharing on migration. Thus the case for a federal Europe becomes stronger as the necessary will and cohesion to make it happen grow weaker.

As a life-long supporter of the European project, I am relieved that support for membership remains strong in most Member States, but it is concerning that, in some Member States, that support rests, not on an acceptance of shared and inviolable rights and obligations, but on what policies suit, or do not suit, individual governments at any particular time. President Macron is one of the few, perhaps the only, EU Head of Government, who seems fully aware of the dangers and who has suggested common approaches. His ideas have not so much been given short shrift, as ignored around the rest of the EU.

The Problem of Britain

An earlier French President, General de Gaulle, was also far-sighted when he predicted that British membership of the European Community would radically change the nature of the organization, partly because of Britain's global, Atlanticist and free-trade outlook, and partly because many others would join in Britain's wake. There is a debate to be had around whether de Gaulle contributed to turning his fears into reality by keeping Britain out of membership for a crucial decade. During that decade, the EEC was shaped to suit French and other interests, thereby making the eventual terms of entry for the UK so unpalatable that the UK was forced to spend a further ten years renegotiating them. That bitter period in turn created a culture of antagonism which permanently soured the UK's relations with her European partners.

I believe that ten-year delay is one significant element in the story of Britain's EEC/EU membership, but only one. I have tried to describe the others in this book. One striking element is vividly analysed in Michael Charlton's book, *The Price of Victory.*[2] The senior British officials who had been involved in the decisions of the 1950s not to take part in either the Coal and Steel Community, or the EEC itself, almost all portrayed to Charlton a political climate in London (under both Labour and Conservative governments) in which any advice that Britain *should* join either organization would have been dismissed as outside the realms of political possibility, let alone desirability. It was not that clever politicians assessed the pros and cons and decided on balance against; on the whole, they saw no issue for them to consider. Their opinion was constrained by the world they had known and

[2] See Chapter 2.

by the future for Britain they envisaged. They were not unaware of Britain's reduced status in a world of two superpowers, but none of the answers to the challenges faced by the United Kingdom was, for them, to be found in the two organizations created by the vision of Monnet, Schuman, and others.

Only as Britain's reality changed, with the loss of empire and its markets, the debacle of Suez, the destabilizing effect of East–West tension, and a clear reorientation of US policy, did thinking evolve. And, with the success of the EEC, thinking inside the British government was forced to evolve in the direction of swallowing hard and accepting a somewhat bitter pill. For the UK, the decision to open negotiations to enter the EEC was an admission of failure. De Gaulle's subsequent treatment of the UK poured salt into the existing wound.

Insofar as, in the 1950s, British Ministers did consider the ECSC and the EEC, the supranational nature of both organizations was a decidedly unpalatable feature. Part of the British EU story is an unwillingness to face up to the true nature of the organization we eventually decided to join. A well-read acquaintance, who voted for Brexit, told me recently that he had, before voting to leave in 2016, read both the Constitutional Treaty and the Lisbon Treaty. 'That', he said, 'convinced me to vote to leave: those treaties are all about mission creep'. He was right, except that 'mission creep' implies something underhand and done by stealth, whereas 'mission creep' is the very essence of the European project. 'Ever closer union' implies just what it says. The agreement of EEC leaders (including Prime Minister Edward Heath) to aim for political and economic union by 1980 was somewhat vague on what political union might mean but clear on the goal of a single currency.

When the House of Commons debated the terms of EEC membership in 1971, MPs were told what the nature of the European institutions would mean. Laws made at EEC level would replace domestic laws and could not be altered or overturned by Parliament, except by a decision to leave the EEC altogether. But the British Ministers of the day believed that power would rest primarily in the hands of governments, especially those of Germany, France, and the UK. They underestimated the extent and depth of the Franco-German relationship, as well as the pervasive change which legislation at EEC level would bring.

The 'sovereignty' issue never went away. Because each piece of EEC legislation entailed a loss of national parliamentary sovereignty and an increase in European Community competence, it posed a domestic problem. Prime Minister Jim Callaghan turned down what was probably the last chance to create an equal partnership between Britain, France, and Germany in part for that reason, when he declined joint ownership of the European Exchange Rate Mechanism. Britain was one of the 'big three' Member States, but never on the same wavelength as the others. We were the odd one out. France and Germany felt a strong historical imperative to cooperate and to make concessions to each other to ensure that the relationship prospered in their mutual interest. Their bilateral relationship represented good domestic politics for each country, as did their joint leadership of the European Community. By contrast, the domestic cost for successive British governments of making the compromises necessary for a successful trilateral relationship was always considered too high. Longstanding, insular, atavistic sentiments still prevailed in British culture and the media. The British governments in the early years of our membership (those of Heath, Wilson, and Callaghan) were domestic failures, with little room for positive manoeuvre within the EEC. The Thatcher government, dominated by the Prime Minister's own combative instincts, used political warfare against the rest of Europe to shore up domestic support at the most controversial period of her economic revolution. By the end of her period in office, the iron had entered into the soul of the Conservative Party.

The government of Tony Blair could have made a difference. It had the huge parliamentary majority to do so. But Blair was constrained by virtue of being beholden to the Murdoch Press. He was also constantly undermined by a Chancellor, Gordon Brown, who used a largely feigned Euroscepticism to burnish his popular credentials in his war of attrition against Blair's leadership. In any case, Blair, while staunchly European, shared the traditional intergovernmental approach of his predecessors. The only EU institution that counted for him was the European Council in which he sat, and he had scant regard for the Community method whose merits I and others sometimes attempted to sell to him.

Blair, like all his predecessors, had his eyes firmly set on the relationship with the United States. He was not the only European post-war leader for whom transatlantic relations were a dominant issue. De Gaulle had sought to establish France as a global player in counterpoise to the United States, and had ultimately failed. In assessing the national interest, all British postwar Prime Ministers, with the possible exception of Heath, thought first of the United States and only secondly of the European Union. British governments were right to see the Anglo-US relationship as vital for the country's (and the West's) security. They were suspicious of French motives in promoting a European security identity which smacked of gesture politics, rather than sound defence policy. But the British relationship with the USA assumed its so-called 'special' nature in UK eyes as much as a political and psychological prop as for its substantive importance. When it came to Iraq, it did not occur to Blair to try to establish an EU policy as a basis for discussion with the USA, as opposed to an Anglo-American policy to take back across the Atlantic to Europe. Traffic across the Atlantic 'bridge' that the UK purported to be, went mostly in one direction.

Successive British governments spoke of leading in Europe but were always placed on the back foot by initiatives for political integration from other Members which were unpalatable to British opinion, all the more so since the rhetoric that accompanied them was often alien to British parliamentary and legal traditions. The case for EU membership was, from the outset, essentially a negative one: Britain had to be a member because she would be worse off outside. This was scarcely a recipe for generating public enthusiasm.

Alongside his two vetoes of Britain's application to join the EEC, De Gaulle did offer the alternative of an Association Agreement: a privileged trading relationship that would have given market access, but without the obligations of full membership. The Wilson government rejected the offer. They doubted de Gaulle's sincerity, fearing that he would allow negotiations to be held, only to veto the outcome, as he had done in 1963. And Wilson and his colleagues clearly saw the huge disadvantage of being rule takers, not rule makers. Their decision reflected the conflict of interest with which successive British governments have wrestled: the European Community was never a very palatable prospect but, after agonized soul-searching, the inescapable conclusion was reached. The EEC was too important economically and politically for the UK, as a European power, not to be a part of it.

Britain's membership of the EEC/EU was never free of friction. And Britain, more than any other member country, found it difficult to accept changes to the original Treaty of Rome even when, as in the case of the Single European Act, they were in her economic interest. In retrospect, a Rubicon was crossed with the British opt-out from the single currency. It looked, at the time, like a success for both sides of the argument: Britain was not forced to participate or to veto, and the other Member States secured their objective without having to resort to an intergovernmental treaty outside the sphere of the Community treaties. But it established the principle, not just of a Europe of different speeds towards the same end goal, but of different ends and obligations. The principle and practice were established, to the point where David Cameron, in 2016, achieved for the UK terms of continued membership which absolved the UK from any commitment to the cornerstone of the European idea: ever closer union. It was scarcely a basis for selling the European project to the electorate, let alone for a wholehearted commitment to the European project had the referendum been won. Today's situation, with the United Kingdom outside the EU and disharmony within the EU, owes a lot, not just to the ill-prepared move to a single currency, but to the abandonment of the idea of the EU as a convoy. Successive German governments had long argued that the EU convoy could not be delayed by the speed of the slowest ship. But, the speed of the slowest ship was a necessary condition for there to be a convoy at all.

The story I have tried to tell is not wholly negative. Successive British governments wanted to make a success of our membership, believing in the undoubted, and vital, role that the European project has played in cementing peace through prosperity among previously warring neighbours. Without pressure from Britain, essential reform of the wastefully unsustainable agricultural policy of the Community would not have happened when it did. It was the British government, under Thatcher, that joined with the European Commission under Jacques Delors to inject urgency into the fulfilment of the Single Market commitment which had lain neglected on the front page of the Treaty of Rome for some thirty years. It was successive British governments who most strongly supported the further enlargement of the European Community. We take for granted the transition from dictatorship to democracy of Greece, Spain, and Portugal. But that transition required the whole-hearted commitment of other European governments. The Callaghan government weighed, and accepted, the economic sacrifice the UK would have to make to help secure democracy and prosperity in those countries.

The same was true for the countries of central and eastern Europe. It is the case that, for the British, enlargement promised to put some water in the wine of those who pressed for a European political union. But the prime British motivation was to underpin the fledgling democracies in the countries finally emerging from Soviet tyranny. In many of those countries, the name of Margaret Thatcher is still revered as their champion. John Major, her successor, had none of her hang-ups about German reunification. He did have a profound conviction that the EU could not be a rich man's club that denied membership, and generous economic support, to those newly liberated nations. Major had accepted the possible pace at which the new accessions would happen at a time when his French opposite number, President Mitterrand, was still willing their deferral to the second decade of the twenty-first century.

One of my former Diplomatic Service colleagues spent much of his career, as I did, engaged in European policy in London, Brussels, and in European capitals. He wrote to me that he felt as if his more than thirty years of public service had been rendered 'a complete waste of time' by Brexit. I understand that feeling all too well. But I do not completely share it. We did our bit to make a success of Britain's membership. The European peace and growing prosperity of the last half century owe much to the combined values, shared interests, and common policies of the EU Member States. Successive British governments played their part in shaping the EU that we have now left.

De Gaulle's veto of Britain's EEC application in 1963, when I was sixteen, convinced me, for idealistic, even more than self-interested, reasons that we had to be a part of the great European project. My parents had lived through two world wars. My father, aged seventeen, had joined up to fight in the first of them. Europe had been the war-torn graveyard of countless numbers of human beings over many centuries. The European project offered—and still offers—a rule-based system for managing the often querulous relations between competitive countries. And it provides a basis on which shared democratic values can be entrenched and deployed for good in the world. For these reasons, I still believe passionately that the United Kingdom should have remained a member. The material loss to the UK from leaving the EU will be quickly measurable, even if much of it escapes public attention. Other, less tangible but potentially more important, losses will have to be assessed over a longer period.

In her 1988 speech in Bruges, Margaret Thatcher described the European Community as 'a practical means by which Europe can ensure the future prosperity and security of its people in a world in which there are many other powerful nations and groups of nations'. Her words have stood the test of time, even if our collective sense of our national interest has not.

Index

For the benefit of digital users, indexed terms that span two pages (e.g., 52–53) may, on occasion, appear on only one of those pages.